BLACKS IN THE NEW WORLD
August Meier, Series Editor

Medicine and Slavery

MEDICINE AND SLAVERY

The Diseases and
Health Care of Blacks in
Antebellum Virginia

TODD L. SAVITT

UNIVERSITY OF ILLINOIS PRESS
Urbana   Chicago   London

Library of Congress Cataloging in Publication Data

Savitt, Todd L., 1943-
 Medicine and slavery.

 (Blacks in the New World)
 Bibliography: p.
 Includes index.
 1. Medicine—Virginia—History—19th century.
 2. Afro-Americans—Diseases—Virginia—History—
 19th century. 3. Slavery in the United States—
 Virginia—Condition of slaves. 4. Public health
 —Virginia—History—19th century. I. Title.
 II. Series. [DNLM: 1. History of medicine—
 Virginia. 2. Blacks—History—Virginia. WZ80.5.B5
 S267m]
 R345.S28   362.8'4   78-8520
 ISBN 0-252-00653-4 (cloth)
 ISBN 0-252-00874-X (paper)

FOR CAROLE

Contents

Illustrations

Tables

Figures

Abbreviations

Periodicals and Reports

AHR	*American Historical Review*
BHM	*Bulletin of the History of Medicine*
BMSJ	*Boston Medical and Surgical Journal*
Cotton Planter	*American Cotton Planter and the Soil of the South*
ELA *Annual Report*	*Annual Report of the Court of Directors of the Eastern Lunatic Asylum*
FR	*Farmer's Register*
H of D *Jl.*	Virginia, House of Delegates, *Journal*
JAMA	*Journal of the American Medical Association*
JHM	*Journal of the History of Medicine and Allied Sciences*
JNH	*Journal of Negro History*
JSH	*Journal of Southern History*
Leg. Docs.	Virginia, *Governor's Message and Annual Report of the Public Officers of the State . . . of Virginia*
Mon. Steth.	*The Monthly Stethoscope and Medical Reporter*
MVMJ	*Maryland and Virginia Medical Journal*
NOMSJ	*New Orleans Medical and Surgical Journal*
SMR	*Southern Medical Reports*
SMSJ	*Southern Medical and Surgical Journal*
Steth.	*The Stethoscope and Virginia Medical Gazette*
VMHB	*Virginia Magazine of History and Biography*
VMJ	*Virginia Medical Journal*
VMSJ	*Virginia Medical and Surgical Journal*
WLA *Annual Report*	*Annual Report of the Board of Directors of the Western Lunatic Asylum*

Books

Blanton, *17th Century*—Wyndham B. Blanton, *Medicine in Virginia in the Seventeenth Century* (Richmond, 1930).

Blanton, *18th Century*—Wyndham B. Blanton, *Medicine in Virginia in the Eighteenth Century* (Richmond, 1931).

Blanton, *19th Century*—Wyndham B. Blanton, *Medicine in Virginia in the Nineteenth Century* (Richmond, 1933).

Blassingame, *Slave Community*—John W. Blassingame, *The Slave Community: Plantation Life in the Ante-Bellum South* (New York, 1972).

Fogel and Engerman, *Time*, I—Robert W. Fogel and Stanley L. Engerman, *Time on the Cross: The Economics of American Negro Slavery* (Boston, 1974).

———, *Time*, II—Robert W. Fogel and Stanley L. Engerman, *Time on the Cross: Evidence and Methods—A Supplement* (Boston, 1974).

Greene, ed., *Carter Diary*—Jack P. Greene, ed., *The Diary of Colonel Landon Carter of Sabine Hall, 1752–1778* (Charlottesville, 1965).

Mullin, *Flight and Rebellion*—Gerald W. Mullin, *Flight and Rebellion: Slave Resistance in Eighteenth Century Virginia* (New York, 1972).

Olmsted, *Seaboard*—Frederick Law Olmsted, *A Journey in the Seaboard Slave States, with Remarks on Their Economy* (New York, 1856).

Postell, *Health of Slaves*—William Dosite Postell, *The Health of Slaves on Southern Plantations* (Baton Rouge, 1951).

Stampp, *Peculiar Institution*—Kenneth M. Stampp, *The Peculiar Institution: Slavery in the Ante-Bellum South* (New York, 1956).

Starobin, *Industrial Slavery*—Robert S. Starobin, *Industrial Slavery in the Old South* (New York, 1970).

Wade, *Slavery in the Cities*—Richard C. Wade, *Slavery in the Cities: The South, 1820–1860* (New York, 1964).

Manuscript Repositories

CW	Research Library, Colonial Williamsburg Foundation, Williamsburg, Va.
Duke	Perkins Library, Duke University, Durham, N.C.
Harvard (Baker)	Baker Library, Harvard University, Cambridge, Mass.
LC	Library of Congress, Washington, D.C.
MCV	Tompkins-McCaw Library, Medical College of Virginia, Richmond, Va.

UNC	Southern Historical Collection, University of North Carolina, Chapel Hill, N.C.
UVA	Alderman Library, University of Virginia, Charlottesville, Va.
VHS	Virginia Historical Society, Richmond, Va.
VSL	Virginia State Library, Richmond, Va.
WSH	Office of the Medical Director, Western State Hospital, Staunton, Va.
W&M	Earl Gregg Swem Library, William and Mary College, Williamsburg, Va.
Wisconsin	State Historical Society of Wisconsin, Madison, Wisc.

Preface

Sickness and death were constant worries of nineteenth-century Americans, especially in the disease-ridden antebellum South. Whether one lived in a crowded city or on a large, isolated plantation, whether one was white or black, one could not totally escape the ravages of endemic and epidemic disease. Health was a ubiquitous topic of conversation among businessmen, artisans, planters, laborers, and agricultural workers of both races. Those who could write recorded their own and their neighbors' states of health in medical and agricultural journals, personal diaries and letters, and newspapers. Remaining alive and well was an ever-present concern for these people—one which had to be faced day in, day out.

For the white man in the South this problem of sickness and health was often compounded by the fact that he was overseer not only of his own and his family's well-being, but also of that of his black slaves. The slaveowner or hirer met this responsibility with varying degrees of enthusiasm. Despite the monetary investment represented by each slave, not all those in charge of the slave's care fulfilled their obligations adequately or humanely. Medical knowledge was at such a state in the early and mid-nineteenth century that helpful medical intervention was, in many cases, a questionable matter. Because enslaved blacks had few legal rights and no social standing in the antebellum South, they became wards of their masters, unable, for instance, to call for professional medical aid when they deemed it necessary; often unable to apply their own remedies to sick loved ones without disobeying the master's orders; and, in a sense, unable to have the final say in their own homes over the care of their own illnesses and death.

Free blacks were in an even less enviable medical position, since they were usually poor and therefore dependent on the good-heartedness of employers, neighboring planters, local white physicians, or city hospitals for health care. Generally inadequate medical attention and high mortality rates resulted among the free black population.

This book is not merely an analysis of the kinds of diseases which afflicted the Old South's black population. It is a description of medical conditions as they existed at that time, and a history of the relationship between black health and white society. In addition to introducing the reader to various maladies and their symptoms, I have attempted to apply basic principles of public health to antebellum living and working conditions, and to relate the reactions of whites to real, expected, and feigned ill health among slaves and free blacks. Because accurate figures regarding morbidity and mortality are not available, statistical analysis has been limited, but not eliminated.

Except in chapter 1, where a general overview of black-related diseases is presented, my focus is on Virginia from the Revolution to the Civil War. Health conditions in the Old Dominion at that time were, in many respects, typical of those prevailing throughout the antebellum South. Residents suffered from malaria, parasitic worm diseases, and dysentery just as Mississippians or Georgians did. Yellow fever struck its major ports, though not as severely or as frequently as at Charleston, Mobile, or New Orleans. Virginia's position on the northern fringe of the slave South perhaps lessened the intensity and duration of warm-weather diseases, but not enough to render its diseases significantly different from those in the Lower South.

During the time span under consideration the black population and the health picture in Virginia were relatively stable. The slave trade had ended, there was little black immigration into the state, and tropical diseases brought from Africa and unable to survive in the new environment had all but disappeared. As in the rest of the world at that time, infectious diseases produced the greatest mortality. In such a medically hostile atmosphere, white Virginians acted with varying degrees of conviction to protect the health of their slaves and their free Negro neighbors, while openly and clandestinely the blacks themselves often took matters into their own hands.

Acknowledgments

As a first-year medical student at the University of Rochester in 1965 I first learned about a genetic blood disease which almost exclusively afflicted blacks. I also learned that, in Africa, those persons carrying genes for the abnormal form of hemoglobin which caused this disorder were immune to the most virulent malarial fever, falciparum malaria. Four years later, having left medical school to pursue the study of history at the University of Virginia, I had occasion to recall the facts regarding sickle cell anemia and malarial immunity. Planters in the South Carolina Low Country, my professors mentioned in passing, noticed that African slaves appeared to bear up better in the "sickly season" of the year than whites; this fact led some to postulate that blacks possessed an innate resistance to certain miasmatic diseases. I knew that malaria was the disorder and sickle cell genes the shield. The following fall semester (1970/71) I had an opportunity to explore the subject in Visiting Professor Charles B. Dew's southern history seminar. The result appears as a part of chapter 1. From malaria it was only a short step to a dissertation encompassing all of black health care and diseases during the antebellum period.

Many people have provided me with various forms of assistance during the years since this project was initiated. My fellow graduate students at the time, especially Thomas Armstrong, William Ernst, Julie Laird, Ray Luce, Larry Morrison, and P. M. Thomas, gave me valuable suggestions and many pieces of important information which they came across in their own research. Professor Robert Brugger of the University of Virginia, who read the entire manuscript, and Professor Josef Barton, now of Northwestern University, who read chapter 8, provided thoughtful guidance, suggestions, and comments.

The staff of the Alderman Library (University of Virginia) Manuscript Department gave me innumerable suggestions on sources which would never have otherwise come to my attention. My special thanks go to Michael Plunkett, Gregory Johnson, Vesta Gordon, Ann Stauffenberg, and Douglas Tanner, whose knowledge of the collections, willingness to spend time searching for all manner of hidden material, and warm friendship made it easy for the University of Virginia Manuscript Room to become my second home for many months. Others who provided special assistance with manuscript collections were Margaret C. Cook (William and Mary College), William G. Ray and John W. Dudley (Virginia State Library), Patricia Gibbs, Nancy Merz, and Linda Rowe (Colonial Williamsburg, Inc., Research Library), and Dr. Hobart Hansen (Western State Hospital). Thanks must also go to the staffs of manuscript departments at Duke University, the University of North Carolina, Library of Congress, Petersburg Public Library, Medical College of Virginia Library, and the Virginia Historical Society.

For things medical I wish to acknowledge three people. Dr. Wilhelm Moll, director of the University of Virginia Medical Library, was a friend and benefactor during my graduate-student career. Through his kindness I was provided the opportunity to supplement my family's income while performing a job which introduced me to virtually every aspect of medical history—from handling medical artifacts to writing historical papers. Mrs. Nell B. Fuller, also of the University of Virginia Medical Library, was my very own wizard of medical references. She managed to answer questions and produce materials which others could not. Dr. Gert H. Brieger, then director of the history of medicine program at Duke University, willingly and cheerfully took on an unofficial student when I wished to increase my knowledge of his field of expertise. He read and criticized the entire manuscript, adding his unique medical and historical perspective.

Mr. and Mrs. William Jarratt of Petersburg, who still possess the papers of their ancestors (free blacks in Petersburg), showed great kindness during my visit to their home. Not only did they allow me to use these manuscripts, but they also answered many questions and introduced me to several people associated with Virginia State College. I spent a delightful hour in the home of Doctors Edna Colson and Amaza Lee Meredith, both retired from the Virginia State College faculty, listening to reminiscences of a previous era and learning about home remedies which had been handed down through their families.

This research was supported by grants from the National Library of Medicine of the National Institutes of Health, numbers LM 02071 and LM 02477.

To Willie Lee Rose, now at Johns Hopkins University, goes a special acknowledgment. She willingly undertook the direction of a research project in a field distant from her own—medical history. Her criticisms have prevented me from inundating the reader with medical language and terminology which would have been unintelligible, and from making unsupported assumptions, drawing unwarranted conclusions, and committing careless blunders. She has been an advisor and warm friend.

My parents, who initially accepted my sudden change of career in 1968 with some reservations, nevertheless continued to provide both moral and intellectual support as I pursued my new studies. Though they may not have known it, I appreciated it.

Finally for Carole, to whom this work is, as it should be, dedicated. She well knows what I feel about all we have experienced since I chose to end my medical career and enter graduate school in history. Her investment in this book is at least as great as my own. Her support, prodding, flexibility, cheerfulness, and sympathy eased the task immeasurably. She also typed it, edited it, and developed every disease mentioned as she read descriptions of the symptoms. Allyson and Jodey are still too young to appreciate either my need for, or enjoyment of, them during these years. To all three of my girls: thanks.

Durham, North Carolina   —T. L. S.

CHAPTER 1

Introduction: Were Blacks Medically Different from Whites?

"Scarcely any observant medical man, having charge of negro estates, fails to discover, by experience, important modifications in the diseases and appropriate treatment of the white and black race respectively." Thus wrote the editor of a prominent Virginia medical journal in 1856, in an attempt to impress upon the state's physicians the importance of providing adequate health care to slaves.[1] He could very well have been speaking to all southern doctors, many of whom believed that medical differences existed between blacks and whites. The issue was of both practical and political importance: it involved not only the health care of an entire racial group in the South, but also the partial justification for enslaving them.

Those physicians who treated slave diseases had a pecuniary and professional concern with the subject. Their recorded opinions in medical, commercial, and agricultural journals, as well as in personal correspondence, attest to the seriousness with which they approached black health. The politically minded physicians (all of whom practiced medicine) were also resolutely committed to their cause. They, too, published for the medical, commercial, and lay public. Men like Josiah Clark Nott of Mobile and Samuel

[1] Editorial, *Mon. Steth.*, I (1856), 162–63. As stated in the preface, the material presented in this chapter is not strictly limited to Virginia but deals with the entire South.

A. Cartwright of New Orleans utilized their knowledge of black medicine to rationalize the necessity and usefulness of slavery. These apologists for the peculiar institution, in order to prove that slavery was humane and economically viable in the South, argued that blacks possessed immunity to certain diseases which devastated whites. Slaveowners, they said, did not sacrifice blacks every time they send them into the rice fields or canebrakes. Nor could physicians adequately treat blacks without knowledge of their anatomical and physiological peculiarities and disease proclivities. Blacks were medically and mentally inferior to whites, they asserted, and the Negro race was actually a distinct species with a separate origin from the Caucasian.

Other whites, too, were interested in the medical differences between the races. Slaveowners wished knowledge of the diseases to which blacks showed most susceptibility, and the best means of preventing their occurrence, in order to protect their costly investments in human chattel. They cared little about physicians' theoretical debates over Negro susceptibility, immunity, and origins of species. They were not impressed with hypotheses, or even with scientific observations of health conditions, in other areas of the South. What each planter noticed was the incidence of disease on his and his neighbors' plantations and the treatments which effected the quickest cures. A physician's statement that "the African is less susceptible to malarious influences than the white" had little meaning to the planter whose three or four best black workers had just been laid up with cases of malaria.[2]

The issue of medical differences between the races has even crept into historical discussions. Ulrich Bonnell Phillips asserted in 1918 that in the rice country whites were highly susceptible to malaria, though their slaves "were generally immune."[3] Most historians of slavery since then have simply repeated the statements of antebellum writers regarding the immunity of blacks to malaria and yellow fever, and their increased susceptibility to respiratory diseases, scrofula, dysentery, and other maladies, without further investigating the scientific basis for such claims.[4] In

        [2] E. M. Pendleton, "On the Susceptibility of the Caucasians and Africans to the Different Classes of Disease," *SMR*, 1 (1849), 339.
        [3] U. B. Phillips, *American Negro Slavery* (New York, 1918), 90–91.
        [4] A few such writers were Minnie Clare Boyd, *Alabama in the Fifties: A Social*

1956 Kenneth Stampp attempted to refute this notion that racial differences existed with regard to health: "The slave of tradition was a physically robust specimen who suffered from few of the ailments which beset the white man. A tradition with less substance to it has seldom existed. In the South, disease did not discriminate among men because of the color of their skins; wherever it was unhealthful for whites to live it was also unhealthful for Negroes."[5] Following Stampp's example, a recent historian of malaria in the New South has also denied that any differences existed in the susceptibility of whites and blacks to particular diseases.[6]

But others who have studied the evidence have found differences, indicating that Phillips and the Old South writers were at least partially correct in their conclusions. Julian H. Lewis, a pathologist at the University of Chicago, wrote a lengthy book in 1942 delineating the medical, anatomical, biochemical, and physiological characteristics of the Negro, concentrating on American blacks.[7] William Dosite Postell, Wyndham B. Blanton, John Duffy, Weymouth T. Jordan, and Peter H. Wood, among others, have also pointed to racial differences in the reactions of individuals to diseases.[8] Modern medical scientists have in fact shown that such ethnic variations do exist.

History (New York, 1931), 178–95; F. Garvin Davenport, *Ante-Bellum Kentucky: A Social History, 1800–1860* (Oxford, Ohio, 1943), 80–106; Martha Carolyn Mitchell, "Health and the Medical Profession in the Lower South, 1845–1860," *JSH*, 10 (1944), 424–46; Richard H. Shryock, "Medical Practice in the Old South," *South Atlantic Quarterly*, 29 (1930), 160–78; Charles S. Sydnor, *Slavery in Mississippi* (New York, 1933), 45–53; Rosser H. Taylor, *Ante-Bellum South Carolina: A Social and Cultural History* (Chapel Hill, N.C., 1942), 90–106. For a more complete list of writings on southern and Negro medicine, see Weymouth T. Jordan, "Plantation Medicine in the Old South," *Alabama Review*, 3 (1950), 84n–85n.

[5] Stampp, *Peculiar Institution*, 296.

[6] James Rodney Young, "Malaria in the South, 1900–1930" (Ph.D. dissertation, University of North Carolina, 1972), 154.

[7] Julian H. Lewis, *The Biology of the Negro* (Chicago, 1942), ix.

[8] Postell, *Health of Slaves*, esp. 74–89; Blanton, *18th Century*, 157; John Duffy, "A Note on Ante-Bellum Southern Nationalism and Medical Practice," *JSH*, 34 (1968), 274–76; Weymouth T. Jordan, *Ante-Bellum Alabama Town and Country* (Tallahassee, 1957), 84–105; Peter H. Wood, *Black Majority: Negroes in Colonial South Carolina from 1670 through the Stono Rebellion* (New York, 1974), 76–91.

White Southerners View the Negro

In certain obvious physical ways Negroes varied greatly from Caucasians. Old South writers particularly commented on facial features, hair, posture and gait, skin color, and odor. One school of American scientists spent much time and effort investigating cranium and brain size, as well as other characteristics, in part to demonstrate that blacks were inferior to whites.[9] Physicians, slaveowners, and other interested persons detected distinctions in the medical reactions of the two races both to diseases and to treatments.

Some white Southerners engaged in an occasionally bitter controversy over the supposed differences between the races. During the 1840's and 1850's Dr. Samuel A. Cartwright, a vociferous advocate of Negro inferiority, published several articles on "The Diseases and Physical Peculiarities of the Negro Race"; these sparked rejoinders from many who thought he had exaggerated the differences.[10] But he and Josiah Clark Nott were only the best known of a number of southern physicians who wrote about racial medicine.[11] In a sense, all those who wrote on the subject were

[9] William Stanton, *The Leopard's Spots: Scientific Attitudes toward Race in America, 1815–59* (Chicago, 1960); J. H. Van Evrie, *Negroes and Negro "Slavery"* (New York, 1861), 88–104; J. C. Nott and G. R. Gliddon, *Types of Mankind . . .* (Philadelphia, 1854).

[10] For more on this subject, see John S. Haller, Jr., "The Negro and the Southern Physician: A Study of Medical and Racial Attitudes, 1800–1860," *Medical History*, 16 (1972), 247–51; Duffy, "A Note on Ante-Bellum Southern Nationalism," 268–73, Jordan, *Ante-Bellum Alabama*, 88–92; Stanton, *Leopard's Spots*, 73–81.

[11] Details of some other physicians' arguments and references to their works may be found in Haller, "The Negro and the Southern Physician," 238–53; Jordan, "Plantation Medicine," 83–107; Shryock, "Medical Practice in the Old South," 168–69. The major writers included: Daniel Drake, "Diseases of the Negro Population," *SMSJ*, NS 1 (1845), 341–43; S. L. Grier, "The Negro and His Diseases," *NOMSJ*, 9 (1853), 752–63; E. M. Pendleton, "On the Susceptibility of the Caucasian and African Races to the Different Classes of Disease," *SMR*, 1 (1849), 336–42; A. P. Merrill, "An Essay on the Distinctive Peculiarities of the Negro Race," *SMSJ*, 12 (1856), 21–36, 80–90, 147–56; Samuel A. Cartwright, "The Diseases and Physical Peculiarities of the Negro Race," *SMR*, 2 (1850), 421–29; Cartwright, "Report of the Diseases and Physical Peculiarities of the Negro Race," *De Bow's Review*, 11 (1851), 64–69, 209–13, 331–36, 504–8; W. G. Ramsay, "The Physiological Differences between the European (or White Man) and the Negro," *Southern Agriculturalist*, 12 (1839), 286–94, 411–18; John Stainback Wilson, "The Peculiarities and Diseases of Negroes," *Cotton Planter,*

providing a defense for slavery. In applying their theories, men like Cartwright and Nott ventured further than most physicians from the strictly medical into the political realm to justify the white southern point of view; but each of the physician-authors wrote as a resident of the slaveholding section.[12] Nor were physicians the only ones who noticed medical and physical differences between whites and blacks. Slaveowners also encountered problems of racial distinctions when they attempted to treat their bondsmen's diseases without professional assistance. Numerous medical manuals were written to guide those who preferred to care for their own and their family's illnesses, but none was directed specifically at treatment of the black population.[13] Though some people called for the publication of such a volume, none appeared before the Civil War.[14] Consequently,

---

NS 2 (1858), 355; NS 3 (1859), 67–68, 92–93, 197–98, 228–29; NS 4 (1860), 46–47, 79–80, 126–28, 173–76, 222–24, 270–72, 319–20, 366–68, 415–16, 463–64, 510–12, 557–60. For a listing of many eighteenth- and nineteenth-century books and medical journals in all languages on blacks and medicine, see United States, Surgeon General's Office, *Index Catalog of the Library of the Surgeon General's Office,* 1st series (Washington, D.C., 1888), IX, 695–97.

[12] Cartwright, "How to Save the Republic, and the Position of the South in the Union," *De Bow's Review,* 11 (1851), 184–97, was originally a letter sent to Secretary of State Daniel Webster. Nott's activities are mentioned throughout Stanton, *Leopard's Spots,* and in Jordan, *Ante-Bellum Alabama,* 88–92.

[13] Jordan, "Plantation Medicine," 84, and Haller, "The Negro and the Southern Physician," 246–47, mention some of these manuals. See, e.g., James Ewell, *The Planter's and Mariner's Medical Companion* (Baltimore, 1813); Samuel K. Jennings, *A Compendium of Medical Science, or Fifty Years' Experience in the Art of Healing* (Tuscaloosa, Ala., 1847); Ralph Schenck, *The Family Physician: Treating of the Diseases Which Assail the Human System at Different Periods of Life . . .* (Fincastle, Va., 1842); A. G. Goodlett, *The Family Physician, or Every Man's Companion, Being a Compilation from the Most Approved Medical Authors, Adapted to the Southern and Western Climates . . .* (Nashville, 1838); J. Hume Simons, *Planter's Guide, and Family Book of Medicine: For the Instruction and Use of Planters, Families, Country People . . .* (Charleston, S.C., 1849); John C. Gunn, *Gunn's Domestic Medicine, or Poor Man's Friend* (Madisonville, Tenn., 1835); Isaac Wright, *Wright's Family Medicine, or System of Domestic Practice . . .* (Madisonville, Tenn., 1833).

[14] G. D. Harmon, "Dr. Wilson's Hand-Book of Health," *Cotton Planter,* NS 3 (1859), 311, 356, 383. The only books produced in English describing the specific medical treatment of blacks for individual diseases were written by British physicians. They directed their remarks to planters and slaveowners in the British West Indian sugar colonies who constantly added new African bonds-

every southern master was left to his own devices to determine what modifications were necessary when applying remedies to slaves. Sometimes the situation inspired attempts at humor, as when a Virginia planter vaccinated white and black household members in 1829: "I shall finish the greater part of the vaccinating to day, [he wrote to a relative,] and shall be out of practice entirely by Weddensday. I have performed the operation on Miss Maria [a white] and was so much accustomed to the thick skins of the negroes that I went into her meat before I thought I had made any impression." [15] At other times, however, the slave's life was at stake and the choice of treatment had far-reaching consequences. The application of so-called heroic treatment (extensive bleeding, purging, and vomiting) to blacks was just such an issue.

Thomas Jefferson made an entry in his Garden Book in 1773, under the title "articles for contracts with overseers," which expressed his antipathy toward venesection. It read, "Never bleed a negro." [16] Though Jefferson's position on bloodletting was extreme, most southern physicians and planters who wrote on the subject agreed that blacks could not withstand the loss of as much blood as whites. Dr. James Lyons of Hanover County, Virginia, reported in the late eighteenth century that though blacks in that area demanded venesection "for the most trifling Diseases," to the point that "it is often difficult to persuade them of their recovery from any disorder without opening a vein," yet they could not bear depletion of the amount recommended

---

men to their work forces. Though the books might have proved useful to slave-owners in the United States, there is no evidence to indicate that they had widespread circulation or popularity here. See, e.g., A Professional Planter (Dr. Collins), *Practical Rules for the Management and Medical Treatment of Negro Slaves, in the Sugar Colonies* (London, 1811); James Thomson, *A Treatise on the Diseases of Negroes, as They Occur in the Island of Jamaica; with Observations on the Country Remedies* (Jamaica, 1820).

[15] St. George Tucker Coalter to John Coalter, 15 March 1829, Brown-Coalter-Tucker Collection, W&M. I wish to thank Margaret Cook, curator of manuscripts at Swem Library, William and Mary College, for bringing this letter to my attention.

[16] Edwin M. Betts, ed., *Thomas Jefferson's Garden Book, 1766–1824* (Philadelphia, 1944), 41 (22 May 1773).

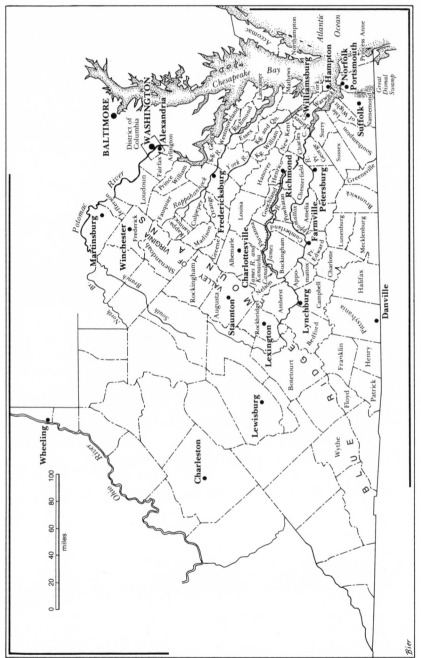

Virginia

Bier

by a leading medical authority.[17] Even northern physicians such as the respected Philadelphian, Nathaniel Chapman, professor of the theory and practice of medicine at the University of Pennsylvania, cautioned that the Negro "rarely bears blood-letting or depletion in any form." Josiah Clark Nott, John Stainbach Wilson, W. G. Ramsay, Samuel A. Cartwright, and other southern physicians corroborated Chapman's statement.[18] Nevertheless, despite injunctions against excessive use of the lancet and depletive medicines when treating blacks, physicians employed these popular techniques frequently. Most issues of antebellum southern medical journals contained articles written by doctors who routinely purged, puked, and bled their black patients, often to unconsciousness.

Though reports of these and other Negro medical "peculiarities" appeared in antebellum periodicals and pamphlets, none could be found in any standard textbook for student doctors or practitioners. Some articles on the subject of treatment provided vague information, such as: "The Caucasian seems to yield more readily to remedies . . . than the African," or, "It is much more difficult to form a just diagnosis or prognosis with the latter [African] than the former [white], consequently the treatment is often more dubious." [19] Only a few journal writers cogently explained specific racial differences and their medical consequences. For example, in 1853 Carter Page Johnson, professor of anatomy at the Medical College of Virginia, described a case in which skin color played an essential role. A slave traveled twenty miles through the country to the teaching hospital to receive treatment for a fluid-filled scrotum which Johnson first diagnosed as simple hydrocele (a collection of fluid in the scrotum). Upon more care-

[17] "Copy of a Letter from Dr. James Lyons," in William Currie, *An Historical Account of the Climates and Diseases of the United States of America . . .* (Philadelphia, 1792), 286.

[18] Chapman's remarks are quoted in J. C. Nott and George R. Gliddon, eds., *Indigenous Races of the Earth; or New Chapters of Ethnological Inquiry* (Philadelphia, 1857), 368, 369; Wilson, "The Negro—His Peculiarities as to Disease," *Cotton Planter,* NS 3 (1859), 229; Ramsay, "Physiological Differences," 416; Cartwright, "Report on the Diseases and Peculiarities of the Negro Race," 67. These claims regarding Negroes and bloodletting have no scientific or medical basis.

[19] Pendleton, "On the Susceptibility of the Caucasian and African Races," 336–37.

ful examination, however, Johnson discovered that the fluid was not clear and translucent as he had expected, but was cloudy and had originated in the abdomen. He was actually dealing with a much more serious problem—strangulated hernia. Johnson explained the implications of this case to his medical colleagues in a professional journal: "Any other than a most accurate examination of this case . . . would have led the surgeon to the diagnosis of a fluid tumour and to the natural inference of the existence of hydrocele, *especially in the negro where the test of [scrotal skin] transparency cannot be applied*. If under this impression a trocar had been plunged into the tumour, a hernial sac would have been penetrated, and in all probability a portion of intestine perforated!" [20]

In 1855 an editor of the *Virginia Medical and Surgical Journal* suggested that a Virginian write a book on "the modifications of disease in the Negro constitution." The subject, he proclaimed, stood "invitingly open"; no medical student, "fresh from Watson or Wood [textbooks of the day], with his new lancet and his armory of antiphlogistics," had been properly trained to treat many of the diseases to which the black man was subject: "Has he been taught that the African constitution sinks before the heavy blows of the 'heroic school' and runs down under the action of purgatives; that when the books say blood letting and calomel, the black man needs nourishment and opium?" Appealing to the pride of Virginia's old and established medical profession, the editor urged that "the medical society of the largest slaveholding state in the Union be the first" to sponsor such a useful and necessary enterprise.[21] But neither the medical society nor any individual doctor answered the *Journal's* challenge.

Many southern medical writers put forth urgent pleas for medical school courses and books on black medicine.[22] Most eloquent was the statement of a Mississippi physician, S. L. Grier. He decried the use of northern and English textbooks which

[20] Carter P. Johnson, "A Report of Two Cases Illustrative of the Difficulty Occasionally Met with in the Diagnosis of Scrotal Tumours," *VMSJ*, 1 (1853), 11–12 (italics added).

[21] Editorial, "The Medical Society of Virginia," *VMSJ*, 4 (1855), 256–58.

[22] See, e.g., editorial in *Mon. Steth.*, 1 (1856), 128–30; Cartwright, "Report on the Diseases and Peculiarities of the Negro Race," 211–12; Duffy, "A Note on Ante-Bellum Southern Nationalism," 271–73.

described diseases rarely seen in the South and ignored the maladies common among residents of the slaveholding states. Grier believed that it was incumbent upon southern physicians to learn all they could about black medical "peculiarities" because Negroes played such a vital role in the development and way of life of their section of the country: "In all . . . that relates to the welfare of the negro race, we have a common and abiding interest and in regard to it, the medical profession has its appropriate duty to perform. Let us beware, lest we prove recreant and fail to meet the claims that are upon us." [23]

Despite southern statements to the effect that "our medical literature cannot be manufactured for us abroad," [24] not one medical writer in the entire region ventured beyond the publication of a few articles on the subject of black medicine, and few produced books describing southern diseases (in which blacks were mentioned only infrequently and tangentially).[25] John Stainbach Wilson, a Columbus, Georgia, physician who had spent years practicing medicine in southern Alabama, came closest to actually producing a textbook on black health. Its advertised title indicated the wide scope of the proposed contents: *The Plantation and Family Physician; A Work for Families Generally and for Southern Slaveowners Especially; Embracing the Peculiarities and Diseases, the Medical and Hygienic Management of Negroes, Together with the Causes, Symptoms, and Treatment of the Principal Diseases to Whites and Blacks.*[26] But apparently the outbreak of hostilities in 1861 interrupted Wilson's plans. It was not until more than one hundred years later, in 1975, that the first textbook on Negro diseases was finally published, written this time by black physicians.[27]

---

[23] Grier, "The Negro and His Diseases," 759. For more on the movement for a distinctive southern medicine, see Duffy, "A Note on Ante-Bellum Southern Nationalism," 266–76.

[24] Grier, "The Negro and His Diseases," 759.

[25] See, e.g., Thompson McGown, *A Practical Treatise on the Most Common Diseases of the South* . . . (Philadelphia, 1849).

[26] Wilson, "The Peculiarities and Diseases of Negroes," *Cotton Planter*, NS 4 (1860), 560.

[27] Jordan, "Plantation Medicine," 90–107; Richard Allen Williams, ed., *Textbook of Black-Related Diseases* (New York, 1975).

Why did no definitive and widely accepted work on the diseases and treatment of blacks appear during the antebellum period? The answer lies in the political rather than medical nature of the issue. Medical practice, especially in rural areas, was a matter of trial and error rather than of application of set procedures learned in medical school. Practitioners and slaveowners soon learned that each Negro responded to treatments differently, rather than as a racial group. Men like Cartwright, Nott, and Wilson were writing for an audience who wished to hear that blacks were distinct from whites. This was, after all, a part of the proslavery argument. Medical theory and practice were still in such a state of flux in the late eighteenth and early nineteenth centuries that there was little risk of any true scientific challenge to a medical system based on racial differences. Observers were correct in noting that blacks showed differing susceptibility and immunity to a few specific diseases and conditions. They capitalized on these conditions to illustrate the inferiority of blacks to whites, to rationalize the use of this "less fit" racial group as slaves, to justify subjecting Negro slaves to harsh working conditions in extreme dampness and heat in the malarious regions of the South, and to prove to their critics that they recognized the special medical weaknesses of blacks and took these failings into account when providing for their human chattel. But in terms of an overall theory of medical care predicated on racial inferiority, the issue was a false one. It is instructive to note here, for example, that no writer ventured beyond vague and cautious statements about bleeding or purging blacks less than whites. None presented a numerical account of the amount of blood loss or the dose of medicine which was optimal for blacks. Remarks on the subject were always couched in terms which placed whites in a position of medical and physical superiority over Negroes, perfect for polemics and useless to the practitioner.

Slavery, Sickle Cell, and Malaria

White physicians and slaveholders not only claimed that blacks reacted uniquely to certain medical procedures; they also asserted that Negroes manifested increased susceptibility to, and more severe cases of, several diseases, and, conversely, greater resistance to other illnesses, when compared with Caucasians. Their observations were usually accurate, but at times they allowed racial prejudice to cloud their views.[28]

One of the most fascinating subjects about which Old South medical authors wrote was black resistance to malaria. Also called intermittent and/or remittent fever, periodic fever, fever and chills, marsh fever, and autumnal fever, malaria was the focus of constant comment during the antebellum period because the black man's liability to it appeared to vary from region to region, plantation to plantation, and individual to individual. Physicians openly disagreed with one another on the subject. Dr. Daniel Drake, eminent practitioner and medical professor of the Upper Mississippi Valley, warned his readers:

> Intermittent, and remittent fevers . . . are the greatest outlets of human life among the people of whom I am speaking [Negro slaves]. They [fevers] return every year in the latter part of summer and in autumn, and one attack is no security against another. When they do not prove fatal, they leave behind them diseases of the spleen, and dropsy. In the following winter those [who] were down in the autumn, are tender, and often die of inflammation of the lungs.[29]

On the other hand, David Ramsay, a respected South Carolina physician and historian, assured planters in his state: "Their [Negroes'] common intermittent fevers are easily cured and seldom require more than a smart emetic." [30]

Malaria is a parasitic disease caused by the colonizing within red blood cells of a one-celled animal, plasmodium. When an infected anopheles mosquito takes a blood meal from a human, these malarial parasites pass from the mosquito's salivary glands into the human bloodstream. From there the immature forms

[28] Numerous articles appeared in antebellum medical and agricultural journals on this topic. For citations and discussions, see Haller, "The Negro and the Southern Physician," 238–53; Jordan, "Plantation Medicine," 83–107; U.S. Surgeon General's Office, *Index Catalog*, IX, 695–97.

[29] Drake, "Diseases of the Negro Population," 342.

[30] David Ramsay, *History of South Carolina, from Its First Settlement in 1670 to the Year 1808* (Newberry, S.C., 1858), II, 52.

enter liver cells, multiply, and reenter the bloodstream by rupturing the host cells. They then invade red blood cells, where a similar multiplication and destruction cycle occurs, releasing more parasites into the circulation. White blood cells (phagocytes) ingest and destroy many of the plasmodia in the blood vessels, lymph nodes, liver, and especially in the spleen, where massive enlargement usually occurs. The crowding of small blood vessels with red cell debris, large numbers of parasites, and phagocytes occasionally causes vascular occlusion. Of the three major types of malarial parasites, only one, *Plasmodium falciparum,* tends to cause death, due to blockage of blood vessels to the brain, heart, or intestines. The other two forms are generally more benign and self-limiting in their destruction, though they tend to remain for longer periods within the human body, and cause lingering or recurrent illnesses. These latter types, *Plasmodium vivax* and *Plasmodium malariae,* may reinvade liver and blood cells several times before the body produces sufficient amounts of antibodies to resist them. If death does not intervene, untreated *P. falciparum* infections usually persist for six to eight months, but no longer than two years, while *P. vivax* may continue to multiply for five years and *P. malariae* for up to thirty years.[31]

The onset is characterized by a period of chills which cannot be relieved even by large numbers of blankets, followed by an episode of extremely high fever, frequent nausea, vomiting, and severe headache. Profuse sweating begins and continues for up to five hours as the fever abates. Finally a nonfebrile interval of from one (*P. falciparum*) to four (*P. malariae*) days, during which the parasites multiply within red blood cells, allows the patient respite from the paroxysms of the disease. This cycle may repeat itself for several weeks, and then recur months or years later, depending on the type of parasite and the patient's condi-

[31] Harold W. Brown and David L. Belding, *Basic Clinical Parasitology* (New York, 1964), 71–87; Ernest Jawetz, Joseph L. Melnick, and Edward A. Adelberg, *Review of Medical Microbiology* (Los Altos, Calif., 1966), 460–63. The best work on all aspects of malaria is Mark F. Boyd, ed., *Malariology* (Philadelphia, 1949).

tion.[32] The conclusion of each paroxysmic cycle leaves the patient in a weakened state, ripe for infection from other animal, bacterial, or viral parasites. In this regard, Dr. Drake's assessment of the disease was certainly an accurate one.

The three major concerns of the plantation slaveowner regarding malaria were that it would kill his slaves during the initial attack; that it would incapacitate susceptible bondsmen during the height of the harvest season; and that it would cause relapses resulting in loss of time from work, or death from weakness and infection. The unpredictability of the disease was a source of great frustration to planters during important seasons.[33] Unfortunately for the slaveowner, harvest time for many crops coincided with the period of greatest activity for the anopheles mosquito—late summer and early fall. The marshes and shallow streambeds deep in shady forests were ideally suited to this insect's breeding needs. The large numbers of whites and blacks already harboring malarial parasites in their livers and bloodstreams served as reservoirs from which uninfected mosquitoes could draw additional supplies to continue the life cycle of the plasmodium. Some planters, though unaware of the diseases carried by these small insects, did issue "Mucheto Bars" (nets) to slaves to keep the pesky creatures from biting, all the while complaining of "10 sick [with] 'Fevers' . . . [I] never have been so out done with sickness before in my life." [34]

Virginia, though an Upper South state, did not escape the trials of malarial invasion. The disease was prevalent in the Tidewater and Southside regions, location of many old and large estates.[35]

[32] Paul F. Russell et al., *Practical Malariology* (London, 1963), 380–85; Brown and Belding, *Basic Clinical Parasitology*, 78–82; Jewetz, Melnick, and Adelberg, *Medical Microbiology*, 462–63. For an excellent discussion of the malarial cycle and its implications for American medical and demographic history, see Darrett B. Rutman and Anita H. Rutman, "Of Agues and Fevers: Malaria in the Early Chesapeake," *WMQ*, 3rd series, 33 (1976), 31–60.

[33] See, e.g., Franklin L. Riley, ed., "Diary of a Mississippi Planter, January 1, 1840, to April 1863," *Publications of the Mississippi Historical Society*, 10 (1909), 333–34.

[34] Edwin A. Davis, ed., *Plantation Life in the Florida Parishes of Louisiana, 1836–1846, as Reflected in the Diary of Bennet H. Barrow* (New York, 1943), 204–5 (23, 26, 27 July 1840).

[35] Governor's Message [Thomas M. Randolph], in H of D Jl., 1822/23, p. 6; E., "Great Improvements in Charlotte County," *FR*, 5 (1837), 2.

Hill Carter's Shirley Plantation, for instance, abutting the James River (and swampland) in Charles City County, annually experienced malarial fevers. Some years it arrived earlier than expected, as in mid-July of 1823, when Carter complained: "Ague and Fever begun already—a few cases." At times malaria seemed to affect his entire white and black family: "Very sickly, every body having the ague & fever." In early September 1855, Carter reported that no cases of ague and fever had yet appeared. The mosquitoes compensated for that oversight by infecting eleven slaves in nine days later that month.[36]

The fact that so-called intermittent and remittent fever was usually a self-limiting disease which caused fewer deaths among slaves than typhoid, pneumonia, or cholera did not prevent planters from worrying about it. Malaria was more of a nuisance, and caused more economic waste in terms of time lost, than other, usually fatal diseases which occurred only in widely spaced epidemics.[37] And since malaria was endemic throughout most of the slave South, it posed a constant threat to health year in and year out, weakening the stricken so that other diseases often killed them.

The physicians who treated the slaves' diseases recorded their opinions on immunity and treatment of malaria in agricultural, commercial, and medical journals, as well as in personal correspondence. The practitioner's interest in the theoretical question of Negro susceptibility actually far exceeded the planter's. Some of the most prominent names in southern medicine contributed articles or statements to important journals giving their opinions on intermittent fever and the Negro. The discussion was not, for the most part, over whether blacks were immune, since it was obvious to most that slaves suffered from malaria just as whites

[36] Shirley Farm Journals, 15 July 1823, 20 September 1826, 7, 22 September–1 October 1855, LC. See also Thomas Shepherd to David Jameson, 14 September 1798, Dismal Swamp Papers, Duke.
[37] Postell, on the other hand, found "comparatively few instances in which malarial fevers were mentioned" in planters' records, and postulated that "since the mortality from malarial fevers was not great the planter was more concerned with those diseases which left a heavy mortality toll than with a chronic ailment" (*Health of Slaves*, 75). For its effects on the development of the New South, see Young, "Malaria in the South, 1900–1930."

did. In dispute was the degree of susceptibility and the virulence of the disease in Negroes: Could slaves acquire some resistance to malaria by living in constant proximity to its supposed source? Were some slaves natually immune? Did slaves have milder attacks of the disease than whites?

At one extreme were the few physicians who held steadfastly to the belief that blacks were, in fact, immune to malaria, or nearly so. The South Carolina planter-physician Philip Tidyman stated in a Philadelphia scientific journal:

> The negroes who reside on large rice plantations and other places in the vicinity of stagnant water, generally enjoy through the hot months as good health as they would do if placed in the mountains. Intermittent fever, so hostile to the constitution of the white inhabitants, has no terror for the negro, who when attacked, requires but little medicine to rid him of this insidious enemy, and to secure him against a return.[38]

Oddly enough, the following two pages of Dr. Tidyman's article describe several medical treatments for intermittent and remittent fever. As shown above, Dr. David Ramsay, the Charleston historian and physician, agreed with Tidyman's observations.

In total opposition to the conclusions of men like Tidyman and Ramsay was another small group of physicians. They believed not only that blacks were just as susceptible to malaria as whites, but also that the attacks were as severe, and, in one case (Dr. Nott), that acquiring resistance to the disease in some regions was impossible. The physicians of this persuasion were careful to confine their remarks to the up-country interior of the southern states, specifically excluding discussion of South Carolina and Mississippi River Low Country Negroes because of their reputed ability to acclimate themselves to marsh fevers.[39]

[38] Philip Tidyman, "A Sketch of the Most Remarkable Diseases of the Negroes of the Southern States," *Philadelphia Journal of the Medical and Physical Sciences,* 12 (1826), 315–16. For similar views, see Thomson, *A Treatise on the Diseases of Negroes in Jamaica,* 14; Dr. Ferguson, quoted in "Acclimation; and the Liability of Negroes to the Endemic Fevers of the South," *New Orleans Medical News and Hospital Gazette,* 5 (1858–59), 84.

[39] Josiah C. Nott, "Liability of Negroes to the Epidemic Diseases of the South," *SMSJ,* NS 14 (1858), 253–54. He wrote extensively on comparative susceptibility to disease in Nott and Gliddon, eds., *Indigenous Races,* 353–401. See also Dr.

The majority of southern physicians, however, took a more moderate stance on the issue of racial immunity and the virulence of malarial fevers, claiming that blacks were less susceptible than whites, though some did note that those living in the Low Country had a much greater resistance than slaves from other areas.[40] One of the few southern physicians who actually took the trouble quantitatively to determine the comparative incidence of malaria in whites and blacks was Alfred G. Tebault of London Bridge, Princess Anne County, Virginia. He made an elaborate study of intermittent and remittent fevers during 1833, 1834, 1835, and 1841, observing the race of those afflicted, as well as their sex, age, and length of residence in the Tidewater area. His results confirmed the moderates' position: "The blacks are by far less liable to fever both intermittent and remittent than the whites and when they are attacked their cases are generally milder and very easily relieved. . . ." Tebault published his findings in the prestigious *American Journal of the Medical Sciences* (Philadelphia) and included a table [41] to illustrate his point:

> During four years, in which I kept a record of cases of periodic fevers, occurring in a population of equal portions of white and black inhabitants, the proportion of attacks stood thus:

Year	Blacks		Whites
1	26	to	100
2	15	"	100
3	40	"	100
4	33	"	100

"D's" statement quoted in Felice Swados, "Negro Health on the Ante-Bellum Plantations," *BHM*, 10 (1941), 464. Swados cites her source as *SMSJ*, NS 2 (1846), 448, but Dr. "D" is not there. For an opinion similar to that of Dr. "D," see "Acclimation," 81.

[40] Merrill, "Distinctive Peculiarities and Diseases of the Negro Race," 150. See also Samuel H. Dickson (Charleston, S.C.) to J. C. Nott, 16 May 1856, in Nott and Gliddon, eds., *Indigenous Races*, 380–81; Ramsay, "Physiological Differences," 414; Drake, "Diseases of the Negro Population," 342; Richard H. Shryock, ed., "Selections from the Letters of Richard D. Arnold, M.D.," *Bulletin of the Johns Hopkins Hospital*, 40 (1928), 178; Pendleton, "On the Susceptibility of the Caucasian and African Races," 339.

[41] Notebook #3, pp. 6–9 (quote on p. 8), Alfred G. Tebault Papers, UVA (#9926); Tebault, "Practical Remarks on Diseases of the Spleen," *AJMS*, NS 31 (1856), 350.

Those physicians who believed that some slaves had natural
or acquired immunity, or contracted less severe cases of malaria,
made some endeavor to explain this phenomenon. Nott and some
of his followers postulated that Low Country blacks suffered less
from marsh fevers than other slaves because there was a "difference in [the] types of those malarial fevers which originate in
the flat tide-water rice ilands, and those of the clay-hills, or
marsh fevers of the interior." The author of an article in the
New Orleans Medical News and Hospital Gazette (possibly one
of the editors, Drs. D. Warren Brickell or Erasmus Darwin
Fenner) disagreed with Nott and proposed his own theory,
which, like Nott's, was surprisingly close to one of the probable
explanations:

> Now, to our apprehension, the attainment of more perfect acclima-
> tion in the latter region [the Low Country] is more justly attributable
> to the *steady continuance* [of endemic fevers throughout the season]
> than to any *peculiarity* of the febrific cause [as suggested by Nott];
> for we find no material difference in the types of fever prevailing
> here and in the uplands.
>
> There are malarious *seasons* as well as malarious regions, and it
> appears to us that in those climates and localities where the morbific
> cause is most continuous, the effects should be most durable. . . .
>
> It requires longer exposure and often numerous attacks before the
> human system becomes seasoned to the deleterious influence of
> malaria.[42]

Modern science has answered many of the questions of immunity and prevention of malaria with which doctors and
planters struggled in the antebellum period. We now know, for
instance, that malaria is spread by the anopheles mosquito, indicating that the use of mosquito netting and the placement of
plantation living quarters away from swamps and stagnant waters
were of some efficacy in reducing the chances of infection with
the malarial parasite. But nineteenth-century planters did not
always follow these two procedures of modern malarial prevention, so the disease took its toll in economic loss and human
suffering. One exception to this general ignorance and apathy

[42] Nott, "Liability of Negroes to Epidemics," 254; "Acclimation," 81–82.

was the work of that indefatigable farmer and loyal Southerner, Edmund Ruffin of Prince George County, Virginia. Articles in his influential agricultural journal, the *Farmer's Register*, constantly reiterated the usefulness of marling and of stagnant millpond drainage in reducing the incidence of malaria among both blacks and whites. Some heeded his advice, but many did not and continued to experience high worker morbidity.[43]

Several factors contributed to the phenomenon of malarial immunity. As will be discussed below, many blacks did possess an inherited immunity to one or another form of malaria. But for Caucasians and those Negroes without natural resistance to a particular plasmodium type, it was possible to acquire malarial immunity or tolerance only under the conditions stated by the author of the article in the *New Orleans Medical News and Hospital Gazette*—by suffering repeated infections of the disease over a period of several years. For this to occur, one species of plasmodium had to be present constantly in the endemic region so that, with each attack, a person's supply of antibodies was strengthened against future parasitic invasions. Interruption of this process, such as removal to non-endemic areas for the summer (when exposure to the parasite was useful in building immunity), or for several years (during schooling or travel), prohibited the aggregation of sufficient antibodies to resist infection. In truly endemic areas, acquiring immunity this way was a risky affair: unprotected children struggled for their lives, adults suffered from relapses of infections contracted years ago, and partially immune adults worked through mild cases. It is no wonder, then, that slaves sold from, say, Virginia, where one form of malaria was prevalent, to a Louisiana bayou or South Carolina rice plantation where a different species or strain of plasmodium was endemic, had a high incidence of the disease. Even adult slaves from Africa had to go through a "seasoning"

[43] See, e.g., Edmund Ruffin, "Desultory Observations on the Police of Health in Virginia," *FR*, 5 (1837), 159–60; E., "Great Improvements in Charlotte County," *ibid.*, 2; [Ruffin,] "On the Sources of Malaria, or Autumnal Diseases, in Virginia, and the Means of Remedy and Prevention," *ibid.*, 6 (1838), 216–28; [Ruffin,] "General Remarks on the Causes of and Means of Preventing the Formation of Malaria, and the Autumnal Diseases Which Are the Effects of It, in Virginia," *ibid.*, 5 (1837), 41–43.

period, because the strains of malarial parasites in this country differed from those in their native lands.[44]

Generally speaking, most malaria in the Upper South and in inland piedmont areas was of the milder vivax type, while vivax and the more dangerous falciparum malaria coexisted in coastal and swampy inland portions of both the Lower and Upper South. Rare pockets of the *P. malariae* type (quartan fever) were scattered across the South.[45] Of course, epidemics of one type or another could strike any neighborhood, resulting in sickness and death even to those who had acquired resistance to the endemic variety. *P. falciparum* usually caused such epidemics, especially in the temperate regions of the South. In Virginia, where *P. vivax* usually predominated, for instance,[46] epidemics of what must have been falciparum malaria struck in 1803, 1822, and the late 1840's and early 1850's, causing many deaths and great losses of work time and business.[47] Some observers here noticed that many blacks suffered only mildly from endemic or epidemic malaria, but they were at a loss to explain it: "Every year [inhabitants] on the [Rappahannock] river side [of Essex County, Virginia], and perhaps half the people in the forest, had intermitting fevers of some type. Negroes were as much affected by tertians and double tertians as the whites, though I do not recollect any negro having bilious fever." [48]

[44] Russell et al., *Practical Malariology*, 426–28.

[45] Ernest Carroll Faust, "The Distribution of Malaria in North America, Mexico, Central America and the West Indies," in Forest Ray Moulton, ed., *A Symposium on Human Malaria* (Washington, D.C., 1941), 8; William Sydney Thayer, *Lectures on the Malarial Fevers* (New York, 1897), 97, 103, 119, 130; Frank B. Livingstone, *Abnormal Hemoglobins in Human Populations: A Summary and Interpretation* (Chicago, 1967), 98; "Copy of a Letter from Dr. James Lyons," in Currie, *An Historical Account*, 282; Notebook #3, p. 9, Alfred G. Tebault Papers, UVA (#9926).

[46] Alexander Somervail, "On the Medical Topography and Diseases of a Section of Virginia," *Philadelphia Journal of the Medical and Physical Sciences*, 6 (1823), 280; "Copy of a Letter from Dr. James Lyons," in Currie, *An Historical Account*, 282, 289; Louisa Barraud Cocke to Mrs. Louisa Cocke, 20 December 1822, in Cocke Deposit, Cocke Papers, UVA; [A. D. Galt,] *Practical Medicine: Illustrated by Cases of the Most Important Diseases*, ed. John M. Galt (Philadelphia, 1843), 10–137; Notebook #3, p. 9, Alfred G. Tebault Papers, UVA (#9926).

[47] James Grimes to Col. John Jamieson [sic], 11 December 1803, Dismal Swamp Papers, Duke; "Governor's Message," H of D Jl., 1822/23, p. 6; A. T. P. Merritt, "An Abstract of an Essay on Congestive Fever," *Steth.*, 1 (1851), 61.

[48] Alexander Somervail, "Medical Topography of Virginia," 280.

The major reason for black immunity to vivax and/or falciparum malaria relates not to acquired resistance, but to selective
genetic factors. At least three hereditary conditions prevalent
among blacks in parts of modern Africa appear to confer immunity to malaria upon their bearers.[49] Recent medical research
indicates that the red blood cells of persons lacking a specific
factor called Duffy antigen are resistant to invasion of P. vivax.
Approximately 90 percent of West Africans lack Duffy antigens,
as do about 70 percent of Afro-Americans. This inherited, symptomless, hematologic condition is extremely rare in other racial
groups. All evidence points to the conclusion that infection by
P. vivax requires the presence of Duffy-positive red blood cells.
Since most members of the Negro race do not possess this factor,
they are immune to vivax malaria. It can be safely assumed that
the vast majority of American slaves and free blacks were likewise resistant to this form of the disease.[50]

Some antebellum blacks had additional protection against
malaria resulting from the abnormal genetic hemoglobin conditions, sickle cell disease (a form of anemia) and sickle cell trait
(the symptomless carrier state of the sickling gene). People with
either of these conditions had milder cases of, and decreased risk
of mortality from, the most malignant form of malaria, falciparum. But many of those who had sickle cell *disease* died from
its consequences before or during adolescence. Blacks who had
sickle cell *trait*, however, lived entirely normal lives and could
then transmit the gene for sickling to their offspring. Since people
with the trait had one normal gene and one abnormal gene for
sickling, while those with the disease had two of the abnormal
genes, offspring could inherit sickle cell anemia only when each
parent contributed a gene for sickling. The incidence of sickle

[49] *Journal of Parasitology*, 41 (1955), 315–18; Arno G. Motulsky, "Hereditary
Red Cell Traits and Malaria," *American Journal of Tropical Health and Hygiene*,
13 (1964), 147–58; Frank B. Livingstone, "Malaria and Human Polymorphisms,"
Annual Review of Genetics, 5 (1971), 33–64. For a recent, excellent application
of the important relationship between sickle cell and immunity to malaria in the
South Carolina Low Country, see Wood, *Black Majority*, ch. 3.

[50] Louis H. Miller et al., "Erythrocyte Receptors for (*Plasmodium knowlesi*)
Malaria: Duffy Blood Group Determinants," *Science*, 189 (1975), 561–63;
Miller et al., "The Resistance Factor to *Plasmodium vivax* in Blacks: The
Duffy-Blood-Group Genotype, FyFy," *New England Journal of Medicine*, 295
(1976), 302–4.

cell trait among the present-day tribes of the former slave coast
(from Senegal to Angola) ranges up to 25 and 30 percent of the
population in portions of Nigeria and the Congo, while sickle cell
anemia occurs in only about 1–2 percent (see maps).[51] Because
the sickle cell condition was not discovered until 1910, physicians
in the antebellum South were unaware that this was one reason
why some slaves on plantations appeared to be immune to
malarial infections.

Scientists have evidence that one other genetic condition
probably affords some malarial resistance: deficiency of the
enzyme glucose-6-phosphate dehydrogenase (G-6-PD deficiency).[52] It is a sex-linked trait like hemophilia (i.e., the
gene controlling this defect lies on the "X" or female chromo-
some, which determines an individual's sex). Medical investigators have not examined the incidence of G-6-PD deficiency in
Africa nearly as extensively as the incidence of sickle cell genes,
but those who have done so already report a high incidence
within the former slave-trading region (see maps).[53]

Despite the fact that slaves moved about with increasing frequency as the internal slave trade assumed greater importance
during the nineteenth century, it is possible to determine the
approximate original distribution of red blood cell defects among

[51] G. C. Ezeilo, "Sickle Cell Trait Frequency in Zambia," *Tropical and Geographical Medicine*, 22 (1970), 189, 196; J. Vandepitte, "The Incidence of
Haemoglobinoses in the Belgian Congo," in J. H. P. Jonxis and J. F. Delafresnaye,
eds., *Abnormal Haemoglobins: A Symposium* (Oxford, 1959), 275; J. Vandepitte
and J. Stijns, "Haemoglobinopathies in the Congo (Leopoldville) and the
Rwanda-Burundi," in J. H. P. Jonxis, ed., *Abnormal Haemoglobins in Africa*
(Philadelphia, 1965), 320–21. For general discussions of the sickle cell diseases,
see G. C. DeGruchy, *Clinical Haematology in Medical Practice* (Philadelphia,
1964), 283–85; Alvin E. Lewis, *Principles of Hematology* (New York, 1970),
179–94; or any recent hematology textbook.
[52] Thomas Botler, "G-6-PD Deficiency and Malaria in Black Americans in
Vietnam," *Military Medicine*, 138 (1973), 153–55.
[53] Livingstone, *Abnormal Hemoglobins*, 17–21; Livingstone, "Malaria and
Human Polymorphisms," 48; Motulsky, "Hereditary Red Cell Traits and Malaria,"
147–55; L. Luzzatto, "New Developments in Glucose-6-Phosphate Dehydrogenase
Deficiency," in Bracha Ramot, ed., *Genetic Polymorphisms and Diseases in Man*
(New York, 1974), 358–72; Luzzatto, "Studies of Polymorphic Traits for the
Characterization of Populations; African Populations South of the Sahara," *ibid.*,
55–68.

eighteenth-century Virginia and South Carolina blacks. To do this, one must assume that present-day African Negroes have not significantly changed their places of residence since that time—a relatively safe assumption. The largest concentrations of blacks with Hemoglobin S (sickle cell hemoglobin) in modern Africa are in the Senegambia, Sierra Leone, and eastern Windward Coast regions. Somewhat smaller pockets of persons with high sickle cell frequencies also exist along the former Gold Coast, the Bights of Benin and Biafra, and the inland areas of the Congo (see maps and Table 1). G-6-PD deficiency is less generally distributed, though future studies may show new areas of concentration in the slave-trading region. Using Philip Curtin's tabulations of the African homes of slave imports into Virginia (1710–69) and South Carolina (1733–1807), and present-day maps of African gene frequencies, a remarkable overlap can be discovered. Modern studies of Hemoglobin S in Charleston and Sea Island blacks confirm this correlation,[54] as do other studies of the incidence of genetic blood defects in American Negroes.[55]

It is impossible to provide an exact calculation of sickle cell and G-6-PD deficiency gene prevalence among antebellum southern blacks. However, an estimate might be ventured based on known gene frequencies among present-day Afro-Americans and those Africans residing in former slave-trading areas. One leading medical authority on abnormal hemoglobins has estimated that at least 22 percent of Africans first brought to this country possessed genes for sickling. Over the generations this figure decreased somewhat as miscegenation diluted the Negro with Indian and Caucasian genes. At present the incidence of the sickling gene in the American black population is about 10 percent.[56] Other medical scientists have determined that approxi-

[54] Philip Curtin, *The Atlantic Slave Trade: A Census* (Madison, Wisc., 1969), 156–58; Livingstone, *Abnormal Hemoglobins*, 82, 86; W. S. Pollitzer, "The Negroes of Charleston (S.C.): A Study of Hemoglobin Types, Serology, and Morphology," *American Journal of Physical Anthropology*, NS 16 (1958), 241–48, esp. 247.

[55] See, e.g., Arno G. Motulsky, "Frequency of Sickling Disorders in U.S. Blacks," *New England Journal of Medicine*, 288 (1973), 31–33.

[56] A. C. Allison, "Aspects of Polymorphism in Man," *Cold Spring Harbor Symposia on Quantitative Biology*, 20 (1955), 240–45; Allison, "Notes on Sickle-Cell Polymorphism," *Annals of Human Genetics*, 19 (1954–55), 47.

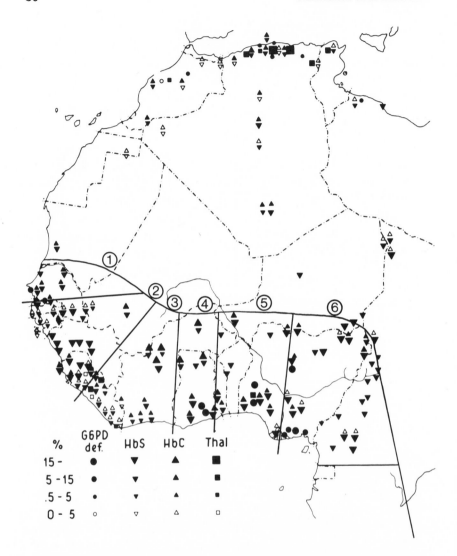

Incidence of Red Blood Cell Defects in Modern Africa.

Numbers refer to regions of origin in Table 1.
G6PD def. = Glucose-6-Phosphate Dehydrogenase deficiency
HbS   = Sickle Cell

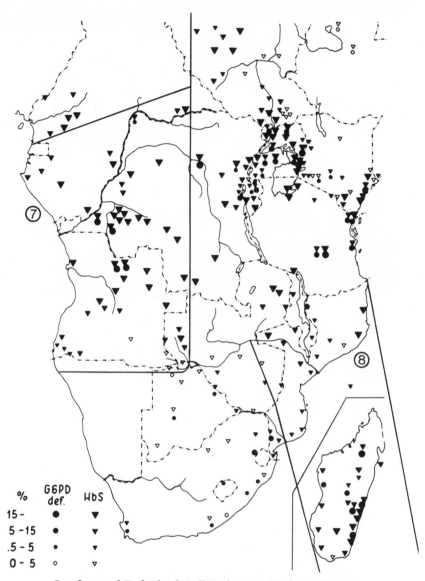

Incidence of Red Blood Cell Defects in Modern Africa.

Numbers refer to regions of origin in Table 1.

G6PD def. = Glucose-6-Phosphate Dehydrogenase deficiency
HbS   = Sickle Cell

SOURCE: Frank B. Livingstone, *Abnormal Hemoglobins in Human Populations* (Chicago, 1967), 82, 86.

Table 1. African Origins of U.S. Slaves, 1690–1807

Percent of slaves of identifiable origin imported by

		Virginia 1710–69	South Carolina 1733–1807	British trade 1690–1807	Estimated percent of total imported into North America
1	Senegambia	14.9	19.5	5.5	13.3
2	Sierra Leone	5.3	6.8	4.3	5.5
3	Windward Coast	6.3	16.3	11.6	11.4
4	Gold Coast	16.0	13.3	18.4	15.9
5	Bight of Benin	—	1.6	11.3	4.3
6	Bight of Biafra	37.7	2.1	30.1	23.3
7	Angola	15.7	39.6	18.2	24.5
8	Mozambique-Madagascar	4.1	0.7	a	1.6
	Unknown	—	—	0.6	0.2
	Total	100.0	100.0	100.0	100.0

a Included in Angola figure.

SOURCE: Philip Curtin, *The African Slave Trade: A Census* (Madison, Wisc., 1969), 157.

mately 20 percent of West Africans have genes for G-6-PD deficiency, while only 10 percent of modern Afro-Americans have it.[57] Overall, then, using conservative figures, approximately 30–40 percent of newly arrived slaves had one or both of these genes, with a slow decrease in incidence over time. Recent evidence points to a higher than expected frequency of the G-6-PD gene in patients with sickle cell disease, perhaps reducing this estimate by a few percent.[58] Thus a large proportion of Negro servants were immune to the severe effects of falciparum malaria—a fact which planters and physicians in the South could not help but notice.

When black Africans from the middle western and eastern coasts unwillingly immigrated to the New World as slaves, they

[57] P. L. Workman, "Gene Flow and the Search for Natural Selection in Man," *Human Biology*, 40 (1968), 272; Curt Stern, *Principles of Human Genetics* (San Francisco, 1960), 234–35.

[58] Ernest Beutler et al., "Prevalence of Glucose-6-Phosphate Dehydrogenase Deficiency in Sickle-Cell Disease," *New England Journal of Medicine*, 290 (1974), 826–28.

naturally brought their diseases with them. Aside from the testimony of some planters and physicians that many slaves appeared to be immune to malaria, there is little concrete evidence to show that the diseases associated with the sickle cell or G-6-PD genes occurred in the antebellum South. Some antebellum records do hint, however, at probable instances of these diseases, though the non-distinctiveness of their symptoms make them difficult illnesses to identify positively. First, many planters complained of the high rate of spontaneous abortion among their slave women.[59] Since young women with either sickle cell anemia or sickle cell–Hemoglobin C disease (another genetic condition related to sickle cell anemia) are known to have a higher rate of miscarriage, the presence of these diseases among bondswomen probably accounted for a portion of the abortions noted.[60] Second, all the abnormal hemoglobin diseases produce mild to severe joint pains which were probably labeled rheumatism by planters, physicians, and slaves alike. Older adults no doubt normally experienced such pains, especially during damp weather; but when children suffered from them, the cause in some cases must have been sickle cell anemia. Third, a partial reason for the notoriously high mortality rates among slave children in the antebellum South was the fact that about half of the children with sickle cell anemia died before reaching the age of twenty.[61] Fourth, in partial explanation of the extreme sensitivity of blacks to all infections of the lungs, recent findings indicate that sickle cell anemia and sickle cell–Hemoglobin C disease predispose individuals to severe pneumococcal infections.[62] Finally, the occurrence of

[59] See, e.g., John H. Morgan, "An Essay on the Causes of the Production of Abortion among Our Negro Population," *Nashville Journal of Medicine and Surgery*, 19 (1860), 117–23; E. M. Pendleton, "On the Comparative Fecundity of the Caucasian and African Races," *Charleston Medical Journal and Review*, 6 (1851), 351–56.

[60] William J. Williams et al., *Hematology* (New York, 1972), 418.

[61] Motulsky, "Frequency of Sickling Disorders in U.S. Blacks," 32.

[62] See, e.g., Robert W. Gibbes, "Southern Slave Life," *De Bow's Review*, 24 (1858), 323; Davis, ed., *Diary of Barrow*, 322 (entries of 6, 8, 9, 11 April 1844); John Duffy, "Eighteenth Century Carolina Health Conditions," *JSH*, 18 (1952), 300. The relationship between abnormal hemoglobin diseases and pneumococcal infections is discussed in Sherwin A. Kabins and Charles Lerner, "Fulminant Pneumococcemia and Sickle Cell Anemia," *JAMA*, 211 (1970), 467–71.

chronic leg ulcers among slaves also hints at the existence of sickle cell disease.[63]

If it is true that approximately 30–40 percent of all American slaves and free blacks were carriers of genetic red blood cell defects, why did men like Dr. Josiah Clark Nott state that slaves in some regions of the South showed immunity to malaria, while those in other areas appeared to be quite susceptible to that disease? He pointed specifically to the Carolina rice plantations along the Atlantic coast as the area where slaves were born with, or were able to develop resistance to, periodic fevers; Dr. A. P. Merrill of Memphis mentioned the cotton and sugar plantations of the Lower Mississippi Valley in a similar vein. Of course, slaves in both areas became sick with, and even died from, malaria, but in smaller numbers than would normally be expected. Both of these areas were probably endemic for falciparum malaria, while in the interior and piedmont regions malaria was due mostly to *P. vivax*. Since the sickle cell gene conferred immunity only to falciparum malaria, and many blacks possessed natural immunity to vivax malaria, those slaves who lived in regions where one species of plasmodium was not endemic were subject to infection by the other species. Furthermore, *P. vivax* was probably not endemic throughout much of the hill country, preventing the residents of these parts from acquiring resistance through repeated infections. When an epidemic of malaria struck, unprotected blacks were quite susceptible. In this sense, Nott was close to the truth when he postulated the existence of two different types of marsh fever, one for the lowlands and one for the hilly interior.

In the end, then, several of the Old South's physicians had remarkably valid theories regarding the immunity of slaves to malaria. Though unable to predict the existence of the genetic diseases which protected blacks, these men did present reasonably accurate descriptions of acquired immunity and the various types of endemic malaria present in the South. They were less well grounded in their suggestions for the prevention of the disease. As with the weather, in those days planters and physi-

[63] See, e.g., Thomson, *Diseases of Negroes in Jamaica*, 103, 106–7, though some of this may be due to nutritional deficiency or hookworm.

cians talked a lot about malaria, but there was precious little anyone could do about it.

Tolerance of Cold and Heat

"The African races are very susceptible of cold, and are as incapable of enduring a northern climate, as a white population are of supporting the torrid sun of Africa," concluded a South Carolina doctor after reviewing the experimental work of several English residents of Caribbean islands.[64] As with malaria, planters and physicians speculated publicly on this subject but could never adequately prove their contentions. It was the confirmed opinion of many white Southerners that blacks could not withstand cold weather to the same degree as whites because of their dark skin and equatorial origins.[65] Dr. A. P. Merrill, in fact, based his entire system of medical treatment of blacks upon the observation that "the negro race is physiologically constituted for the enjoyment of a hot climate." [66] Consequently these writers, as well as those publishing in agricultural journals, enjoined slave owners to provide blacks with adequate clothing and shelter for cold weather.[67]

Their major concern was that blacks seemed to resist and tolerate respiratory infections less well than whites. The editor of a Richmond journal, *The Monthly Stethoscope and Medical Reporter*, expressed this view in an editorial: "As a single illustration . . . [any observant medical man] will say at once, that an amount of disease of the respiratory organs, from which a white man would recover, would be fatal to the negro. . . ." Daniel Drake, the famous Mississippi Valley physician, agreed that inflammation of the lungs was "among the most destructive diseases of the colored population," and added that it often left patients with "permanently unsound" lungs. A Georgia doctor,

[64] Tidyman, "A Sketch of the Most Remarkable Diseases of Negroes," 306–14.
[65] See, e.g., Nott and Gliddon, eds., *Indigenous Races*, 363–67, esp. 366.
[66] Merrill, "Distinctive Peculiarities of the Negro Race," 25.
[67] "Management of Slaves, &c.," *FR*, 5 (1837). 32–33; Wilson, "The Negro—His Mental and Moral Peculiarities," *Cotton Planter*, NS 4 (1860), 46; Franklin, "On the Preservation of the Health of Negroes," *American Farmer*, 2 (1820), 242.

referring to local mortality statistics, confirmed the fact that blacks were "much more subjected to pulmonary affections" than whites.[68]

Since the germ theory had not yet been accepted, these men and others explained their observations with a combination of medical, anthropological, and scientific logic—and occasionally with unfounded theories. Blacks, natives of a tropical climate, were physiologically ill suited for the cold winter weather and cool spring and fall nights of the temperate zone. They breathed less air, dissipated a greater amount of "animal heat" through the skin, and eliminated larger quantities of carbon via liver and skin than whites. In addition, blacks were exposed to the elements for much of the year, placing a strain on heat production within the body. One medical extremist, Samuel A. Cartwright of New Orleans, even claimed that Negroes' lungs functioned inefficiently, causing "defective atmospherization of the blood." Some pointed to the then commonly known observation that slaves often slept with their heads (rather than their feet) next to the fire and entirely covered by a blanket; this was seen as proof that they required warm, moist air to breathe and to survive in this climate. Blacks were, these men concluded, physiologically different from whites.[69]

Even today there is some confusion among medical authorities regarding the susceptibility of Negroes to severe pulmonary infections. Some claim a racial or genetic predisposition, while others deny it. Historically, blacks have shown higher incidence and more severe manifestations of respiratory illness than have whites. Explantions for this phenomenon are numerous. First, Negroes did not experience bacterial pneumonias until the coming of the Caucasian. The entire newly exposed population was thus exquisitely sensitive to these infections, and developed much more serious cases than whites who had had frequent

[68] Editorial, Mon. Steth., 1 (1856), 162–63; Drake, "Diseases of the Negro Population," 342; Pendleton, "On the Susceptibility of the Caucasian and African Races," 337.

[69] Merrill, "Distinctive Peculiarities of the Negro Race," 25–28; Cartwright, "Diseases and Peculiarities of the Negro Race," 209–10; McGown, A Practical Treatise on the Most Common Diseases of the South, 28; "Medico-Chirurgical Society of Richmond," VMSJ, 1 (1853), 35.

contact with the bacteria since childhood. Second, black African laborers who today move from moist tropical to temperate climates (e.g., to the gold mines of South Africa) contract pneumonia at a much higher rate than whites. Though the incidence of disease decreases with time, it always remains at a more elevated level than among Caucasians. The same phenomenon probably operated during slavery. At first the mortality rate from penumonia among newly arrived slaves was probably inordinately high, but with time the figure decreased somewhat, though it is still now higher than in Caucasians. Third, there appears to be a close relationship between resistance to pulmonary infection and exposure to cool, wet weather. Slaves, who worked outdoors in all seasons and often lived in drafty, damp cabins, were therefore more apt to suffer from respiratory diseases than their masters. Finally, overcrowding and unsanitary living conditions caused an increased incidence of respiratory diseases. Slaves living in small cottages or grouped together in a large community at the quarters, where intimate and frequent visiting was common, stood a greater chance of contracting airborne infections than did the more isolated whites. Undoubtedly, all these factors combined to increase the occurrence of respiratory illness among southern blacks.[70]

The most serious nonfatal manifestation of cold intolerance was frostbite. At least one proslavery apologist claimed that the Negro race was more susceptible to this condition: "Almost every one has seen negroes in Northern cities, who have lost their legs by frost at sea—a thing rarely witnessed among whites, and yet where a single negro has been thus exposed doubtless a thousand of the former have." [71] No records of the differential racial incidence of frostbite exist for antebellum Virginia (and probably not for any other southern state), but the private letters and

[70] P. E. C. Manson-Bahr and Charles Wilcocks, *Manson's Tropical Diseases* (London, 1966), 14; Ivan L. Bennett, Jr., "Pneumococcal Infections," in T. R. Harrison et al., eds., *Principles of Internal Medicine* (New York, 1966), 1504; Roderick Heffron, *Pneumonia, with Special Reference to Pneumococcus Lobar Pneumonia* (New York, 1939), 312–16. Paul D. Hoeprich, "Bacterial Pneumonias," in Hoeprich, ed., *Infectious Diseases* (New York, 1972), 313, states: "There is no racial predisposition to pneumococcal pneumonia."

[71] Van Evrie, *Negroes and Negro "Slavery,"* 25.

journals of some residents of the Old Dominion provide evidence of this condition. Thomas Jefferson hired a slave one winter who, contrary to orders, went "down the country" for a few days and returned with both feet frostbitten. The man spent the next six months recovering. He lost his great toe and nearly lost both his legs from the resultant gangrene; Jefferson informed his owner, "I doubt if they will ever again be sound." [72] The condition was a serious one, especially for slaveowners who stood to lose the labor of valuable workers. One Amherst County planter paid his physician 300 pounds of tobacco in 1777 to cure a slave with frostbite. The treatment was painful, as an entry in this doctor's account book will attest: "To Scarifying Negroe Christmass Foot & Legs when Mortified & Frostbit, removing Skin & flesh & three times dressing the Negroe." [73]

Blacks are more susceptible to cold injury than whites. Studies conducted during and after the Korean War indicate that blacks have a poorer adaptive response to cold exposure than do whites in the followings ways: their metabolic rates do not increase significantly until after whites', and even then they do not rise as much; their first shivers (one of the body's defensive responses to cold) occur at a lower skin temperature than for whites; and their incidence of frostbite is higher and their cases more severe than those of whites. Even after blacks have acclimated to cold (and they do so in a manner physiologically similar to whites), they are then only slightly less liable to sustain cold injury than they had been previously.[74] Those antebellum observers who

[72] Thomas Jefferson to General William Chamberlayne, 17 August 1810, 6 January 1811, in Edwin Morris Betts, ed., *Thomas Jefferson's Farm Book* (Princeton, 1953), 30–33.

[73] Medical Journal of Dr. Edmund Wilcox, 1776–83, entry for 20 January 1777, Hubard Family Papers, vol. 13, p. 23, UNC. For other cases, see *Enos Hord v. S. F. and W. H. Jordan*, in Rockbridge County Court House, Lexington, Va., #74, especially M. Eskridge to Enos Hord, 16 March 1855, and S. F. and W. H. Jordan to E. Hord and J. D. Tulloss, 26 March 1855; *Dabney v. Taliaferro*, 4 Randolph 256.

[74] Russell W. Newman, "Cold Acclimation in Negro Americans," *Journal of Applied Physiology*, 27 (1969), 316–19; Thomas Adams and Benjamin G. Covino, "Racial Variations to a Standardized Cold Stress," *ibid.*, 12 (1958), 9–12; David Weiner et al., "Cold Hemagglutinins and Frostbite," *Army Medical Research Laboratory, Fort Knox, Kentucky, Reports*, 90 (1952), 1–18; Kenneth D. Orr et al., "Cold Injury—Korea 1951–52," *ibid.*, 113 (1953), 205–568,

warned against overexposure of slaves to cold were essentially correct.

Racial differences also exist with regard to heat tolerance, but these may be modified under certain conditions. Again, ante-bellum observers agreed that blacks, having originated in an area known for its heat and humidity, were ideally suited for labor in the damp, warm South. One northern physician, John H. Van Evrie, explained the black man's resistance to heat in both religious and physiological terms:

> God has adapted him, both in his physical and mental structure, to the tropics. . . .
> His head is protected from the rays of a vertical sun by a dense mat of woolly hair, wholly impervious to its fiercest heats, while his entire surface, studded with innumerable sebaceous glands, form-ing a complete excretory system, relieves him from all those climatic influences so fatal, under the same circumstances, to the sensitive and highly organized white man. Instead of seeking to shelter him-self from the burning sun of the tropics, he courts it, enjoys it, de-lights in its fiercest heats.[75]

The 1850 mortality census seemed to bear out these contentions. According to the census-takers, whites died of "heat" at three times the rate of blacks (8.6 per 10,000 white deaths vs. 3.4 per 10,000 black deaths).[76] Even more striking are the New Orleans Board of Health figures for 1850. According to this report, only one black died of heatstroke during that year (7 per 10,000 black deaths) compared with 67 whites (110 per 10,000 white deaths).[77]

These figures do not portray a true picture of the occurrence of heatstroke, however, since not every person who collapsed from the heat died and became a mortality statistic. In the fourteen British West Indian colonies between 1817 and 1836,

---

esp. 374; Peter W. Post et al., "Cold Injury and the Evolution of 'White' Skin," *Human Biology*, 47 (1975), 65–80.

[75] Van Evrie, *Negroes and Negro "Slavery,"* 251, 256.

[76] J. D. B. De Bow, *Mortality Statistics of the Seventh Census of the United States, 1850* (Washington, D.C., 1855), 28.

[77] J. C. Simonds, "Annual Report of the New Orleans and Lafayette Board of Health, for the Year 1850," *SMR*, 2 (1850), 74–77.

for instance, black African troops serving the Crown suffered
from sunstroke at the same rate as white soldiers (51 per million
black soldiers vs. 53 per million white soldiers), though their
mortality rates were quite different (0 per million black soldiers vs. 9 per million white soldiers). Furthermore, though the
morbidity rates for the two races were similar, blacks would
undoubtedly have suffered less from heatstroke had they performed labor equivalent to that of their white counterparts.
Instead, they worked, as one army officer explained in submitting his medical report, "on the public works and heavy fatigue
duties," and took "such of the guards [duties] as are most likely
to prove prejudicial to the health of whites." Even under these
adverse circumstances blacks fared better than whites.[78]

Modern medical investigators have discovered that under
normal living conditions Negroes in Africa and the United States
are better equipped to tolerate humid heat than whites. However, both races possess the same capacity to acclimatize to hot,
humid conditions.[79] The physiological mechanisms by which the
human body acclimatizes to heat can be readily observed and
measured. Increased external temperature causes the body to
perspire more, resulting in a greater evaporative heat loss, a decline in skin and rectal temperatures, and a drop in the heart rate
from its initially more rapid pace. When whites and blacks are
equally active in the same environment over a period of time,
there is little difference in heat tolerance.[80]

From this information it can be assumed that, in the Old South,
slaves and free blacks possessed a higher *natural* tolerance to
humid heat stress than did whites. In addition, Negroes became
quickly acclimatized to performance of their particular tasks

[78] [Alexander M. Tulloch,] *Statistical Report on the Sickness, Mortality, and
Invaliding among the Troops in the West Indies* . . . (London, 1838), 4 and
Abstracts I, XIII, XXV, XXVI of Appendix. This report is also printed in Great
Britain, Parliament, House of Commons, *Sessional Papers*, XL, 417.

[79] Paul T. Baker, "Racial Differences in Heat Tolerance," *American Journal of
Physical Anthropology*, NS 16 (1958), 293; Joel M. Hanna, "Responses of Native
and Migrant Desert Residents to Arid Heat," *ibid.*, NS 32 (1970), 187.

[80] C. H. Wyndam, "Heat Reactions of Different Ethnic Groups," in UNESCO,
*Environmental Physiology and Psychology in Arid Conditions: Proceedings of the
Lucknow Symposium* (Liege, Belgium, 1964), 143–45; N. B. Strydom and C. H.
Wyndam, "Natural State of Heat Acclimatization of Different Ethnic Groups,"
Federation Proceedings, 66 (1963), 806–7.

under the prevailing climatic conditions of the region. This natural and acquired acclimatization enabled black laborers to withstand the damp heat of summer better than could whites, who were unused to physical exertion under such severe conditions. White farm and general laborers, however, also must have adjusted to the heat and fared as well as blacks. One physiological difference between Caucasians and Negroes which might have affected work performance in the hot, humid South was the latter's inherent ability to discharge smaller amounts of sodium chloride and other vital body salts (electrolytes) into sweat and urine. Excessive loss of these salts leads to heat prostration and heatstroke. Thus conservation of needed electrolytes provided slaves with an advantage over laboring whites, whose requirements for replacement of the substances were greater.[81] In the case of heat tolerance, then, white observers were correct in noting a racial difference, but they tended to ignore the fact that many whites did become acclimatized to the hot, humid environment and worked quite as well as slaves. They only needed a bit more salt.

Other Medical Differences

Whites detected, or thought they detected, distinctive variances in black susceptibility to several other medical conditions common in the antebellum South. Many believed that slave women developed prolapsed uteruses at a higher rate than white women, though modern anatomists have shown that Negroes are actually less prone to this affliction than Caucasians (see Chapter 4). Observers also noted that slaves were frequent sufferers of typhoid fever, worms, and dysentery, though we now know that the reason for this high prevalence was environmental rather than racial or genetic (see Chapter 2). Blacks did, however, have a greater resistance to the yellow fever virus than whites (see Chapter 7).

One disease which drew great attention because of its fre-

[81] This phenomenon was noted by at least one antebellum physician. See W. G. Ramsay, "Physiological Differences," 413. William S. S. Ladell, "Terrestrial Animals in Humid Heat: Man," in D. B. Dill et al., eds., *Handbook of Physiology: Adaptation to the Environment* (section 4) (Washington, 1963), 625–59.

quency and virulence was consumption (pulmonary tuberculosis). It was the leading cause of death in nineteenth-century America for members of both races. A particular form of the disease struck blacks so commonly that it came to be known as Negro Consumption or Struma Africana. It was characterized by extreme difficulty in breathing, unexplained abdominal pain around the navel (from which a third name for the disease arose, Negro Poisoning), and rapidly progressing debility and emaciation, usually resulting in death.[82] In all likelihood most of the cases which white Southerners described as Negro Consumption were miliary tuberculosis, the most serious and fatal form of the disease known, in which tubercles are found in many body organs simultaneously, overwhelming what natural defenses exist. The reason why rapidly fatal varieties of the disease (so-called galloping consumption) afflicted Negroes more frequently than Caucasians may be related to the fact that Caucasians (like Mongolians) had suffered from tuberculosis for many hundreds of years and had developed a strong immune response to the infection, whereas Africans (and American Indians and Eskimos) had been exposed to tuberculosis only since the coming of the white man and had not yet built up this same effective resistance. Others have discounted racial immunity as an explanation and have argued that, as a "virgin" population, blacks were highly susceptible to serious first attacks of tuberculosis. Additional factors such as malnourishment, pre-existing illness, or general debility also contributed to the apparent black predisposition to tuberculosis.[83]

There is little doubt that tuberculosis was an important cause of slave deaths throughout the Old South, despite the statement

[82] John R. Hicks, "African Consumption," *Steth.*, 4 (1854), 625–29; Haller, "The Negro and the Southern Physician," 242–43. For complete case histories, see Peter R. Reamey, "Post-Mortem Examination of a Case of Tabes Mesenterica," *Steth.*, 2 (1852), 380–81; "Medico-Chirurgical Society of Richmond, March 1st [1853]," *VMSJ*, 1 (1853), 33–35; L. P. Yandell, "Remarks on Struma Africana, or the Disease Usually Called Negro Poison, or Negro Consumption," *Transylvania Journal of Medicine*, 4 (1831), 83–103.

[83] Wintrobe et al., eds., *Harrison's Principles of Internal Medicine*, 866, 868. For more on the response of previously unexposed populations to epidemic diseases, see Alfred W. Crosby, "Virgin Soil Epidemics as a Factor in the Aboriginal Depopulation in America," *WMQ*, 3rd series, 33 (1976), 289–99.

of a recent medical historian, William D. Postell, that white "southerners were to a large extent in agreement . . . [on] the rarity of tuberculosis in the Negro prior to the Civil War."[84] He based his statement on the authority of several postbellum writers who emphasized the marked increase in tuberculosis among newly emancipated freedmen.[85] A look at the available figures indicates that the facts are otherwise. The 1850 census, for example, recorded 125 tuberculosis deaths among blacks and 237 among whites in Alabama, for proportionate mortality rates per 10,000 deaths of 263 (black) and 547 (white). The South Carolina rates are 267 (black) and 452 (white) per 10,000 deaths, while in Virginia they were 571 (black) and 1,045 (white).[86]

Despite the fact that white Southerners seemed to die at a somewhat higher rate than blacks from consumption, figures from four areas of Virginia indicate that more Negroes died from the disease at a younger age. (See Table 2.) Almost 72 percent of the 208 slaves and free blacks who contracted and died of tuberculosis were under 40 years old, compared with 56 percent of the 416 whites in Petersburg, Staunton, Augusta County, and Southampton County between 1853 and 1860.[87] This confirms current medical thinking regarding the virulence of consumption among blacks.

The most convincing figures regarding the susceptibility of Negroes to tuberculosis come from reports on the African and British troops stationed in the West Indies between 1817 and 1836. Here, in an area where blacks relatively new to a disease only recently introduced into Africa worked next to whites from an area where that disease was endemic, the former died from consumption more than three times as often as the latter (1,302 blacks vs. 448 whites per 10,000 deaths). This despite the fact that morbidity rates differed very little (71.7 hospital admissions per 10,000 living black troops vs. 74.3 per 10,000 white troops).[88]

[84] Postell, *Health of Slaves*, 79.
[85] *Ibid.*, 189–90.
[86] De Bow, *Mortality Statistics, 1850*, 28, 50–51, 252–53, 290–91.
[87] Register of Deaths, 1853–60, VSL.
[88] [Tulloch,] *Statistical Report*, Abstracts I, XIII, XXV, and XXVI of the Appendix.

Table 2. Age at Death from Tuberculosis of Black and White Residents of Petersburg, Staunton, Augusta County and Southampton County, Virginia, 1853–60 [a]

Race	Age groups	Number of deaths	Percent of deaths	Cumulative percent of deaths
Negro	0–9	17	8.1	8.1
	10–19	44	21.1	29.2
	20–29	55	26.3	55.5
	30–39	34	16.3	71.8
	40–49	19	9.1	80.9
	50–59	19	9.1	90.0
	60 & up	21	10.1	100.1
		209	100.1	
Caucasian	0–9	23	5.5	5.5
	10–19	33	7.9	13.4
	20–29	100	24.0	37.4
	30–39	76	18.3	55.7
	40–49	68	16.4	72.1
	50–59	51	12.3	84.4
	60 & up	65	15.6	100.0
		416	100.0	

[a] Compiled from Register of Deaths, 1853–60, VSL.

Another form of tuberculosis which antebellum observers noted particularly among Negroes was scrofula ("white swelling" or "king's evil," derived from the English tradition that the royal touch would cure the disease). Scrofula was characterized by a massive tubercular swelling of lymph glands in the neck and then in other parts of the body, followed by a generalized slow wasting culminating in death. Whites, primarily those living in impoverished circumstances, also suffered from scrofula. The author of one home remedy manual commented that the disease was most common "among the children of the poor and negroes, who are ill fed, ill lodged and ill clothed." [89]

Had antebellum medical observers included scrofula deaths with those from other forms of tuberculosis, the black mortality

[89] Ewell, *Medical Companion*, 204. See also "Cartwright on the Negro Constitution," *Steth.*, 2 (1852), 699.

rate from tuberculosis would have equaled or exceeded that of whites. According to the 1850 national mortality census 45 of every 10,000 white deaths were caused by scrofula, compared with 113 of every 10,000 black deaths.[90] In Staunton, Petersburg, Augusta County, and Southampton County, between 1853 and 1860 the reported gap between white and black scrofulous deaths was even wider—35 per 10,000 (white) vs. 171 per 10,000 (black).[91] Tuberculosis, then, may be included with those diseases which indicated to antebellum Southerners that blacks were medically different from whites.

There were many diseases and conditions about which physicians of the early nineteenth century knew nothing. One of these then-undiscovered medical problems, lactase deficiency, played an important role in the nutritional status of slaves and free blacks. Medical scientists are fond of pointing out that a majority of the world's population cannot drink milk because they do not possess sufficient quantities of the enzyme, lactase, necessary for the proper digestion of milk sugar (lactose). People suffering from this condition develop severe diarrhea upon drinking more than a very small amount of milk. Lactase deficiency (also called lactose intolerance) exists among large numbers of West Africans from former slave-trade areas, and among many American Negroes descended from these Africans. Specifically, over 95 percent of individuals tested from Ibo and Yoruba tribes in Nigeria, and about 70 percent of Afro-Americans, are lactose intolerant. A few Nigerian groups do resemble Northern Europeans in their ability to digest milk sugar (78 percent of one nomadic tribe, the Fulani, are lactose tolerant), but they contributed only a small portion of slaves to the international trade.

Debate continues in scientific circles as to the basis of this condition. Is it hereditary or adaptive? Historically, most West Africans were not dairying peoples; perhaps the low level of lactase simply reflects an environmental adaptation to the lack

[90] De Bow, *Mortality Statistics, 1850*, 27. The proportion in New Orleans during that same year was 13.5/10,000 (white) vs. 36.3/10,000 (black); Simonds, "Annual Report of the New Orleans and Lafayette Board of Health, for the year 1850," 75.

[91] Registers of Deaths, 1853–60, VSL.

of milk stimulus. But the trait also seems to run in families and ethnic groups, pointing to a genetic component. Regardless of the mechanism, many American slaves must have been lactase deficient, since their descendants today still possess that characteristic, as do modern Africans from the old slave-trading area. Though antebellum planters made little reference to any connection between milk drinking and diarrhea among their human chattel, it is reasonable to assume that the condition existed and that it prevented a large majority of adult slaves from consuming cow's milk in any quantity. (Lactase deficiency had no effect on breast feeding.[92]) This explains, in part, why milk was not an important component of most adult slaves' diets.

The diseases discussed above represent only some of the several to which Negroes show a higher predilection. The remainder are difficult to trace back to slavery times either through direct records or by implication through comparative West African medicine. Among those not mentioned, the most important is hypertension (high blood pressure). Others include polydactyly (six or more fingers per hand), umbilical hernia, cancers of the cervix, stomach, lungs, esophagus, and prostate, and toxemia of pregnancy.[93] At the same time, Negroes are much less susceptible to hookworm disease, cystic fibrosis, and skin cancer than Caucasians.

Blacks are not the only racial or ethnic group possessing increased immunity and susceptibility to specific diseases. Jews are less prone to contract tuberculosis, but more subject to Niemann-Pick Disease and Gaucher's Disease. Other vulnerabilities exist among Swedes (sarcoidosis, porphyria, and pernicious anemia), South Africans of Dutch descent (porphyria cutanea

---

[92] Norman Kretchmer, "Memorial Lecture: Lactose and Lactase—A Historical Perspective," Gastroenterology, 61 (1971), 805–13; T. D. Bolin and A. E. Davis, "Primary Lactase Deficiency: Genetic or Acquired?" ibid., 62 (1972), 355–57; Frederick J. Simoons, "New Light on Ethnic Differences in Adult Lactose Intolerance," American Journal of Digestive Diseases, 18 (1973), 595–98; Kretchmer, "Lactose and Lactase," Scientific American, 227 (October 1972), 71–78.

[93] Williams, ed., Textbook of Black-Related Diseases; Lewis, Biology of the Negro. See also Victor A. McKusick, "Clinical Genetics at a Population Level: The Ethnicity of Disease in the United States," Alabama Journal of the Medical Sciences, 3 (1966), 408–24.

tarda hereditaria), Ulster Scotsmen (nephrogenic diabetes insipidus), and Italians, Greeks, Syrians, and Armenians (thalassemia). For residents of the Old South, though, the only group whose medical differences mattered were Negroes. Whites built a partial justification of slavery on the observed variations between themselves and blacks. These physicians and slaveowners were correct in stating that blacks were medically different from whites, but this was only true for certain specific diseases and conditions. For the most part, the illnesses and treatments of blacks were identical to those of whites.

CHAPTER 2

Health and the Slave Quarters

Though blacks were, in some specific instances, medically different from whites, they generally suffered from the same diseases. Infectious and parasitic diseases, maladies presently associated with poor living conditions, were the major causes of illness and death for both groups in antebellum Virginia. Sanitation, housing, food, clothing, and the extent of interracial contacts at all levels of society were major determinants of individual health. To understand the state of black health in the Old Dominion, it is necessary to understand the relationship between public and personal health.

Contagion in the Slave Community

According to federal census figures, between 1790 and 1860 blacks constituted 40–50 percent of Virginia's population. The vast majority of Negroes were slaves, though by 1860 free blacks formed a sizable community (10.5 percent of all blacks). Most slaves lived and worked on farms or plantations performing agricultural labor, assisting in the maintenance of the land and buildings, or working indoors as servants to the master and his family. A smaller number of bondsmen resided in the urban areas of Virginia, either as hirelings from rural farms or as permanent residents attached to their masters' homes. Free blacks also lived in both rural and urban settings. Those Negroes who did not work on farms or in the homes of white town-dwellers usually found employment as skilled artisans or as laborers for one of Virginia's industrial concerns. Many firms were located in towns, but others—public works projects, iron forges, furnaces and foundries, shingle-gathering operations, and coal mines—were not.

Wherever blacks worked, the continuance of their good health depended largely on the conditions which existed in and around their places of residence. Overcrowding and poor sanitary facilities created situations which threatened the well-being of all those living nearby. Rural whites usually resided at a distance (sometimes measured in miles) from their slaves, or, in the case of whites without slaves, often entirely isolated from neighbors. But bondsmen on plantations, farms, and rural industrial sites tended to live in a well-defined area known as the quarters. In 1860, for instance, the Halifax County census-takers recorded that between 5 and 9 slave dwellings stood on each of 60 farms, 10–19 cabins on 19 other farms, and 20–30 houses on 6 large plantations.[1] Throughout the period from 1790 to 1860 about 70 percent of Virginia's slaves lived on holdings which contained 10 or more bondsmen, and about 45 percent lived on holdings with 20 or more slaves.[2] Here was an ideal setting for the spread of disease, similar to the situation which existed in most antebellum urban areas. What was considered personal illness in a white rural family became, in a three- or ten- or thirty-home slave community, a matter of public health and group concern.

At the slave quarters sneezing, coughing, or contact with improperly washed eating utensils and personal belongings pro-

[1] United States, Bureau of the Census, Manuscript Schedule 2 of the Eighth Census, Halifax County, Va., 1860. Other Virginia counties demonstrated similar breakdowns: e.g., Amelia County—5–9 dwellings, 77 farms; 10–19 dwellings, 21 farms; more than 20 dwellings, 6 farms.

[2] Louis C. Gray, *History of Agriculture in the Southern United States to 1860* (Washington, D.C., 1933), I, 5, 531. Fogel and Engerman, *Time*, II, 99–100, broach the subject of population density among slaves but compare it with conditions in northern cities among free urban workers, rather than with free rural whites in the South. Though they point out that overcrowding and poor sanitation in the North resulted in ill health and death, they neglect the public health problems of the slave quarters.

moted transmission of disease-causing micro-organisms among family members. Poor ventilation, lack of sufficient windows for sunshine, and damp earthen floors merely added to the problem by aiding the growth of fungus and bacteria on food, clothing, floors, and utensils, and the development of worm and insect larvae. Improper personal hygiene (infrequent baths, hair-brushings and haircuts, unwashed clothes, unclean beds) led to such nuisances as bedbugs, body lice (which also carried typhus germs), ringworm of skin and scalp, and pinworms. In a house-hold cramped for space, these diseases became family, not indi-vidual, problems. And when two or more families shared homes and facilities, as occurred, for instance, on some James River plantations,[3] the problem of contagion became further aggravated.

Contacts outside the home also facilitated the dissemination of disease. Children who played together all day under the super-vision of a few older women, and then returned to their cabins in the evening, spread their day's accumulation of germs to other family members. Even mere Sunday and evening socializing in an ill neighbor's cabin was enough to "seed" the unsuspecting with disease. Contaminated water, unwashed or poorly cooked food, worm larvae–infested soil, and disease-carrying farm ani-mals and rodents also contributed their share to the unhealthful-ness of the quarters.

The two major types of seasonal diseases which afflicted Old Dominion blacks reflected living conditions within most slave communities (see Figure 1). Respiratory illnesses prevailed dur-ing the cold months, when slaves were forced to spend much time indoors in intimate contact with their families and friends. As warm weather arrived and workers spent more time outdoors, intestinal diseases caused by poor outdoor sanitation and close contact with the earth became common. A closer look at the specific maladies in each season will explain this variation.

Several important contagious diseases were spread through contact with respiratory system secretions, including tuberculosis, diphtheria, colds and upper respiratory infections, influenza, pneumonia, and streptococcal infections (including sore throats

[3] Olmsted, *Seaboard*, 111–12.

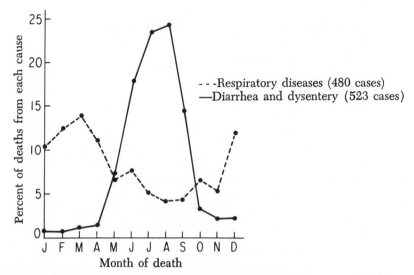

Figure 1. Seasonal Variation of Deaths from Respiratory Diseases [a] and from Diarrhea and Dysentery [b] in Four Virginia Localities,[c] 1853–60.

[a] For diseases included in this classification, see Table 9, note 23.
[b] For diseases included in this classification, see Table 9, note 22.
[c] From Registers of Deaths for Augusta County, Southampton County, Petersburg, and Staunton, VSL.

and scarlet fever).[4] Tuberculosis is not usually thought of as a malady common to rural areas of the South or to Negro slaves, but because blacks lived in clusters on many plantations the infection spread easily, not just among members of one household, but from family to family in the quarters. The common cold was also high on the list of pulmonary complaints, though it rarely caused death. Each winter slaveowners made entries in farm books complaining of the presence of upper respiratory illnesses on the farm: "Myself & several of the coloured people have bad coles," or "Hands & children have suffered very much from colds—in fact cold has been quite an epidemic." Indicative of the frequency with which colds affected Virginia's slaves was this statement in

[4] For an excellent introduction to the nature of communicable diseases from a public health standpoint, see Charles V. Chapin, *The Sources and Modes of Infection* (New York, 1916); Gaylord W. Anderson, Margaret G. Arnstein, Mary R. Lester, *Communicable Disease Control: A Volume for the Health Officer and Public Health Nurse* (New York, 1962).

Charles Friend's diary at the close of the 1855 frost season: "We have all escaped sickness [this past winter] and have had very few or no colds." [5]

Pleurisy and influenza also struck blacks in rural Virginia,[6] but the most serious acute respiratory malady was pneumonia. Epidemics affected not only individual rural plantations, but entire neighborhoods. During the spring of 1852, for instance, pneumonia was reported in such disparate portions of the state as Petersburg, Madison Court House, Surry, Prince George County, and a district of Rockingham County in the Valley of Virginia. This epidemic struck Charles Friend's plantation in Prince George County, incapacitating at least seven of his thirteen adult hands at one time.[7]

Another group of respiratory diseases was also significant—the many sore throats of which both whites and blacks frequently complained. The majority were probably manifestations of viral colds and as such disappeared with the illness. But scarlet fever and other streptococcal infections occurred often and ravaged households and plantations throughout the state. When the organism struck, slaves grouped together in the quarters could hardly avoid infection. Scarlet fever was a much more serious disease in the nineteenth century than it is today, causing severe illness and, frequently, death. Dr. Alfred G. Tebault wrote a memorandum in which he described what must have been a streptococcal outbreak in Princess Anne County near London Bridge. A fifteen-year-old Negro girl developed a mild sore throat and skin rash

[5] John Walker Diary, 7 February 1835, UNC; Edmund Ruffin, Jr., Diary, February 1851, UNC; White Hill Plantation Books, 1 March 1855, UNC.

[6] Edward T. Tayloe to B. O. Tayloe, 17 January 1832, Tayloe Papers, UVA (#38–630); Blanton, *19th Century*, 247; Cary Charles Cocke to John Hartwell Cocke, 8 January 1849, Shields Deposit, Cocke Papers, UVA; Greene, ed., *Carter Diary*, I, 379 (2 April 1770); ——— to ———, 6 June 1823, Irvine-Saunders Papers, UVA (#38–33); "Sick List from 1st June, 1841," White Hill Plantation Books, UNC; John Walker Diary, 1, 8, 15, 22 February 1845, UNC.

[7] Editorial, "Epidemics of Virginia," *Steth.*, 2 (1852), 277–78; White Hill Plantation Books, 15 February to 3 March 1852, UNC. Other mention of pneumonia among blacks may be found in "Mortality of the City of Richmond," *VMSJ*, 1 (1853), 172; Samuel Drewry to John Buford, 18 April 1854, Buford Papers, Duke; Dr. B. H. Walker Diary, 16 to 25 January 1858, VSL; J. F. Peebles, "The Result of Cases of Pneumonia Treated Chiefly by Tartar Emetic," *AJMS*, NS 15 (1848), 338–48.

which lasted for five or six days during early December 1842. Shortly afterward, another slave, age four, "in the same kitchen," came down with a severe case of scarlet fever from which she died eighteen days later. An infant in the household was attacked with mild tonsillitis, but her twenty-three-year-old mother contracted ulcerated sore throat, malignant scarlet fever, and pneumonia, succumbing in six days. Five members of this same household who had nursed the sick now became ill with sore throats. All recovered. Other persons elsewhere in the neighborhood also developed manifestations of this epidemic disease, including a black boy, age fourteen, from whom Dr. Tebault then caught the infection. He passed it on to his two-year-old daughter (in a much more violent form), who in turn spread sore throats of varying intensity to all nine of the people who, at one time or another, attended her in sickness.[8]

Streptococcus was related to two other severe types of illnesses that occurred with some frequency among blacks. Rheumatic fever, an infection of the joints, often followed attacks of scarlet fever or sore throat. It caused damage to the heart (rheumatic heart disease) and so rendered adult slaves useless to their masters. Some victims never survived to adulthood. John Walker of King and Queen County recorded in his diary a case of what was probably acute rheumatic fever:

> The negro girl Elen was taken sick Tuesday and has been very sick since once thought she would soon die she is still very ill we tried different medicines all to little or no effect   she lays helpless still Docr Henley was sent to for to see her he says her disease is the Rheumatism she has no use of her legs they are lifeless cant move them at all no medicine has as yet gone through her stomach a great deal has been given her when moved has very severe & excruciating pains in her arms and breast she is more strangely diseased than I ever saw any person labouring under disease before

[8] Alfred G. Tebault Papers, Lecture Notebook #3, p. 117, UVA (#9926). See also Edward Tayloe Journal, 25 October, 2 November, 4 December 1861, UVA (#38–62); White Hill Plantation Books, 1 March, 6 April 1859, UNC; M. H. Houston, "Remarks on Scarlet Fever," *Steth.*, 1 (1851), 301; John Walker Diary, 15 November to 20 December 1845, UNC; Edwin A. Morrison, "On the Use if Quinine in Scarlet Fever," *VMJ*, 11 (1858). 89–91; R. D. Buford to John Buford, 26 October 1854, Buford Papers, Duke.

Ellen died five days later.[9]

The other important streptococcal disease was erysipelas, a rapidly spreading affliction of the skin which often invaded internal organs and caused death. One Fauquier County woman lost seven of her nine servants to erysipelas during an epidemic. Though an infrequent visitor to the Old Dominion, it struck with frightful virulence upon its arrival, especially among those living in close proximity to one another. The quarters were a perfect target.[10]

Streptococcus was not the only widespread cause of severe sore throats among Virginia's rural slaves. Diphtheria, also called croup and sometimes putrid sore throat, struck almost annually and affected large numbers of children and some adults. Masters knew that close contact with diphtheric patients often resulted in spread of the disease, so they attempted to isolate the sick whenever possible. Dr. Charles Minor illustrated the importance of separating the sick from the well in a report on a diphtheria outbreak in Albemarle County in 1854. Ten members of a twelve-person slave household on a large plantation contracted the disease; only two others, both of whom lived in a small house 400 yards away and "had 'used' at this cabin" where the twelve resided, took sick. Blacks living 50–75 yards from the infected house remained healthy because they shunned any contact with their sick neighbors. All ten in the first house recovered; one of the infected slaves in the second house died.[11]

The community life of the slave quarters provided excellent surroundings for dissemination of several year-round diseases contracted through respiratory secretions. People today tend to

[9] John Walker Diary, 26 December 1846, UNC.

[10] Alban S. Payne, "Report on Epidemics of Piedmont District, for the Years 1846 and 1872 Inclusive," *Transactions of the Medical Society of Virginia* (1872), 50. See also J. F. Peebles, "Facts, in Relation to Epidemic Erysipelas, as It Prevailed in Petersburg, Virginia, during the Winter and Spring 1844–45," *AJMS*, NS 11 (1846), 23–44; WLA *Annual Report, Leg. Docs.,* 1851–52, pt. I, doc. #9, p. 35.

[11] Blanton, *19th Century,* 135; Mariana D. Bagley, "History of the Public Health of Norfolk, Virginia, up to 1860" (M.A. thesis, Duke University, 1939), 16–17; R. T. Hubard to James Hubard, 15 November 1860, Randolph-Hubard Papers, UVA (#4717, 5885); Charles Minor, "Case of Diphtherite—Croupe Chez l'Adulte," *VMJ,* 6 (1856), 100–102.

regard these illnesses—whooping cough, measles, chicken pox, and mumps—as limited to the younger population, but adult slaves who had never experienced an outbreak of, say, measles in Africa or the United States were quite susceptible to infection and even death. Measles and whooping cough are still important causes of fatality in developing countries, as they were in antebellum Virginia.[12] A typical whooping cough epidemic broke out on John Walker's King and Queen County farms, Chatham Hill and Locust Grove, during the summer of 1853. Walker's own children first contracted it in mid-June at Sunday school and brought it home. It soon spread to a few of Walker's slave children, and then to the adults. No deaths occurred during the epidemic, though at least twenty-two Negroes became sick. His slaves were more fortunate than many others.[13]

Masters' fears were not solely for the health of their bondsmen; the "great house" also stood on the plantation. Any sick slave who entered the owner's or overseer's home might expose the white family to the same diseases as the Negroes. House slaves, too, could carry back to the quarters the germs of an illness currently infecting the white family. When measles swept through the Negro quarter of Edgehill, the Albemarle County plantation home of Thomas Jefferson's daughter, Martha, and son-in-law, Thomas Mann Randolph, the white family fully expected the contagion to reach their children "thro the servants." When none of her children took sick, Martha wrote disappointedly to her father:

[12] For evidence of epidemics of childhood diseases, see any page in the manuscript Register of Deaths for any county in the state, VSL. Charles Wilcocks and P. E. C. Manson-Bahr, *Manson's Tropical Diseases* (Baltimore, 1972), 392; John Duffy, *Epidemics in Colonial America* (Baton Rouge, 1953), 169.

[13] John Walker Diary, 25 June-22 October 1853, UNC. For other examples of whooping cough in Virginia, see John Hartwell Cocke to Joseph C. Cabell, 31 August 1826, Cabell Papers, UVA; Henry St. George Tucker to St. George Tucker, 9 May 1819, Tucker-Coleman Collection, W&M; "Extracts from the Diary of Francis Taylor, of Orange County, Va.," in Blanton, *18th Century*, 413; William Fuqua to Major John Ambler, 9 February 1808, 10 November 1809, Ambler Family Papers, UVA (#1140); Edward Tayloe Journal, 1859, pp. 19, 22, UVA (#38–62). Examples of measles may be found in Greene, ed., *Carter Diary*, II, 792–93, 812; H. D. Taliaferro Diary, April and May 1847, "Notes of Cases," VHS; Frances A. Buford to John Buford, 5 May 1855, Buford Papers, Duke; William K. Scarborough, ed., *The Diary of Edmund Ruffin* (Baton Rouge, 1972), I, 204, 215, 216, 219.

"I regret extremely my children have missed it. The season was so favorable and it [the disease] was so mild generally that no time or circumstance for the future can ever be as favorable again, besides having had the anxiety for nothing." [14]

Blacks, captives of the slave quarters, did not have the option of leaving the plantation to escape a severe epidemic or of remaining when it was mild. Whites like Martha Randolph had the freedom to take action against contagion. Robert T. Hubard of Chellow Plantation in Buckingham County, for example, fearing that the diphtheria epidemic which had already prostrated several of his slaves might spread to his own children, "had Charity & her family moved to the house 200 yds west of Sam's house, as I did not like to have the sick negroes so near my dwelling house." [15] Another rural slaveowning family simply left the plantation for several weeks after the death of one slave and the sickness of several more from a "fever." Mary Watts Morris of Taylors Creek (near Richmond?) abandoned home, she wrote to her mother, "not only on account of my self but for the safety of my children." The slaves were left, epidemic or not, to care for the farm.[16]

Contagious diseases spread quite easily through the slave communities of antebellum Virginia because, even in rural areas, the population density was often quite high on plantations and farms. Overcrowding of individual slave houses, then, was not the sole prerequisite for the occurrence of epidemics at the quarters. Germs were also transmitted among bondsmen in different households during the course of everyday life, aided by general uncleanliness and people's ignorance of the causes of disease.

Sanitation in the Slave Community

Not all major illnesses were spread by direct communication between people. Some human parasites required an inter-

[14] Martha Jefferson Randolph to Thomas Jefferson, 10 July 1802, in Edwin M. Betts and James A. Bear, Jr., eds., *The Family Letters of Thomas Jefferson* (Columbia, Mo., 1966), 233.

[15] Robert T. Hubard to James Hubard, 15 November 1860, Randolph-Hubard Papers, UVA (#4717, 5885).

[16] Mary Watts Morris to Mrs. Mary Watts, 3 August 1820, Irvine-Saunders Papers, UVA (#38–33).

mediate phase to develop their full destructive capabilities, or a
second host to transport them to new humans. As warm weather
arrived, respiratory diseases decreased in frequency and insects
became important culprits in the spread of disease—particularly
maladies of the digestive tract and various "fevers." What more
could a mosquito or housefly wish than a large concentration of
human beings, decaying leftover food scraps, scattered human
feces, or a compost heap? Mosquitoes discharged yellow fever
or malarial parasites while obtaining fresh blood from their victims. Flies transported such bacteria as *Vibrio* (cholera), *Salmonella* (food poisoning and typhoid), and *Shigella* (bacillary
dysentery), the virus which causes infectious hepatitis, and the
protozoan *Entameba histolytica* (amebic dysentery) from feces
to food. Trichina worms, embedded in the muscles of hogs inhab-
iting yards often shared with bondsmen, were released into a
slave's body when the meat was not completely cooked. Finally,
there were the large parasitic worms, a concomitant of primitive
sanitation.

Intestinal disorders were at least as common among antebellum Virginia's blacks as were respiratory diseases. The human
alimentary tract is distinguished among all other body systems
in that it receives daily large amounts of foreign material, usually
in the form of food, which it must sort and assimilate into a usable
form. In Virginia and the Old South, where living conditions were
generally unhygienic, seemingly good food and drink often concealed pathogenic organisms ranging from viruses to worm
larvae. Hands entering mouths sometimes contained the germs
that others had cast off in feces, urine, or contaminated food. It
is not surprising to find that dysentery, typhoid fever, food poisoning, and worm diseases afflicted large numbers of Virginians,
especially those living in the poorest, most crowded circumstances, without sanitary facilities or time to prepare food
properly. Slaves and free blacks often fit into this category.

Though in the sixteenth century Queen Elizabeth of England
had a water closet installed in her palace, the use of running
water to facilitate the disposal of human excreta was slow in
coming to the South. Most rural people continued to use privies,
latrines, cans, or the woods for nature's calls until the 1920's and

even 1930's.[17] The problem was that unless privies were lined with non-porous material, the semi-solid, putrefying contents passed through the soil, saturating the adjacent land and releasing disease-causing micro-organisms and worm larvae into the ground. If, as frequently happened, waste water seeped into the drinking water supply, an epidemic of cholera, dysentery, diarrhea, typhoid, or hepatitis might ensue.

In rural nineteenth-century Virginia, as well as in most other agricultural areas of the South, even privies were infrequently used. An eminent Charlottesville physician, James L. Cabell, conducted a survey of sanitary facilities during the early 1870's and reported to the American Medical Association in 1877 that among a great many Virginians "there are absolutely no special conveniences, the male members of a family resorting to the woods, the females using chamber vessels which are emptied into a brook if one be close at hand, or into the garden or stable yard." [18] Dr. C. S. Morton, a practitioner in Appomattox County, wrote to Cabell that in the antebellum period "there were no privies used in the country as a general thing." [19] Those privies that did exist were usually found in the homes of the white masters, and only rarely in Negro cabins.[20]

Few antebellum southern medical, commercial, or agricultural writers even raised the subject of rural sanitation, and only one,

[17] In 1876 two-thirds of Savannah's homes (3,366 of 5,000) contained privies, and only one-third of those with water closets (500 of 1,759) actually connected to waste sewers, the remainder going to sealed vaults called dry wells. James J. Waring, *A Communication to the City Council on the Privy System of Savannah* (Savannah, 1877), 3; George Rosen, *A History of Public Health* (New York, 1958), 155–56; L. L. Lumsden, "The Privy as a Public Health Problem," *America Journal of Public Health* (1920), 45–48.

[18] James L. Cabell, "Etiology of Enteric Fever," *Transactions of the American Medical Association,* 28 (1877), 418.

[19] *Ibid.,* 432. In 1910, the Rockefeller Sanitary Commission surveyed 1,000 Virginia farms and found that only 15 percent had a privy of any kind: Harry Frank Farmer, "The Hookworm Eradication Program in the South, 1909–1925" (Ph.D. dissertation, University of Georgia, 1970), 26.

[20] Thomas Jefferson, whose home near Charlottesville displays many of his applications of practical science, had a receptacle several feet below the commode seat in his bedroom which, when full, was pulled (by rope) fifty yards through a tunnel to be emptied under the East Front of Monticello. No information regarding the slave quarters at Monticello is available. Personal communication from James A. Bear, Jr., resident director and curator of Monticello, 16 July 1974.

Dr. J. Hume Simons of South Carolina, in his plantation handbook on medicine, made a special plea for conveniences for slaves: "One sleeping room, at least, in every [slave] house, should have a seat with a hole and cover, for the calls of nature; because there are seldom or never any conveniences in the way of chambers [chamber pots]; and if they had them they would immediately break them." It was common practice, according to Simons, for blacks "to go into the open air for the calls of nature, in all kinds of weather," thereby exposing themselves, when ill, to relapses or retarded recovery.[21] In those days of overconcern with the state of patients' bowels, the plight of a "dosed" (with laxatives) slave on a rainy, cold, or snowy day was unenviable.

Inconvenience aside, many Virginia planters took advantage of their slaves' primitive sanitary practices by using the waste material as night soil. One physician living in Richmond in 1876 recalled that "around the old [slave] houses . . . all accumulations of filth were regularly scraped up, and hauled off to enrich the land."[22] This was recommended practice throughout the Old South, especially for large slaveholders. Dr. John Stainbach Wilson of Columbus, Georgia, described the procedure and its usefulness to readers of his series on Negro health and diseases in the *American Cotton Planter and the Soil of the South:*

> [T]here should be at least one raking every year, to remove the accumulations that will gather about all inhabited places, and more especially the habitations of negroes. These rakings should be thorough, extending beneath the houses, and embracing the yard, and all its surroundings. By pursuing this course you will obtain some rich additions to your compost heap; and at the same time, you will do much towards the protection of your negroes from disease. . . .[23]

If the accumulations of waste were not removed regularly, however—and needless to say once a year was not often enough—

[21] J. Hume Simons, *Planter's Guide and Family Book of Medicine* (Charleston, S.C., 1849), 208.

[22] Report of Dr. R. T. Coleman to James L. Cabell, in Cabell, "Etiology of Enteric Fever," 445.

[23] John S. Wilson, "The Peculiarities and Diseases of Negroes," *Cotton Planter,* NS 4 (1860), 222.

the danger of disease was great. Children constantly played near the ground around cabins, providing ample opportunity for ingestion (fingers in the mouth), penetration (through the skin), or further spread (fingers on food prepared for others) of pathogenic organisms which had been discharged in feces. Rain often washed contaminated droppings into streams from which drinking water was obtained. Germ-laden material also saturated the soil around cabins and entered subsurface well water supplies. Finally, waste sometimes contaminated the fruits and vegetables which many slaves cultivated on plots near their homes. Farmers using night soil on crops similarly stood the risk of poisoning their families, workers, or customers with unclean produce.

A good example of the danger courted by slaves living in unsanitary conditions was an occurrence on a mid-nineteenth-century northern Albemarle County farm containing about seventy-five slaves. The Negroes' cabins were built on a flat area higher than, and 50–100 yards away from, Buck Mountain Creek, the major source of drinking water. Hogs and children played in close proximity to one another, and all residents (human and animal) used the land for normal body functions. Only periodic rains cleared away the filth, sweeping it into the creek. When typhoid erupted on the farm, no doubt from contaminated water, about fifty slaves and several whites suffered its ravages.[24]

Typhoid fever was often called "continued fever" because of its characteristic unremitting elevation of body temperature for two to three weeks. One of the two major epidemic intestinal diseases of the Old Dominion (dysentery was the other), it occurred regularly on plantations. It was transmitted from person to person in contaminated food, water, and feces. Flies and other insects, or unclean hands, also carried the bacteria from exposed human waste products to food. Infection resulted if contaminated eatables were then served and ingested uncooked. *Salmonellae*, the causative bacteria, survived in milk, ice cream, and water, as well as in shellfish living in polluted estuaries. Improper sewage disposal, common in antebellum Virginia, was usually the major

[24] Report of Dr. W. G. Rogers in 1876 to James L. Cabell, in Cabell, "Etiology of Enteric Fever," 435–36. For another typhoid epidemic, see U. B. Phillips, *Life and Labor in the Old South* (Boston, 1929), 235–36.

cause of epidemics. Carriers, both symptomatic and asymptomatic, were also a source of infection.

In the typical epidemic, a sick slave, hired out or visiting relatives in another neighborhood, was returned home and nursed by members of the family. Many of those who visited and ministered to the patient eventually contracted the disease, either by direct contact with infected feces, or by ingesting food or drink contaminated from flies, fingers, or a freshly polluted water supply. Once infected, the new patients returned to their homes on the same or a nearby farm to continue the cycle of contagion. Few ever recognized the source of infection, so the epidemic usually ran its course unabated through a section of the state. Among outbreaks reported were those in central piedmont Virginia, Bedford, Greenesville, Henrico, and Halifax counties, and the neighborhood around Hampton. It is noteworthy that all the epidemics mentioned here occurred in rural areas rather than in towns, indicating that individual carriers probably brought the disease with them from other places and subsequently infected friends, relatives, and masters.[25]

In addition to typhoid fever, *Salmonellae* caused less serious diseases, primarily bacterial food poisoning. Cattle or pigs as well as eggs, cheeses, milk, and ice cream harbored the bacteria and passed them on to humans who consumed them. Though cases cannot be documented, there is little doubt that outbreaks of acute diarrhea and abdominal pain among many slaves on a plantation occurred as the result of food poisoning, given the lax food handling and preservation methods which encouraged the growth and spread of pathogenic organisms.[26]

Unsanitary living conditions also promoted the dissemination

[25] Charles W. Ashby, "On the Pathology and Treatment of Typhoid Fever," *VMSJ*, 4 (1855), 360–61; L. B. Anderson, "Treatment of Typhoid Fever," *ibid.*, 5 (1856), 364–65; John P. Little, "Abstract of an Essay on Typhoid Fever," *Steth.*, 1 (1851), 121–22; James E. Reeves, *A Practical Treatise on Enteric Fever . . . Embracing a Partial History of the Disease in Virginia* (Philadelphia, 1859), 89–91; R. A. Gholson, "Continued Fever of Southern Virginia," *VMJ*, 9 (1857), 1–20; Robert G. Jennings, "Remarks on the Use of the Tampon in Uterine Hemorrhage, with a Report of Two Cases," *Steth.*, 3 (1853), 209; James L. Cabell, "Etiology of Enteric Fever," 422–24.

[26] R. L. Huckstep, *Typhoid Fever and Other Salmonella Infections* (Edinburgh, 1962), 252–57; Wilcocks and Manson-Bahr, *Manson's Tropical Diseases*, 543–44.

of another frequently fatal disease, dysentery or "bloody flux."
It existed in two forms (though antebellum physicians did not
recognize this), bacillary *(Shigella)* and amebic *(Entameba histolytica).* Both were transmitted in contaminated feces to the alimentary tract by fingers, foods, fluids, fomites, and flies, though
epidemics were usually caused by the bacillary type. Bloody
stools were the hallmark of the disease. If not controlled, the
results of dysentery were intestinal hemorrhage, dehydration,
perforation of the bowel, liver abscess, peritonitis, and death. It
took lives in the state every year and disabled many others for
periods ranging from several days to several weeks. Epidemics
struck both towns and farms, particularly during warm moist
seasons. Severe outbreaks occurred, for instance, in Petersburg
each summer between 1846 and 1849, in the south central counties
(Patrick and Henry, along with the town of Martinsburg) during
May 1853, and in the Northern Neck in July 1770. Thomas Jefferson's Monticello slaves felt the effects of dysentery in round-robin
fashion one summer. The former president recounted to a relative: "We have now in our family, both in doors and out, more
sickness than I have ever had since I was a housekeeper. . . .
Without doors two or three are taken of a day, so that all the
houses of the negroes are mere hospitals requiring great and constant attendance and care; all of an epidemic dysentery now
prevailing thro' the neighborhood. . . ."[27]
Dysentery and typhoid fever were warm weather epidemic
disorders, and respiratory illnesses were winter maladies. But
worms seemed invariably present at the quarters regardless of
the season. They turned up in lungs, liver, blood vessels, lym-
phatics, gall bladder, vagina, anus, and skin, as well as in the
intestines. Diagnosis and treatment of other diseases became confused or excessively complicated owing to the presence of these

[27] P. R. Reamey, "Observations on the Epidemic Dysentery of Henry County,
Virginia, as It Prevailed during the Summer of 1853," *Steth.*, 3 (1853), 557–64;
J. J. Thweatt, "On the Use of Nitrate of Silver in Certain Forms of Dysentery in
Adults and Diarrhea in Children, with Cases and Remarks," *ibid.*, 1 (1851), 10;
Greene, ed., *Carter Diary*, 1, 452 (23 July 1770); Thomas Jefferson to Mrs. M.
B. Jefferson, 2 August 1815, in Edwin M. Betts, ed., *Thomas Jefferson's Farm
Book* (Princeton, 1953), 39. See also Bagley, "History of Public Health of
Norfolk," 19, 23.

parasites. The discharge of a few or many worms in feces usually meant not that one was now free of infestation, but that large numbers still resided within the bowels and other organs. How many lost workdays and human lives resulted from parasitic infections cannot be counted, but the toll was high. It is safe to say that at least half (probably more) of Virginia's black population harbored worms during their lifetimes.

A detailed discussion of all the worms which might have infested antebellum Virginia's slaves would serve little purpose when proof of their existence is lacking and contemporary descriptions are too vague for historical diagnosis. This discussion will instead concentrate on the several varieties of parasites known to have afflicted Negroes during this period. Writers of the day generally differentiated five varieties of intestinal worms in their popular family medicine books: the long roundworm (*Ascaris*), long threadworm (*Trichuris* or maw worm), short threadworm, broad (fish) tapeworm, and narrow (pork or beef) tapeworm. In no case did they understand the means by which patients contracted worm infections.[28]

The most frequently found variety, no doubt recognized because of its tremendous size (4–15 inches), was *Ascaris lumbricoides*, an intestinal roundworm. It is still one of the commonest human parasites, involving, by some estimates, one-fourth of the world's population and up to 3 million persons in the American South. *Ascaris* occurs where sanitation and personal hygiene are poor. The damp clay soil found in much of Virginia favored growth of *Ascaris* eggs implanted in the feces which infected persons deposited (see Figure 2). Children playing on the ground then came in contact with this contaminated soil and unknowingly picked up large numbers of eggs on their hands. The man-to-man cycle was completed when dirty fingers entered mouths and the eggs were swallowed. Young slave children living at the quarters

[28] See, e.g., W. H. Coffin, *The Art of Medicine Simplified, or a Treatise on the Nature and Cure of Diseases, for the Use of Families and Travelers* (Wellsburg, Va., 1853), 49–51; Ralph Schenck, *The Family Physician: Treating of the Diseases Which Assail the Human System at Different Periods of Life . . .* (Fincastle, Va., 1842), 439–42; J. Hume Simons, *Planter's Guide and Family Book of Medicine . . .* (Charleston, S.C., 1849), 170–73; A. G. Goodlett, *The Family Physician, or Every Man's Companion . . .* (Nashville, 1838), 588–92.

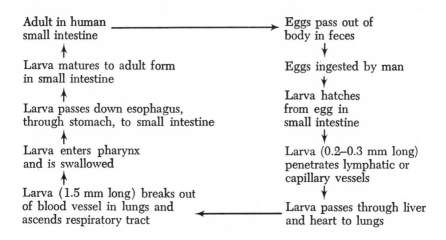

Figure 2. Life Cycle of *Ascaris lumbricoides*.
SOURCE: adapted from Harold W. Brown and David L. Belding, *Basic Clinical Parasitology* (New York, 1964), 123.

on rural farms were particularly exposed to parasite-laden soil. But adults, too, made frequent contact with the earth, both during their leisure hours at home, where promiscuous defecation occurred constantly, and in the fields, where recent human droppings added to the night soil some planters collected and distributed as fertilizer. Food grown with infected fertilizer often harbored eggs ripe for transmission to consumers. Agricultural and rural dwellers thus had ample opportunity to contract ascariasis. So, too, did urbanites living in towns with unpaved streets and exposed sewage or in homes without toilet facilities of any kind. Most towns and cities in the Old Dominion fit that description before 1860.

One further source of roundworm infection was dirt-eating (geophagy). Though rarely mentioned as a problem in Virginia among whites or blacks (the 1850 mortality census reported only three deaths ascribed to this cause in the Old Dominion, one in whites and two in blacks), the practice undoubtedly occurred. Physicians and slaveowners in states further south complained often and bitterly—though helplessly—about its frequency among their patients and wards. Historians now believe that geophagy was merely a habit or custom, rather than a symptom of hookworm disease or dietary deficiency.[29] Regardless of the cause, these people undoubtedly ingested millions of tiny roundworm eggs along with the clay.

Ascaris was one of the most common parasitic worms in the antebellum South. Examples of patients harboring them abound in the medical and plantation literature. A sickly seven-year-old slave boy living in Accomack County provides a typical case history. He had suffered from colicky pains for some time and eventually developed a lump six or seven inches long, bulging from his abdomen. The owner took him to a physician in town (Accomack Court House), who diagnosed the malady as worms and administered cathartics and anti-helminthic (worm-destroying) drugs. The boy soon discharged a convoluted mass containing 46 large lumbricoids. The abdominal lump disappeared immediately. Had these worms not been expelled, the child would probably have developed intestinal obstruction and died (see illustration).[30]

A second common worm parasite was the tapeworm. Slaves in the Old Dominion consumed large quantities of beef, pork, and freshwater fish during the year. The beef, pork, and fish tapeworms reached blacks from poorly cooked or raw infected meat or fish (see Figure 3), found their way to the small intestine, and successfully competed with their human hosts for nutrients

[29] W. M. Carpenter, "Observations on the Cachexia Africana or the Habits and Effects of Dirt-eating in the Negro Race," *New Orleans Medical Journal*, 1 (1844–45), 146–68; J. R. Cotting. "Analysis of a Species of Clay Found in Richmond County [Georgia], Which Is Eagerly Sought After and Eaten by Many People Particularly Children," *SMSJ*, 1 (1837), 288–92; P. Mustacchi, "Cesare Bressa (1785–1836) on Dirt Eating in Louisiana: A Critical Analysis of His Unpublished Manuscript *De la Dissolution Scorbutique*," *JAMA*, 218 (11 October 1971), 229–32; D. Dickens and R. N. Ford, "Geophagy (Dirt Eating) among Mississippi Negro School Children," *American Sociological Review*, 7 (1942), 59–65; Robert W. Twyman, "The Clay Eater: A New Look at an Old Southern Enigma," *JSH*, 37 (1971), 439–48.

[30] L. S. Joynes, "Mechanical Obstruction of the Intestinal Canal, Produced by Worms," *Steth.*, 1 (1851), 271–73. See also Jesse Lewis to Drs. Brown or Jameson, 2 August 1814, Charles Brown Papers, W&M.

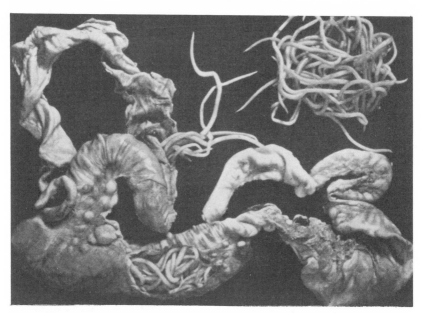

Ascarids Impacted in Small Intestine, Causing Fatal Obstruction.
SOURCE: Charles Wilcocks and P. E. C. Manson-Bahr, *Manson's Tropical Diseases*
(Baltimore, 1972), 249.

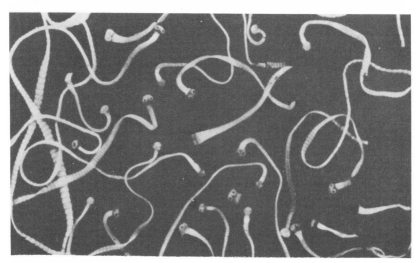

Taenia saginata, the Beef Tapeworm. Note proglottids (segments) and
heads which attach to intestinal wall.
SOURCE: Ernest Carroll Faust, Paul Farr Russell, and Rodney Clifton Jung, *Craig
and Faust's Clinical Parasitology* (Philadelphia, 1970), 536.

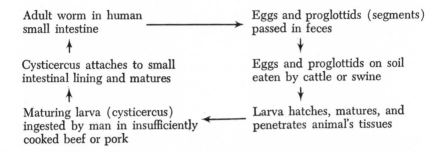

Figure 3. Life Cycles of Beef and Pork Tapeworms (*Taenia saginata* and *Taenia solium*).
SOURCE: adapted from Brown and Belding, *Basic Clinical Parasitology*, 167, 172.

from ingested food.[31] The results were usually vague abdominal pains, occasionally constipation or vomiting, increased hunger, and undefined sensations of discomfort. Landon Carter recorded the occurrence of one severe case of tapeworm on the plantation and indicated that he had seen many more. His slave Windsor was seized one day with such violent pains across his abdomen as to cause him to "run mad" and require restraint "from killing himself." Carter suspected worms and administered anti-helminthic drugs. This "brought off large quantitys of Slimy goard seeds such as all experience pronounce to be parts [segments] of the Joint [tape]worm" (see illustration). The worm had apparently become so long and convoluted that it had caused an acute obstruction of his intestine.[32]

Other worms also infected Virginians, though physicians either mistook them for one of the varieties mentioned above or could not see them because of their size or concealment during the life cycle. The two most important were the trichina worm, *Trichinella spiralis*, and the hookworm, *Necator americanus*.

Trichinosis must have occurred frequently in the Old South,

[31] Coffin, *Art of Medicine Simplified*, 49–50; Goodlett, *Family Physician*, 589-91; Harold W. Brown and David L. Belding, *Basic Clinical Parasitology* (New York, 1964), 159–63, 167–73.
[32] Greene, ed., *Carter Diary*, I, 205–6 (17 March 1758); Schenck, *Family Physician*, 439.

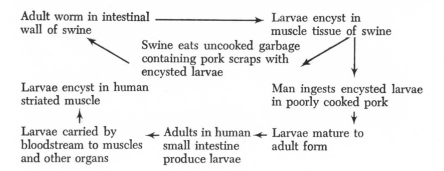

Figure 4. Life Cycle of Trichina Worm (*Trichinella spiralis*).
SOURCE: adapted from Brown and Belding, *Basic Clinical Parasitology*, 96.

given the amount of pork consumed daily. *T. spiralis* was transmitted to those who ate poorly cooked pork muscle in which encapsulated larvae dwelled (see Figure 4). Hogs contracted the disease by eating garbage containing uncooked pork scraps, or from infected rats residing around slaughterhouses or eateries. In this way neither urban nor rural pork consumers escaped infestation. Though grain-fed pigs stood much less chance of ingesting *T. spiralis* larvae than those fed garbage, animal control in cities and on farms during the antebellum period was notoriously poor. Leftovers from the table and the slaughter pen were readily accessible to the unrestrained hogs. Though unrecognized in the Old Dominion, trichinosis undoubtedly accounted for many of the cases treated as typhoid fever, malaria, food poisoning, rheumatism and arthritis, respiratory illnesses, brain fever, and heart disease.[33]

Hookworm, unlike the other worm parasites discussed here, did not enter its host through the mouth. Instead its larvae, which developed on the ground from eggs which infected humans had discharged in feces, penetrated through the skin to small blood vessels. Barefooted slaves, field workers who touched the soil with their hands, and slave fishermen who sat on soil along river banks were thus quite susceptible to hookworm invasion. Once

[33] Brown and Belding, *Basic Clinical Parasitology*, 94–101.

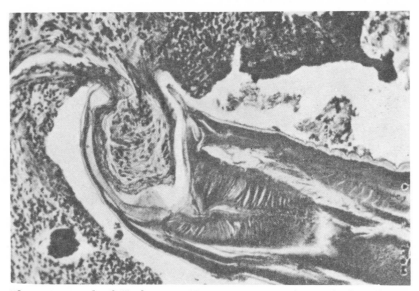

Photomicrograph of Hookworm (*Necator americanus*) Attached to Human
Small Intestine. A portion of the intestinal lining has been sucked into the
hookworm's mouth.
SOURCE: Faust, Russell, and Jung, *Craig and Faust's Clinical Parasitology*, 308.

in circulation, the larvae followed a route identical to *Ascaris*,
passing through the heart to the lungs, up the respiratory tree,
and down into the intestines as the host swallowed. Symptoms
included itching ("ground itch" or "dew itch") as larvae penetrated the skin, transient pneumonia or bronchitis during larval
migration through the pulmonary tract, and severe anemia associated with the destruction of red blood cells by the adult worm
attached to intestinal mucosa (see illustration). Chronic sickness
was the lot of those infected, accompanied by an enormous appe-
tite, retarded mental, physical, and sexual growth among children, extreme lethargy, generalized edema (swelling), and
chronic leg ulcers. Neither eggs nor worms could be seen in
stools without close scrutiny.

Portions of Virginia were ideally suited for the growth and
development of the hookworm larvae. During the eradication
campaign of 1909–25 investigators discovered large numbers of
cases in both the eastern part of the state, from Tidewater to the
Blue Ridge, and the southwest, where moist, loose, sandy or

loamy soil predominated. *N. americanus* larvae survived best in these kinds of soils. Given the poor sanitary habits of the residents, the hookworm had no difficulty locating a host and maintaining itself. Again, as with trichinosis, there is no real medical testimony to confirm the presence of hookworm among Virginia's slaves (other than an occasional comment about laziness or tenacious leg ulcers). But based on its African origin and its prevalence when discovered at the turn of the twentieth century, there is little doubt of its existence in antebellum Virginia.[34]

Proper disposition of wastes was a major component of the public health problem in any slave community. Leftover food, decaying exposed in the sun or under a slave cabin, formed an excellent breeding ground for bacteria and animal parasites, as well as for worm and insect larvae. Children who touched this rotting food and then put their fingers in their mouths stood a good chance of contracting intestinal diseases or worse. Farm animals devouring the decomposed food scraps often developed parasitic diseases, especially tapeworm and trichinosis, which were then dispatched to slaves in poorly cooked meat.[35]

In contemporary accounts or reminiscences few planters or slaves mentioned the presence of rats, a common resident of places filthy and crowded. They were present in antebellum Virginia, however, as were such vermin as bedbugs, body lice, and pinworms. In slave quarters cramped for space, these animals became family and community problems.[36]

[34] *Ibid.*, 109–17; Farmer, "Hookworm Eradication," 10, 17, 19, 21, 28–29, 38, 106–7; W. A. Plecker, "The Failure of Physicians to Diagnose Hookworm Disease," *Virginia Medical Semi-Monthly*, 16 (1911–12), 601–5; Allen W. Freeman, "The Prevalence and Prevention of Hookworm Disease in Virginia," *ibid.*, 57–61.

[35] Simons, *Planter's Guide*, 207, mentions the common slave practice of pouring leftovers onto the ground under the cabin through a hole in the floor.

[36] On rats and rat bites in the slave quarters, see R. L. Madison, "Chloroform— Its External and Internal Uses," *Steth.*, 3 (1853), 632–33; and Augusta County Register of Deaths for 1856, VSL—a six-month-old male slave was "killed by rats in bed." On body lice, see Gordon W. Jones, "Doctor John Mitchell's Yellow Fever Epidemics," *VMHB*, 70 (1962), 46. For evidence that Southerners suffered from these minor pestilences, see any of the domestic medicine guides, e.g., Goodlett, *Family Physician*, 425–27; Schenck, *The Family Physician*, 412–16. See also Lynchburg *Daily Virginian*, 7 September 1860, reproduced on cover of *American Historical Review*, 79 (April 1974).

The greatest threat to health under these circumstances was typhus, a scourge of worldwide proportions until quite recently. It is caused by one of a group of small organisms that is neither virus nor bacteria, called rickettsia. Two types of rickettsiae—*R. mooseri* and *R. prowazeki*—probably afflicted antebellum Virginians, causing endemic (murine) and epidemic typhus respectively. Body lice transmitted the latter from one infected individual to another, while fleas carried the former from rats to humans. Public sanitation and personal hygiene played a significant role in the epidemiology of typhus. Slaves heavily laden with body lice, or resident in filthy quarters infested with rats, required only the introduction of rickettsiae from some outside source to trigger the cycle of typhus contagion. Judging from the occasional mention of rats at some slave quarters, the frequent references of slaveholders and physicians to poorly kept slave cabins, and the slave's lack of adequate time or inclination to wash clothing, this disease should have affected many towns and farms.[37]

Typhus fever appears to have struck Virginia several times during the antebellum period.[38] John Hartwell Cocke provided an excellent history of an epidemic on his Bremo Plantation and in the surrounding Fluvanna County countryside which possessed all the hallmarks of typhus. It commenced during late August 1821, taking its victims with sudden chills, severe headaches, pains in the back and limbs, and a steady fever which remitted slightly each morning. Some patients developed respiratory symptoms, especially coughs, while others vomited often. By 7 September there were twenty-nine cases among his blacks and eight in the fourteen-member white family. Some three hundred persons in the neighborhood contracted the "strange disease," as Cocke

[37] Wilcocks and Manson-Bahr, *Manson's Tropical Diseases*, 603–16.
[38] For the eighteenth century see John Mitchell, "Yellow Fever as It Appeared in Virginia in 1741 and 1742," *Philadelphia Medical Museum*, 1 (1804), 1–20; Jones, "Doctor Mitchell's Yellow Fever," 43–48; Edmund Wilcox Ledger, vol. 13, Hubard Family Papers, 5 January, 6, 10 March, 5, 13 May 1778, UNC; Hunter Dickinson Farish ed., *Journal and Letters of Philip Vickers Fithian 1773– 1774: A Plantation Tutor of the Old Dominion* (Williamsburg, Va., 1957), 68 (25 March 1774). For discussion of typhus in colonial America, see Duffy, *Epidemics in Colonial America*, 229–32.

called it, though few died. None of the more than one hundred Bremo Plantation residents who suffered the illness—which may have been the mild, flea-borne murine typhus—lost their lives. Cocke's respite from disease was brief, however, lasting from the end of October 1821 to March 1822, when a typhus-like epidemic again struck his people. Concurrently a more fatal epidemic, perhaps louse-borne typhus, was infecting residents of Brunswick County, where Cocke acted as executor of several estates. During 1821 and 1822 mortality here was higher and the suffering more intense than in Fluvanna. The following year an epidemic which from its name, "negro quarter fever," was presumably this same virulent strain of typhus fever, struck several plantations in Louisa County, killing numerous bondsmen.[39]

Parasitic diseases were rife at the slave quarters for the same reasons that directly communicable illnesses were so prevalent. Individuals living in a community cannot limit such disorders to themselves or their families without knowledge of the mode of transmission. Contaminated food and water, nonexistent sanitary facilities, and haphazard garbage disposal encouraged the establishment of parasites in the ecological system of the slave quarters. Private health was thus a matter of concern for the entire community.

Yaws, Syphilis, and Gonorrhea

Another disease associated with primitive living conditions afflicted Virginia's plantation Negroes for the first two centuries of their enslavement and then rapidly disappeared by the Civil War. Yaws, though not a venereal disease, is caused by a spirochete, *Treponema pertenue,* related to the spirochete of

[39] "1821 Sept. 4, List of Invalids"; "Cure for Strange Epidemic Disease," 5 September 1821; William Bolling to John H. Cocke, 27 October 1821; John D. Wilkins to Cocke, 20 April 1822; all in Cocke Deposit, Cocke Papers, UVA; Nicholas Faulcon to Cocke, 21 April 1822, Shields Deposit, Cocke Papers, UVA; Cocke to Editors of the *Richmond Enquirer,* 31 September and 1 October 1821, reprinted in Norfolk *American Beacon,* 8 October (p. 2) and 10 October (p. 2) 1821; E. Pendleton to Col. John Ambler, 9 May 1823, Ambler Family Papers, UVA (#1140). An epidemic in 1834 among Fauquier County slaves described by Alban S. Payne, "Report on Epidemics of Piedmont District," 68, as typhoid fever may have been typhus instead.

syphilis, *T. pallidum.* Slaves carried this disease with them from Africa. It remained prevalent in areas of the New World which had a constant influx of West Africans, possessed a tropical climate for much or all of the year, and whose people lived in suitably poor conditions. Though sporadic cases occurred in the colonial period as far north as Rhode Island, New York, and Pennsylvania, the major pockets of disease were limited to the South.

Yaws is an ugly but usually not fatal malady characterized by papillomas and raspberry-like (framboesia) open ulcers over many portions of the body (see illustration); these remain for several months and then disappear. Repeated physical contact with such sores often leads to transmission of the disease, especially among families or playmates. Filth and damp heat tend to prolong the course of yaws and hence increase the chance for new infections. Serious deformities of bones, nose, and palate may occur in advanced stages (see illustration). The use of clothing, soap and water, and wound dressings remarkably decrease the incidence of yaws.[40]

Despite the protestations of Virginia's medical historian, Wyndham Bolling Blanton, that "probably few true cases of yaws were found among Virginia slaves," enough evidence exists to doubt that conclusion and to speculate that the disease existed in a number of white and black Virginians during colonial and post-Revolutionary times. Blanton based his assumption on the confusion of syphilis and yaws by physicians of the period. Both diseases produced a "great pox" (as distinguished from smallpox) and bone lesions, but syphilis often manifested the distinctive venereal chancre and yaws the "mother yaw" or large ulcer, which helped to distinguish one from the other.[41]

In 1728 William Byrd described a condition occurring frequently among residents of the Virginia–North Carolina border: "First it seizes the Throat, next the Palate, and lastly shews its spite to the poor Nose, of which tis apt in a small time treacher-

[40] Wilcocks and Manson-Bahr, *Manson's Tropical Diseases,* 566–79; Thomas C. Parramore, "Non-Venereal Treponematosis in Colonial North America," *BHM,* 44 (1970), 571–73.
[41] Blanton, *18th Century,* 156.

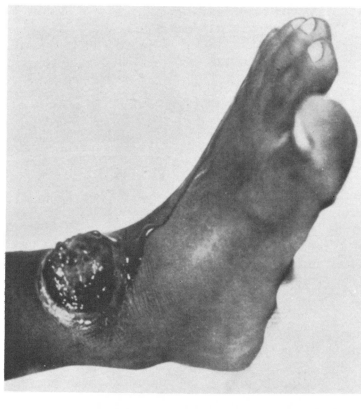

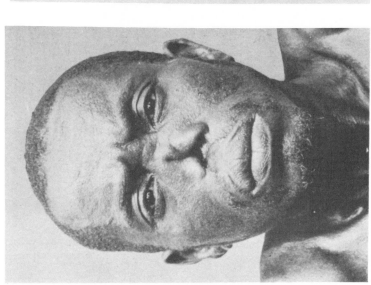

Disfigurements Caused by Yaws. Tertiary yaws may destroy nose and palate. Also shown is the typical raspberry ulcer (framboesia) of yaws.

SOURCE: Wilcocks and Manson-Bahr, *Manson's Tropical Diseases*, 571, 567.

ously to undermine the Foundation." [42] This disease must have been yaws. The following year Governor William Gooch granted freedom to the slave Papan of New Kent County, who had revealed to the government his secret cure for yaws and syphilis. This discovery, members of the Council felt, "may be of great benefit to mankind, and more particularly to the preservation of the lives of a great number of Slaves belonging to the Inhabitants of this Country, frequently infected" with the disease. Another early writer, Robert Beverley, mentioned the presence of yaws in his 1705 history of the colony. There is also substantial evidence from the Revolutionary period, in an Amherst County physician's record book. Of the several patients whom Edmund Wilcox diagnosed as displaying yaws between 1776 and 1778, at least two stand out as probable true cases: one slave woman with an ulcer on her breast and others affecting her bones and neck region, and a male slave with "yaws and ulcer in his Nose." This physician did not doubt his own ability to distinguish between the lesions of yaws and syphilis, as he also entered "Lues Veneria" (syphilis) in his case book when he felt it to be the appropriate diagnosis. Even Landon Carter knew of yaws. He assumed that a family of three siblings, one of whom had been "subject to gross ulcers," all died "from a mere family disorder . . . presumptively the yaws or hereditary pox." [43]

Unquestionably the two diseases were confused in colonial Virginia. It is curious, however, that the term "yaws" disappears from casebooks, diaries, and home medicine manuals by the turn of the nineteenth century. Either people suddenly began indiscriminately to label all cases of both diseases as syphilis, or yaws died out at this time. The latter seems a more likely explanation, for the cessation of the slave trade coincides remarkably well with this changeover in terminology. Without reinforcements from

---

[42] Parramore, "Non-Venereal Treponematosis," 575.
[43] William K. Boyd, ed., *William Byrd's Histories of the Dividing Line betwixt Virginia and North Carolina* (Raleigh, 1928), 54; Louis B. Wright, ed., *The History and Present State of Virginia by Robert Beverley* [1705] (Chapel Hill, N.C., 1947), 306; "Virginia Council Journals, 1726–53," *VMHB*, 34 (1926), 103–4; Edmund Wilcox Ledger, Hubard Family Papers, vol. 13, 10 September 1776, 26 April 1777 (also 20 January, 1777, 26 January 1778), UNC; Greene, ed., *Carter Diary*, II, 1059 (16 July 1776).

Africa, *T. pertenue* could not spread as rapidly or as easily in a hostile environment. Virginia was hot and damp for only a portion of the year. Slaves wore clothing most of the time, which effectively covered infective ulcers and prevented contagion. In addition, though neither whites nor blacks observed particularly heathful sanitary habits, they did have their wounds washed and dressed regularly, further retarding *T. pertenue*'s spread to new hosts. As tropical yaws died out, its cousin, venereal syphilis, took over as the leading spirochete in Virginia.[44]

Syphilis and its bacteriologically unrelated associate, gonorrhea, are not transmitted through filth or unsanitary living conditions, but they were public health problems in antebellum Virginia nonetheless. Unlike yaws, venereal diseases became, if anything, more prevalent in the 1800's than they had been during the previous two centuries. Though morbidity figures for Virginia's whites and blacks do not exist, the frequency with which these two diseases appeared in physicians' casebooks points to a rate which may be, as one historian has stated, "startling."[45] Masters knew that venereal disease (used here to denote gonorrhea and syphilis) was disseminated by intimate sexual contact, but they also knew how difficult it was to prevent contagion by recognition and isolation of infected individuals.

Both diseases were a nuisance to antebellum Virginia masters and a discomfort to the many slaves who contracted them. Two examples from the Northern Neck area will serve to illustrate the easy mode of spread among plantation hands. Dinah, one of Landon Carter's slaves, complained for some time of illness before her master discovered that she was suffering from "the great Pox [syphilis] which she is quite rotten with indeed." One of the slaves on a nearby plantation had transmitted the infection to her, and Carter, aware of the danger of contagion, wished (in his diary) that "this bitch may not have given it to some of my boys." He had already treated three other neighborhood slaves

<hr>

[44] An example of the care used in dressing the ulcers of yaws may be found in Edmund Wilcox Ledger, Hubard Family Papers, vol. 13, p. 23 (20 January 1777), UNC.

[45] Eugene Genovese, "The Medical and Insurance Costs of Slaveholding in the Cotton Belt," *JNH*, 45 (1960), 151.

for similar complaints, indicating that syphilis was not a rarity in that part of the state during the Revolutionary period. Sixty years later, in nearby King and Queen County, the pious, God-fearing John Walker became understandably outraged upon learning of several cases of adult and congenital (childhood) venereal disease among the residents of his farm. Some female slaves, Walker belatedly discovered, had been sneaking over to a white neighbor's house for the previous ten years "to whore it" with members of both races. Though he felt he had ended this practice by exposing and whipping those blacks involved, at least two other cases of venereal disease developed among his slave women some years later. How many men and women contracted gonorrhea or syphilis from infected individuals is a significant question. Regardless of race or sex, those who picked up the infection took it back to their homes and, no doubt, exposed others to it. The potential for a full scale "silent" epidemic existed, as incidents such as these were common throughout the state.[46]

Venereal disease was not confined to blacks or to rural areas. Doctor James T. Hubard, who practiced medicine in the port town of Petersburg, treated five servants and twenty-six different whites for syphilis and gonorrhea during 1800. Dr. Edmund Wilcox of Amherst County recorded two instances of gonorrhea in whites and two of syphilis, one in a white male and the other in a slave woman, between March 1777 and March 1778. In addition, unfaithful spouses occasionally brought home convincing evidence of their extramarital liaisons by transmitting venereal infections to their legal partners: two slave couples on different Amelia County farms contracted gonorrhea, as did Wesley and Sarah in Madison County, and a white Petersburg pair. Industrial slaves, especially those living in cities, were prime targets for venereal disease from prostitutes and casual liaisons. Bondsmen hired from the country then carried their newly acquired infections back to the plantation, where others might soon share it. Virtually every physician who noted the kinds of diseases he

[46] Greene, ed., *Carter Diary*, II, 1073 (4 February 1777), also 1074 (9 February), 1088 (4 April), 1097–98 (23 April); John Walker Diary, 5, 8 July, 21 October, 12 November 1834, 10 January 1835, 4 November 1848, 5 July 1850, UNC.

treated listed some patients suffering from either syphilis or gonorrhea.[47] The two major discernible complications of venereal disease were urethral strictures and congenital syphilis. The former usually presented few medical problems once the diagnosis had been made, but little could be done to cure the latter. John Walker claimed to have lost three children to congenital syphilis; an Amherst County doctor treated a child "born with a Lues Veneria & scars & Ven'l Warts"; and several other practitioners recorded similar cases. How many people died or lived lives of pain due to undiagnosed or untreatable complications of veneral disease cannot be determined.[48]

Physicians' records tell only part of the story of gonorrhea and syphilis in antebellum Virginia. For each case that was recorded, there were many which were not, because people treated the disease themselves or waited until it disappeared. They did not realize the potential hazards of concealment to personal and public health. Venereal disease may have been more common among slaves than among whites because of promiscuity engendered by the slave system. However, the fact remains that in each

[47] See, e.g., "James T. Hubard's Day Book," and Edmund Wilcox Ledger, Hubard Family Papers, vols. 33 and 13, UNC; accounts of Mrs. Francis Tabb and Mr. Thomas Goode with Dr. James H. Conway, Conway Account Book (Amelia County), VSL; accounts of Thornton Fry and Joseph Edwards with Dr. George Thrift, Thrift Ledgers (Madison County), UVA (#9153d); account of James Calliss with Dr. Thomas H. Dunn, Dunn Account Books (Middlesex County), VSL (vol. 1, p. 16); account of Mr. Azel French with Dr. Lewis W. Chamberlayne, Chamberlayne Account Book (Richmond), VHS; Edmunds Mason, "Use of Alum on Bougies in Stricture," VMJ, 13 (1859), 109–10 (factory hand); medical account of John Buford with Dr. T. E. Dunn, 1855–56, Buford Papers, Duke (railroad hand); account of John Enders with Dr. Charles J. F. Bohannan, Bohannan Ledgers (Richmond tobacco factory hand), VSL; medical account of Leslie and Brydon with John Bragg, 1831–32 (Petersburg tobacco factory hands), Leslie Papers, Duke.

[48] R. H. Baylor, "Bridle and Permanent Stricture Successfully Treated," VMSJ, 4 (1855), 376–78; Mason, "Use of Alum," 109–10; account of Abraham Tinsley with Dr. George Thrift, Thrift Ledgers, UVA (#9153d); John Walker Diary, 21 October, 12 November 1834, 10 January 1835, UNC (there is some doubt as to the correctness of Walker's diagnosis); Edmund Wilcox Ledger, Hubard Family Papers, vol. 13, 2 March 1778, UNC; account of Mrs. Francis Tabb with Dr. James H. Conway, Conway Account Book, VSL; account of Miss Ann Wiglesworth with Dr. Nelson S. Waller, Waller Account Book (Spotsylvania County), VSL.

county venereal diseases probably occurred with a frequency which could be considered epidemic. Each newly reported case arose from a person already harboring the micro-organisms; that person, in turn, probably had spread the germs to several other unsuspecting victims.

Urban and Industrial Slave Communities

The public health aspects of urban slave life were similar to those found on plantations. Town-dwelling slaves also experienced the problems of overcrowding and poor housing. Bondsmen usually resided in houses located behind their masters' dwellings, though hired slaves were sometimes permitted to seek their own lodgings elsewhere in the city. This latter practice occasionally caused difficulties for both the Negro and the owner: slaves were found living in dark, filthy, tiny shanties or rooms, poorly clothed, and sometimes sick, with no one to aid them. But even the quarters provided by the master were often cramped and unhealthy.[49]

Urban life favored the outbreak of epidemics even without slumlike housing conditions; poor housing only increased the risk. One man moved his large white and black family to a house in a Virginia town and lost twenty-two or twenty-three members (mostly slaves) within a few months. A friend attributed the deaths to the poor housing facilities provided the slaves: "The Lot was small, and the Back yard so much crowded with out houses, and trees, as to exclude the Sun almost entirely. The cellars of course must have been exceedingly damp, and in them the Negroes lodged." [50] Several eminent Richmond physicians, outraged at the amount of sickness occurring in town among those hirelings who obtained their own living quarters (usually in the worst houses of the city in order to reduce costs), published an exposé in the state's only medical journal. One doctor, summoned to treat an ill servant, "after considerable difficulty . . . found him in a *loft* of a miserable out house, on the premises of low peo-

[49] A more detailed account of urban slave housing may be found in Wade, *Slavery in the Cities*, 56–59.
[50] Eliza B. Watts to Miss Alice Watts Saunders, — June 1820, Saunders Family Deposit, UVA.

ple. . . . The patient was ill, and only covered with a few rags, on the floor, and could get no assistance." [51] A Williamsburg physician discovered that he could not examine the tongue of his slave patient because she lived in so dark a loft.[52]

Besides providing poor lodgings for some urban slaves, town slaveholders also furnished Negroes with inadequate sanitary facilities, though whites in most antebellum Virginia towns found conditions equally unhealthy. In Norfolk, Richmond, and Williamsburg pit privies were the general rule, and these were emptied by hand only periodically. Although some whites no doubt had water closets once running water and sewer systems were built, a postbellum public health officer described Richmond's sanitary situation as it had existed in 1855:

> The city was then unsupplied with sewers. All the waste water from lots passed along or stagnated in the badly graded gutters, which, in a few hours, became offensive to sight and smell. No provision was made for the removal of garbage or refuse matter from the lots. Every one was allowed to employ unreliable scavengers, who, in the secrecy of the night, dumped the offensive material in the ravines in the city, or in many cases, buried it on the lots.[53]

It is not surprising that cholera struck Richmond four times (1832, 1834, 1849, 1854) before the Civil War, most viciously in the poorer, valley sections of the city where sewage and garbage were dumped. Generally the public health problems described for plantation slave communities also prevailed in Virginia's towns.

The quality of housing at industrial sites varied widely. Firms at permanent locations such as ironworks, gold and coal mines, and tobacco factories provided reasonably well constructed dormitory accommodations. Public works contractors, whose jobs shifted constantly from one section of a canal, railroad, or turnpike to another, provided their laborers with temporary shanties. The

[51] Editorial, "Practice on Hirelings," *Steth.*, 1 (1851), 677.

[52] [A. D. Galt,] *Practical Medicine: Illustrated by Cases of the Most Important Diseases*, ed. John M. Galt (Philadelphia, 1843), 168.

[53] *Annual Report of the Board of Health of the Births, Marriages and Deaths in the City of Richmond, for the Year 1878* (Richmond, 1879), 7; Bagley, "Public Health of Norfolk," 12; personal communication from Patricia A. Gibbs, research assistant, Colonial Williamsburg Foundation, 17 July 1974.

100-150 workmen at the Vaucluse Gold Mine in Orange County lived in cabins "all in good order and new," while those at the Culpeper Gold Mine, eighteen miles west of Fredericksburg, found their accommodations "framed substantially, and clapboarded." William Weaver, owner of the Union Iron Forge in Rockbridge County, built a stone cabin for his Negro employees. Most railroad contractors had their slaves build houses on the right-of-way before going to work on the road. Many urban-based industries permitted slave workers to find their own quarters in town, but the Tredegar Company housed its laborers in tenements at the ironworks.[54]

If anything, health conditions at temporary sites were probably worse than at permanent industrial locations. This was one reason why slaveowners were reluctant to hire out their blacks to public works contractors. Though specific evidence is not available, poor sanitation and housing at temporary labor camps no doubt increased the incidence of intestinal, respiratory, skin, and parasitic diseases.[55]

Living conditions of slaves were thus an important matter. Masters were forced to consider not only the well-being of an individual slave, but also the public health of the entire plantation, household, or industrial community. The slaves had to remain healthy to work. A report such as the one which Colonel John Ambler received from the overseer of his Louisa County estate, Mill Farm, pointed up the difficulty of attaining that goal: "Capt Joseph Winstons negroes is dying with the negro quarter Fevour the quarters yours lives in keeps them in good health." [56]

[54] For a general discussion of industrial slave housing, see Starobin, *Industrial Slavery*, 57–62; *Plan and Description of the Vaucluse Mine, Orange County, Virginia* (Philadelphia, 1847), 8; B. Silliman, "Remarks on Some of the Gold Mines, and on Parts of the Gold Region of Virginia, Founded on Personal Observations, Made in the Months of August and September, 1836," *American Journal of Science*, 32 (1837), 117; Forge Inventory (doc. 17—Accounts), in *Weaver v. Mayburry*, Augusta County Court House, Staunton, Va. (#239); I. W. Leftwich to John Buford, 13 May 1854, Buford Papers, Duke; Charles W. Turner, "The Virginia Railroads, 1828–1860" (Ph.D. dissertation, University of Minnesota, 1946), 205.

[55] See, e.g., J[ulius] B. Buford to John Buford, 8 July 1855, Buford Papers, Duke; Turner, "The Virginia Railroads," 154.

[56] E. Pendleton to Col. John Ambler, 9 May 1823, Ambler Family Papers, UVA (#1140).

CHAPTER 3

Clothing, Food, and Working Conditions

The major medical problem at the quarters was communicable disease. However, in the course of each day bondsmen faced other health problems unrelated to contagion or parasites. Inadequate clothing and food, poor working conditions, harsh physical punishment, pregnancy, and bodily disorders also made slaves sick or uncomfortable, often rendering them useless to their masters and burdensome to their friends and family.

Clothing

Though adequate clothing was important for slaves, it did not play as crucial a role in the maintenance of health as housing did. Of course clothing covered and protected the body from exposure to wind, sun, rain, snow, cold, and insects. It also limited the severity of many minor falls to cuts, scrapes, and bruises, and of some industrial accidents to burns over small areas. But only a few disorders are spread by contact with infected clothing (smallpox, body lice, impetigo, typhus) or by contact of exposed skin with other objects (tetanus, yaws, hookworm, brucellosis). Common decency and antebellum society's moral standards dictated that all people, especially adults, be ade-

quately covered. Some slaveowners counted appearance heavily
(i.e., no worn or disheveled clothing), but others allowed their
slaves to wear ill-fitting, dirty, or torn garments. Children often
ran naked during the hot seasons.[1] Except in cases where slaves
were truly underclothed in winter, possibly causing decreased
resistance to respiratory ailments, the danger of contracting disease owing to inadequate or dirty wearing apparel was relatively
small.

Virginia's cold, even snowy, winters made the issuance of warm
clothing to slaves a necessity. Given our present knowledge that
Negroes withstand cold poorly and suffer more frequently from
exposure and frostbite than do Caucasians, adequate protection
from winter weather was essential (see chapter 1). Unfortunately,
slaves were quite vulnerable to their owners' whims in the matter of clothing. Food could be obtained from the (locked or
unlocked) storehouse, chicken coop, or hog pen, and holes in
cabins could be patched with mud, dirt, or wood. In contrast,
cloth and leather usually had to be purchased—they could not be
found on the plantation in sufficient surplus quantities. If the
master did not provide clothing or the material needed to make
it, the Negro had to tolerate the cold.[2] One former Southampton
County slave woman emphasized the typical slave's helplessness
as she recalled the contrast between her attire and that on a
neighboring plantation:

> Of course we slaves were given food and clothing and just enough
> to keep us goin good. Why Master would buy cloth by the loads and

[1] Fogel and Engerman, *Time*, I, 116–17; Stampp, *Peculiar Institution*, 289–92;
Mullin, *Flight and Rebellion*, 50–51; Wade, *Slavery in the Cities*, 125–31; Starobin, *Industrial Slavery*, 54–57.

[2] Many examples of good and bad practices might be cited to illustrate the
varieties of slave winter attire in Virginia. See, e.g., George P. Rawick, ed., *The
American Slave: A Composite Autobiography* (Westport, Conn., 1972), XVI,
Virginia Narratives, 10, 15; Olmsted, *Seaboard*, 112; contract, Robert T. Hubard
and George Jones [overseer], 1 June 1839, Hubard Papers, UVA; [George E.
Harrison,] "Slavery in Virginia: Extract from *Slavery in the United States*—by
J. K. Paulding being a letter to the author from a farmer of lower Virginia,"
VMHB, 36 (1928), 279; S. Sydney Bradford, "The Negro Ironworker in Ante
Bellum Virginia," *JSH*, 25 (1959), 201; [William McKean to James Dunlap,]
2 March 1811, Roslin Plantation Records, VSL; receipt of Martha Holmes, 14
November 1832, Dismal Swamp Papers, Duke; receipt of Susan M. Walton, 17
December 1844, Randolph Papers, Box 11, LC.

heaps, shoes by the big boxfull; den he'd call us to the house and give each on us our share. Plenty to keep us comfortable, course it warn't silk nor satin, no ways the best there was, but 'twas plenty good 'nough for us, and we was plenty glad to get it. Then we would look and see how the slaves on the 'jining farm was fareing, 'twould almost make us shed tears. It made us feel like we was gitting 'long most fine.[3]

Of articles of clothing which masters provided their bondsmen, shoes were probably the most important in terms of health and disease. Not only did they provide warmth in the winter to feet and toes highly susceptible to frostbite, but they also protected slaves against hookworm penetration, scrapes, scratches, burns, and some puncture wounds which would otherwise have caused tetanus. Not all Virginia slaves wore shoes, however. In addition to children, who usually went barefooted in warm weather, adult bondsmen at scattered farms and industries across the state also went unshod. Without this protection slaves frequently injured their feet and lost time from work. "Moses foot sore from sand burrs so he is minding cows," ran a typical plantation master's complaint.[4] Shoes were particularly important for ironworkers, because they labored in the mountains on rough, often wet terrain. A lack of footwear here meant time lost, as the supervisor at one ore bank complained: "Spott is laying up at Bank for the want of a par [of shoes]. The bank is very wet, it is so rough they cannot work with out them. . . . Two of the Car's boy is barefooted they will be layed up if they are not shod."[5]

Virginia masters usually refrained from distributing warm winter shoes (and other winter clothing) until the weather actually turned cold, in order to reduce the frequency of repairs and replacements. Though some fall days and most fall nights were rather chilly throughout the state, slaves did not receive warm shoes until November or December, even from the most humane owners. It was, for instance, the explicit order of a Halifax County man who hired his slaves to a tobacconist in Danville:

[3] Interview of Mrs. Marriah Hines, 26 March 1937, in Rawick, ed., *The American Slave*, XVI, Virginia Narratives, 27–28. Mrs. Hines, born on 4 July 1835, had lived as the slave of James Pressman of Southampton County until emancipation.

[4] White Hill Plantation Books, 11 November 1853, UNC.

[5] W. W. Rex to Daniel Brady, 21 September 1860, Weaver Papers, Duke.

"I dont wish them furnished with shoes until the time they ought to receive their Winter Shoes & if Convenient would prefer your giving them Shoes early in December ... [so] they will go through the Winter."[6] Hill Carter of Shirley Plantation distributed his slaves' shoes in early November but "ordered them not to put them on until given permission," which came more than a month later.[7] Apparently slaves found ways of protecting their feet from the cold during these chilly November weeks, for planters persisted in this practice of late fall shoeing throughout the antebellum period. Aside from the necessity of providing slaves with warm outerwear and shoes to protect them against frostbite and exposure in winter, the role of clothing in preventing disease was relatively minor.

Food for Plantation Slaves

As illustrated by recent historical literature,[8] facts regarding slave diet are difficult to obtain, evidence of dietary deficiency diseases or lowered resistance to other diseases due to poor

[6] Jno. B. Carrington to Jno. M. Sutherlin, 5 April 1858, Sutherlin Papers, Duke. Examples of planters providing shoes in November are: White Hill Plantation Books, 15 November 1841, 26 November 1853, 29 November 1855, 20 November 1857, 18 November 1859, UNC; John Walker Diary, 10 December 1832, 10 December 1833, 12 November 1834, 12 December 1835, UNC. See also account of Dismal Swamp Land Company with Benjamin D. Smith, 27 October 1848–27 March 1849, Dismal Swamp Papers, Duke.

[7] Shirley Farm Journals, 6 November and 8 December 1824, LC.

[8] See, e.g., Richard Sutch, "The Treatment Received by American Slaves: A Critical Review of the Evidence Presented in *Time on the Cross*," *Explorations in Economic History*, 12 (1975), 395–96; Fogel and Engerman, *Time*, I, 109–15, II, 90–99. Though Fogel and Engerman's conclusion that most slaves received adequate nutrition may be correct, the methods and assumptions used in arriving at the figures presented raise several questions. The "disappearance technique," whereby the amounts of various foods remaining after use for feed, seed, and sale are assumed to have been fed to slaves, is quite appealing and ingenious. But, as the authors admit, it works best only when the number of slaves on a plantation is large enough to render the error resulting from the proportion of food consumed by whites inconsequential. Can we generalize from the figures obtained on several large (more than fifty slaves) plantations in the Deep South that bondsmen throughout the South, on all sizes of farms, ate in a similar manner? And are these figures valid in the first place? Though Fogel and Engerman "overfed the whites" with all types of foods raised on the plantation, and decreased the amount of beef and pork available for slave consumption by 15–30

nourishment among slaves is often tenuous and unconvincing, and interpretations of the nutritional adequacy of the slave diet based on modern metabolic research are complex, confusing, and often subject to debate. Most of the deficiency diseases presently known have symptoms which mimic other disorders, making it difficult to recognize them in antebellum medical descriptions. For example, a historian of slave health in the Deep South, William Dosite Postell, surveyed manuscript books and journals of many plantations, speculating in 1951 that "the great number of dental caries, sore eyes, sore mouths, sore feet and legs, and skin lesions [found among slaves] is suggestive of p[e]llagra and other dietary-deficiency diseases." Though the symptoms described do suggest vitamin malnutrition, one cannot conclude that this is the proper diagnosis. Bad teeth, skin rashes, eye, leg, and mouth lesions—common ailments of both blacks and whites—could have been caused by other conditions or seasonal diseases. These descriptive terms are too vague to permit diagnosis as dietary deficiency disease.[9]

---

percent in order to account for any possible sales to urban markets, they did not include in their procedural description any indication that they reduced the stated amount (1860 census) of milk, butter, sweet and Irish potatoes, peas, corn, wheat and other grains raised, which might have been sold to neighbors. In Virginia large planters like Hill Carter often used a portion of their crops to pay debts to, or earn cash from, other farmers or providers of services. Unless Fogel and Engerman can produce evidence from the records of those large plantations used in their study which state the quantities of produce retained for slave use, can they assume with any validity that a large portion of some of the foods were not sold off the plantation?

[9] Postell, *Health of Slaves*, 85. Stampp, *Peculiar Institution*, 282, makes vague references to "slaves who . . . suffered from dietary deficiencies," but presents no evidence to substantiate their existence. Leslie Howard Owens, *This Species of Property; Slave Life and Culture in the Old South* (New York, 1976), 50–69, discusses slave diet and its effect on behavior. He asserts that dietary deficiency diseases existed to a much greater extent than historians have heretofore admitted. As with Postell, however, Owens's evidence is unconvincing both for making diagnoses and for assessing the extensiveness of these disorders among the slave population.

A recent, important article which was published too late for inclusion in the body of this book is Kenneth F. and Virginia H. Kiple, "Slave Child Mortality: Some Nutritional Answers to a Perennial Puzzle," *Journal of Social History*, 10 (1977), 284–309. The Kiples present convincing evidence that slave children suffered not infrequently from nutritional deficiency, especially of iron, calcium,

One recently discovered description of a disease prevalent among underfed, hard-working Louisiana sugar plantation slaves does, however, provide evidence to support Postell's assertion that nutritional inadequacy occurred in the Old South. Cesare Bressa (1785–1836), a respected Italian physician who practiced medicine in New Orleans and on nearby sugar plantations between 1818 and 1829, provided to the French-speaking medical society of that city a detailed composite case history, with autopsy results, of a fatal disease which a modern physician has diagnosed as beriberi (thiamine deficiency). The general diet on these plantations was cornmeal with a small amount of putrid, decaying, salted meat. Bressa cured his patients in 40-60 days with rest and a varied diet of nutritious foods. An excellent recent study by Kenneth and Virginia Kiple also demonstrates that some slaves did develop symptoms of what was probably incipient pellagra during the winter and spring months of the middle 1840's, poor agricultural years in several regions of the South. These were seasons when supplements to the basic cornmeal and pork diet were minimal, even in good times. Those who had previously survived the winters on a poor but passable nutritional intake now lacked enough niacin and its metabolic precursors, and so developed manifestations of the disease. White physicians and slaveowners often called it "black tongue," owing to one of its common signs, and counted it as a new disease.[10]

Some Virginia slaves undoubtedly received inadequate diets from their masters. During the colonial and early post-Revolution-

---

and phosphorus. They demonstrate how complex interdependent factors in nutrient metabolism, environmental and geographical conditions, and lack of medical knowledge by slave owners all conspired against the good health of antebellum black children. The Kiples list several common causes of infant death which they believe were actually nutritional in origin but which physicians and lay people alike either mislabeled (neonatal tetanus, teething, and smothering), or assumed had other etiologies (convulsions, rickets, and dirt-eating). Their arguments are convincing, though some of their medical data is not yet conclusive, especially with regard to magnesium deficiency as a factor in crib death.

[10] Piero Mustacchi, "Cesare Bressa (1785–1836) on Dirt Eating in Louisiana: A Critical Analysis of His Unpublished Manuscript *De la Dissolution Scorbutique*," *JAMA*, 218 (1971), 229–32. The 1825 manuscript was discovered in the Library of the Academy of Sciences, Torino, Italy. Kenneth Kiple and Virginia Kiple, "Black Tongue and Black Men: Pellagra and Slavery in the Antebellum South," *JSH*, 43 (1977), 411–28.

ary periods meat was not regularly provided to bondsmen, a deficiency which could have led to protein malnutrition or anemia.[11] One Charlotte County planter actually stated in 1837 that he had seen bondsmen who appeared undernourished and sickly, but he also denied that many masters permitted this to occur: "I believe that there are extremely few masters who starve their slaves to actual suffering; in fact, I am unacquainted with any such. But, I have no doubt that the slow motion, and thin expression of countenance, of many slaves, are owing to a want of a sufficiency of nourishing food. . . . There is, however, a great change for the better, in the article of diet to negroes, within the last ten or fifteen years." [12]

Two additional factors must be taken into account when assessing the adequacy of slave diets. First, nutritional deficiencies do not produce diseases immediately. The body is able to store varying amounts of nutrients during times of adequate feeding and to release them from the tissues in periods of insufficiency. Proteins in the form of essential amino acids cannot, as a rule, be stored more than a few hours, whereas calcium reserves will last an average person for several years (see Table 3). Virginia slaves who ate sufficient foods except perhaps during midwinter months, when green vegetables were often lacking, would most likely show only slight, early, and temporary signs of dietary deficiency diseases like pellagra.[13]

Second, certain parasitic intestinal worms interfere with the body's normal utilization of various nutrients (iron, protein, and Vitamins A, B_{12}, and C).[14] More than half of the blacks of antebellum Virginia hosted worms sometime in their lives; those

[11] See references in Mullin, *Flight and Rebellion*, 50; Greene, ed., *Carter Diary*, I, 299 (15 May 1766), II, 871 (10 October 1774).

[12] Charlotte County [pseudonym], "Management of Slaves," *FR*, 5 (1837), 32.

[13] Norman Jolliffe, "The Pathogenesis of Deficiency Disease," in Jolliffe, ed., *Clinical Nutrition* (New York, 1962), 1–4. Even in winter, however, sweet potatoes and other vegetables were available.

[14] Children infected with 13 to 40 *ascaris* roundworms lose significant amounts of protein (4 grams in a diet containing 35–50 grams). Ascariasis may also cause deficiencies of vitamins A and C. The whipworm, *Trichuris trichiura*, mentioned frequently by Old South medical writers, and the hookworm, *Necator americanus*, both suck blood from intestinal blood vessels, causing anemia. The fish tapeworm, *Diphyllobothrium latum*, competes with its human host for Vitamin B_{12} in ingested food, resulting in pernicious anemia.

Table 3. Nutrient Reserves in an Adequately Fed Male Adult [a]

Amino Acids [b] (labile)	A few hours
Carbohydrates	13 hours
Fat (at 12% of body weight) [c]	27 days
Thiamine	30–60 days
Ascorbic acid (Vitamin C)	60–120 days
Niacin (Nicotinic acid)	60–180 days
Riboflavin	60–180 days
Vitamin A	90–365 days
Iron (menstruating woman @ 12 mg/day)	125 days
(man and menopausal woman @ 2.0 mg/day)	750 days
Iodine	1,000 days
Calcium (based on 25% loss of a total of 1,000 gm @ 0.1 gm/day)	2,500 days

[a] Based on approximate daily nutrient expenditure of a 70 kg (154 lb) adult. These reserves vary with the person's activity, temperature regulation, and health. SOURCE: Norman Jolliffe, ed., *Clinical Nutrition* (New York, 1962), 4.
[b] Amino acids are the building blocks from which the body manufactures proteins.
[c] Average percentage of fat is lower in black males and higher in females.

harboring such parasites required increased amounts of foods rich in the lost nutrients. Though slaveowners sometimes detected the presence of worms, they did not realize that they needed to raise food allowances to compensate for this loss. Bondsmen living on a barely adequate diet soon became deficient in some nutrients as worm infestation increased. This may have been true among the anemic, listless slaves Bressa described in Louisiana, as well as among those noted by the Charlotte County planter. Intestinal parasites cannot be ignored as a factor in evaluating slave diets.

Because of their availability, low cost, and supposed nutritional value, pork and corn constituted the primary foods for most Virginia slaves. Both could be raised on the farm. Pork was, as one historian of eating habits in the Old South described it, "the undisputed 'king of the table,'" and corn was its "companion food." [15] Slaves and whites consumed both in all forms and in great quantities. On Virginia plantations the usual amount for a working male hand varied between a peck and a peck-and-a-half of corn per week (1-1.5 quarts per day), most often already ground into meal, and 3.5 pounds of bacon or pork per week

[15] Sam Bowers Hilliard, *Hog Meat and Hoecake: Food Supply in the Old South, 1840–1860* (Carbondale, Ill., 1972), 41, 48.

(half a pound per day). Female fieldhands and some indoor servants received proportionally less, with the weekly figure sinking below one peck of corn and two pounds of bacon on some plantations.[16] Had these been the only foods which bondsmen received each day, then the response of a young northern tutor living on Robert Carter's Nomini Hall Plantation (Westmoreland County) in 1773 would have been entirely justifiable: "Good God! are these Christians?" [17]

Based on current dietary standards, one quart of whole ground, dry, bolted cornmeal, prepared from white corn (the South's favorite), and half a pound of cured, medium-fat ham with no bone or skin, could not have provided enough essential nutrients to sustain a moderately active, twenty-two-year-old male or female, much less a hard-working laborer or a pregnant or lactating woman (see Table 4).[18] Fieldhands fed this diet alone (with water) would soon have become emaciated and sickly and would have shown symptoms of several nutrient deficiencies. It is highly unlikely that any slave could have survived very long on a diet consisting solely of pork and cornmeal.

Most Old Dominion masters provided supplements to the basic hogmeat and cornmeal, a practice most urgently recommended by agricultural writers throughout the state. Vegetables topped the list of required additional foods. Planters could, if they planned ahead, have a ready supply of at least one or two varieties

[16] Entries in plantation journals for Buffalo Farm, Nelson County, ca. November 1845 and November 1846, vol. 54, Hubard Family Papers, UNC; "List of Names of the People of Upper Bremo withe each ones allowance of meal weeckley," 17 February 1837, and "Memorandum of Corn for Recess in the yer 1825," Cocke Deposit, Cocke Papers, UVA; "Weekly allowance of Meat and Meal at L[aurel] S[pring]," vol. VI, p. 128, Cox Account Books, UNC; [William Cabell Rives, Jr.,] Plantation Books, Memorandum #2, p. 164, Rives Papers, LC; "Day Book No. 1," Leslie Papers, Duke; ——— to Mr. Cooke, 2 February 1848, Barker-Cooke Papers, W&M; [Harrison,] "Slavery in Virginia," 278.

[17] Hunter Dickinson Farish, ed., *The Journal and Letters of Philip Vickers Fithian 1773–1774: A Plantation Tutor of the Old Dominion* (Williamsburg, Va., 1957), 38 (23 December 1773).

[18] See Hilliard, *Hog Meat and Hoecake*, 55–58, for preparation of cornmeal and cuts of pork. Charles Frederick Church and Helen Nichols Church, *Food Values of Portions Commonly Used* (Philadelphia, 1966), 13, 121. Values for other, relatively fatty pork cuts (except salt pork) do not differ significantly from cured ham.

Table 4. Daily Slave Nutrition Based on a Cornmeal [a] and Pork [b] Diet

	Calories [c] (kcal)	Protein (gm)	Calcium (mg)	Phosphorus (mg)	Iron (mg)	Thiamine (mg)	Niacin (mg)	Vitamin A (IU)	Riboflavin (mg)	Vitamin C (mg)
Amount supplied	2,348	82	103	1,420	14	3.0	18	1,132 [h]	0.8	0
Amount recommended [d]										
Male [e]	2,700	56	500 [i]	800	10	1.4	18	5,000	1.6	45
Female [f]	2,000	46	500 [i]	800	18	1.0	13	4,000	1.2	45
Female pregnant [g]	2,300	76	1,200	1,200	18+	1.3	15	5,000	1.5	60
Female lactating [g]	2,500	66	1,200	1,200	18	1.3	17	6,000	1.7	80

[a] 1 quart whole ground, dry, bolted, cornmeal. Church and Church, *Food Values*, 13.

[b] ½ pound cured, medium fat ham with no bone or skin. *Ibid.*, 121.

[c] kcal = kilocalories; gm = grams; mg = milligrams; IU = international units.

[d] Food and Nutrition Board, National Academy of Sciences, *Recommended Dietary Allowances* (Washington, 1974), 129. These are recommended rather than required daily allowances of nutrients. Thus, "even if a person habitually consumes less than the recommended amounts of some nutrients, his diet is not necessarily inadequate for those nutrients" (*ibid.*, p. 12).

[e] 23–50 year old, 154 pound, 69 inch male.

[f] 23–50 year old, 128 pound, 65 inch female (menstruating).

[g] 23–50 year old, 128 pound, 65 inch female (pregnant or lactating).

[h] White cornmeal, preferred by Southerners, contains only a trace of Vitamin A. Yellow cornmeal contains 566 IU of this vitamin per cup. The amount given here is based on a diet of half yellow and half white cornmeal.

[i] Food and Nutrition Board, *Recommended Dietary Allowances*, 84–85.

throughout the year. Also recommended were fish, fresh meat, molasses, milk, and buttermilk.[19] Those owners who provided their chattel with large quantities of fresh meat as a change from salted, pickled, or smoked pork also helped prevent anemia resulting from insufficient iron intake. Robert Hubard, for instance, allowed his slaves at Buffalo Farm in Nelson County twice as much fresh as cured meat.[20] Planters like Hill Carter annually slaughtered several beeves during the late fall when the pork supply ran low, in order to continue feeding slaves meat during the harvest and clean-up season.[21] Slaveowners who furnished no meat at all to their bondsmen had to supplement the cornmeal ration with year-round vegetables in order to maintain their Negroes' health. Landon Carter, for instance, served meat only to reward favored slaves, to induce slaves to work, or to treat his slaves at irregular times during the year. The basic diet included cornmeal (or wheat when the corn ran short), cowpeas, vegetables in season, and offal (sweetbreads and chitterlings).[22]

Some of the foods which Virginia slaveowners furnished their slaves were more nutritious than others. Sweet potatoes, a vegetable popular among bondsmen, was particularly nourishing and was easily preserved over the winter months. A small sweet potato

[19] Charlotte County [pseudonym], "Management of Slaves," 32. H[ill] C[arter], "On the Management of Negroes," FR, 1 (1834), 565; H., "Remarks on Overseers and the Proper Treatment of Slaves," ibid., 5 (1837), 302; Plantation and Farm Instruction, Regulation, Record, Inventory and Account Book, for the Use of the Manager on the Estate of   , and for the Better Ordering and Management of Plantation and Farm Business in Every Particular, by a Southern Planter (Richmond, 1852), 6, in Hairfield Plantation Records (Orange County, Va.), UVA (#2198). Others who used this book were Philip St. George Cocke at Belmead, Powhatan County (VHS), and Thomas Edward Cox at Laurel Spring, Henrico County (UNC).

[20] Entry in Plantation Journal, ca. November 1846, vol. 54, Hubard Family Papers, UNC. See also Day Book No. 1, Roslin Plantation (Chesterfield County), Leslie Papers, Duke; Hilliard, Hog Meat and Hoecake, 44, 59.

[21] Shirley Farm Journals, 21, 28 October, 11, 18, 25 November 1827, and for that same period each year during the 1820's, LC.

[22] Greene, ed., Carter Diary, I, 299 (15 May 1766), 314 (6 July 1766), 467 (14 August 1770), 494 (19 September 1770); II, 602 (31 July 1771), 871 (10 October 1774); Mullin, Flight and Rebellion, 50; George Washington to William Pearce, — December 1793, in Moncure D. Conway, ed., George Washington and Mount Vernon, in Memoirs of the Long Island Historical Society, 4 (1889), 24.

contained about 1.5 times the minimum daily requirement of Vitamin A and one-third of the required amount of Vitamin C, both nutrients almost entirely lacking in pork and white corn-meal.[23] One former slave of a Lunenburg County family recalled (some seventy-two years after emancipation) that sweet potatoes were a staple of his diet: "We had plenty of food such as 'twas—cornbread, buttermilk, sweet potatoes, in week days." [24] Molasses and honey, like sweet potatoes, often found their way to Virginia slaves' tables.[25] Unknown to the slaves or their owners, molasses served not merely as a sweetener and food flavoring (though this was undoubtedly the reason for its popularity): five tablespoons supplied almost half of an adult male's, and nearly one-quarter of an adult female's, minimum daily iron requirement, as well as over 250 much-needed calories. It added significantly to the value of many slaves' diets.[26]

Wheat, too, was eaten by slaves in the form of bread, cakes, and pancakes, all of which required the addition of milk. Because it was not nearly as popular as cornmeal, wheat was consumed in smaller quantities—most fortunately, since unenriched bolted flour without the germ or bran (the kind most whites used) had far less food value than cornmeal. Hill Carter, for example, reserved only 60 bushels of his wheat annually for the slaves. This amounted to about five unmilled quarts per day for his slave force of over a hundred.[27]

One major source of nutrients for Virginia's enslaved blacks was fish. The Potomac, York, Rappahannock, James, and Appo-

---

[23] Hilliard, *Hog Meat and Hoecake*, 51, 65; Fogel and Engerman, *Time*, I, 113–15; Postell, *Health of Slaves*, 85–86; Church and Church, *Food Values*, 85. Fogel and Engerman, *Time*, I, 113, ignoring the fact that Southerners preferred white corn (which has only traces of Vitamin A) to yellow corn, state that "corn has more Vitamin A" than wheat.

[24] Rawick, ed., *The American Slave*, XVI, Virginia Narratives, 10, interview with Mr. Charles Crawley, 20 February 1937.

[25] [Harrison,] "Slavery in Virginia," 279; John Hartwell Cocke to Louisa Cocke, 8 June 1839, Cocke Deposit, Cocke Papers, UVA; John Driver to David Jameson, 26 January 1791, Dismal Swamp Papers, Duke.

[26] Church and Church, *Food Values*, 72; Postell, *Health of Slaves*, 85–86. Honey is not nearly as high in iron, though it furnishes over 300 calories.

[27] Hilliard, *Hog Meat and Hoecake*, 50; Shirley Farm Journals, 24 August 1824, 1 August 1825, 8 August 1827, LC.

mattox Rivers, as well as the Atlantic Ocean, Chesapeake Bay, and the many smaller rivers and streams throughout the state, supported a wide variety of seafood. Fish were so plentiful that Landon Carter bragged in his diary one October day: "I may say that if we are without fish this day it is the first day we have missed them since this year began, winter or sumer before." [28] Some slaveowners purchased or preserved fish for distribution year round, while others simply set out nets and apportioned the daily catch among their Negroes. Thomas Jefferson often economized by replacing pork with fish (usually salted herring) for a period of time during the year. He found that "a barrel of fish, costing 7. D. [dollars] goes as far with the laborers as 200 lb of pork worth 16. D." Two fish, Jefferson's usual ration per slave, provided substantial amounts of essential protein, minerals, and vitamins, as well as variety from monotonous meals of salt pork.[29] Slaves also fished for their own meals in nearby streams, with or without the permission of overseer or master. Young boys not yet working full-time in the fields or the big house, and elderly "retired" slaves, had the most opportunity to catch a little extra food for the family dinner.[30]

Many agricultural authors and slavemasters indicated in their writings that blacks often raised vegetables, poultry, and even pigs on their own plots of land near the quarters. The assumption was that extra food from this source would supplement rations supplied by the master. Surprisingly, however, some of these same writers also pointed out that slaves usually sold what they

[28] Greene, ed., *Carter Diary*, II, 876 (13 October 1774). Many of the patients of both races whose cases appear in [A. D. Galt,] *Practical Medicine: Illustrated by Cases of the Most Important Diseases*, ed. John M. Galt (Philadelphia, 1843), had eaten fish at regular meals, indicating that Tidewater residents took advantage of the many fish-filled waterways in their vicinity.

[29] Edwin M. Betts, ed., *Thomas Jefferson's Farm Book* (Princeton, 1953), pt. I, 57, 77, pt. II, 186–87. John Hartwell Cocke of Bremo, Jefferson's friend, also purchased salted fish for his slaves (Cocke to Maria Cocke, 8 June 1839, Cocke Deposit, Cocke Papers, UVA). See also George Washington to William Pearce, — December 1793, in Conway, ed., *George Washington and Mount Vernon*, 24; John Walker Diary, 21, 28 March 1835, UNC; [Harrison,] "Slavery in Virginia," 278.

[30] H. C. Bruce, *The New Man: Twenty-nine Years a Slave, Twenty-nine Years a Free Man* (York, Pa., 1895; reprinted, New York, 1969), 24; Greene, ed., *Carter Diary*, II, 834 (25 July 1774).

raised to the master or at the marketplace, thereby defeating the major purpose of the plan.[31] In all likelihood the slaves did not dispose of all their produce, but saved some for future needs. The fact that there were bondsmen who sold rather than kept food indicates that, other than those saving every available penny to purchase their freedom, some slaves received sufficient nutrition from their regular rations, supplemented by homegrown food, to feel quite comfortable relying on their masters for proper nutrition.

The diet of slave children often varied from that of adults, for several reasons. Not only were masters usually more solicitous of the wants and desires of young ones,[32] but slave parents, as much as they were able, no doubt put their offsprings' nutritional needs before their own. Some children, left all day in the care of elderly slave women or siblings, were, as a recent historian of slavery asserted, "fed irregularly or improperly." There is no evidence, however, that poor feeding of children was the general rule in Virginia, or that this was the reason why "young black children suffered from a variety of ills" (none of which the writer specified) and "died in droves." [33] There is no question that cooking for groups increased the chance for rapid dissemination of such epidemic intestinal diseases as typhoid, dysentery, and food poisoning. But no proof exists that this occurred regularly on most plantations. Nor was noontime the only meal of the day; mothers could make up for any perceived deficiencies in their children's daily diet during the evening meal. Neither malnutrition nor food contaminated by nannies killed slave children "in droves" on Virginia plantations.

[31] Olmsted, *Seaboard*, 108; Hilliard, *Hog Meat and Hoecake*, 46–47, 59–60; [Harrison,] "Slavery in Virginia," 277; C[arter,] "On the Management of Negroes," 565; John S. Bassett, ed., "The Westover Journal of John A. Seldon, Esqr., 1858–62," *Smith College Studies in History*, 6 (1921), 270 (19 August 1858); Plantation Book: Memoranda 1852 (#1), p. 71 (22 March 1853), Rives Papers, LC; John Walker Diary, 1 April 1837, UNC; Greene, ed., *Carter Diary*, II, 840 (27 July 1774), 1095–96 (20 April 1777); White Hill Plantation Books, 6 May 1854, UNC.

[32] Plantation Journal, ca. November 1845, vol. 54, Hubard Family Papers, UNC; Greene, ed., *Carter Diary*, I, 952 (27 September 1775); Peggy Nicholas to Sydney Smith Nicholas, 17 June 1819, Edgehill-Randolph Papers, UVA.

[33] Blassingame, *Slave Community*, 94.

If, as planters (and many historians) claimed, slaves received food enough for their dietary needs, why was thievery so common? Masters complained, cursed, and cried about this recurring problem. While some whites described the adequacy of their "people's" diets,[34] others silently fumed or punished slaves for stealing extra food.[35] Part of the reason for food theft was, obviously, hunger. Nineteenth-century slave narratives and early twentieth century former slave interviews attest to this. H. C. Bruce, writing in the 1890's of his own enslavement in Prince Edward County, recalled that "some slave owners did not feed well, causing their slaves to steal chickens, hogs and sheep from them or from other owners." Charles Grandy, born a slave in 1842 on Hickory Ground Farm near Hampton, explained why and how he stole to a WPA interviewer in 1937: " 'Cose we knowed it was wrong to steal, but de niggers had to steal to git somepin' to eat. I know I did. Dey had plenty o' food dere. Hawgs, cows, chickens an' ev'thing was plentiful. Sometimes dey kill two an' three hundred hawgs but dey sell 'em. Didn give me any. I got so hungry I stealed chickens off de roos'. Yessum, I did, chickens usta roos' on de fence den, right out in de night. We would cook de chicken at night, eat him an' bun'n de feathers." [36]

Hunger is a subjective sensation as well as a physiological signal. Its major "purpose" is to protect the human organism from starving body tissues. All foods are actually combinations of chemical substances which the digestive system liquifies, chemically alters, and passes on to the blood for further distribution. Cells in each particular organ (e.g., brain, heart, kidneys) utilize these chemicals to perform their specific functions within the body. If the chemicals are present in sufficient quantities, all systems operate normally. Often, however, the hunger signal acts out of psychological habit, disregarding the actual state of the

[34] Letitia M. Burwell, *A Girl's Life in Virginia before the War* (New York, 1895), 2; Thomas B. Merritt, "An Essay on the Autumnal Fever of Brunswick, Virginia," *American Medical Recorder*, 7 (1824), 285.

[35] John Walker Diary, I, 78 (17 November 1829), UNC; White Hill Plantation Books, 11, 12 June and 13 December 1841, UNC; Greene, ed., *Carter Diary*, II, 712 (16 August 1772).

[36] Bruce, *New Man*, 26; interview of Charles Grandy, 18 May 1937, WPA Folklore Files, UVA (#1547).

body's nutritional supplies. The sight or thought of food, stressful situations, or habitual behavior such as eating three meals a day when only two are necessary, or constantly overeating at mealtimes, may trigger the mental rather than the physiological mechanism and cause inappropriate hunger pangs. Hunger, for slaves as for free people, may have been, at times, a reflection of such psychological needs.

Planters recognized that slaves "will steal if they are not well fed," and that "the very best remedy for hog stealing is to give the rogues a plenty of pork to eat." [37] But even provision of extra pork, meal, molasses, fruit, or whatever did not effectively curtail thievery. Slaves also stole as a means of silently resisting the system and of expressing frustration at the limitations of their diets. They could not eat all they saw their master eating, yet they worked hard to produce it for him. The master could eat as many chickens, eggs, hams, potatoes, or peaches as he wished, whenever he wished. Slaves had to eat what was supplied to them and eat it at specified times of the day. If bondsmen became hungry in the fields, they had no recourse but to withstand the pangs until mealtime. Evening snacks came from their own private supplies of leftovers or homegrown produce, if they had any. Whites, on the other hand, partook of a wide variety of slave-grown and imported foods eaten whenever desired. The weekly distribution of rations constantly reminded slaves that they did not have the freedom to choose the type, quantity, or quality of the food they consumed. This was why slaves stole despite the "lavishness" of some masters' provisions.

Food for Industrial Slaves

Industrial slaves fared both better and worse than their plantation brethren, depending on location and individual policy. In addition to the ubiquitous cornmeal and pork ration, some industrialists provided slaves with a variety of vegetables and meats, or with the opportunity to purchase extra food with cash earned on the job. Others barely served enough at table to maintain health. Like hard-working fieldhands, industrial bondsmen

[37] H[ill] C[arter], "On the Management of Negroes," 565.

who performed heavy labor required larger than average quantities of calories and some nutrients. If all ate as well as John Hartwell Cocke's carpenters and stonemasons who were hired out to a Lynchburg man in 1829, industrial slaves would have been a uniformly healthy lot. Those particular slaves received bacon "not inferior to any used in this place and for which is paid 8 cents per pound," beef three times a week, peas, bread, "and half a pint of the best whiskey which can be bought here."[38]

Urban industrialists, when willing and financially able, could supply their workers with adequate amounts and some variety of foods simply because marketplaces were located in towns. This did not assure the slave of ample nourishment, however, since food was one of the most expensive items for masters. Some managers skirted the problem of provisions by giving slaves board money and sending them off on their own. While bondsmen living under this system did not always eat balanced meals, they did have a freedom of choice unknown to plantation hands.[39]

The food supply was less certain for slaves living at rural railroad and canal labor camps, iron forges and furnaces, and mines. Though the directors of the Dismal Swamp Land Company and a few ironmasters, notably David Ross and William Weaver, attempted to overcome this difficulty by raising crops and animals on nearby farms, they did not always succeed in harvesting enough for all workers. Available records indicate that laborers at Weaver's iron enterprises in the Rockbridge County mountains were often short of food. Supervisors there constantly wrote frantic letters requesting beef, flour, pork, and corn for the hands.[40] On the plantation owned by the Dismal Swamp Land

[38] Albert Stein to John Hartwell Cocke, 30 June 1829, Cocke Deposit, Cocke Papers, UVA.

[39] Starobin, *Industrial Slavery*, 50–51; Editorial, "Practice on Hirelings," *Steth.*, 1 (1851), 677; A Manufacturer, "Treatment of Cholera on a Large Scale," *Richmond Enquirer*, 5 October 1832, p. 3; Joseph C. Robert, *The Tobacco Kingdom: Plantation, Market and Factory in Virginia and North Carolina, 1800–1860* (Durham, N.C., 1938), 203–5.

[40] *Lynchburg Star*, 3 September 1811, advertisement regarding David Ross's Oxford Iron Works, William Bolling Papers, Duke; Starobin, *Industrial Slavery*, 52; C[harles] G[orgas] to Uncle [William Weaver], 27 July 1859, Weaver-Brady Papers, UVA (#38–98). For more on Weaver's food problems, see Starobin, *Industrial Slavery*, 52–53.

Company near Suffolk, the overseer during the 1780's frequently reported food shortages. Not enough could be raised to maintain the slaves who gathered shingles in the swamp and worked the farmland; this situation necessitated the purchase of pork from outside sources and the shortening of corn rations. By the 1830's the company was purchasing all its supplies.[41] Other companies experienced much less difficulty obtaining provisions. Those railroad contractors who worked the eastern portion of Virginia avoided the logistical problem of transporting stores through the mountains. Here, in the flatlands, wrote one Richmond builder to a business friend, there were "plenty [of] *Corn & Negroes.*" [42] The James River and Kanawha Canal Company hired many slaves each year, promised to feed them well, and apparently succeeded, as did many other rural industrial employers.[43]

Records kept by the proprietors of Graham's Forge in Wythe County illustrate the manner in which rural industrial slaves were fed. Graham hired both slave and free white laborers for his iron operation; he fed them in separate boardinghouses for at least the period between mid-June 1857 and mid-October 1858.[44] The very extensive and specific daily journal entries listing foods obtained for both houses provide an unusual opportunity to view the differences in nourishment that each group received. Unfortunately, there is no extant record of the number of workers at the establishment during this period, so individual food allotments cannot be determined precisely. The variety of foods

[41] Jacob Collen to David Jameson, 26 December 1784; Jameson to Collen, 30 December 1784; John Driver to Jamieson [*sic*], 25 February 1787, 11 February, 2 June 1788, 8 June 1789, 19 May 1791; Bills and Receipts, 1830's; all in Dismal Swamp Papers, Duke.

[42] A. S. Burton to John [Buford], 10 November 1854, Buford Papers, Duke. For examples in Southwest Virginia, see bills and receipts in Buford Papers, Duke.

[43] E. L. [Chirn?] to Dr. A. G. Grinnan, 25 March 1855, Grinnan Family Papers, UVA (#49); Elijah Fletcher to Calvin Fletcher, 18 August 1849, in Martha von Briesen, ed., *The Letters of Elijah Fletcher* (Charlottesville, Va., 1965), 219; Charles W. Turner, "The Virginia Railroads, 1828–1860" (Ph.D. dissertation, University of Minnesota, 1946), 205.

[44] Graham-Robinson Ledgers, vol. 9, UVA (#38–107). See also Charles B. Dew, "Disciplining Slave Ironworkers in the Antebellum South: Coercion, Conciliation, and Accommodation," *AHR,* 79 (1974), 406–11; Bradford, "Negro Ironworker in Virginia," 202; S. Sydney Bradford, "The Ante-Bellum Charcoal Iron Industry of Virginia" (Ph.D. dissertation, Columbia University, 1958), 88.

served, however, reflects not only the superior nourishment (by nineteenth-century standards) of the white workers' diet over that of the blacks, but also the seasonal shortages of two staples, corn and pork. Vegetables, fruit, and poultry appear on neither list, indicating that laborers purchased or raised these themselves, or that Graham supplied them as they became available.

All the men ate large quantities of pork, beginning at hog-killing time in late December and continuing until they depleted the supply the following September or October. Based on the amount given the few slaves who lived there year round and who occasionally received individual portions of food, six to seven pounds per week appears to have been the usual allotment to blacks. White proportions cannot be determined. The journal writer at the forge did not enter cuts of pork served at table, simply calling everything "bacon," with two exceptions. During June 1857 the forge owners suddenly substituted "jolls" for bacon in the Negro laborers' rations, supplementing the white workers' bacon with small quantities of the same. Apparently whites preferred their "bacon" to pork jowls, and got it; blacks had no choice. Jowls, along with shoulders and sides, comprised what one Cincinnati meat-packer called "prime pork," considered a secondary grade of meat often sent to southern plantations.[45]

In addition to "jolls," the ironworkers also received "offal" shortly after December hog-killing. This was probably the pancreas, thymus, other soft organs, and intestines (chitterlings) of freshly slaughtered pigs. Whites appear to have eaten it only as a stopgap measure when they could obtain no other meat, as occurred in early March 1858, as well as in December 1857 just prior to Christmas. Blacks consumed "offal," in the absence of other meat, from 8 December 1856 until 14 February 1857, while the whites ate bacon. In the context of the period, "offal" was considered a less desirable cut of pork, despite the fact that sweetbreads contain more protein, minerals, and vitamins per pound than most other parts of the pig.[46] In the fall, when Graham could obtain only small quantities of bacon for his laborers, he served beef as a supplement and occasionally as a substitute

[45] Hilliard, *Hog Meat and Hoecake*, 58.
[46] Church and Church, *Food Values*, 56.

meat. Though not highly regarded by most Southerners, fresh beef did provide a change of taste from the preserved pork consumed almost all year. Once January arrived, however, both slaves and whites preferred to resume their usual habit of eating a pound or so of their favorite bacon each day.

As with meats, so with grains. The workers at Graham's Forge regularly consumed great quantities of cornmeal, though not always to the exclusion of other cereals. Not one month passed in either boardinghouse without some distribution of this staple. The usual slave ration was one-quarter bushel or eight quarts per week; the individual white worker's share, again, was not entered in the account book. Along with cornbread, both blacks and whites quite frequently ate foods made with flour—usually bread, pancakes, pastries, and cakes. Other than for a three-month period in the summer of 1857, the free laborers were served such dishes continuously; slaves did not receive flour regularly with their boardinghouse fare until May 1858. The Negroes also ate "shorts," consisting of such unmilled and discarded portions of the wheat kernel as bran and germ, something which the white laborers at the forge apparently shunned. Though not included routinely in the slaves' diet, "shorts" appeared in their food at least once a month between February and September 1858. Ironically, wheat bran and germ (like sweetbreads) are more nutritious (in protein, iron, and vitamins) than the bolted unenriched flour preferred by whites.[47] Graham also occasionally added a small amount of rice to the white workers' fare, something he neglected to do for his slave employees.

According to the account book no other foods were served at the Negro boardinghouse. Several other food items were, however, listed for the white boardinghouse: sugar, lard, pepper, tea, ginger, molasses, honey, eggs (each spring), and coffee. Additional food had to be purchased from Graham on a cash or credit basis. Those who worked hard and saved carefully could thus enjoy a few extras. Some slaves chose to spend their cash on food, while others bought clothing, fiddle strings, and trinkets for wives, lovers, or children. Most purchased sugar, coffee, molasses,

---

[47] *Ibid.*, 19; Carl Voegtlin, M. X. Sullivan, C. S. Myers, "Bread as a Food," *Public Health Reports,* 31 (1916), 936–37.

and spices such as cinnamon and pepper. Though these items did not constitute what modern nutritionists could call a balanced diet, they did contain some of the nutrients necessary to maintain health.[48]

John Buford, a railroad contractor in southwest Virginia, did not keep detailed records of his black and white employees' diets, but did retain the receipts enumerating the types of foods purchased from local farmers and merchants for these men. Like Graham, Buford relied heavily on bacon and corn to sustain his workers, though he supplemented these with eggs, butter, molasses, flour, and spices. It is not known whether Buford withheld eggs, flour, or other foods from blacks in favor of white laborers as Graham did. He substituted beef for all or part of the meat ration during the autumn months, and, like Graham, purchased small amounts of pork jowls at various unpredictable times of the year. Vegetables and fruit were not ordered, though workers may have purchased them at the company store.[49]

The nutritional status of each slave—industrial, urban, or agricultural—depended upon several factors. Most important, of course, was the quality of the food provided by the master and by the bondsman himself. When the basic cornmeal-and-pork diet was supplemented with vegetables and dairy products, slaves were usually well protected against nutrient deficiency disorders. However, if a slave suffered from certain parasitic worm infections, the normal diet was not sufficient. Pregnant or lactating women, as well as people employed at strenuous labor, also required additional food. Plantation and some urban slaves had better opportunities to supplement inadequate diets than did most industrial bondsmen, especially those in rural areas. The latter had to rely on supplemental earnings to purchase extras at company-owned stores.

Working Conditions

The good health of a slave depended on conditions both at home and at work. Nineteenth-century newspapers empha-

[48] Graham-Robinson Ledgers, vol. 9 (entries for Trial, Matt Hill, and Granville Graham), UVA (#38–107).

sized dramatic mine disasters, steamboat explosions, railroad accidents, and mishaps involving urban industrial laborers, while they tended to ignore the hazards of farm and rural work. Yet it was in the countryside that the majority of Virginia's slaves lived and toiled, often under unsafe and unhealthy conditions. Accidents were not the only cause of work-related illnesses either in towns or on farms. Climatic and other external situations also exacted their toll.

Though warm weather helped the crops grow, it did not always have the same effect on the black Virginians who tended them. Planters recording the effects of excessive heat on their fieldhands made it clear that even though Negroes originated in tropical Africa, they were not immune to sunstroke.[50] Hill Carter of Shirley Plantation wrote, for instance, during the 1825 wheat harvest: "Hotest day ever felt—men gave out & some fainted." [51]

Slaveowners also recognized the potential hazards of overexertion and exposure. Some indulged their slaves by easing their tasks; others found this impossible, especially at certain times of the year. Hill Carter and no doubt many others worked their Negroes in intense heat when necessary to harvest a crop. Charles Friend of Prince George County, on the other hand, had second thoughts when the ditching operation to which he had assigned many slaves evolved into a messy and unhealthy job: "We have the ditchers knee deep in water and mud. If I had known how bad it was I should not have put them to work at it but hired labor to do it." [52] One master did just that, as Frederick Law Olmsted observed while traveling in the countryside between Richmond and Petersburg. He met a farmer who had hired Irish laborers to drain a field to be used for tobacco culture, instead of risking his slaves' lives at such "dangerous work." [53]

Another potential danger for plantation slaves was exposure

[49] Bills and Receipts, 1850's, Buford Papers, Duke.

[50] They could, however, endure heat longer than many whites because of acclimation to work under hot, humid conditions and because of an inherent ability to conserve vital body salts (see ch. 1).

[51] Shirley Farm Journals, 23 June 1825, 5 June 1850, LC. See also John B. Garrett Farm Journal, 19 July 1830, UVA.

[52] Quoted in Blanton, 18th Century, 161.

[53] Olmsted, Seaboard, 90–91.

to disease from the animals with which they worked. Among these diseases brucellosis, leptospirosis, and anthrax were probably the most important.[54] Brucellosis (undulant fever, Malta fever), a disease of goats, cattle, and pigs, infected humans through several routes, one of the most common being direct contact of skin wounds with infected carcasses. People were especially exposed to the disease at hog-killing time (usually in late December) and whenever beeves were slaughtered. Because the signs and symptoms of brucellosis were so similar to those of malaria, observers in the Old South undoubtedly classified the disease as a type of intermittent fever. Leptospirosis (mud fever), also a disease of domestic animals, was spread by contact of wounds, skin, nose, or mouth with the organism *Leptospira* in animals' urine on the ground, or in food or fresh water. Slaves working in Deep South rice and sugar fields were thus particularly susceptible, though Virginia's blacks laboring in swamps and muddy farm pastures no doubt contracted it, too. Usual symptoms included fever and headache as the *Leptospirae* invaded the blood and spinal fluid, and severe muscle pain.[55] Anthrax, a disease of cattle, pigs, and other domestic animals, is a threat in the United States even today. Known outbreaks occurred in several areas of the antebellum South, including Kentucky, Louisiana, Mississippi, and the Gulf states, among both animals and man. It was caused by a bacterium which cattle, sheep, goats, and horses (the most common hosts) ingested with their vegetable food. People who handled the animals' hide or hair, or who ate infected meat, developed skin pustules, fever, vomiting, diarrhea, and general malaise, depending on the route of infection. Some persons died of meningitis and septicemia.[56] Virginia

[54] For complete catalog and description of all diseases potentially dangerous to farm hands, see Thomas G. Hull, ed., *Diseases Transmitted from Animals to Man* (Springfield, Ill., 1963).

[55] Charles Wilcocks and P. E. C. Manson-Bahr, *Manson's Tropical Diseases* (Baltimore, 1972), 482–99, 596–602.

[56] *Ibid.*, 548–50; Robert P. Hanson, "The Earliest Account of Anthrax in Man and Animals in North America," *Journal of the American Veterinary Medical Association*, 135 (1959), 463–65; Clarence D. Stein, "Anthrax," in Hull, ed., *Diseases Transmitted from Animals to Man*, 82–105. An outbreak of "Watery Murrain" among Landon Carter's cattle in 1753 and again in 1757 may well have been anthrax. Greene, ed., *Carter Diary*, I, 148–49.

plantation slaves undoubtedly contracted these diseases as they worked with animals on farms.

Farm accidents did not possess the spectacular and often brutal qualities of industrial mishaps; since the equipment was usually less sophisticated and powerful, mass injuries rarely occurred. Falls, overturned carts, runaway wagons, drownings, limbs caught in farm machines, kicks from animals, and cuts from axes or scythe blades were the commonest types. Occasionally slaves suffered more remarkable mishaps, as when a 260-pound Culpeper County fieldhand jumped eight feet from a hay loft onto a pile of hay in which a wooden pitchfork, sharpened handle up, lay concealed. The point punctured the man's scrotum and passed into his abdominal cavity, but miraculously pierced no internal organs. Thanks to prompt surgical attention he was doing "light work" around the plantation about three weeks later.[57]

As with agricultural hands, industrial slaves were exposed to the extremes of climate. At the Dismal Swamp summer heat, an unprecedented dry spell, and the appearance of swarms of insects forced suspension of shingle-gathering during August and September 1838. The company agent, headquartered near Suffolk, reported that workers could not obtain enough drinking water even to venture into the swamp for long. Railroad, canal, and road workers were no better off, as the best seasons for construction coincided with the hottest months of the year. Those in tobacco factories were at least shielded from the sun's rays and direct heat, though the temperatures there were often unbearable.[58]

[57] Charles R. Kemper, "Case of Injury from the Penetration of a Hay Fork into the Abdomen—with Recovery," Steth., 4 (1854), 9–11. See also Edward Tayloe Journal, 17 January 1852, UVA (#38–62); G. A. Strange to John Hartwell Cocke, 8 August 1832, Cocke Deposit, Cocke Papers, UVA (accidental falls); Frances A. Buford to John Buford, 7 July 1855, Buford Papers, Duke; "Births, Deaths, &c. of my negroes," in Freedmen Account Book, Watson Papers, UVA; John Walker Diary, 26 October 1839, UNC (cart and wagon accidents); Shirley Farm Journals, 17 May 1823, LC; Frances Taylor Diary, 18 August 1786, UNC (drownings); Shirley Farm Journals, 4 August 1824, LC; White Hill Plantation Books, 30 July 1859, UNC; James T. Gibson to Colonel John Ambler, 3 January 1828, Ambler Family Papers, UVA (#1140); interview of Charles Grandy, in Rawick, ed., The American Slave, XVI, Virginia Narratives, 22 (limbs caught in machines and cuts from blades).

Warm weather, however, did not usually injure slaves for long periods of time. It was cold which permanently disabled industrial blacks—probably more often than agricultural slaves in Virginia because of the seasonal nature of outdoor farm work. Slaves hired to an industry for a year worked the entire twelve months (Christmas excepted), regardless of the temperature. In addition to the danger of developing frostbite while working outdoors, there existed the problem of prolonged exposure to winter cold during the journey to and from the industrial site in January and December. Iron entrepreneurs frequently hired slaves in eastern Virginia and transported them across the Blue Ridge to mountain forges and furnaces. Owing to inclement weather, one group of slaves spent thirty days reaching their destination; once there, though not frostbitten, they fell ill for several days, no doubt from a combination of fatigue, exposure, and decreased resistance to infection.[59]

The tobacco factory environment posed other kinds of health hazards, the greatest being lung diseases and constant inhalation of tobacco fumes. Tobacco dust affected beginners more often than veteran tobacco hands, and bothered bale unloaders and unpackers more than other workers. The dust irritated eyes, causing excessive tearing; a combination of dust and tobacco juice from the leaves also caused rashes on the face and backs of hands. All tobacco workers constantly inhaled nicotine and some, no doubt, suffered acute poisoning, characterized by insomnia, headache, watery eyes, nausea, and vomiting. Recent research indicates that chronic nicotine poisoning is rare among tobacco factory hands, and that most of the effects of tobacco dust and juice soon disappear. However, the dust liberated during the dry-

---

[58] Joseph Holladay to Dr. Robert Butler, 31 July, 31 August, 30 September 1838, Dismal Swamp Papers, Duke; Thomas Leftwich to John Buford, 14 July 1854, Buford Papers, Duke. Starobin, *Industrial Slavery*, 65–67, describes instances of sunstroke in industries in Louisiana and Mississippi. Robert, *Tobacco Kingdom*, 197, states that dippers in tobacco factories often worked "stark naked in their rooms near the drying roofs."

[59] Negro Time Book, 1837–52, entries for 7–15 February 1840, Graham Papers, UVA (#38–106); Bradford, "Negro Ironworker in Virginia," 197. See also S. Farrer to William W. Davis, 29 January 1850, Jordan and Davis Papers, Wisconsin; Samuel Drewry to John Buford, 20 January 1854, Buford Papers, Duke.

ing and stemming processes contains enough respirable-sized silica particles to cause a lung disease, tobacosis, similar to the black lung disease of miners. Since skilled black laborers often learned their trades at an early age and remained at their tasks in the factories for years, the prevalence of tobacosis and other chronic respiratory diseases among these hands must have been greater than among most other agricultural and industrial workers except miners.[60]

Each industry exposed workers to different types of dangers. The hazards of coal mining included methane (marsh) gas explosions, black lung disease (not then recognized), suffocation from lack of oxygen, drowning in flooded mine shafts, and flash fires. Falling trees and rocks, steep cliffs, hot furnaces and forges, unsafe equipment, and nonexistent safety practices also threatened the lives of laborers at public works projects, ironworks, and railroad yards. Even at smaller industrial operations the working conditions did not favor health of the laborers. James, a brickyard worker in Richmond, developed diarrhea and swollen legs and feet after working ten months, a physician recorded, "in mud and water." James Dabney, a slave hired out to learn the building trade, complained that his "business is to work in the mortar hole." His master objected that "he will learn but little of the trade in that position besides being worked beyond his strength." Despite this and James Dabney's two long bouts with illness during the year, he was rehired to the same man the following January.[61] A few slaveowners placed restrictions on the type of work which hired slaves could perform, but this was not the usual practice:

> Davy Says that Working in the furnace is Injurious to his Eyes therefore I do not wish him to work there against his Will

[60] Donald Hunter, *The Diseases of Occupations* (Boston, 1969), 1071–72; William Patterson to Robert Leslie, 9 December 1830; Jno. A. Branden to Leslie & Brydon, 12 January 1831, both in Leslie Papers, Duke; Robert, *Tobacco Kingdom*, 197–98.

[61] Thomas L. Hunter, "Notes of Clinical Lectures, Delivered at the Infirmary of the Medical College of Virginia," *MVMJ*, 15 (1860), 436; Cary Charles Cocke to John Hartwell Cocke, 8 January 1849, Shields Deposit, Cocke Papers, UVA. See also A. S. Brockenbrough to Cocke, 15 April 1825, Cocke Deposit, Cocke Papers, UVA.

I think it necessary to inform you that I am verry unwilling for him [Phill] to work in the ore on blowing Rock as he has been so much injuerd by it and he is verry dissattisfied at it. but he is willing to work at anything that thear is not so much danger.[62]

One recent historian counted only three slaves of fifty-two hired to a Rockbridge County iron furnace whose masters prohibited labor in the ore pits.[63]

Slaves suffered accidental injuries of various kinds at industrial sites. It is not necessary to enumerate them, though the details of one particularly gruesome case may serve to emphasize the safety problem. A forty-year-old Richmond hand fell on his forehead while carrying a 150-pound bar (used in pressing tobacco) across his shoulders. The man could not break his fall because his hands were on the bar. Doctor James Bolton, called to the factory, reported that "the blood spouted from his nose and mouth, and in a few minutes he was dead." He described the injury as "the most extensive and terrible fracture I have ever witnessed." [64]

Only rarely did higher state courts hand down decisions that dealt with on-the-job dangers to slaves, but in two relevant cases the personal rights of bondsmen received noteworthy mention along with the property rights of masters. In the first instance, a slave named Monroe, hired as an agricultural slave in Wood County, was placed on an Ohio River flatboat to assist with navigation. He somehow drowned on the journey to New Orleans, and his owner sued for damages. The state Court of Appeals, meeting in Lewisburg in July 1837, agreed with the plaintiff and interpreted the law for all slave-hirers to know: "If he [the owner] hires him [the slave] with a reasonable expectation that he

[62] R. Brooks to Messrs. Jordan and Irvine, 2 January 1812; Nancy Matthews to Colonel John Jordan, 18 January 1831, Jordan and Irvine Papers, Wisconsin. See also J. R. Anderson to Messrs. Anderson, Shank, and Anderson, 14 December 1843, in Outgoing Letterbook, Tredegar Papers, VSL; Samuel Drewry to Capt. Paschal Buford, 13 December 1853, Buford Papers, Duke; Starobin, *Industrial Slavery*, 131–34; Bradford, "Negro Ironworker in Virginia," 199.

[63] Bradford, "Negro Ironworker in Virginia," 199n.

[64] *Steth.*, 3 (1853), 399–400. See other accident reports in Time Book of D. and H. Forrer, Shenandoah Iron Works (Page County), 18 October 1857, W&M; William Staples to William Weaver, 3 January 1860, Weaver Papers, Duke; James Bolton, "Bellevue Hospital Reports," *Steth.*, 5 (1855), 131–32; Starobin, *Industrial Slavery*, 37–50.

will be employed in a business comparatively healthy and free from danger to life, it ought not to be permitted to the bailee [hirer] to immure him in an unhealthy mine, or to subject him to the hazards of distant voyages, and the perils of business he has never followed." Then followed a dual explanation for this ruling, based on the needs and desires of the two groups most hurt by such a situation: "Humanity to the slave requires this, and the security of the rights of property imposes other restrictions on the bailee, for the sake of the owner." The second case concerned a hired slave who drowned in a coal pit mine when overcome by noxious fumes which suddenly appeared. His owner claimed negligence on the part of the owner for providing only one bucket with which to lift slave workers out of the single seventy-foot shaft, and for trusting the judgment of a slave foreman, who had preceded the miners into the pit, that no fumes were present. In 1836 the judges of the Richmond Court of Appeals found for the slave-owner, noting that they would not have done so had the mine operator taken proper safety precautions. In both cases the slave's right to life was considered at least as important as the owner's property rights.[65]

All laborers, white and black, were susceptible to accidental injuries and exposed to hazardous or unhealthy working conditions. Negroes comprised a majority of the labor force at most farms, tobacco factories, mining operations, iron forges and furnaces, and public works projects, where supervisors did not usually emphasize safety or overly concern themselves with the comfort of their workers. Under these conditions the good health of blacks in antebellum Virginia was often endangered.

[65] *Spencer* v. *Pilcher*, 8 Leigh 565; *Randolph* v. *Hill*, 7 Leigh 383 (both in *Virginia Reports*).

CHAPTER 4

Other Health Problems
and Conditions

Whipping

The whip was an integral part of slave life in the Old Dominion. Those bondsmen who had not experienced its sting firsthand were acquainted with persons, usually friends or relatives, who had. Whites held out the threat of whipping as a means of maintaining social order. When strong discipline was called for, so, very often, was the lash. Even the mildest and most God-fearing of masters permitted application of this painful instrument in extreme cases, though some insisted that the slave's skin not be cut or that there be a responsible witness present when punishment was administered.[1] The whip originally consisted of a narrow strip of hard cowhide, or, in the case of the lash, of tough whipcord. Sometimes the fearful cat-o'-nine-tails was employed. As owners began to object to the scars left on slaves' backs, two new implements were introduced to replace those which removed the skin with each stroke. One was the broad strap of soft leather; the other was a kind of paddle. The latter, purported to be the invention of a Virginian, was made of

[1] John Walker Diary, 17 November 1829, UNC; ——— to ———, n.d., Austin-Twyman Papers, folder 165, W&M; Jno. W. Carrington to Jno. M. Sutherlin, 27 September 1858, Sutherlin Papers, Duke.

a broad, flat piece of hard wood punctured through in many places with small holes. Neither of these tools of punishment lacerated the victim's skin.[2]

From a medical point of view, whipping inflicted cruel and often permanent injuries upon its victims. Laying stripes across the bare back or buttocks caused indescribable pain, especially when each stroke dug deeper into previously opened wounds. During the interval between lashes, victims anticipated the next in anguish, wishing for postponement or for all due speed, though neither alternative brought relief. In addition to multiple lacerations of the skin, whipping caused loss of blood, injury to muscles (and internal organs, if the lash reached that deep), and shock. (Rubbing salt into these wounds, often complained of as a further mode of torture, actually cleansed the injured, exposed tissues and helped ward off infection.) The paddle jarred every part of the body by the violence of the blow, and it raised blisters from repeated strokes. In addition to the possibility of death (uncommon), there was the danger that muscle damage inflicted by any of these instruments might permanently incapacitate a slave or deform him for life. And yet, an overseer's instruction book published in Richmond advised whipping as punishment for a first offense.[3] The results of flogging at its worst were evident on the bodies of slave and free black state prisoners returning to Richmond in 1861 from labor on Virginia's public works projects. The penitentiary surgeon advised the governor and legislature that Jim (slave) had "numerous scars and extensive callous ridges on his back, constituting permanent injury"; John Gaines (free black) suffered with "numerous scars, from severe whipping, over almost every part of his body"; and Sam (slave) was "very feeble, badly used, and much whipped." [4]

[2] R. G. Van Yelyr, *The Whip and the Rod: An Account of Corporal Punishment among All Nations and for All Purposes* (London, 1941), 157.

[3] *Plantation and Farm Instruction, Regulation, Record, Inventory and Account Book, for the Use of the Manager on the Estate of   , and for the Better Ordering and Management of Plantation and Farm Business in Every Particular, by a Southern Planter* (Richmond, 1852), 10. For locations of copies of this volume, see ch. 3, n. 19. The second offense was punished by making the slave stand in the stocks for the weekend or holidays with only bread and water for food. For a third misdemeanor a slave would lose his meat ration.

[4] Report of the Surgeon of the State Penitentiary, in Penitentiary *Annual Report* (1861), *Leg. Docs.* 1861–62, doc. 13, p. 41.

An unsual case arose in Jefferson County (now part of West Virginia) which illustrates the painfulness and medical effects of whipping. Henry, a slave, stabbed Harrison A. Anderson, a white man, with a knife and was sentenced to receive "five hundred lashes, on his bare back, well laid on." The court ordered that this harsh punishment be carried out thirty-nine stripes at a time, under the direction of the jail's physician. The doctor, not willing to see such a severe sentence carried out, immediately resigned his position, as did four others over the subsequent fifteen months. When Dr. John B. Johnson finally accepted the post, he found that Henry had already withstood two sets of thirty-nine lashes. The jailor informed Johnson that Henry had not endured the punishment well, and would have fallen to the prison floor had he not commanded the slave to sit down. The physician refused to permit further flogging and, along with a group of local citizens, filed a petition with the governor asking for a pardon. Dr. Johnson explained how repeated floggings, even with long intervals allowed for healing, left the skin more sensitive to pain, and hence more subject to "constitutional suffering" than before. The governor accepted this and other arguments and rescinded the sentence within a few weeks.[5]

Not all whippings were administered as severely as the one in this case, of course. They could be quite as mildly applied, Fogel and Engerman point out in their recent book, "as the corporal punishment normally practiced within families today." Though these writers included a numerical survey of whippings on one Louisiana plantation, one is forced to conclude from their statement that it is not the frequency of whipping which is important from a medical point of view, but the effect of each beating upon the slave's body.[6] The only way to measure the amount of injury caused by whipping slaves is to count the number of sick days taken immediately following an instance of corporal punishment.

[5] Pardon of Slave Henry, 7 March 1854, in Executive Papers, March–May 1854, VSL.

[6] One antebellum physician (a Georgian, not a Virginian), H. A. Ramsay (*The Necrological Appearance of Southern Typhoid Fever in the Negro* [Thompson, Ga., 1852], 16), claimed that in the black man "the nervous system with reference to sensation is less developed than in the white," basing his statement on the reputed painlessness with which slaves bore whippings.

Fogel and Engerman assert: "Planters preferred whipping to incarceration because the lash did not generally lead to an extended loss of the slaves' labor time. In other words, whipping persisted in the South because the cost of substituting hunger and incarceration for the lash was greater for the slaveowner than for the northern employer of free labor." [7]

But was the lash cheaper than hunger and incarceration? An Old Dominion slave who experienced the sting of the paddle recalled years later: "You be jes' as raw as a piece of beef an' hit eats you up. He loose you an' you go to house no work done dat day." [8] No work done that day or, in many cases, for several days. Ellick, a rebellious member of Charles Friend's White Hill Plantation slave force, was slapped one day "for not being at the stable in time this morning," and "soundly whipped" the next day for running away and for not submitting to a flogging earlier that morning. He spent the next week recovering in bed, only to receive another whipping upon his return to work. This time he ran off for two days before settling back into the plantation routine. Another of Friend's slaves lost a week from work after a severe whipping in August 1845.[9] Caroline Hunter, a former slave near Suffolk, had vivid memories of floggings and time lost from work: "I can' never forgit how my massa beat my brothers cause dey didn' wuk. He beat 'em so bad dey was sick a long time, an' soon as dey got a smatterin' better he sold em. . . ." [10] Numerous other examples of slaves who lost extended periods of time from work due to whippings are available. Unfortunately, no planter in Virginia kept close records of beatings and subsequent time lost. Nor were physical injuries from whippings the only cause of lost labor. Some pretended to have sustained wounds simply to get back at their masters, while others ran off

[7] Fogel and Engerman, *Time*, I, 145, 147. For other criticisms of Fogel and Engerman on the whipping issue, see Herbert G. Gutman, *Slavery and the Numbers Game: A Critique of "Time on the Cross"* (Urbana, Ill., 1975), 14–41.

[8] Interview of William Lee, n.d., WPA Folklore File, UVA (#1547). See also Stampp, *Peculiar Institution*, 175–76.

[9] White Hill Plantation Books, 6–20 July 1849, 3 August 1852, 13 August 1845, UNC.

[10] Interview of Caroline Hunter, 8 January 1937, WPA Folklore File, UVA (#1547). See also Henry Box Brown, *Narrative* (Boston, 1849), 24–25.

for several days or weeks out of anger or wounded pride. Both incarceration without food and whipping with one device or another could produce the same effect on a slave—time lost from work.[11]

Women and Children

The daily routines of slave women and children were often upset by health conditions peculiar to these groups. Pregnancy, childbirth, and menstruation caused female slaves to suspend their normal activities for periods of time. And slave children, like all youngsters, were highly susceptible to common infectious diseases; they took sick more often than adults and required special attention.

Female slaves probably lost more time from work for menstrual pain, discomfort, and disorders than for any other cause. Planters rarely named illnesses in their diaries or daybooks, but the frequency and regularity with which women of childbearing age appeared on sick lists indicates that menstrual conditions were a leading complaint. A Fauquier County physician considered the loss of four to eight workdays per month not unusual for slave women.[12] Among the menstrual maladies which afflicted bondswomen most often were amenorrhea (lack of menstrual flow), abnormal bleeding between cycles (sometimes caused by benign and malignant tumors), and abnormal discharges (resulting from such conditions as gonorrhea, tumors, and prolapsed uterus).[13]

[11] See, for injury due to whipping, Graham Family Papers, Account Book, 11 September 1829, UVA (#38–106); and Brown, *Narrative*, 24–25; for pretended illness following whipping, Greene, ed., *Carter Diary*, I, 369 (15 March 1770), II, 1093 (6 August 1774).

[12] Alban S. Payne, "Report of Obstetrical Cases," *Steth.*, 3 (1853), 204. For an example of frequent female morbidity, see White Hill Plantation Books, UNC.

[13] For examples of these conditions, see William G. Craghead, "Case of Catamenial Retention from Imperforated Hymen," *Steth.*, 5 (1855), 193; Payne, "Report of Obstetrical Cases," 203–6; John B. Davies, "Remarks on Amenorrhea, with Cases," *Steth.*, 1 (1851), 142–44; Senex, "A Case of Metritis, Followed by Obstinate Vicarious Menstruation," *ibid.*, 5 (1855), 527–31; Edmund Wilcox Ledger, Hubard Family Papers, vol. 13, 22 March 1777 (Silvia), 30 October 1776 (slave of Roderick McCulloch), UNC; R. L. Madison, "Case of Fibrous Polypus of the Uterus," *VMSJ*, 3 (1854), 185–89; T. Stanly Beckwith, "Case of Polypus Uteri Successfully Removed," *VMJ*, 8 (1857), 187–91.

Some servants took advantage of their masters by complaining falsely of female indispositions. One unnamed Virginian who owned numerous slaves complained to Frederick Law Olmsted about such malingering women:

> The women on a plantation . . . will hardly earn their salt, after they come to the breeding age; they don't come to the field, and you go to the quarters and ask the old nurse what's the matter, and she says, "oh, she's not well, master; she's not fit to work, sir;" and what can you do? You have to take her word for it that something or other is the matter with her, and you dare not set her to work; and so she lays up till she feels like taking the air again, and plays the lady at your expense.[14]

Whites found it impossible to separate the sick from the falsely ill; as a result they often indulged their breeding-aged women rather than risk unknown complications. Thomas Jefferson, for instance, ordered his overseer not to coerce the female workers into exerting themselves because "women . . . are destroyed by exposure to wet at certain periodical indispositions to which nature has subjected them." [15]

If white Virginians treated women's gynecological complaints with a certain delicacy, they regarded pregnancy as almost holy. In addition to the fact that slave women received time off from work, avoided whippings, and were even able to feign pregnancy to gain their ends, expectant women were protected from execution in capital offenses until after parturition. At least three cases arose between the Revolution and the Civil War in which slave women obtained execution postponements for this reason, though all were presumably put to death following delivery.[16]

Masters disliked granting time off to working slaves, of course,

[14] Olmsted, *Seaboard*, 190.

[15] Thomas Jefferson to Joel Yancey, 17 January 1819, in Edwin M. Betts, ed., *Thomas Jefferson's Farm Book* (Princeton, 1953), 43.

[16] Adelaide M. Hunter, "The Punishment of Crimes in Virginia" (M.A. thesis, Duke University, 1947), 15; *Commonwealth* v. *Sall and Creasy*, 14 April 1806, described in James Hugo Johnston, *Race Relations in Virginia and Miscegenation in the South, 1776–1860* (Amherst, Mass., 1970), 22; "Message IV [of Governor Henry Wise] Relative to Reprieves and Pardons, to the General Assembly of Virginia," 7 December 1857, *Leg. Docs.*, 1857–58, pt. I, doc. 1, p. clxxvi; Legislative Petitions, Richmond [City], 23 December 1857, VSL.

but they could do little else with pregnant women. David Ross, owner of the Oxford Iron Works and several hundred slaves in Campbell County, felt the severe pinch on labor during the war of 1812: "We are lazy enough at the Oxford factory which has been much reduced no less than seven women at the Furnace & Ore Banks so far advanced in pregnancy they can't do their duty indeed some are delivered others confined all the stoutest spinning girls have been drawn out to supply their place, one of the weavers Jeany has been sick ever since you left the works which ended in an abortion & still confined." Even when Nature took its due course, impatient masters cursed its slowness. Landon Carter, awaiting the confinement of a slave woman, commented in his diary: "There is one big bellyed woman that has seemed to be near her time about 2 months." Charles Friend of Prince George County seemed to suffer right along with his slave Aggy during her difficult pregnancy, though probably for a different reason. In Friend's mind Aggy's condition, which he called "miseries," was "that plague to all farmers," no doubt because she had done almost no work for the previous several months.[17]

Childbirth was a dangerous procedure for both mother and infant, regardless of race. If the 1850 mortality census can be trusted, the death rate from complications of pregnancy was slightly lower in slaves than in whites (see Figure 5).[18] Among the problems women faced were convulsions, retention of placenta, ectopic pregnancy, breech presentation, premature labor, and uterine rigidity. Sometimes the life of mother or child had to be sacrificed to save the other. Occasionally, both died. An eighteen-year-old Richmond bondswoman began convulsing at the start of her labor. Neither bleeding nor laxatives relieved her, nor could the unborn child pass through her only slightly dilated cervix. Two attending physicians attempted unsuccessfully to

[17] David Ross to John Duffield, 9 January 1813, David Ross Letterbook, VHS; Greene, ed., *Carter Diary*, I, 204 (16 March 1758); White Hill Plantation Books, 26 February, 23 April 1845. Examples of time off for pregnancy and confinement may be found in Edmund Ruffin, Jr., Diary, 11 June 1851, UNC; N. B. Layne's Monthly Report for August 1856 to William Cabell Rives, Jr., in Agriculture [Book] III, p. 61, Rives Papers, LC; numerous entries throughout the White Hill Plantation Books, UNC.
[18] Fogel and Engerman, *Time*, I, 123.

remove the baby with long forceps and finally decided to save the mother at the expense of the child. The common procedure at that time involved destruction of the infant's skull and removal of the brain (craniotomy) so that its head (the largest part of a fetus's body) would pass through the cervix and vagina. This was performed without injury to the mother, permitting her to recover within a few days.[19]

Virginia's black women played an important role in the development of Caesarean section, a surgical procedure designed to save both mother and child in certain difficult births. Usually this operation was attempted if the baby could not pass through its mother's contracted or occluded pelvis naturally. Though this type of procedure had a long history throughout the world, most attempts had been unsuccessful because of the septic techniques used and the failure to re-suture the uterus once the fetus had been removed. Old Dominion physicians reported performing six Caesarean operations prior to the Civil War, four on blacks and two on whites. The first took place near Occoquan, Fairfax County, in 1828 before several physicians and leading citizens. Mrs. Payne, a free Negro, had suffered months of pain beyond term without delivering her child, due to a blockage at the uterine os. An irregular practitioner (an empirical surgeon) performed the procedure successfully, removing the dead fetus and carefully stitching up the surgical wounds. Mrs. Payne, however, died suddenly during what had been an otherwise rapid and uneventful convalescence, purportedly from peritonitis after eating improper food. (Infection or hemorrhage are more likely causes.)

In 1855, Dr. William G. Smith removed a living child by Caesarean section from Maria, a Northampton County slave who suffered from vaginal occlusion. Though the child was still alive fifteen months later, the mother died within six days. Of three operations performed during 1856, all on dwarfs (two black

---

[19] A. Sneal, "Report of a Case of Puerperal Convulsions," *Steth.*, 2 (1852), 28–33. For other examples of complications of pregnancy, see S. H. Harris, "Case of Delivery of a Foetus through the Abdominal Parieties," *AJMS*, 20 (1837), 77–81; John A. Cunningham, "Case of an Extra-Uterine Foetus, Retained Forty Years," *VMSJ*, 4 (1855), 94–95; Thomas K. Clarke to Dr. Charles Brown, 31 August 1814, Brown Papers, W&M; Nathaniel H. Ryan to Edmund W. Hubard, 18 August 1841, Hubard Family Papers, UNC; Mr. Daniel Williams account with Dr. William B. Price, Price Account Books, I, 1843, Duke.

[Richmond] and one white [Norfolk]), only one mother and her child survived; in the others either the baby or the mother died.[20]

Some women never carried their children to term, losing them during the first or second trimester of pregnancy. Miscarriages and threatened abortions were major crises for both the master and the slave family because two lives were at stake. Often, however, there was little a doctor could do but treat the patient after miscarriage had already occurred.[21] There is some indication that slaves suffered more frequent abortions and miscarriages than whites, but reliable figures are not available for either race.[22]

Antebellum women were subject to two common complications of childbirth, puerperal (childbed) fever and prolapsed uterus. The former, an infection of the reproductive organs during or after parturition, occurred either singly or in epidemics, depending upon the mode of infection. When a midwife or doctor delivered several children in a single day without cleansing hands between visits, several cases of this malady might arise simultaneously in a confined area. All too often the result was death.[23] Uterine prolapse, a weakening of pelvic supporting tissue result-

[20] J. L. Miller, "Caesarean Section in Virginia in the Pre-asceptic Era, 1794–1879," *Annals of Medical History*, NS 10 (1938), 23–25; M. L. Weems, "Case of Caesarean Section," *AJMS*, 18 (1836), 257–58; William G. Smith, "Case of Caesarean Operation," *VMJ*, 7 (1856), 203–8; Charles S. Mills, "Caesarean Section," *Mon. Steth.*, 1 (1856), 425–36; Editorial, "Caesarean Section," *VMJ*, 7 (1856), 169–71; Robert P. Harris, "Gastro-Hysterotomy in Virginia," *Virginia Medical Monthly*, 6 (1879–80), 186–91. Contrary to most statements on the subject, Jesse Bennet did not perform the first Caesarean section in Virginia (on his wife in 1794, while living in Rockingham County). Arthur G. King, "The Legend of Jesse Bennet's 1794 Caesarian Section," *BHM*, 50 (1976), 242–50.

[21] Bezaleel Brown to Dr. Charles Brown, 4 July 1816; Minoah Via to Drs. Brown or Raglin, 15 October 1818, both in Brown Papers, W&M; Edmund Wilcox Ledger, Hubard Family Papers, vol. 13, 29 March, 20 July 1777, 17, 23 February, 28 April 1778, UNC.

[22] See Eugene D. Genovese, "The Medical and Insurance Costs of Slaveholding in the Cotton Belt," *JNH*, 45 (1960), 151; Felice Swados, "Negro Health on the Ante-Bellum Plantations," *BHM*, 10 (1941), 468–69.

[23] For examples of puerperal fever, see C. R. Harris, "The Epidemic Puerperal Fever of Mount Solon and Vicinity," *Steth.*, 2 (1852), 376–80; journal of Dr. James Hubard, 8–9 January 1811, Hubard Papers, UVA (#8708a); A Young Practitioner, "Report of a Case of Disease Supposed to Be Peritonitis," *Mon. Steth.*, 1 (1856), 361–65; White Hill Plantation Books, 13 January 1842, UNC; William Michie to Dr. Charles Brown, 12 April 1814, Brown Papers, W&M; Dr. B. H. Walker Diary, 30–31 August 1858, VSL; Olmsted, *Seaboard*, 83; *Steth.*, 1 (1851), 204–9; *VMJ*, 11 (1858), 292–95.

ing in partial or complete protrusion of the uterus through the vagina, debilitated both slave and white women who had borne children. No figures as to its incidence in antebellum Virginia exist; nor do mortality statistics provide any hint, since it did not usually cause fatalities. A South Carolina medical student asserted in his dissertation in 1837 that among South Carolina Low Country slave women prolapsed uterus was "quite a common disease"; other observers reported similar findings. These statements run counter to recent studies which conclude that prolapse is less common among blacks than whites in the United States and South Africa, perhaps due to a greater elasticity of the abdominal wall which protects the pelvic supporting tissues among Negro women. If those who noted a higher prevalence of prolapse in antebellum blacks had actually counted cases and compared the numbers, their conclusions might have been different.[24]

Children, like women, were exposed to certain unique disorders which caused illness or death. Though their labor did not usually account for much, young slaves' serious illnesses did mean time lost from work for mothers watching over them at home or distractedly worrying about them while performing daily tasks. In addition to the usual ailments common to all children—mumps, measles, chicken pox, diarrhea, "teething" (not really a disease, but considered a cause of sickness and death prior to the twentieth century), diphtheria, respiratory diseases, and whooping cough (see Table 5)—slave children suffered more frequently from some illnesses than whites, owing to different living conditions.

Neonatal tetanus (also called *trismus nascentium*) was a common cause of death among newborn slaves throughout the South. Slaveowners and physicians, who recognized its origin in the improper handling of the umbilical stump, often discussed it

[24] H. Perry Pope, "A Dissertation on the Professional Management of Negro Slaves" (M.D. thesis, Medical College of South Carolina, Charleston, 1837), 14; Postell, *Health of Slaves*, 118; William F. Mengert, "Alterations of Uterine Position," in Robert A. Kimbrough, ed., *Gynecology* (Philadelphia, 1965), 176–77; O. S. Heyns, "Genital Prolapse," in G. P. Charlewood, *Bantu Gynecology* (Johannesburg, 1956), 102; R. B. Durfee, "Management of Genital Organ Prolapse," *Clinical Obstetrics and Gynecology*, 9 (1966), 994. For more on the care of slave women, see ch. 5.

Table 5. Leading Known Causes of Infant [a] Death in Staunton, Petersburg, Augusta County and Southampton County, Virginia, 1853–60, by Race [b]

White (N=332)	Percent	Slave (N=189)	Percent	Free Black (N=33)	Percent
1—Diarrhea [c]	31.5	1—Diarrhea [c]	18.5	1—Teething	18.2
2—Nervous system diseases [c]	12.6	2—Nervous system diseases [c]	14.3	2—Nervous system diseases [c]	18.2
3—Respiratory system diseases [c]	10.5	3—Whooping cough	10.6	3—Diarrhea [c]	18.2
4—Digestive system diseases [c]	8.7	4—Respiratory system diseases [c]	10.6	4—Whooping cough	18.2
5—Whooping cough	7.5	5—Suffocation	9.0	5—Digestive system diseases [c]	9.1
6—Diphtheria [c]	5.1	6—Diphtheria [c]	5.8	6—Accidents	6.1
7—Scarlet fever [c]	4.2	7—Teething	5.3	7—Immaturity	3.0
8—Immaturity	4.2	8—Immaturity	4.8	8—Diphtheria [c]	3.0
9—Teething	2.7	9—Measles	4.2	9—Suffocation	3.0
10—Measles	2.1	10—Sudden death	3.7		
11—Tuberculosis [c]	1.8	11—Digestive system diseases [c]	3.2		
12—Erysipelas	1.5	12—Tuberculosis [c]	1.6		
13—Typhoid [c]	1.2	13—Accidents	1.6		
14—Sudden death	0.6	14—Scarlet fever [c]	1.6		
15—Accidents	0.6	15—Typhoid [c]	1.6		
		16—Dropsy	1.1		

(Missing or unknown causes: 307 whites, 341 slaves and free blacks)

[a] Under one year of age.
[b] Register of Deaths, 1853–60, VSL.
[c] For names of diseases included in these categories, see Table 9, notes 21–28, 34.

in their writings.[25] It still kills large numbers of children in unde-
veloped countries. *Clostridium tetani,* the same bacterium which
caused tetanus in older children and adults, also infected new-
borns through the unwashed and frequently touched umbilical
stump. In a typical antebellum case, related by Dr. A. Snead of
Richmond to his colleagues at a medical society meeting in 1853,
an eight-day-old black child first refused her mother's breast
and gave a few convulsive hand jerks. Soon the baby's entire
muscular system was rigid, with her head bent back, fists and
jaws clenched, and feet tightly flexed, as the bacterial toxin
affected central nervous system tissue. Death, of suffocation
owing to respiratory muscle paralysis, did not intervene until the
eighteenth day (though it usually occurred within seven to ten
days).[26]

One cause of death which Virginians did not consider a disease
and which seemed to occur almost exclusively among the slave
population was "smothering," "overlaying," or "suffocation."
Observers assumed that sleeping mothers simply rolled onto or
pressed snugly against their infants, cutting off the air supply, or
that angry, fearful parents intentionally destroyed their offspring
rather than have them raised in slavery. Modern medical evidence
strongly indicates that most of these deaths may be ascribed to
a condition presently known as Sudden Infant Death Syndrome
(SIDS) or "crib death." [27] The Second International Conference
on Causes of Sudden Death in Infants (1970) defined SIDS as
"the sudden death of any infant or young child which is unexpected by history, and in which a thorough post-mortem examination fails to demonstrate an adequate cause of death." [28] SIDS is,
at present, responsible for 10–30 percent (45 percent, in one
study) of deaths between the ages of two weeks and eleven

[25] See, e.g., W. Duncan, *Tabulated Mortuary Record of the City of Savannah,
from January 1, 1854, to December 31, 1869* (Savannah, 1870), 15, 29; Postell,
Health of Slaves, 122. For a recent, excellent article on slave child mortality, see
reference in ch. 3, note 9.

[26] Alexander M. Earle and W. Larimer Mellon, Jr., "Tetanus Neonatorum: A
Report of Thirty-two Cases [in Haiti]," *American Journal of Tropical Medicine
and Hygiene,* 7 (1958), 315–16; "Medico-Chirurgical Society of Richmond, [1
March 1853]," *VMSJ,* 1 (1853), 35.

months, clearly establishing it as a leading killer of children under one year of age.[29]

Typical cases of overlaying share several of the unmistakable hallmarks of SIDS. Compare a twentieth-century physician's description of the latter with an overseer's and a planter's remarks on the former:

> An apparently thriving two-month-old boy is found dead face down in his crib. Except for a brief mild rhinorrhea during the previous week, the child has been in excellent health from birth. At a routine well-baby check by the family doctor a few days prior to the event, he appeared robust and free of problems. On the night of death, he took his formula eagerly and was put down in his crib about 10 P.M. His mother looked in before retiring; he was sleeping peacefully on his abdomen with his face to the side. When found at 6:30 A.M., he had obviously been dead for several hours.[30]

> I [Nathaniel Ryan, overseer] am sorry to inform you [Edmund Hubard, slaveowner] that Matilda has lost her youngest child she over laid it, it was well and hearty when she went to bed and found it dead sometime in the night.[31]

[27] For more on suffocation throughout the South, see Fogel and Engerman, *Time*, I, 124–26; II, 101. Their conjecture (II, 101) that the significantly higher death rates of present-day black children over white children from SIDS explains the difference between antebellum free and slave suffocation rates is probably incorrect. There may be a racial predisposition to SIDS, but scientists now believe that most of the differences between races can be better explained on a socioeconomic basis relating to living conditions. The best reviews of research and current thinking regarding SIDS are J. Bruce Beckwith, "The Sudden Infant Death Syndrome," *Current Problems in Pediatrics*, 3 (June 1973); and Eileen G. Hasselmeyer and Jehu C. Hunter, "The Sudden Infant Death Syndrome," *Obstetrics and Gynecology Annual*, 4 (1975), 213–36.

[28] Abraham B. Bergman, J. Bruce Beckwith, and C. George Ray, eds., *Sudden Infant Death Syndrome: Proceedings of the Second International Conference on Causes of Death in Infants* (Seattle, 1970), 18.

[29] Marie Valdes-Dapena et al., "Sudden Unexpected Death in Infancy: A Statistical Analysis of Certain Socioeconomic Factors," *Journal of Pediatrics*, 73 (1968), 388; John W. Melton et al., "Sudden and Unexpected Deaths in Infancy," *Virginia Medical Monthly*, 95 (1968), 63. The 45 percent figure was reported in Abraham B. Bergman et al., "Studies of the Sudden Infant Death Syndrome in King County, Washington. III. Epidemiology," *Pediatrics*, 49 (1972), 861.

[30] J. Bruce Beckwith and Abraham B. Bergman, "The Sudden Death Syndrome of Infancy," *Hospital Practice*, 2 (November 1967), 44.

[31] Nathaniel Ryan to Edmund W. Hubard, 15 December 1841, Hubard Family Papers, UNC.

Last week [wrote Robert Hubard to his brother Edmund] Tilla over-
laid/when asleep/and killed her youngest child—a boy 6 or 7 months
old. This was no doubt caused by her own want of care and attention.[32]

Most people, both today and a century ago, automatically assume
that the fault lies with the parent and that death is preventable.
This is not true. Physicians now know that children cannot be
smothered as long as there is any circulating air available, even
when the infant is beneath the covers or wedged against the
sleeping mother.[33]

In addition to this descriptive similarity between SIDS and
overlaying, there is a remarkable epidemiological correspondence,
both in age and in seasonal variation. Crib death does not occur
among children of all age groups. Those under two weeks and
over one year are almost entirely spared; those between two
weeks and four months are prime targets. In two recent studies,
conducted in King County (Seattle), Washington, and Richmond, Virginia, 85 percent and 63 percent, respectively, of the
victims were between one and four months old. The majority of
these deaths occurred during the colder six months of the year
(October through March).[34] The figures obtained from an
analysis of the manuscript register of births for twenty-six Virginia
counties between 1853 and 1860 corroborate the King County and
Richmond studies. Of the 226 children whose demises the parent
or slaveowner attributed to overlaying, smothering, or suffocation,
54 percent were between one and four months of age. Furthermore, 56 percent of the deaths occurred between October and
March (see Figures 6-9).[35]

The recorded incidence of overlaying was much lower in

[32] Robert T. Hubard to Edmund W. Hubard, 21 December 1841, *ibid.*

[33] Beckwith and Bergman, "Sudden Death Syndrome," 50–51.

[34] Bergman et al., "Studies of Sudden Infant Death Syndrome in King County,"
863; Melton et al., "Sudden and Unexpected Deaths in Infancy," 64–65.

[35] Registers of Death, 1853–60, Accomac, Albemarle, Amelia, Arlington, Au-
gusta, Bedford, Botetourt, Brunswick, Cumberland, Essex, Fairfax, Fauquier,
Floyd, Frederick, Greene, Greensville, Halifax, Hanover, Henrico, Henry, Isle of
Wight, Lancaster, Pittsylvania, and Southampton Counties; Petersburg and
Staunton Towns, VSL. The oldest child in the survey to die of suffocation was
six years.

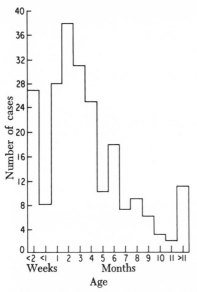

Figure 5. Age Distribution of 226 Cases of Smothering, Suffocation, and Overlaying in Virginia, 1853–60.

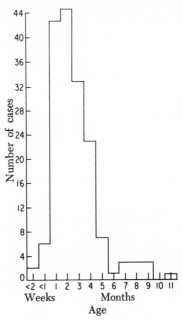

Figure 6. Age Distribution of 170 SIDS Cases in King County, Washington, 1965–67.

SOURCE: Bergman *et al.*, "Studies in the Sudden Infant Death Syndrome in King County, Washington, III. Epidemiology," *Pediatrics*, 49 (1972), 863.

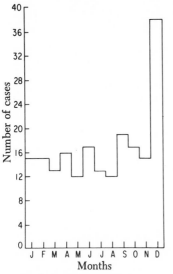

Figure 7. Months of Death of 202 Cases of Smothering, Suffocation, and Overlaying in Virginia, 1853–60.

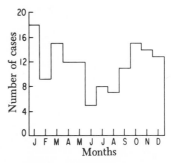

Figure 8. Months of Death of 170 SIDS Cases in King County, Washington, 1965–67.

SOURCE: adapted from Bergman *et al.*, "Studies in SIDS," 863.

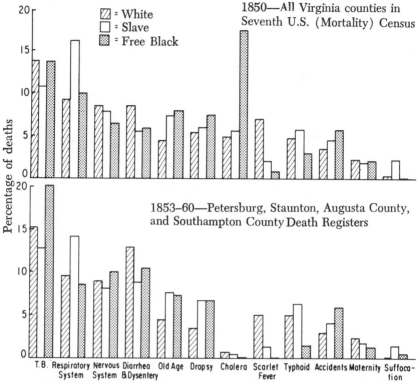

Figure 9. Race-Specific Proportional Mortality Rates for Selected Diseases in Virginia, 1850–60.

antebellum Virginia (about 4 percent of infant deaths) than that of SIDS in presentday America (10–30 percent of infant deaths) for several reasons. Since people did not understand the cause of sudden infant death, they classified it as "unknown" in most mortality lists. Today we cannot explain this phenomenon of unexpected death in young babies, but, rather than lump it with other unknown causes of death, medical scientists have provided us with the descriptive but no more helpful term "Sudden Infant Death Syndrome." Another important factor was the marked underreporting of white suffocation deaths (only about 2 percent of the total from this cause), probably due in part to the social stigma associated with child smothering. White parents and physicians likely attributed many sudden deaths among these children to teething, pneumonia, and "unknown causes." Though present studies indicate that blacks do in fact have a higher incidence of SIDS than whites, as do all members of lower socioeconomic groups regardless of race (possibly owing to poor sanitary conditions and overcrowding),[36] the 98 percent figure for antebellum Virginia blacks (229 black of 232 total smothering deaths) is much too high.[37]

Smothering was not a problem confined solely to the plantation, though one early southern writer asserted that the peculiarities of the slave system increased its incidence: "Not a few [babies] are overlaid by the wearied [slave] mother, who sleeps so dead a sleep as not to be aware of the injury to her infant." [38] Overlaying occurred also in the North, where it was reported with much less frequency, again no doubt due to social pressures, and in European countries.[39]

Certainly not all cases of suffocation among slave children can be attributed to crib death. Nineteenth-century physicians rarely performed autopsies and probably misdiagnosed some of their cases simply because they lacked the requisite knowledge. In addition, some slave mothers did actually commit infanticide, though without their master's knowledge. The information presented here, however, indicates that the majority of infant deaths attributed to suffocation, smothering, and overlaying were actually cases of Sudden Infant Death Syndrome.

The question of infanticide cannot be dismissed lightly. Some historians have argued that most infanticides reflected the desire

[36] Valdes-Dapena et al., "Sudden Unexpected Deaths in Infancy," 390–92.

[37] It is interesting to note that, in the latest available Department of Health, Education, and Welfare national survey, underreporting continues to be a problem. Less than half of the estimated infant deaths attributable to SIDS (based on recent epidemiological studies) were classified as such on 1968 death certificates. Among the reasons for this were the lack of acceptance of SIDS as a disease entity, and subjectivity on the part of the local certifier—a condition remarkably similar to that which existed in antebellum Virginia. Noel S. Weiss et al., "Problems in the Use of Death Certificates to Identify Sudden Unexpected Infant Deaths," *Health Services Reports*, 88 (1973), 555–58.

[38] Thomas Affleck, "On the Hygiene of Cotton Plantations and the Management of Negro Slaves," *SMR*, 2 (1851) 435.

[39] Bureau of the Census, *Mortality Statistics of the Seventh Census of the United States, 1850* (Washington, D.C., 1855), 28.

of slave parents to avoid watching their children grow up in bondage. Though this may have been true in some cases, the evidence presented in several Virginia court hearings and petitions to the governor provides other explanations for at least some of the murders. Parental influence and fear of discovery of an illegitimate child by the couple's parents or owners were given as reasons in four of the six slave cases reported. Seventeen-year-old Charlotte, hired in Richmond, murdered her newborn at least partially out of a desire to conceal the birth from her employers. Lucy, fourteen, destroyed her infant "to hide her shame," while the mother of another Lucy acted in a similar manner "to hide the shame of the [unmarried] daughter." Most masters vouched for the previous "good character" of the women who had perpetrated such brutal acts (one mother struck her child's head with a blow "sufficient to drive in the skull," and another murdered by "strangling and suffocating" the infant).[40] Though the underlying motives in these cases may have been humanitarian (saving the child from slavery), available evidence points to the contrary. Infanticide was not a phenomenon limited solely to slaves. The causes of infanticide sometimes involved factors other than a simple hatred of slavery.[41]

As has already been discussed (see chapter 2), a disease which struck black children frequently was worms. The poor sanitary conditions at many antebellum Virginia slave quarters were conducive to the development of these parasites in the soil. Children playing in the dirt inevitably picked up worm larvae as they put

[40] Fogel and Engerman, *Time*, I, 124–26; "Communication from the Governor Relative to Reprieves, Pardons and Commutations, 1852-3," *Leg. Docs.*, 1852–53, pt. II, doc. 65, p. 5 (Lucy); Richmond *Daily Dispatch*, 10 August 1854, p. 2 (Charlotte); "Reprieves, Pardons, Etc.," *Leg. Docs.*, 1855–56, pt. V, doc. 29, pp. 9–10; Richmond Hustings Court Minutes, 10 April 1855, VSL (film); petition of Samuel Ellis to Governor Joseph Johnson, Executive Papers, April 1855, VSL (all three for the case of the other Lucy); "Message IV Relative to Reprieves and Pardons, to the General Assembly of Virginia," 7 December 1857, *Leg. Docs.*, 1857–58, pt. I, doc. 1, p. clxxviii (Opha Jane), and p. clxxxv (Suckey); Powhatan County Order Book, 7 April 1856, VSL (film) (Opha Jane again); "Communication Relative to Reprieves, Pardons, Etc., December 23, 1859," *Leg. Docs.*, 1859–60, pt. VI, doc. 35, pp. 24–25 (Marietta).

[41] Other infanticides in Virginia: H of D *Jl.*, 1827/28, p. 23 (Documents Accompanying the Governor's Message); *Leg. Docs.*, 1848–49, doc. 33, p. 4.

fingers in mouths. Failure to use, or lack of, privy facilities only served to spread worm diseases to other residents of the quarters and to visiting slaves, who then carried these parasites to their own plantation quarters.

Some black children had overt sickle cell disease (see chapter 1), with irregular hemolytic crises, severe joint pains, chronic leg ulcers, and abdominal pains. The medical records relating to antebellum Virginia do not provide any clear descriptions of the disease, probably because its symptoms resemble so many other conditions and because the sickness was not known until 1910. These children were often the "sickly" ones, useless for field work or heavy house duties, expensive to maintain because of frequent infections, and often unable to bear children if they survived puberty. Their lot was a poor and painful one.

Slave children also developed diseases which no one could identify or treat. John Walker's young servants appeared one day with "head ach sweled faces & belly diseases"; Colonel John Ambler's evidenced swollen feet and faces, and bones cutting through the skin, and Landon Carter's had "swelling of the almonds of . . . [their] ears which burst inward and choaked . . . [them]." The white tutor at Nomini Hall, Philip Vickers Fithian, noticed that one slave mother on this Westmoreland County estate had lost seven children successively, none of whom had even reached the age of ten: "The Negroes all seem much alarm'd. . . ." Childhood was generally the least healthy period of a slave's life in antebellum Virginia.[42]

Other Diseases and Conditions

Infectious diseases caused the most illnesses among antebellum Virginia's black population. Those discussed in previous sections constituted the most common complaints, with the exceptions of cholera, yellow fever, and smallpox (see chapter 7).

[42] John Walker Diary, 23 April 1853, UNC; Levi P. Clarke to Colonel [John] Ambler, 2 June 1829, Ambler Family Papers, UVA (#1140); Greene, ed., *Carter Diary*, I, 377 (31 March 1770), 379 (2 April 1770); Hunter Dickinson Farish, ed., *Journal and Letters of Philip Vickers Fithian 1773–1774: A Plantation Tutor of the Old Dominion* (Williamsburg, Va., 1957), 182.

Though it may seem surprising to find cancer, heart disease, and stroke missing from the list, it must be remembered that, in the days before acceptance of the germ theory, people were ignorant of true causes or proper cures of infectious diseases. Furthermore, cancer, heart disease, and stroke are usually disorders of middle and later life, ages which many in the population never reached. If hypertension prevailed among blacks as much then as it does now, stroke and heart disease may have caused more slave and free black deaths than we previously suspected.

Though doctors knew that tumors might occur anywhere in the body, almost all those described in the medical literature of Virginia appeared on skin or bone or in the female genital system. Neither proper techniques nor instruments existed to diagnose internal cancers (i.e., of liver, gastro-intestinal tract, bladder, spleen, lymph nodes, brain, or blood), nor were autopsies performed frequently or carefully enough for physicians to correlate the signs and symptoms of disease during life with post-mortem changes in the appearance of affected organs. In addition, few doctors had the time, inclination, or training to make proper use of that most important tool of the pathologist, the microscope. The result was a dearth of cancer diagnoses for internal organs. External tumors, however, were eminently treatable by excision, so physicians proudly publicized their successes. Several cases found their way into state medical journals, some with pictures of slaves (see illustrations), while others appeared in the lay press. One article included the drawing of black woman, naked to the waist, sadly displaying her cancerous shoulder growth. Tumors of the jawbone predominated; others included the shoulder, breast, lips, eye, and skin over ankle.[43]

[43] A. E. Peticolas, "College Infirmary Cases," *VMJ*, 12 (1859), 381–84 (2 jaw cases); Charles Bell Gibson, "Osteo-Sarcoma of Lower Jaw—Amputation—Cure," *AJMS*, NS 4 (1842), 277–80; John N. Broocks, "Cases Treated in the Armory and Penitentiary Hospitals, with Remarks," *Steth.*, 1 (1851), 101–2 (jaw and breast cases); A. E. Peticolas, "Case of Osteo Sarcoma of the Inferior Maxilla," *VMJ*, 13 (1859), 283–84 (jaw); Frank Cunningham, "Surgical Cases at the Medical College of Virginia," *VMJ*, 9 (1857), 21–23 (jaw); A. E. Peticolas, "Case of Osteoid Cancer, with Remarks," *VMSJ*, 2 (1854), 380–83 (shoulder); S[ocrates] Maupin to Dr. William A. Maupin, 9 April 1841, Maupin-Washington Manuscripts, UVA (#2769a) (jaw); Petersburg *Daily Express*, 15 December

As with internal cancers, cardiovascular diseases were difficult for pre–Civil War physicians to diagnose. Heart attacks and arteriosclerosis probably occurred much less frequently than at present. The major heart diseases recognized at that time were malfunctions of the valves, rupture, and cardiac enlargement, though their causes were not known. Consequently, few Virginia doctors or slaveowners reported upon cases of cardiovascular disorders in medical journals, casebooks, or plantation diaries. Despite the fact that dropsy (edema), the accumulation of body fluids in the chest, abdomen, face, and extremities, often signifies disturbances of the cardiovascular system, especially within the heart and the lungs, practitioners of this period understood little of internal body-fluid dynamics and so attributed such illnesses and deaths simply to dropsy.[44]

Diseases of the nervous system posed similar problems. Other than epilepsy and apoplexy (stroke), the medical profession was unable to diagnose specific brain disorders. Instead, such terms as "brain fever," "softening of the brain," "inflammation of the brain," "nervous fever," and "fits" were used. There was no way to identify or treat the true causes of these maladies: brain tumors, infectious diseases (especially meningitis and neurosyphilis), toxic substances in the blood, and nerve diseases. One of the more common diagnoses, nervous fever, may actually have

---

1857, p. 1 (eye), 10 November 1858, p. 1 (breast); P. M. Tabb & Son to R. L. T. Beale, 9 June 1854, Beale Letter Book, UVA (#38–105), (unspecified site); Isham Cheatham to Col. John Ambler, 16 May 1829, UVA (#1140), (shoulder); account of John G. Dulany with Dr. George Thrift, Thrift Ledgers, UVA (#9153d), (breast); account to Corbin Warwick with Dr. Charles J. F. Bohannan, Bohannan Ledgers, VSL (lip); account of Samuel Thompson with Dr. George W. Clement, Clement Account Book, Pocket Plantation Papers, UVA (#2027), (ankle).

[44] For examples of cardiac and vascular illnesses in Virginia blacks, see Sallie Carter Randolph to Isaetta Randolph Hubard, 1 March [1861], Randolph-Hubard Papers, UVA (#4717, 5885); F. W. Roddey, "On Fatty Degeneration of the Heart—with the Report of a Case," *Steth.*, 3 (1853), 446–62; Doctor's Account Book, 1846–53, entry for 2 April 1848, p. 114, Louthan Family Papers, UVA (#38–34); Charles [Gorgas] to [William Weaver], 1 May 1860, Weaver Papers, Duke. Dropsy: White Hill Plantation Books, 29 September, 29 October 1848, UNC; Garland Garth to Dr. Charles Brown, 16 August 1816, Brown Papers, W&M. There are many more examples of dropsy throughout the antebellum medical and slave literature.

Virginia Slave with Tumor of Jawbone. Man (age 30) is shown before and after surgical excision at Medical College of Virginia Infirmary.

SOURCE: Frank Cunningham, "Surgical Cases at the Medical College of Virginia," *VMJ*, IX (1857), facing p. 1.

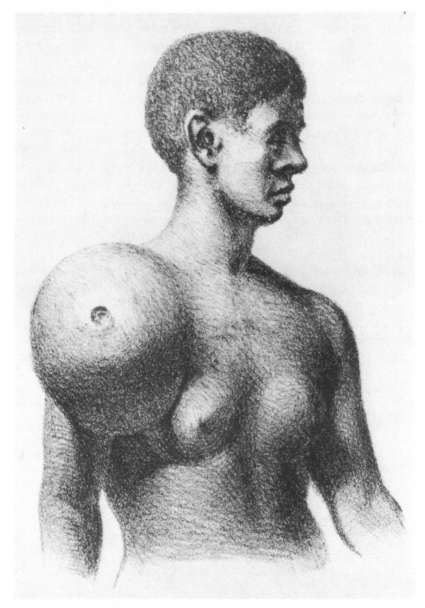

Virginia Slave with Bony Tumor at Shoulder Joint. Woman (age 25) is shown before surgical excision at Medical College of Virginia Infirmary. She died subsequent to the operation.

SOURCE: A. E. Peticolas, "Case of Osteoid Cancer, with Remarks," *VMSJ*, II (1854), facing p. 380.

been a manifestation of typhus or typhoid fever in the central nervous system. And the very nondescriptive term "fits," used so often to describe slaves' illnesses, includes such a wide range of possible diseases that historical guesses are impossible.[45]

As for ocular problems, in addition to the usual number of medically unenlightening symptoms—red eyes, ophthalmia, sore eyes, swollen eyes, and eye pain—the major disease was cataract, which physicians cured regularly with surgery.[46]

Hernia ("rupture") was a frequent cause of pain and of lost workdays among black male laborers. Males possess a potential space on both sides of the lower abdominal wall through which, during severe physical exertion, a portion of the small intestine may pass. The resulting condition, known as inguinal hernia, may be felt in or near the scrotum. If not immediately returned to its proper position within the abdomen, this sac of bowel often becomes entrapped as the space through which it originally entered the inguinal canal contracts, causing strangulation. With its blood supply cut off, the incarcerated intestine cannot survive; gangrene sets in, the remaining small intestine within the abdomen ceases to function properly, and a life-threatening situation arises. Only surgical intervention can cure a strangulated hernia, whereas

[45] Thomas Jefferson to Joel Yancey, 25 June 1819; "Roll of the negroes in the winter of 1798–9;" both in Betts, ed., *Thomas Jefferson's Farm Book*, 44 (nervous fever), 57 (epileptic slave); M. M. Robinson to John Hartwell Cocke, 20 September 1820, Shields Deposit, Cocke Papers, UVA (nervous fever); Edmund Wilcox Ledger, Hubard Family Papers, vol. 13, 29 January, 31 July 1777, UNC (fits); Petersburg *Daily South Side Democrat*, 8 August 1854, p. 2 (fit); account of A. Kennedy with Dr. William B. Price, account of Daniel Williams with same, Price Account Books, I, Duke (epilepsy); John Wharton, "Case of Chorea," *American Medical Recorder*, 9 (1826), 100; Thomas Pollard, "Bellevue Hospital Reports," *VMJ*, 10 (1858), 286 (brain softening).

[46] *Lynchburg Press*, 31 August 1821, p. 4 (runaway ad—slave's "eyes are often affected with redness"); *ibid.*, 27 April 1821, p. 3 (runaway ad—slave "has recently had a phelm on the left eye, which has nearly destroyed the sight"); account of Miss Anna Robinson with Dr. Charles Bohannan, Bohannan Account Book, p. 152, VSL (ophthalmia); J. T. Hubard to Mrs. Wilcox, 9 April 1811, Hubard Family Papers, box 3, folder 33, UNC (unidentified eye problem); William Selden to [L. W. Tazewell?], 22 January 1839, Galt Family Papers (Medical), CW (unidentified eye problem); T. P. Mayo, "Clinical Reports of the Richmond College Infirmary," *VMSJ*, 2 (1854), 276–77 (cataracts); James Bolton, "Bellevue Hospital Reports," *Steth.*, 4 (1854), 459–63, 5 (1855), 67–69 (cataracts).

prompt attention at the first occurrence of herniation will prevent the progression of events to gangrene.

These facts were common knowledge to most slaveowners and to many adult male slave sufferers, who usually sought medical advice or wore trusses to impede a repetition of the condition. The editors of the *Virginia Medical Journal* emphasized the importance of caring for hernias among the slave labor force. They calculated from statistics among whites in the United States, England, and France that "not less than *one hundred and fifty thousand negroes* are afflicted with hernia." Were a permanent cure found for this condition, they further declared, "*twenty millions* [would be added] to the present value of this species of property, besides greatly increasing its productive force." Though the figures may have been exaggerated, the significance of the condition was not.[47]

Disorders of bones, muscles, joints, and skin tended to incapacitate workers, rather than to kill them. Many suffered from rheumatism and arthritis, which were exacerbated by cold, damp weather. Others complained of boils, skin ulcerations (especially on the legs), cysts, abnormal bone growths or deteriorations, abscesses, and joint conditions. There were also the usual aches and pains, sore fingers, hands, arms, legs, and feet, "risings" of hands, breasts, or other parts, weak knees, and other vague but real disturbances of the integument and organs of movement. The bites of bees, snakes, dogs, spiders, and hornets wasted many workdays, as did painful bladder stones ("gravel"), and that most annoying of conditions, the toothache.[48]

Mortality Statistics

Prior to 1850 neither the state nor the federal government undertook to enumerate mortality figures within their jurisdic-

[47] Editorial, "Radical Cure of Hernia," *VMJ*, 10 (1858), 344–46; *Richmond Enquirer*, 21 August 1832, p. 1; James Bolton, "Two Cases Simulating Hernia," *Mon. Steth.*, 1 (1856), 625–28; Charles Bell Gibson, "Notes of Surgical Cases," *VMJ*, 13 (1859), 16–19; Thomas Jefferson to Nathaniel H. Hooe, 20 October 1810, 3 November 1811, in Betts, ed., *Thomas Jefferson's Farm Books*, 31–32, 34.

[48] Examples of these ailments can be found in any plantation journal, physician's casebook, or medical journal of the antebellum period.

tions. In that year, however, the U.S. Bureau of Census required that its fieldworkers inquire of each household head whether any deaths had occurred in his or her family unit during the preceding twelve months. Though this was a rather imprecise approach to the matter, it was a start. Despite the unknown number of forgotten and concealed fatalities, and the gross inaccuracies which inevitably resulted from relying on lay descriptions of causes of death, the 1850 mortality census stands as the only published antebellum federal enumeration listing deaths by disease and race. (For some unknown reason the bureaucrats in Washington chose not to tabulate the 1860 mortality figures by race—a most unfortunate decision.)

Spurred by both the 1850 census and the prodding of the state's medical profession, legislators in Richmond called for an annual collection of births, marriages, and deaths from each county beginning in 1853. County commissioners of revenue were to gather the data from individual residents, physicians, and coroners, record them on sheets which the state provided, and send them to county clerks, who copied and indexed them before submission (by 1 March of the following year) to the state auditor for compilation. For their efforts the commissioners of revenue and clerks each received as compensation three cents per entry. As with the federal enumeration, this statewide registration lacked completeness and accuracy. Some county clerks even failed to respond each year. The state auditor's published collations and tabulations of submissions were of limited value, not only because of missing data but also because the reports included no breakdown of diseases by race. In addition, some of the figures submitted were patently incorrect and misleading. For example, the clerks in Lynchburg failed to differentiate between free and slave blacks; the city of Richmond reported only 10 free Negro deaths in 1857 while Petersburg, with a comparable population of freedmen, reported 54, and Alleghany County submitted a return in 1856 listing a total of 6 deaths out of a population of about 5,000 for a rate of 1.2 deaths per 1,000 people, compared to the 10 percent rate of Bath, an adjoining county.[49]

One might assume that, in reporting to the census-takers or

county commissioners, slaveowners would have tended to remember deaths of members of their immediate families more clearly than fatalities among bondsmen, especially when the number of slaves was large and the time since death was long. This would have increased the relative number of white deaths shown in such enumerations and rendered any comparisons between deaths in the white and black populations inaccurate. But according to the superintendent of the Seventh United States Census, James D. B. De Bow, slave mortality was much less underreported than free black and white mortality. Cliometric historians have accepted De Bow's assessment and have proceeded to calculate life tables and death rates for slaves and whites based on the 1850 census returns. This is a rather risky business, especially when comparisons with state returns such as the Virginia Registration of Deaths demonstrate entirely different figures.[50]

An additional problem involves the use of returns that were undoubtedly atypical. The census year 1850 (which ran mid-1849 to mid-1850) coincided with the outbreak of a major nationwide epidemic of cholera (summer and fall of 1849). If Virginia is illustrative of the situation in other states, black mortality far exceeded white in areas where cholera struck (see chapter 7), distorting any true picture of supposedly typical comparative mortality rates. Furthermore, Edward Jarvis, the nineteenth-century physician-statistician who wrote the official analysis of the 1860 mortality returns, felt that the enumeration of children under the age of five had been so incomplete in 1850 as to render

---

[49] Virginia, *The Code of Virginia, Second Edition, Including Legislation to the Year 1860* (Richmond, 1860), 526–29; "Report of the Auditor of Public Accounts, Relative to Marriages, Births and Deaths," *Leg. Docs.*, 1855–56, pt. II, doc. 64 (for 1853–54); *Leg. Docs.*, 1857–58, pt. V, doc. 50 (for 1855–56); *Leg. Docs.*, 1859–60, pt. I, doc. 5 (for 1857–58). No compilations were published for the years 1859–61.

[50] J. D. B. De Bow, *Statistical View of the United States . . . Compendium of the Seventh Census . . .* (Washington, D.C., 1854), 92; Paul H. Jacobsen, "An Estimate of the Expectation of Life in the United States in 1850," *Milbank Memorial Fund Quarterly*, 35 (1957), 197–201; Robert Evans, Jr., "The Economics of American Negro Slavery, 1830–1860," in Universities–National Bureau Committee for Economic Research, *Aspects of Labor Economics* (Princeton, 1962), 208–13; Fogel and Engerman, *Time*, II, 100.

any use of it entirely misleading.[51] Not only would death rates for the population under age five be inordinately high, but any attempt to assign differential mortality rates to whites and blacks in this age group would also be deceptive because the racial distribution of those uncounted children is unknown.[52] Any use of 1850 mortality or child population returns should be made with these caveats in mind so that correctives can, when possible, be applied. Reference to antebellum state or municipal censuses and registries of deaths would help to reduce potential errors.

In evaluating causes of death as reported by federal census-takers or county officials, several other factors become important. Certain diseases possessed an inherent class bias in early nineteenth-century society. Mention has already been made of the prejudice against reporting sudden unexplained white infant deaths as suffocation or overlaying. Scrofula (tuberculosis of lymph glands in the neck) was another disease considered by the better classes of whites as a malady of the poor and the black. So, too, with the epidemic scourges cholera and yellow fever (see chapter 7).

Terminology is another problem. It is doubtful that early nineteenth century physicians or laymen could accurately differentiate among cases of pneumonia, pleurisy, bronchitis, lung cancer, and consumption; or colic, dyspepsia, gastritis, enteritis, appendicitis (the existence of which was unrecognized), and other abdominal organ diseases. Nervous fever, a condition which they classified as a separate fever, could have been typhoid, typhus, or an encephalitis, among other things. The safest approach to listing nineteenth-century causes of death is to classify them by groups such as tuberculosis—all forms; digestive system diseases; respiratory system diseases; and central nervous system diseases (a poor but inescapable category in which to include nervous fever). This method of broad categorization also tends to

[51] Edward Jarvis, "Mortality Statistics: Introduction, Commentary, and Compilation from Tabular Portion of Mortality, Eighth Census," in U.S. Bureau of the Census, *Statistics of the United States . . . in 1860 . . .* (Washington, D.C., 1866), [IV,] 285–86.

[52] But Fogel and Engerman, *Time*, I, 123–24, II, 101, used the 1850 population returns for children under age one year to calculate comparative infant mortality for whites and blacks.

minimize the error inherent in listing the class- or race-biased diseases mentioned above.

By using classifications of causes of deaths, rather than specific diseases, and by assuming that, though deaths were perhaps under-enumerated, the reporting of types of diseases in both races remained constant, it is then possible (though still risky) to determine such information as the leading causes of death for whites and blacks, the race-specific comparative mortalities for disease categories, and differential disease-specific mortalities for each race when living in urban or rural settings. One qualification must be added here: though those reporting deaths to enumerators may have stated the cause as accurately as possible, they did not know the actual cause as frequently when blacks were involved. This phenomenon occurred nationally. A larger number of unknown causes of death exists for blacks than for whites in every federal, state, and municipal antebellum mortality return. How many of these unknown fatalities were actually due to such diseases as tuberculosis, pneumonia, etc., cannot be determined. However, if they were labeled "unknown" because no one had examined the individual at the time of death, rather than because reporters were reluctant to admit to certain types of diseases, it is reasonable to assume that these deaths were due to diseases occurring regularly in the general population, which killed at the same rate as those already listed in the bills of mortality. This "unknown" group can then be ignored in determining the relative importance of specific causes of deaths among residents of a city, state, or county.

In the present study, mortality data from four Virginia localities —Staunton, Augusta County, Petersburg, and Southampton County—have been analyzed for the period 1853 to 1860 from the manuscript registers of deaths at the Virginia State Library in Richmond.[53] Clerks of the four localities under consideration collected data on 6,156 deaths during eight years, of which 5.6 percent (340) were free blacks, 36.7 percent (2,261) were slaves, and 57.7 percent (3,554) were whites (see Table 6). As Table 7

[53] Fogel and Engerman are presently compiling data from both the 1850 and 1860 manuscript federal censuses which will provide a much larger number of observations and cover several southern states.

indicates, the cause of death in each case was not always provided, with the bias in favor of the white population. The quality of data varied for each locality during each year; Petersburg and Augusta provided the most consistent information, Staunton the least. Not all deaths were reported, especially in the first and latter years of the series; therefore these figures are useless in any attempt at comparing mortality rates among the three groups— unless one assumes, as have previous writers, that all were equally underreported. If this assumption is accepted, then free blacks died at about two-thirds the rate of whites and half the rate of slaves, a very surprising figure, since the 1850 census shows a higher death rate for free blacks (140/10,000) than for whites

Table 6. Deaths Reported in Augusta and Southampton Counties, Petersburg and Staunton, Virginia, 1853–60, by Race [a]

	Whites	Slaves	Free Blacks	Unknown	Total
Augusta	1,425	499	16	0	1,940
Southampton	566	670	90	1	1,327
Staunton	248	117	16	0	381
Petersburg	1,315	975	218	0	2,508
Total	3,554	2,261	340	1	6,156
(Percent)	(57.7)	(36.7)	(5.6)		(100.0)

[a] Register of Deaths, VSL.

Table 7. Number of Known and Unknown Causes of Death in Virginia Mortality Returns, 1850–60, by Race

	1850 [a]			1853–60 [b]		
	Number of deaths	Number of known causes	Percent of known causes	Number of deaths	Number of known causes	Percent of known causes
Whites	9,897	8,014	81.0	3,554	2,862	80.5
Slaves	8,400	6,284	74.8	2,261	1,537	68.0
Free Blacks	762	558	73.2	340	221	65.0

[a] United States, Bureau of the Census, *Mortality Statistics of the Seventh Census of the United States, 1850* (Washington, 1855), 295.

[b] Register of Deaths for Augusta County, Southampton County, Petersburg and Staunton, Virginia, 1853–60, VSL.

(111/10,000), though the rate for slaves remains the highest (178/10,000) (see Table 8).

Despite the obvious drawbacks of these early tabulations, it is possible to learn something about the health conditions of Vir-

Table 8. Mortality Rates from Two Sources Compared, for White, Slave, and Free Black Virginians (Per 10,000 of Each Group in Population)

Year	Whites	Slaves	Free Blacks
	Rural and Urban		
1850 [a]	111	178	140
1853 [b]	111	172	80
1855 [b]	105	151	71
1857 [b]	97	152	65
1858 [b]	95	146	65
	Urban		
1850 [a,c]	205	133	222
1853 [b,d]	120	80	87
1855 [b,e]	97	54	41
1857 [b,f]	121	109	112
1858 [b,g]	76	74	49
	Rural		
1850 [a,h]	106	180	127
1853 [b]	111	184	79
1855 [b]	106	156	76
1857 [b]	93	154	58
1858 [b]	93	150	70

[a] Calculated from mortality returns of Seventh Federal Census, 1850.

[b] Calculated from published tabulations of the State Auditor; not all cities or counties submitted returns.

[c] Alexandria, Norfolk, Richmond, Portsmouth, Petersburg.

[d] Fredericksburg, Lynchburg, Norfolk, Petersburg, Richmond, Staunton, Williamsburg.

[e] Danville, Fredericksburg, Lynchburg, Petersburg, Richmond, Staunton, Williamsburg, Winchester. Norfolk was excluded because excessive mortality during the yellow fever epidemic would have distorted the figures.

[f] Danville, Lynchburg, Norfolk, Petersburg, Richmond, Staunton, Williamsburg, Winchester.

[g] Danville, Fredericksburg, Lynchburg, Norfolk, Richmond, Staunton, Williamsburg, Winchester.

[h] Includes several urban areas which could not be isolated from the figures— e.g., Lynchburg, Fredericksburg, Danville, Winchester, Staunton, and Wheeling. Only Wheeling was attacked by cholera.

ginians during the decade prior to the Civil War. Most striking is the overwhelming prevalence of tuberculosis among members of both races (see Tables 9a, b). Infectious diseases in general were much more significant causes of mortality than they are at present, with respiratory and gastro-intestinal conditions at the head of the list. It is interesting to note that old age, respiratory illnesses, and suffocation were listed as the cause of a much higher proportion of black than white deaths (see Figure 9), while the opposite was true of scarlet fever. Dropsy (accumulations of fluid in the abdominal, thoracic, and/or other body cavities) did account for more deaths among Negroes than among Caucasians, but the meaning of the data is uncertain because dropsy occurs secondary to underlying, primary conditions such as chronic vascular, respiratory, or liver disease which the data did not specify. The differential mortality due to accidents is perhaps best explained by the more dangerous jobs which many blacks performed in towns, on farms, and at industrial sites.

Diarrhea and dysentery in Augusta and Southampton counties caused proportionally almost twice as many Negro deaths as they did in Petersburg and Staunton. This variation did not hold true for Caucasians (see Figure 10) and may reflect the effect that rural concentrations of blacks living in unsanitary conditions in slave communities had on health. Place of residence seemed to have little effect on black mortality due to old age or respiratory ailments, but may have influenced the percentage of deaths from tuberculosis.

A major problem in using the census and registration figures is, as already discussed, reliability of data. This is most effectively that free blacks, because of their usually indigent economic status and low social positions, died at a higher rate than either slaves or whites. According to the 1850 federal mortality census returns slaves lead the list in Virginia, followed by freedmen and whites (see Table 8). Locally gathered statistics for all counties reporting to the state auditor in 1853, 1855, 1857, and 1858 indicate, however, that free blacks had a consistently lower mortality rate than either Caucasians or bondsmen. These differences can perhaps be explained as resulting from the inordinate number of free Negro cholera fatalities during the 1849 epidemic (see

Table 9a. Leading Known Causes of Death in Virginia, 1850 [1], by Race [3]

White (N=8,014)[4]	Percent	Slave (N=6,284)[4]	Percent	Free Black (N=558)[4]	Percent
1—Tuberculosis [5]	13.8	1—Respiratory diseases [6]	16.1	1—Cholera [11]	17.2
2—Respiratory diseases [6]	9.2	2—Tuberculosis [5]	10.7	2—Tuberculosis [5]	13.8
3—Nervous system diseases [7]	8.6	3—Nervous system diseases [7]	7.9	3—Respiratory diseases [6]	10.0
4—Diarrhea [8]	8.5	4—Old age	7.3	4—Old age	7.9
5—Scarlet fever [9]	6.9	5—Dropsy [10]	6.0	5—Dropsy [10]	7.5
6—Dropsy [10]	5.5	6—Typhoid [12]	5.7	6—Nervous system diseases [7]	6.5
7—Cholera [11]	4.9	7—Diarrhea [8]	5.5	7—Diarrhea [8]	5.9
8—Typhoid [12]	4.7	8—Cholera [11]	5.5	8—Accidents [15]	5.8
9—Old age	4.5	9—Accidents [15]	4.5	9—Typhoid [12]	2.9
10—Digestive system diseases [13]	4.5	10—Digestive system diseases [13]	3.2	10—Digestive system diseases [13]	2.5
11—Diphtheria [14]	3.5	11—Diphtheria [14]	2.3	11—Whooping cough	2.5
12—Accidents [15]	3.4	12—Suffocation [18]	2.2	12—Maternity [16]	2.0
13—Maternity [16]	2.1	13—Scarlet fever [9]	2.0	13—Worms	2.0
14—Measles	1.5	14—Worms	1.8	14—Teething	1.3
15—Whooping cough	1.4	15—Maternity [16]	1.8	15—Diphtheria [14]	1.1
16—Neoplasms [17]	1.2	16—Measles	1.6	16—Intemperance	1.1
17—Heart disease	0.8	17—Teething	1.5	17—Malaria [19]	0.7
18—Teething	0.8	18—Whooping cough	1.5	18—Scarlet fever [9]	0.7
19—Worms	0.8	19—Homicide	0.9	19—Measles	0.5
20—Erysipelas	0.7	20—Heart disease	0.6	20—Homicide	0.5
Fevers (unclassifiable) [20]	6.5	Fevers (unclassifiable) [20]	5.5	Fevers (unclassifiable) [20]	4.6

(See footnotes following Table 9b.)

Table 9b. Leading Known Causes of Death in Virginia, 1853–60 [2], by Race [3]

White (N=2,862) [4]	Percent	Slave (N=1,537) [4]	Percent	Free Black (N=221) [4]	Percent
1—Tuberculosis [21]	15.2	1—Respiratory diseases [23]	14.1	1—Tuberculosis [21]	20.4
2—Diarrhea [22]	12.9	2—Tuberculosis [21]	12.8	2—Diarrhea [22]	10.4
3—Respiratory diseases [23]	9.6	3—Diarrhea [22]	8.8	3—Nervous system diseases [24]	10.0
4—Nervous system diseases [24]	8.9	4—Nervous system diseases [24]	8.1	4—Respiratory diseases [23]	8.6
5—Digestive system diseases [25]	6.3	5—Old age	7.7	5—Old age	7.2
6—Typhoid [26]	5.0	6—Dropsy [30]	6.8	6—Dropsy [30]	6.8
7—Scarlet fever [27]	5.0	7—Typhoid [26]	6.2	7—Accidents [31]	5.9
8—Diphtheria [28]	4.9	8—Whooping cough	4.0	8—Whooping cough	5.4
9—Old age	4.6	9—Accidents [31]	4.0	9—Teething	4.5
10—Dropsy [30]	3.5	10—Digestive system diseases [25]	3.9	10—Digestive system diseases [25]	2.7
11—Accidents [31]	2.9	11—Diphtheria [28]	2.2	11—Intemperance	2.7
12—Maternity [32]	2.2	12—Measles	2.1	12—Homicide	1.8
13—Whooping cough	1.8	13—Maternity [32]	1.8	13—Maternity [32]	1.4
14—Heart diseases [33]	1.7	14—Teething	1.8	14—Typhoid [26]	1.4
15—Neoplasms [34]	1.4	15—Smothered [35]	1.4	15—Worms	1.1
16—Measles	1.3	16—Scarlet fever [27]	1.2	16—Diphtheria [28]	0.9
17—Intemperance	1.1	17—Heart diseases [33]	0.8	17—Rheumatism [36]	0.9
18—Teething	1.0	18—Rheumatism [36]	0.8	18—Female diseases [37]	0.9
19—Worms	0.9	19—Neoplasms [34]	0.7	19—Measles	0.5
20—Cholera	0.8	20—Urinary system diseases [39]	0.7	20—Smothered [35]	0.5
Fevers (unclassifiable) [38]	3.7	Fevers (unclassifiable) [38]	2.5	Fevers (unclassifiable) [38]	4.5

[1] Includes figures from the entire state. Compiled from mortality statistics of the Seventh Federal Census, 291–95.

[2] Includes figures for Petersburg (1858 missing), Staunton, Southampton County and Augusta County only. Compiled from Registers of Deaths for those localities, on microfilm at VSL.

[3] All figures are percentages of the total number of deaths for that race during the designated time period. Causes listed as "unknown" were excluded from the computations.

[4] The numbers in parentheses reflect the total number of deaths from all known causes for that race. Only leading causes are listed for each race.

[5] Consumption, scrofula.

[6] Asthma, bronchitis, catarrh, catarrhal fever, influenza, disease of lungs, pleurisy, pneumonia.

[7] Apoplexy, disease of brain, chorea, congestion of brain, convulsions, epilepsy, brain fever, inflammation of brain, insanity, neuralgia, paralysis, disease of spine.

[8] Cholera infantum, diarrhea, dysentery, summer complaint.

[9] Scarlet fever, disease of throat, quinsy.

[10] Dropsy, hydrothorax, ascites.

[11] Cholera, cholera morbus.

[12] Typhoid fever was referred to as typhus fever in the list of causes of death in the 1850 census.

[13] Disease of bowels, colic, cramp, dyspepsia, hernia, inflammation of bowels, inflammation of stomach, jaundice, disease of liver, piles, disease of stomach.

[14] Croup.

[15] Burns, drownings, scaldings, explosions, shootings, railroad, unspecified.

[16] Childbirth, puerperal fever.

[17] Cancer, tumor.

[18] Known now as crib death or Sudden Infant Death Syndrome (SIDS).

[19] Intermittent fever, remittent fever.

[20] Bilious fever, congestive fever, inflammatory fever, fever not specified.

[21] Consumption, tabes mesenterica, tuberculous meningitis, white swelling, scrofula, phthisis.

[22] Diarrhea, dysentery, flux, cholera infantum, summer complaint.

[23] Pneumonia, bronchitis, pleurisy, lung abscess, catarrh, catarrhal fever, affection of lungs, congestion of lungs, breast disease, bilious pleurisy, cold, hemorrhage of lungs, asthma.

[24] Hydrocephalus, convulsions, epilepsy, affection of brain, paralysis, congestion of brain, apoplexy, delirium, meningitis, nervous fever, brain fever, inflammation of brain, softening of brain, disease of head, water on the brain, spasms, injury of spine, neuralgia, affection of eyes, palsy, fits.

[25] Affection of bowels, bowel complaint, rupture, intussusception, ulceration, hemorrhage of bowels, congestion of bowels, appendix, affection of liver, bowel abscess, cramp, colic, peritonitis, vomiting, stricture of esophagus, dyspepsia, disease of stomach, gastritis, cirrhosis, jaundice, thrush.

[26] Continued fever, typhoid fever.

[27] Scarlet fever, affection of throat, putrid sore throat, ulcerated sore throat, quinsy, abscess of throat, laryngitis.

[28] Diphtheria, croup.

[29] Disease of kidneys, gravel, bladder disease.

[20] Dropsy, hydrothorax.

[31] Drowning, burns, falls, unspecified, railroad, gunshot, lightning, scalds, stabbings, choked on food, exposure, rats, strangled, suffocation.

[32] Childbirth, childbed fever.

[33] Affection of heart, rupture of aorta, aortic aneurysm, heart enlargement, palpitation of heart.

[34] Cancer, tumors.

[35] Smothered, overlayed, suffocation. Known now as crib death or Sudden Infant Death Syndrome.

[36] Inflammatory rheumatism, rheumatism.

[37] Affection of womb, prolapsed uterus, suppressed menstruation, hemorrhage of womb, dropsy of womb.

[38] Slow fever, cold fever, bilious fever, eruptive fever, typhus fever, congestive fever, congestive chill, bilious inflammation, chills.

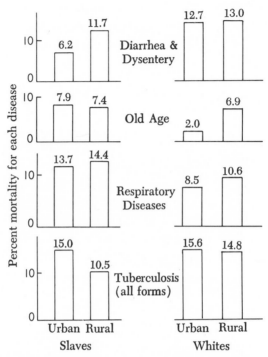

Figure 10. Mortality for Four Specified Causes among Whites and Slaves Living in Rural ᵃ and Urban ᵇ Areas of Virginia, 1853–60.
ᵃ Augusta and Southampton counties
ᵇ Petersburg and Staunton

Table 9a), and by extreme underreporting of free black deaths on the part of local officials between 1853 and 1858. Federal census and registration returns may inform us more about the isolation and anonymity of free blacks, the perseverance of the data-gathers, and the memories of the reporters than about the number of deaths that actually occurred. It is reasonable, then, to doubt the accuracy of much of the statistical data drawn from these returns, but not necessarily to question the broad generalizations made regarding disease categories.

As for morbidity rates, none can be calculated for specific diseases. What can be determined is the number of days lost from work due to illness for agricultural or industrial slaves where such records were kept. William D. Postell found a number of farm journals for the Lower South which enumerated time lost for illness. Fogel and Engerman tabulated Postell's numbers and reported that slaves on 15 Deep South plantations between 1825 and 1860 were absent from work about 12 days per year out of 2,274 man-years of labor time.[54]

Few such records have been located for Virginia plantations, though those that are available corroborate these findings (see Table 10). In addition, data for workers on a section of the James River and Kanawha Canal for 1854 and part of 1855, and for laborers at Paramount Furnace in Wythe County for several years during the 1830's, have been discovered (see Table 10, note). The average number of days lost per year at these two industrial sites was 5.8, though the range extended from 3.9 to 11.1.

[54] Postell, *Health of Slaves*, 148–50; Fogel and Engerman, *Time*, I, 126.

Table 10. Slave Time Lost from Work Due to Illness on Two Farms and at Two Industrial Sites in Virginia

	Date	Man-Years	Days ill	Days lost/ Man-Year
		Farms		
Humphrey [a]	1831	5	53	10.6
Cox [b]	1854	3	33	11
		Industries		
Canal hands [c]	1855	26.0	213.5	8.2
	1856	13.8	53.3	3.9
Furnace hands [d]	1830	11.1	72	6.5
	1831	15.0	166	11.1
	1833	20.0	137	6.9
	1834	20.3	129	6.4
	1835	13.5	139.5	10.3
	1836	17.6	84.5	4.8
Total Industrial		137.3	794.8	5.8

[a] Fountain Humphrey Farm Notebook, "Losstime of hands for 1831," p. 1, UVA (1623).

[b] Thomas Edward Cox Account Books, vols. I, VI, UNC.

[c] Slave Time Book, Paramount Furnace, Wythe County, Va., in Graham Papers, UVA (38–106).

[d] "Time Book for Gwynn Dam and Lock for 1855 and 6, George Roe" (James River and Kanawha Canal), in Austin-Twyman Papers, Folder 164, W&M.

In all statistical work with data as unreliable as those available for the early nineteenth century, extreme caution must be exercised. The calculations and tabulations presented above illustrate the problems.

CHAPTER 5

White and Black Medicine

As a result of their bondage, slaves were in a difficult position with regard to health care. When taken ill they had a limited range of choices. Most masters insisted that, as property, they immediately inform the person in charge when there was any sickness so the malady might be arrested before it worsened. But bondsmen, as people, felt reluctant to submit to the often harsh prescriptions and remedies of eighteenth- and nineteenth-century white medical practice. They preferred self-treatment or reliance on cures recommended by friends and older relatives. Many depended on Negro herb and root doctors, or on influential conjurers among the local black population. This desire to treat oneself, or at least to have the freedom to choose one's mode of care, came into direct conflict with the demands and wishes of white masters, whose trust in black medicine was slight and whose main concern was keeping the slave force intact.

To further compound the problem, unannounced illnesses did not entitle a bondsman to time off from work. To treat his own illness a slave had to conceal it or pass it off to the master as less serious than it actually was. Masters who complained that blacks tended to report sickness only after the disease had progressed to a serious stage often discovered that slaves had treated illnesses at home first. These bondsmen were not, as white Southerners frequently asserted, acting irresponsibly; they were simply declaring some independence. Did the master or overseer, slaves asked themselves, know any better than they did what was medically best? In that day of general reluctance to rely on the skills of a physician, could the whites in authority be trusted not to overdose, over-bleed, or over-purge from ignorance or error? Would it not be preferable to effect one's own cure—to take the responsibility for one's own life, rather than hand it over to another person? The blacks' dilemma, then, was whether to delay reporting illnesses and treat the diseases at home, risking white reprisal; or to submit at once to the medicines of white America and, in a sense, surrender their bodies to their masters. The result was a dual system in which some slaves received treatment both from masters and from black practitioners.

White Medicine—Home Care

When illness afflicted a slave, white Virginians responded in several ways. They almost always applied treatments derived from European experience. Most often the master, mistress, or overseer first attempted to treat the ailment with home remedies. If the patient failed to respond to these home ministrations, the family physician was summoned. Some slaveowners distrusted doctors and called instead "irregular" practitioners—Thomsonians, homeopaths, hydropaths, empirics, eclectics, etc. Masters who hired out their bondsmen to others for a period of time arranged for medical care when signing the hiring bond. Whatever the situation, Virginians often displayed concern for the health of blacks in bondage. The reasons were threefold: slaves represented a financial investment which required protection; many masters felt a true humanitarian commitment toward their slaves; and whites realized that certain illnesses could easily spread to their own families if not properly treated and contained.

Masters expressed their concern for ailing slaves in various ways. George Washington insisted, as did many other owners, that in times of sickness his bondsmen should "want for nothing" in the way of proper medicines and medical attendance.[1] Other

[1] George Washington to William Pearce, 17 April 1796, in Moncure D. Conway, ed., *George Washington and Mount Vernon*, in *Memoirs of the Long Island*

owners spent their own time nursing fieldhands or favorite servants back to health, occasionally even canceling social or business engagements in serious cases.[2] A few expressed their feelings about sick slaves in letters or diaries (though usually such thoughts were reserved for the death of a servant). Sallie Carter Randolph of Albemarle County, for example, lamented the severe illness of Davy in a letter to her daughter: "I feel so concerned for the poor fellow he bore such a high character." [3]

Others displayed more ambivalent feelings, since the illness of a slave also meant time lost from work. Upon hearing of the illness of a slave belonging to his friend Tom McLelland, Dr. B. H. Walker of King and Queen County wrote in his diary of his sympathy for Tom, as "she is the only *valuable* woman he has." The mistress of a large plantation declared, in the presence of a sick slave who would require constant attendance by a fellow bondsman during his convalescence, that the loss of these two hands constituted another in a series of severe *"set backs* in our [crop]" due to illness, from which she scarcely expected to recover. That she strictly obeyed the doctor's orders reflects both her need for the sick man's future labor and her human feelings about his well-being.[4]

Once they found slaves sick, some owners went to great extremes to effect cures. Landon Carter felt he had made a great sacrifice by visiting one of his ill female servants while he was still suffering from "colic" himself. He ordered that the woman be taken out for fresh air in Carter's own carriage because she was too weak to sit unaided on a horse. Mary Austin of Hanover

---

Historical Society, 4 (1889), 239. See also Socrates Maupin to Addison Maupin, 31 May 1849, Maupin-Washington Manuscripts, UVA (#2769a); James L. Hubard to Robert T. Hubard, 21 April 1851, Hubard Papers, UVA (#8039); Blanton, *18th Century*, 166.

[2] Thomas J. Randolph to John Hartwell Cocke, 15 February 1819, Shields Deposit; M. M. Robinson to Cocke, 20, 25 September 1820, Cocke Deposit; all in Cocke Papers, UVA.

[3] Sallie Carter Randolph to Isaetta Randolph Hubard, 1 March [1861], Randolph-Hubard Papers, UVA (#4717, 5885). See also John Walker Diary, 8 October 1853 (but also 15 March 1845), UNC.

[4] Dr. B. H. Walker Diary, 30–31 August 1858, VSL; W., "Contributions of a Country Doctor," *VMJ*, 8 (1857), 5.

County nursed an orphan slave girl back to health, developed "a strong and . . . lasting attachment for her," and finally petitioned the state legislature for her release from bondage.[5] During the nineteenth century the owners of at least eight Old Dominion slaves suffering from lung or rheumatic complaints saw fit to send them to take the waters at several of the exclusive mineral baths and springs which dotted the central and mountain portions of the state.[6] Others sent their ailing bondsmen to Richmond physicians with high reputations.[7] The novelist Elizabeth Meriwether carried this theme of white concern for slave health to absurdity (or perhaps to its logical conclusion) when she had a character in one of her novels about antebellum life attend medical school specifically to learn proper treatment for his bondsmen.[8]

Not all masters took a great interest in the maintenance of their slaves, however. One Virginia escapee to freedom, Henry Box Brown, scoffed at proslavery advocates who praised the virtuous slaveholder for providing good care to the sick: "In many instances the severe toils and exposures the slave has to endure at the will of his master, brings on his disease. . . ."[9] A recent medical historian of the Old South, Richard Shryock, echoed Brown's sentiment in a discussion of slave medical care. As a reason for supplying proper medical care to bondsmen, he asserted, "property interest has only a partial validity,—men have been known to neglect even their own live stock."[10]

---

[5] Greene, ed., *Carter Diary*, II, 996–97; petition of Mary Austin, Hanover County (#6922), Legislative Papers, VSL, quoted in James Hugo Johnston, *Race Relations in Virginia and Miscegenation in the South, 1776–1860* (Amherst, Mass., 1970), 17.

[6] [George E. Harrison,] "Slavery in Virginia: Extract from *Slavery in the United States*—by J. K. Paulding, being a letter to the author from a farmer of lower Virginia," *VMHB*, 36 (1928), 276; Thomas Pollard, "Observations on the Rockbridge and Bath Alum Springs," *Steth.*, 3 (1853), 150; Ulrich Bonnell Phillips, *Life and Labor in the Old South* (Boston, 1929), 247–48; John Spencer Bassett, ed., "The Westover Journal of John A. Seldon, Esqr., 1858–1862," *Smith College Studies in History*, 6 (1921), 306, 308.

[7] Carter P. Johnson, "A Report of Two Cases Illustrative of the Difficulty Occasionally Met With in the Diagnosis of Scrotal Tumors," *VMSJ*, 1 (1853), 11; Bassett, ed., "Westover Journal," 310.

[8] Cited in Weymouth T. Jordan, "Plantation Medicine in the Old South," *Alabama Review*, 3 (1950), 85.

[9] Henry Box Brown, *Narrative* (Boston, 1849), 25.

For those whites who took their responsibilities to sick slaves seriously, however, home treatment was the first step in the restorative process. Virginians recognized that physicians, though possessed of great knowledge of the human body and the effects of certain medicines on it, were severely limited in the amount of good they could perform. Because no one understood the etiology of most diseases, no one could effectively cure them. Astute nonmedical observers could make diagnoses as well as doctors, and could even treat patients just as effectively. Physicians played their most crucial roles in executing certain surgical procedures, assisting mothers at childbirth, and instilling confidence in sick patients through an effective bedside manner. At other times their excessive use of drugs, over-ready cups and leeches, and ever-present lancets produced positive harm in depleting the body of blood and nourishment and exhausting the already weakened patient with frequent purges, vomits, sweats, and diuretics. Laymen often merely followed the same course of treatment that they had observed their physicians using or that they had read about in one of the ubiquitous domestic medical guides. Anyone could practice blood-letting or dosing with a little experience. And a physician's services cost money, even when no treatment or cure resulted from the consultation. Why, then, argued heads of families and slaveowners, should we call for the aid of an expensive, often ineffective, professional, when we can attempt a cure ourselves (or use the local Thomsonian, homeopathic or botanical practitioner) for less money and the same or less risk of life? [11]

Among those who pondered this question was Thomas Jefferson. He held quite decided opinions on the efficacy of physicians and wasted no time in relating these thoughts to newly installed overseers. Dr. Steptoe's presence should be requested, he in-

---

[10] Richard H. Shryock, "Medical Practice in the Old South," *South Atlantic Quarterly*, 29 (1930), 175.

[11] This issue of the usefulness of eighteenth- and nineteenth-century physicians is a difficult one. Certainly they performed their services well enough to earn a living and to convince many patients of the necessity of professional care. Though limited by lack of knowledge in some areas, physicians could cure or relieve the symptoms of many diseases and conditions.

formed Jeremiah A. Goodman at Poplar Forest (Bedford County), only for diseases from which medical practitioners might provide "certain relief": pleurisy, malaria, dysentery, and venereal afflictions. But, Jefferson continued, "in most other cases they oftener do harm than good." Rather than waste money and time, he advised Goodman, administer salts—"they are . . . salutary in almost all cases, & hurtful in none"—a light diet, sugar or molasses, and "kind attention" to restore such Negroes to health. Other masters followed similar policies.[12]

Home care was not an innovation of eighteenth-century Virginians, but one that stemmed from man's natural instinct to relieve his own or his family's illness as quickly as possible. The unavailability of physicians, the inaccessibility of many farms to main highways, and the lack of good roads and speedy means of transportation reinforced such thinking among rural Virginians. Even when a doctor was summoned, hours or even a day passed before his arrival, during which time something had to be done to ease the patient's discomfort. People learned to tolerate pain and to cope with death more readily than twentieth-century Americans because both occurred so frequently, but the mitigation of suffering was still a primary goal. To that end most Virginians stocked their cabinets with favorite remedies (or the ingredients required for their preparation) in order to be well equipped when relief was demanded. On large plantations with many slaves this was a necessity, as Catharine C. Hopley, tutor at Forest Rill near Tappahannock, Essex County, noted: "A capacious medicine chest is an inseparable part of a Southern establishment; and I have seen medicines enough dispensed to furnish good occupation for an assistant, when colds or epidemics have prevailed." Some physicians made a living selling medicine chests and domestic health guides designed specifically for use on southern plantations. Self-sufficiency in medical care was desirable on farms and even in urban households, especially when financial considerations were important.[13]

[12] Thomas Jefferson to Jeremiah A. Goodman, Poplar Forest Memorandum, December 1811, in Edwin M. Betts, ed., *Thomas Jefferson's Garden Book, 1766–1824* (Philadelphia, 1944), 467. See also ——— to Mr. Cooke, 2 February 1848, Barker-Cooke Papers, folder 1, W&M; "Addressed to My Sons, R. T. Hubard, 1846," Hubard Papers, box 10, UVA (#8708); Blanton, *18th Century,* 169.

By the eighteenth and nineteenth centuries the medical armamentarium of disease-fighting drugs had become quite large and complicated, especially for those who prepared their own remedies. There were, however, certain favorites which slaveowners repeatedly ordered from suppliers or drug houses in the market towns. Calomel, castor oil, ipecac, jalap, laudanum, opium, camphor, and quinine led the list, though others had their uses and found their ways into many homes. Accessories such as lancets, spatulas, scales, blister powders and paper for plasters, cupping instruments, mortars, and syringes (injection, not hypodermic) were also important in the practice of domestic medicine. Of course no home was complete without a copy of Simon's *Planter's Guide and Family Book of Medicine,* Ewell's *Medical Companion,* or South's *Household Surgery,* all of which presented specific instructions on the treatment of many diseases, the proper dosages of drugs for each age group, the best uses for most medicines, and assorted miscellania of medical and agricultural importance (see illustration).[14]

Armed with quinine [15] and other drugs in the plantation or

[13] Landon Carter treated his slaves and often differed openly with the attending physician; e.g., Greene, ed., *Carter Diary,* I, 241, 242, 316. [Catharine C. Hopley,] *Life in the South: From the Commencement of the War* (London, 1863), I, 103, Mary Louise Marshall, "Plantation Medicine," *Bulletin of the Medical Library Association,* 26 (1938), 57; White Hill Plantation Books, I, 8, UNC.

[14] Lists of medicines ordered for plantations, homes, etc., may be found in Hubard Papers, receipts, UVA (#8708); Cocke Papers, receipts, UVA; City of Alexandria Papers, poor house and public dispensary, UVA (#7146); Hubard Family Papers, Account Book 1837–54, vol. 54, UNC; Graham-Robinson Ledgers, vol. 8, p. 1, UVA (#38–107); Madden Family Papers, account of Willis Madden with James R. Brown, 1848–52, UVA (#4120); Charles Gorgas to ———, 9 September 1859, Weaver-Brady Papers, UVA (#38–98); [William B. Randolph to Mr. Striker,] 18, 19 February 1850, Randolph Papers, LC; John Walker Diary, 22 November 1854 and passim, UNC. For a list of domestic medicine books, see ch. 1, n. 13.

[15] This was the most important medicine of the period. It had great effect both on the practice of medicine and on the existence of slavery, for without it malaria would have disabled the laboring population even more than it did. This drug and its predecessor, cinchona, both of which were used extensively in Virginia, saved slaveowners a fortune in time and money. For more on quinine in Virginia, see J. F. Peebles, "Original Views on the Nature and Varieties of Intermittent Fever . . . ," *Steth.,* 4 (1854), 267–68; Shryock, "Medical Practice in the Old South," 163; Randolph Harrison to John Hartwell Cocke, 12 October 1821, Cocke Deposit, Cocke Papers, UVA; L. Faulkner, "Sulphate of Cinchona Equal to Sulphate of Quinia in the Treatment of Intermittents," *VMJ,* 7 (1856), 293–97.

home dispensary, one person, usually white, had the responsibility of dosing and treating ill slaves. The master, mistress, or overseer spent time each day with those claiming bodily disorders and soon developed a certain facility in handling both patients and drugs. The approach was empirical—if a particular medication or combination of drugs succeeded in arresting symptoms, it became the standard treatment for that malady in that household until a better one came along. Overseers and owners inscribed useful medical recipes into their diaries or journals and clipped suggestions from newspapers, almanacs, and books. The medical sophistication of men like Landon Carter and Robert Hubard rivaled that of their family physicians, at least with regard to the use of drugs.[16]

The plantation overseer found himself in the unenviable position of having to produce as much labor as possible from the slaves under his command, using punishment when necessary, and at the same time of having to care for slaves' illnesses and protect them from exposure, exhaustion, and accident. He was taskmaster, judge, and physician simultaneously—a tremendous and sometimes impossible responsibility. A set of printed instructions for farm managers, published in Richmond during the 1850's, listed the overseer's medical obligations to his slaves. He should be able to determine fevers by pulse, distinguish the intensities of fevers, differentiate one disease from another by its symptoms, apply the correct palliatives in proper amounts for each type of disease or disorder, bleed and cup patients as necessity dictated, and refer to suitable medical guides on proper occasions. The overseer was expected, the directives continued, to attend the sick each morning and as often during the day as the case required. Though he could assign certain duties to a reliable nurse, ultimate responsibility for care rested with him. To facilitate matters, farm proprietors were to provide overseers with a medical library containing books on popular medicine, and a well-stocked medicine chest. Woe to the young overseer who

<hr>

[16] Stampp, *Peculiar Institution,* 316; interview of Baily Cunningham, 14 March 1938, WPA Folklore File, UVA (#1547); "Cure for Dysentery," 12 October 1821, Cocke Deposit, Cocke Papers, UVA; Cure for Chronic Cough in "1855 Richmond Receipts," Hubard Papers, box 5, UVA (#8708).

CATHARTICS, or active Purges—such Medicines as purge out the Bowels briskly.

	FOR A GROWN PERSON.	FOR A CHILD FROM 5 TO 7 YEARS OF AGE.	HOW MANY TIMES A DAY.	IN WHAT TO BE TAKEN.
ALOES—of the extract of Spiked,	8 to 10 grains.	3 to 4 grains.	Once or twice a day.	In pills.
Of the powder,	6 to 8 grains.	3 to 4 grains.	2 or 3 times a day.	Pills, or with sugar.
Of the tincture,	1 to 4 teaspoonfuls.	2 teaspoonfuls.	3 or 4 times a day.	In sugar and water.

Good for costiveness and worms. Aloes are used, also, with calomel and rhubarb, three to four grains in each powder, given three or four times a day, to force the courses when stopped.

COMMON ALOES— (Barbadoes Aloes):				
Of the powder,	15 to 20 grains.	6 to 8 grains.	Once or twice a day.	Pills, or with sugar.
Of the extract,	10 to 15 grains.	5 to 6 grains.	Once or twice a day.	In pills.

Good for obstinate costiveness.

GAMBOGE.

CALOMEL:	5 to 6 grains.	3 to 4 grains.	Twice a day.	In sugar or syrup.

Good for costiveness, biliousness, and a great many complaints. There is, perhaps, no medicine more generally useful than this.

CASSIA (pulp).

COLOCYNTH—powder:	8 to 10 grains.	4 to 5 grains.	Every 3 hours, until it acts freely on the bowels.	In sugar.

Good for costiveness (habitual).

How to bleed.—Let the patient sit up in the bed, or in a chair; make the arm which you are going to bleed from bare. Tie a piece of list or broad tape, by winding it three or four times around the arm, just above the elbow joint, moderately tight, but not so tight as to stop the pulse of that arm. Next, feel the vein in the hollow of the elbow, below the bandage, to try if it has swelled out, and feels tight, grasp the arm with your left hand, and keep your thumb pressed upon the vein, just below where you are going to stick it. Next, hold your lancet in your right hand, and let the point touch the middle of the vein, just above the thumb which is on it. Now push it firmly and steadily into the vein; taking care not to move your thumb, and not to let the point of the lancet go too

straight or too deep down, for you may cut through the other side of the vein; but cut from you upward. A small cut just allowing the point of the lancet to go into the vein is generally sufficient. As soon as you take off your thumb, the blood flies. When you have taken enough, generally from a pint to a pint and a half from a strong grown person, untie the bandage and take it off, then double a small piece of linen rag into four, and put it on the cut; tie the bandage round the arm, over this rag, not too tight.

Part of a List of Useful Remedies, and Instructions for Bloodletting, from *Planter's Guide and Family Book of Medicine*, by John Hume Simons (Charleston, 1849), 31, 204–5.

did not have an experienced slave nurse to assist him the first year![17]

The cardinal rule of home medical care was, "Know Thy Limitations." Overseers realized that plantation owners did not want to pay large doctor bills; nor did masters respond very affably to news of a slave's death from disease. Nathaniel Ryan was a farm manager imbued with the spirit of domestic treatment. He insisted on caring for the sick slaves on Edmund Hubard's Saratoga estate in Buckingham County until the last possible moment, bragging to his employer one cold January that, despite frequent illnesses on the farm, "I have managed all the cases myself without the need of a physician." Six months later Hubard's brother Robert confirmed that Ryan did indeed refrain from requesting professional assistance, even when others felt he should have done so: "Today I rode over to Saratoga. All of your negroes were well except Nancy (your cook) who was quite sick last night, but was today much better and able to walk about. Mr. Ryan said she was not sick enough to need any physician even last night." Nancy's recovery may have been the result of the treatments Ryan had administered and perhaps could have been retarded by a doctor's hand, but Robert Hubard felt that Ryan did not have due regard for the precept regarding knowledge of the limits of one's own expertise.[18] Some overseers were more cautious. When Isham Cheatham, manager of an estate in Henrico County, noticed that the lesion on Liddy's shoulder worsened rather than healed under his care, he admitted his ignorance to Colonel John Ambler and suggested that her condition was more serious than previously suspected: "I think there is something

---

[17] "Instructions to Managers," in *Plantation and Farm Instruction, Regulation, Record, Inventory and Account Book, for the Use of the Manager on the Estate of   , and for the Better Ordering and Management of Plantation and Farm Business in Every Particular, by a Southern Planter* (Richmond, 1852), 5, 6, 11. See ch. 3, n. 19, for locations of this volume. Franklin, "Rules for Overseers," *FR*, 8 (1840), 231, advised managers to visit the sick three times during the day and once at night. See also William K. Scarborough, *The Overseer: Plantation Management in the Old South* (Baton Rouge, 1966), 84–86.

[18] Nathaniel H. Ryan to Edmund W. Hubard, 21 January 1841, and Robert T. Hubard to Edmund W. Hubard, both in Hubard Family Papers, UNC; "Addressed to My Sons, R. T. Hubard, 1846," Hubard Papers, box 10, UVA (#8708).

more Wanting to be done to her sore than I know what to do, as I think it verry probable it may be a cancer." [19]

The overseer's incompetence or negligence was the slave's loss. New and inexperienced farm managers, unskilled in the treatment of illness, necessarily used bondsmen as guinea pigs for their on-the-job training. As a consequence of living on the wrong plantation at the wrong time, same slaves probably lost their lives or became invalids at the hands of newly hired, poorly trained, or simply inhumane overseers.

When the owner was present and willing, he took over as chief medic of the household. He faced the same problems as a novice overseer but may have received previous training from others on the farm. Slaves had no assurance, however, that their master was more adept at treating illnesses than an overseer was—or, for that matter, more sensitive to their needs. Landon Carter often visited and administered medical assistance to his bondsmen, but he also sometimes neglected them or placed too much reliance on his slave assistant, Nassau, an alcoholic who frequently shirked his duties. In addition, on some slaves Carter used harsh drugs which he refused to prescribe for his own family. During an epidemic of "bilious fever" he administered rattlesnake powder (*Polygala senega*) to his bondsmen and their offspring. Though the drug helped, it also produced severe, prolonged sweating, "great discharges of urin," and other untoward side effects which led him to state in his diary, "I wish my own fears did not prevent my giving it to my Children," who were also sick. Charles Grandy, a former slave, recalled in 1937 that his master treated a deep knife wound to the elbow with chimney soot (to stop the bleeding), and then put the arm in a sling. It soon became permanently deformed.[20] One practice through which owners may have knowingly caused suffering, injury, and even death was that of not summoning a physician early in the course of a disease. Both overseers and owners adhered to this policy with untold consequences. For some diseases home treatment probably worked as

[19] Isham Cheatham to Colonel [John] Ambler, 16 May 1829, Ambler Family Papers, UVA, (#1140).

[20] Greene, ed., *Carter Diary*, I, 131 (20 October 1756); interview of Charles Grandy, 26 February 1937, in George P. Rawick, ed., *The American Slave: A Composite Autobiography* (Westport, Conn., 1972), Virginia Narratives, XVI, 22.

well as the doctor's remedies, if not better; in others it was positively deleterious. When no physician was available, planters were certainly justified in relying on their own resources to bring the patient through a medical crisis.

Men did not hold exclusive rights to the care and treatment of sick slaves. The woman of the household, usually the slaveowner's wife or daughter, also tendered aid to the ill in her capacity as superintendent of domestic affairs. Post-Civil War Virginians have tended to over-romanticize her role and her sacrifices as nurse, though she did, like the master, often devote much time, thought, and energy to the condition of blacks. One writer eulogized the mistress as "heroine" of the plantation and "Lady with the Lamp"; another recalled that her "mother and grandmother were almost always talking over the wants of the negroes . . . the principal objects of their lives seeming to be in providing [slaves with] these comforts." [21]

These larger-than-life portraits possess much truth which modern historians have tended to pass over because the pictures appear so exaggerated. Whether or not she was, as one recent women's historian has put it, "chief medical officer," is not as important as the fact that she frequently administered medical assistance to both the white and black households. Masters and overseers were not always willing to spend time at this task, nor could they easily leave the fields or places of business to check a patient's condition several times a day. Overseers' wives should not be ignored, either, especially when their husbands managed the plantations of absentee owners. Their duties included, according to one widely used set of instructions, maintenance of Negro health and comfort, attendance upon the infirm, supervision of the care of slave children, and prescription of medicine to those requiring it. [22]

Two former Virginia slaves described, in the 1930's, their

[21] Victor H. Bassett, "Plantation Medicine," *Journal of the Medical Association of Georgia*, 29 (1940), 118; Letitia M. Burwell, *A Girl's Life in Virginia before the War* (New York, 1895), 7. See also Thomas Nelson Page, *Social Life in Old Virginia before the War* (New York, 1897), 41.

[22] Anne Firor Scott, *The Southern Lady: From Pedestal to Politics, 1830–1930* (Chicago, 1970), 36; *Plantation and Farm Instruction Book*, 5.

memories of two women's nursing skills. Baily Cunningham, who had been owned by a family of German descent near Rocky Mount, Franklin County, remembered that his mistress "had three kinds of medacine that would cure everything." Vinegar nail, a drink resulting from the combination of one pound of iron nails left overnight in a jug of vinegar, cured aches and pains in the stomach or back when taken with two rosin pills (the second home remedy) prepared from raw pine rosin. The third restorative, useful for tooth or ear aches, consisted simply of filling the tooth or ear with tar. Cunningham, who did not mention the mortality rate on the farm, claimed that his mistress never called a doctor. Sister Harrison lived as a child in Portsmouth, where her mother was hired out daily. Her mistress cared for two slave children quite conscientiously, especially during Sister Harrison's recovery from burns sustained in a fall into a hot grate.[23]

When women expressed themselves in writing on the subject of slave care, it was usually negatively or ambivalently in a letter to a friend or an entry in a personal diary. "Our Negroes have all except Billy have been sick, I realy am quite tired of mixing and giving physick," wrote a Williamsburg lady to her brother in Boston. Susan Hubard complained to her husband Robert, in Richmond on business, that she had been engaged all morning "seeing to cloth & weighing out physic &c." Two sisters living in different parts of Virginia penned letters one month apart to their mother in Campbell County. In one case the writer described how an epidemic of "bilious fever" among the slaves had disrupted her household routines, "for I can get no one to help me"; the other exclaimed, "I had my time so much occupied with sick negroes that I scarcely knew what to be at." [24]

[23] Interviews of Baily Cunningham and Sister Harrison, WPA Folklore File, UVA (#1547).

[24] J[udith] P. Galt to Dr. A. D. Galt, 22 October 1810, Galt Family Papers (Personal), reel 1 (microfilm), CW; Susan P. Hubard to Robert T. Hubard, 22 September 1846, Randolph-Hubard Papers, UVA (#4717, 5885); Mary Watts to Mrs. Mary Watts, 18 November 1823, and Alice Watts Saunders to Mrs. Mary Watts, 15 December 1823, both in Irvine-Saunders Papers, UVA (#38–33). See also diary of Louisa H. Cocke, 13–16 October 1830, 9, 23–25 May, 10 June, 15 July 1833, Cocke Deposit, Cocke Papers, UVA; John Walker Diary, 3 October 1846, UNC; James L. Cabell, "Etiology of Enteric Fever," *Transactions of the American Medical Association*, 28 (1877), 423.

An additional feature of Virginia slave medical care was the plantation hospital. Its form varied from farm to farm and probably existed on only some of even the largest slaveholdings in the state. The number of such infirmaries is difficult to determine because few owners made note of them in their letters or records. One can safely assume that a plantation with a slave nurse or medical assistant was likely also to have a slave hospital or unit in which to isolate the unwell. On large estates it was quicker and more efficient to place ailing slaves in one building, where care could be tendered with a minimum amount of wasted movement and where all medicines, special equipment, and other necessary stores could be maintained. Of course, infectious diseases could spread quite rapidly through a hospital, subjecting those with non-contagious conditions to further sickness. Farms containing fewer than five or ten slave dwellings in one central area probably did not require a hospital, though some had them. This institution appears to have been less common in Virginia than in the Deep South, where holdings were generally larger. Among those Virginians who built slave hospitals on their farms were Landon Carter (Sabine Hall, Richmond County), George E. Harrison (Brandon, Prince George County), and George Washington (Mount Vernon, Fairfax County). Other planters referred in journals or letters to sick slaves "in the house," an expression which may have meant a hospital, a portion of a farm building near the quarters, or the master's house itself.[25]

Those in charge of black health often met with one problem which challenged their skills both as managers and as healers: malingering. Large slaveowners and employers believed themselves to be experts on this subject. They developed the attitude that if a slave complained of illness he was acting like "a true negro in being always 'poorly'" to escape work. This placed masters in the ticklish situation of having to decide when a slave

[25] Greene, ed., *Carter Diary*, I, 141, 388, II, 662, 664, 793; "A Peek at the Old Dominion," *American Turf Register and Sporting Magazine*, July 1832, reprinted in *VMHB*, 36 (1928), 206; [Harrison,] "Slavery in Virginia," 279; Phillips, *Life and Labor*, 312; Blanton, *18th Century*, 168; Thomas L. Dicken to Col. John Ambler, 25 January 1826, Ambler Family Papers, UVA (#1140); White Hill Plantation Books, 4 April 1845 and passim, UNC.

was crying wolf and when he was truly ill. A Georgia physician, H. A. Ramsay, claimed he never had difficulty detecting pretended sicknesses among blacks: "The negro is prone to dissemble and feign disease; probably no race of human beings feign themselves ill so frequently, and are so incapable of concealing their duplicity." Some Virginians could not have agreed less with Dr. Ramsay's assessment. William Pearce, George Washington's Mount Vernon overseer during the presidential years, had great difficulty distinguishing between the slaves' real and feigned illnesses. The President's Negroes had become masters of fraud in his absence, causing Washington, who always kept up with affairs at Mount Vernon, to label Betty Davis, the worst offender, a "lazy, deceitful and impudent huzzy" whose equal "is not to be found in the United States." Right through to the Civil War masters and overseers continually scratched their heads and made remarks such as: "We are all well Excep Betsey of amherst She still Complains of a pain in the hip I have not Bin able to find out wheather She is desitfull or not." [26]

There was an art to feigning sickness, and slaves learned it early. Common stomach complaints or general malaise did not usually work, for the medicines given often made a person sicker. Charles Grandy remembered in 1937 how, some eighty years earlier, he had pretended to be ill when the overseer detected him sleeping in the cornfield: "When you gits sick, dey give you some kin' o' medicine called ipicac. . . . Dey make me take dat an' I got sick den sho' 'nough. Got so sick I hadda go to bed. Stayed

[26] Socrates Maupin to Addison Maupin, 31 May 1849, Maupin-Washington Manuscripts, UVA (#2769a); H. A. Ramsay, *The Necrological Appearance of Southern Typhoid Fever in the Negro* (Thompson, Ga., 1852), 14; George Washington to William Pearce, 8, 22 March 1795, in Conway, ed., *Washington and Mount Vernon*, 170, 175–76; James T. Gibson to Philip St. George Ambler, 17 July 1828, Ambler Family Papers, UVA (#1140). For other examples of malingering, see [Jane H. Randolph] to Peggy Nicholas, 14 November 1826, Edgehill-Randolph Papers, UVA; Levi R. Clark to Philip St. George Ambler, 24 [January] 1828, Ambler Family Papers, UVA (#1140); Susan P. Hubard to Robert T. Hubard, 8 March 1843, 22 September 1846, Randolph-Hubard Papers, UVA (#4717, 5885); Francis A. Buford to John Buford, 7 July 1855, Buford Papers, Duke; John Walker Diary, 24 June 1848, 22 March 1851, 31 March 1855, UNC; "Acct of days work of Masons at Buckingham Iron Works," 21 April 1835, Cocke Deposit, Cocke Papers, UVA; William W. Rex to Daniel Brady, 21 December 1859, Weaver-Brady Papers, UVA.

dere three or four days too. So I got clear o' dat whippin." James L. Smith, a slave in Lancaster County who later escaped, had, by the age of ten or so, learned all the tricks. He disliked the job of shooing crows from the cornfield, but he knew that if he acted sick "they will give me something that will physic me to death." In addition, if he complained of a stomach ache his mistress would "make me drunk with whiskey," an experience which, he previously learned, incapacitated him and angered his owners. Smith finally hit upon the scheme of pretending to have severely injured his leg. To make the effect even more realistic, he ate less and remained in his room most of the time. When a fieldhand informed him, two weeks later, that the crows had left the cornfield for the now ripening cherries, Smith "began to grow better very fast." [27]

Malingering often succeeded in excusing a slave from work, but it also endangered the health of all working Negroes. When serious illness did strike, the overseer, master, hirer, or physician could not always believe what the patient said. Slaves were, after all, dependent upon whites for medical care. Most had no wish to die, and they often had to rely on the white man's belief that a particular symptom or disease was serious enough to warrant professional treatment. Malingering only added to the problem of diagnosis and remedy. Dr. W. H. Taylor, called to treat a forty-year-old "healthy looking" Negro blacksmith in "cataleptic condition," illustrates the point. He remembered that "simulation was a characteristic of his [the patient's] race" and therefore "made a rigid examination, the result of which convinced me that there was no deception attempted." In this case, the patient received immediate treatment, though he died anyway. Other slaves could not convince those in charge that they were sick. One strong young fieldhand complained to his master for a week or ten days; nevertheless, a physician later related, he could not "induce the master to think anything serious was the matter with him." He died of typhoid fever shortly thereafter. The same was true of William, a Richmond tobacco factory hand who jumped

<hr/>

[27] Interview of Charles Grandy, 18 May 1937, in WPA Folklore File, UVA (#1547); James Lindsay Smith, *Autobiography of James L. Smith* (Norwich, Conn., 1881; reprinted New York, 1969), 21–24 (see also 9–10).

twelve feet from a platform to escape punishment and later died of a severe concussion. For two full days Dr. Pollard believed the man "was practicing deception." He even visited William at night, unannounced, "thinking I might probably find the mask thrown off, and my patient walking about, or enjoying himself with friends." Only then, when he found William still in bed and sicker than ever, did he begin "to look on the case as serious." Perhaps the patient couldn't have been saved anyway, but malingering among slaves did have its detrimental aspects.[28]

White Medicine—Practitioner Care

One of the certificates of death, written by a "physician of large practice," received at the City Inspector's reads as follows: "Mrs. Karolyne Johnson's dawther aged five months and ate days died with defishency of life to-day under my attendance."—*Lynchburg Virginian*, 8 January 1857, p. 3.

Clearly, slaveowners knew of and used alternative measures to care for their sick bondsmen and did not place their reliance entirely on local medical doctors. Their habit of resorting to the physician only at the last minute, or when all home remedies had failed, did little to endear owners to neighborhood practitioners. How was a man whose reputation and very financial existence depended entirely upon successful treatment of patients to react when the subjects of his trade were so frequently moribund upon his arrival? Robert Carter of Nomini Hall, Westmoreland County, was a prime offender. In one 1787 note requesting Dr. Timothy Harrington's assistance he listed the names of five sick slaves (one of whom "I expect will die in a few hours"), the natures of their illnesses, and the course of treatment Carter had pursued to that point. On another occasion Carter wrote to the doctor: "I do not wish to continue practice any longer on Peter—and I now deliver him over to you." This type of attitude infuriated members of the medical establishment. In the 1850's,

[28] W. H. Taylor, "Case of Catalepsy," *VMJ*, 7 (1856), 51–52; Charles William Ashbury, "On the Pathology and Treatment of Typhoid Fever," *VMSJ*, 4 (1855), 36; Thomas Pollard, "Report of a Case of Hemiplegia, Attended with Ramollissement, Probably the Result of Concussion," *VMJ*, 11 (1858), 347.

when slaveowners complained to Dr. Thomas J. Garden of Wylliesburg, Charlotte County, about his poor cure rate in cases of pneumonia, he angrily countercharged that the planters were at fault. If they would learn to call in physicians earlier, he argued, they would better ensure recovery of their human chattel.[29]

Despite many masters' rather cavalier handling of the established medical profession, there were times when they desperately wished for the doctor's presence. More practitioners should have retained in their files the numerous hastily scrawled notes from frantic slaveowners begging for medical assistance, or kept a record of each verbal summons to a sick slave at a distant farm or village household. For physicians did play important roles, both physiological and psychological, in the treatment of illness. Dr. Charles Brown of Charlottesville, for instance, had a thriving country practice during the early nineteenth century. He handled many types of problems: James Old wanted him to determine whether his slave woman, then "in a strange way," was pregnant or not; Bezaleel Brown needed his opinion "if I must bleed her [Jane, who had a pain in her side and suppression of urine] either large or small in quantity"; and Jemima Fretwell wished Brown to "cutt of[f] the arm" of a four-month-old slave which had been "so very badly burnt" that "the [elbow] joint appears like it will drap of[f]." [30] Sometimes physicians made daily visits to dress slaves' wounds or to keep track of household epidemics. In emer-

---

[29] Robert Carter to Dr. Timothy Harrington, 12 January 1787; Carter to Dr. Walter Jones, 24 January 1787; Carter to Harrington, 30 ———— (n.d.); all in Robert Carter Letterbooks, Duke; J. B. Garden, "Pneumonia," *Steth.*, 5 (1855), 3. For other statements regarding the slaveowner's reluctance to call in a physician, see Greene, ed., *Carter Diary*, I, 213; Stampp, *Peculiar Institution*, 316; Robert Q. Mallard, *Plantation Life before Emancipation* (Richmond, 1892), 33–34; L. S. Joynes, "Remarks on the Report of the Auditor of Public Accounts to the General Assembly of Virginia, Relative to the Registration of Births, Marriages, and Deaths," *VMJ*, 7 (1856), 7; Walter Fisher, "Physicians and Slavery in the Antebellum Southern Medical Journal," *JHM*, 23 (1968), 41–42; Bassett, "Plantation Medicine," 120.

[30] James Old to Dr. Charles Brown, n.d., folder 3; Bezaleel Brown to Dr. Charles Brown, n.d., folder 1; both in Brown Papers, W&M. There are many more examples to be found in this fascinating collection.

gencies some owners panicked and fretted away many hours after learning of their physician's temporary absence.[31]

Between the remedies of the household and the standard treatments of the physician stood "irregular" medicine, often as important but only partially accepted in Virginia. Alien systems of medical care generally did not gain popularity in the United States until the 1820's or later, though individual quacks and informally trained practitioners had provided care to many since the seventeenth century. Aside from these men, however, useful alternative approaches to allopathic (regular) practice rooted themselves and blossomed only about the time of President Jackson. Most important for slaves in Virginia were the Thomsonians and homeopaths.[32]

The main virtue of most irregular health systems was their relative harmlessness, especially when compared with traditional approaches. Homeopathy, developed in Europe by the German Samuel Hahnemann during the 1790's and brought to this country about 1825, used as its motto the Latin phrase *similia similibus curantur*—that is, a small dose of the drug which produces symptoms most similar to the disease being treated will cure that disease. Thomsonians (adherents to the system devised by a New Hampshire farmer turned medical proselytizer, Samuel Thomson) eschewed harsh drugs in favor of herbal and vegetable emetics and tonics. Hydropaths (water therapists) were equally innocuous. But certain so-called empirics, who practiced medicine as they traveled and learned as they practiced, could seriously

[31] See, e.g., Dr. Frank Carr to Thomas Jefferson, 18 March 1816, Carr-Cary Papers, UVA (setting bones); Edmund Wilcox Ledger, Hubard Family Papers vol. 13, UNC (setting bones, frequent visits, etc.); Martin B. Coyner, Jr., "John Hartwell Cocke of Bremo: Agriculture and Slavery in the Ante-Bellum South" (Ph.D. dissertation, University of Virginia, 1961), 137 (frequent visits to a few slaves); Robert Wellford Diary, 20 February 1814, Wellford Family Papers, UVA (#3682) (trepanning slave's head); Petersburg *Daily Express*, 21 November 1859, p. 1 (operation for club foot); Judith Hale to Miss Sarah Watts, 17 July 1820, Irvine-Saunders Papers, UVA (#38–33) (doctor not at home in emergency); diary of Louisa H. Cocke, 23 May 1833, Cocke Deposit, Cocke Papers, UVA (doctor not available until late in the day).

[32] For a survey of nineteenth-century medical sects in Virginia, see Blanton, *19th Century*, 193–203. James O. Breeden, "Thomsonianism in Virginia," *VMHB*, 82 (1974), 150–80, provides an excellent in-depth study of the most popular system.

harm patients. Regular physicians, in their own way, caused more mischief than their less accepted counterparts, as they blistered, purged, puked, poisoned (mercury in calomel, for example), and exsanguinated their patients to further sickness or death. While the irregulars knew just as little as the allopaths and thus did as poor a job of removing the true causes of illness from the body, they at least permitted enough substance to remain for natural defenses to attempt to attack the disease.[33]

In 1847 Carter P. Johnson, a physician, published a report in the *Transactions of the American Medical Association* enumerating the regular and non-diploma-holding medical practitioners of seventy-five Virginia counties and towns. One-third (294 of 972) of the "doctors" had never received diplomas, at least thirty followed the Thomsonian system, and one adhered to homeopathic tenets.[34] These statistics sent shudders down the spines of many allopaths. Thomsonianism, which advocated that every man be his own physician, was undoubtedly even stronger than these numbers indicated.

The impact of alternative movements on the medical care of blacks in Virginia was greater than historians have recognized. Most slaveowners either treated with conventional medicines or called in regular doctors, rejecting the new cults as quackery; but a sizable minority, difficult to estimate, became enthusiastic proponents of at least one system—Thomsonianism. This movement, with practitioners in areas with heavy slave concentrations (64 percent of the Tidewater counties and 66 percent of the Piedmont counties during the 1830's and 1840's) appealed to masters who were fed up with the ineffective and expensive treatments of their regular physicians. One Tidewater resident turned to Thomsonianism after experienced Norfolk physicians had un-

[33] Excellent summaries of Thomsonianism, homeopathy, and other nineteenth-century medical systems may be found in William G. Rothstein, *American Physicians in the Nineteenth Century: From Sects to Science* (Baltimore, 1972), 125–74. See also Martin Kaufman, *Homeopathy in America: The Rise and Fall of a Medical Heresy* (Baltimore, 1971); Alex Berman, "The Impact of the Nineteenth Century Botanico-Medical Movement on American Pharmacy and Medicine" (Ph.D. dissertation, University of Wisconsin, 1954).

[34] Carter P. Johnson, "Report of the Number of Practitioners of Medicine in Virginia," *Transactions of the American Medical Association*, 1 (1848), 362–64.

successfully managed a household scarlet fever outbreak. All twenty cases, the happy slaveowner reported to the editors of a Thomsonian journal, had been cured. Another man, in Goochland County, stated that a local Thomsonian practitioner had cured his slave of a disease which one of the most respected regular physicians of the area had found intractable to the usual blister and salivation treatments. And a Prince Edward County Thomsonian doctor claimed to have cured a ten-year-old slave who had been suffering from rabies (a misdiagnosis, no doubt). With adherents to the sect so widely diffused throughout the state, the services or success stories of practitioners no doubt reached at least a portion of the slaveholding class and influenced its thinking.[35]

Alva Curtis, an important figure in the national Thomsonian movement, got his start during the 1832 Richmond cholera epidemic by treating his own and his neighbors' servants. Some slaves, fearing retribution for taking medicines not sanctioned by their masters, convinced Curtis to administer the drugs secretly. This he did under the assurance, probably well founded, "that my medicine could do no harm." As Curtis's reputation spread, he became the leading Thomsonian in the state. The infirmary which he ran in Richmond, accommodating both black and white patients, remained in existence for several years after his departure for Ohio in 1834. Other infirmaries in Petersburg and Norfolk had similar admission policies.[36]

Typical of the slaveowners who espoused Thomsonianism was John Walker of King and Queen County. As a small farmer and slaveholder Walker had always relied on his own good judgment for most health complaints, and on a trained physician for matters

---

[35] "The Thomsonian Practice," *Thomsonian Recorder*, III (22 November 1834), 57; "To the Editor," *ibid.*, 56–57; "To the Editor," *ibid.* (20 December 1834), 81–84; all cited in Breeden, "Thomsonianism in Virginia," 158, 161.

[36] Breeden, "Thomsonianism in Virginia," 167; *Richmond Enquirer*, 15 October 1833, p. 3; 4 December 1834, p. 2; 19 June 1838, p. 4; 14 July 1846, p. 2; John Walker Diary, 4 February 1837, UNC; *Thomsonian Recorder*, II (26 April 1834), 239–40. Ebenezer Pettigrew, a North Carolina planter, sent his ten-year-old slave girl, Nicey, to Dr. Thomas Nash's Infirmary in Norfolk for rheumatic pains; see Bennett H. Wall, "Medical Care of Ebenezer Pettigrew's Slaves," *Mississippi Valley Historical Review,* 37 (1950), 463–64.

beyond his ken. But he found that neither his own nor his doctor's knowledge, skill, and experience always effected cures, so Walker occasionally resorted to outside assistance. Midwives delivered his wife's and his slaves' children, and "Doctor Lewis," an old black man in an adjoining county, treated two of his bondsmen when all else had failed. Then one day Walker decided to try the Thomsonian system at the urging of local agent Thomas M. Henley. For his $23.87½ the new convert received Thomson's *New Guide to Health,* membership in the neighborhood "Friendly Botanical Society" (which probably held occasional meetings), and the right to purchase genuine Thomsonian medicines. It cost Walker another $1.87½ for these drugs, purchased from nearby Society member William Watts. Armed with the six basic medicines of the system,[37] he commenced his practice. Walker had the assurance that any Friendly Society member would come to his assistance whenever necessary, without charge.[38] He become a fierce proponent of botanical medicine, subscribing to the movement's journal, the *Thomsonian Recorder,* sending his incurably sick slave William (who was scrofulous) to the Thomsonian Infirmary and several Thomsonian doctors in Richmond, attending the 1835 national convention in Richmond, faithfully using Thomsonian medicines through the 1850's, long after the movement had declined, and insisting that his slave Daniel, hired out in Richmond annually, be treated solely by Thomsonian doctors. "The Tompsonian practice," he wrote shortly after the Richmond convention in 1835, "is fast gaining ground and may the Lord hasten on the day that it will overspred the Earth as the waters the great deep." [39]

[37] No. 1, the emetic, lobelia, cleansed the stomach and promoted free perspiration; No. 2, cayenne pepper, dissolved in sweetened hot water, restored lost internal heat; Nos. 3 and 4, various teas and tonics prepared from herbs, roots, barks, etc., restored the proper functioning of bile and digestive system; Nos. 5 and 6, brandies and wines fortified with these same natural ingredients, further strengthened the internal system and the weakened patient.

[38] John Walker Diary, 30 June 1826, 1, 5 June 1833, 3, 17 May, 7, 27 June 1834, including accounts for 1833 and 1834, UNC; Rothstein, *Physicians in the Nineteenth Century,* 132, 139–40.

[39] Walker's diary contains innumerable references to Thomsonian medicine. See esp. the financial statements at the close of each volume (typescript), his remarks on the Thomsonian convention (16 November 1835), his encounters with Rich-

Despite their efforts, slaveowners, overseers, and regular and irregular physicians failed to satisfy the health care needs of Virginia's slave population. Though a Virginia medical historian has pointed out that "wealthy masters demanded the best medical attention for their slaves and were willing to pay well for it," the best was often not good enough. And though some doctors bragged, as did R. Burton of Albemarle County, that they rarely lost a single Negro patient, the majority could not make such a statement.[40] Medical knowledge in antebellum Virginia was, as for the rest of the nation, quite poor except for a few specific diseases and conditions.

Black Medicine

Beyond the master's and overseer's eyes, back in the slaves' cabins, some Virginia blacks took medical matters into their own hands. When under the surveillance of whites, slaves usually (but not always) accepted their treatments. Some even administered them in the name of the master. But others developed or retained from an ancient African heritage their own brand of care, complete with special remedies, medical practitioners, and rituals. The result was a dual system of health care, the two parts of which constantly conflicted with each other.

Masters did not appreciate slaves overusing the plantation infirmary, medicines, or the family doctor, but they preferred this to black self-care for several reasons. Their quarrel with the bondsmen was the same as the physicians' with the masters: slaves waited too long before seeking medical assistance and often misdiagnosed illnesses. Most owners were willing to permit blacks a small amount of freedom to treat minor ailments at home, but lost their patience when the sickness got out of hand. James

mond and Chesterfield County Thomsonians who tried to cure the slave William (4 February, 6 March, 18 May, 4, 11 July, 5 October 1837, 27 December 1838, 11 April 1839), his insistence on Thomsonian doctors for the hired Richmond slave Daniel (1 January 1838, 29 December 1846, and at the start of each year), his wife's refusal of Thomsonian medicines (late September 1845), and his use of the drugs during a cholera epidemic (9 June, 29 September 1849).

[40] Blanton, *18th Century*, 166; Dr. R. Burton to Wilson Cary Nicholas, 24 December 1813, Nicholas Papers, UVA (#2343).

L. Hubard, in charge of his father's lands during the latter's vacation at Alleghany Springs, reported that Daphny had treated her own son with vermifuges (worm medicines) for several days before realizing that the boy was suffering not from worms but from dysentery. He quickly altered the medication and summoned a doctor, blaming the entire affair on "the stupidity of Daphny." An enraged Landon Carter found a suckling child with measles at the slave quarters. "The mother," he wrote in his diary, "let nobody know of it until it was almost dead." [41]

Whites also accused slaves of negligence or incompetence in the care of their fellow bondsmen. Dr. G. Lane Corbin of Warwick County, for instance, promoted the use by slaves of collodion, a syrupy dressing, because it required so little attention once applied: "This I consider of moment in regard to our slave population, whose negligence and inattention to such matters [as the proper dressing of wounds] must have attracted the notice of the most superficial observer." Negroes frequently were charged with irresponsibility, ignorance, slovenliness, and indifference in the management of other blacks' illnesses. "They will never do right, left to themselves," declared one Franklin County planter. [42]

Furthermore, some whites argued, slaves did not even care for their own personal health properly. Recovery was retarded and even reversed, Dr. W. S. Morton of Cumberland County remarked, "by their [slaves'] own stupid perversity in refusing confinement to bed, and to follow other important directions when in a very dangerous condition." Masters and physicians often confirmed this but were powerless to combat it. It was difficult for whites, unless they were present at all times, to force ailing blacks to take medicines or to remain constantly in bed. A most spectacular instance of death following defiance of medical orders occurred in Portsmouth when a black male patient of Dr.

[41] James L. Hubard to Robert T. Hubard, 4 August 1857, Hubard Papers, UVA (#8039); Greene, ed., *Carter Diary*, II, 812 (20 May 1774).

[42] G. Lane Corbin, "Collodion on Stumps of Amputated Limbs," *Steth.*, I (1851), 489; L. G. Cabell to Bowker Preston, 8 October 1834, Hook Collection, UVA (#145). See also Greene, ed., *Carter Diary*, I, 194 (slaves overfeed their children), II, 865 (woman neglects children's health during frequent sexual escapades).

John W. Trugien, confined to bed with a stab wound of the heart, sustained a massive effusion of blood from that organ upon exerting himself by rising from his pallet.[43]

To offset the failures and harshness of white remedies, or the negligence of masters, and, most important, to exert some control over their lives, slaves frequently treated their diseases and disorders or turned to other trusted blacks for medical assistance, with or without the master's knowledge. Charles Friend permitted his Negro women to lose workdays to care for their sick children, a practice which other planters no doubt also followed. Some mothers took advantage of a good thing, however, and raised masters' suspicions. George Washington warned his overseer, William Pearce, to investigate carefully one young man's supposed illness, noting that the youth's mother had once nursed him three months for a minor wound. At other times whites allowed their bondsmen to care for very old or infirm spouses and relatives. However, in regular illnesses among the majority of slaves, planters expected to be informed and involved in the treatment.[44]

Yet black home remedies circulated secretly through the slave quarters and were passed down privately from generation to generation. Most of these cures were derived from local plants, though some medicines contained ingredients which had superstitious value only. Occasionally whites would learn of a partic-

[43] W. S. Morton, "Causes of Mortality amongst Negroes," *Mon. Steth.*, 1 (1856), 290; John W. H. Trugien, "A Case of Wound of the Left Ventricle of the Heart.—Patient Survived Five Days;—with Remarks," *AJMS*, NS 20 (1850), 99–102. See also L. G. Cabell to Bowker Preston, 8 October 1834, Hook Collection, UVA (#145); Green, ed., *Carter Diary*, II, 649 (slave won't stay in bed), II, 942, 943, 993, 994 (slave won't take medicine); John Walker Diary, 14 June 1834 (slave won't take medicine), UNC.

[44] White Hill Plantation Books, 23 June 1851, 29 November 1852, 2 June 1854, 4 August 1856, 6 October 1859, UNC; George Washington to William Pearce, 14 September 1794, in Conway, ed., *George Washington and Mount Vernon*, 109. For examples of black care of infirm and aged relatives, see Thomas Childs to Colonel John Ambler, 19 May 1822, Ambler Family Papers, UVA (#1140); Robert Riddick Papers, pp. 37–44 (Jemmy and Mingo), UVA (#2227); J. R. Anderson to Willis Clayton, 5 February 1846, Tredegar Papers, Letterbook, VSL; Hez Ford to [James E. Cooke], 18 March 1851, Barker-Cooke Papers, W&M; H. C. Bruce, *The New Man: Twenty-nine Years a Slave, Twenty-nine Years a Free Man* (York, Pa., 1895; reprinted, New York, 1969), 60.

ularly effective medicine and adopt it, as when Dr. Richard S. Cauthorn announced in the *Monthly Stethoscope* that an old folk remedy which had been used for years by blacks in the counties north of Richmond worked almost as well as quinine for agues and fevers.[45] Otherwise most whites simply ignored or tolerated the black medical world until something occurred to bring their attention to it—either a great medical discovery or a slave death caused by abuse.

Because blacks practiced medicine in virtually every portion of the Old Dominion and because their methods were based partially on superstition, problems occasionally arose. The main source of trouble was usually not the misuse of home remedies, but the "prescriptions" and activities of so-called conjure doctors. These men and women used trickery, violence, persuasion, and medical proficiency to gain their reputations among local black communities. They were viewed as healers of illnesses which white doctors couldn't touch with their medicines, and as perpetrators of sicknesses on any person they wished—all through "spells." The tradition, explains one Negro historian of the origin of black medicine, was inevitably transferred to the Americas, since conjuration had been "the prevailing practice . . . in Africa." It established itself in the West Indies, where obeah men gained control over the people of their locales through fear, superstition, and injury. Those who suddenly took sick often believed that enemies had engaged conjure doctors to cast spells on them. Slaves brought these traditions with them to the North American colonies, where they again became firmly rooted among the superstitious.[46] Practitioners of the art of conjuring still operate profitable businesses in some parts of the South today.[47]

[45] Richard S. Cauthorn, "A New Anti-Periodic and a Substitute for Quinia," *Mon. Steth.*, II (1857), 7–14. A most interesting compilation of black family remedies was presented to me in 1973 by Miss Amaza Lee Meredith, Box 10, Virginia State College, Petersburg, Va. 23806.

[46] Kelly Miller, "The Historic Background of the Negro Physician," *JNH*, I (1916), 101; James Thomson, *A Treatise on the Diseases of Negroes, As They Occur in the Island of Jamaica: With Observations on the Country Remedies* (Jamaica, 1820), 9–10; Ramsay, *Necrological Appearance*, 15.

[47] See, e.g., Ed McTeer, *The High Sheriff to the Low Country* (Beaufort, S.C., 1971); Wilbert C. Jordan, "Voodoo Medicine," in Richard Allen Williams, ed., *Textbook of Black-Related Diseases* (New York, 1975), 716–25.

Root doctors and conjurers have usually been associated with blacks of the Lower South. But they also practiced in Virginia from at least as far back as 1729, when Governor Gooch emancipated a slave for revealing his secret cure for venereal disease and yaws. By 1748 so many blacks claimed to be doctors—some falsely, in order to procure and prepare poisons against their masters or enemies, both black and white—that the colonial legislature prohibited all slaves, on pain of death, from administering medicines without the consent of the owners of both the "doctor" and the prospective black patient. This law was modified in 1792 to permit acquittal of those slaves who administered medicines with good intention, provided the drugs had caused patients no harm. At least two slaves were brought before the courts and convicted for violations of this law, a male in 1794 and a woman in 1823. There is no record of the punishment meted out to the first offender; the second had her death sentence commuted to sale and transportation from Virginia. The laws never effectively curtailed the activities of black practitioners, however; evidence of their work, both legal and illicit, exists for the entire colonial and antebellum periods.[48]

Robert Carter, among other planters, recognized that black doctors sometimes produced better results than white practitioners, and he willingly sent at least one of his slaves to David, owned by William Berry of King George County, for treatment. Guy, who had been languishing for the previous eighteen months under Carter's care, now, in July 1786, was "very desirous of becoming a Patient of Negroe David." Carter, therefore, consented to "his going up to yr house to be under the care & direction of David." He expected Guy to remain several days for the black doctor to "observe the operation of the first [dose of] medicine," and afterward to return home with the appropriate drugs. Carter himself had owned a Negro—Tom, his coachmen —who had treated slaves throughout the neighborhood in the

[48] Charles Kemper, comp., "Documents Relating to the Boundaries of the Northern Neck, from the Originals in the British Public Records Office," *VMHB*, 28 (1920), 306; Blanton, *18th Century*, 173–74; Virginia, *The Revised Code of the Laws of Virginia . . .* (Richmond, 1819), I, 427; Ulrich B. Phillips, "Slave Crime in Virginia," *AHR*, 20 (1915), 336–40; Virginia; General Assembly, *Acts of Assembly, 1842–43* (Richmond, 1843), 60.

1770's. One white man reported that "the Black people at this place [Taurus farm] hath more faith in him [Tom] as a Doctor than any white Doctr." Benjamin Harrison of Berkeley Plantation also owned a slave doctor (female), while several other eighteenth century planters occasionally employed them according to law.[49]

These black practitioners may have been conjure doctors, or empirics well versed in herb and root medicines. Details of their associations with both whites and blacks are lacking. David and Tom had won the confidence of local slaves and, it appears, at least the approval of their masters. This may indicate that the type of medicine they practiced was acceptable to whites or that slaveowners, when desperate to save the lives of valued servants, were even willing to try mystics. Although Landon Carter is a good source of information on most subjects for this period, he is strangely silent on the matter, perhaps because he and his slave medical assistant, Nassau, never required another black practitioner, and his bondsmen never requested one.

Our information on nineteenth-century root and charm doctors is somewhat fuller. Much of the power which conjurers held over slaves was psychological rather than physical. Henry Clay Bruce, writing after his emancipation from slavery, recalled the remarkable influence these men had over his superstitious acquaintances in Prince Edward County: "There have been cases where Colored people took sick from some cause, and imagined themselves tricked or poisoned by some one, and the white doctor, unable to do them any good, gave up the case, and the patients believing themselves poisoned and therefore incurable, have died, when they might have been saved, if the white doctor had only . . . announced himself a conjurer, and proceeded to doctor the patient's mind." Bruce described one old, white-haired, crippled man who "claimed to be able to do many mysterious and impossible things." When his master moved from Virginia to Missouri, those who lived on the new plantation "believed and feared"

[49] Robert Carter to William Berry, 31 July 1786, Robert Carter Letterbooks, Duke; Louis Morton, *Robert Carter of Nomini Hall: A Virginia Tobacco Planter of the Eighteenth Century* (Williamsburg, Va., 1941), 115; Blanton, *18th Century*, 173.

him; nevertheless, others in the neighborhood "denounced him as an old humbug." [50]

Superstition was a powerful force within the slave community, and a difficult one for white non-adherents to understand or overcome. For instance, the older brother of a slave patient of Dr. A. D. Galt of Williamsburg observed to the doctor that his medicines were useless because Gabriel "had been tricked" and "must have a Negro Doctor" to reverse the progress of the illness. Galt soon claimed to have cured the man, though he did admit that Gabriel suffered frequent relapses, "probably from intemperance in drink." In another case, a slave woman took sick and eventually died on a plantation near Petersburg from what her fellow bondsmen believed were the effects of a conjurer. Some slaves speculated that the young man whom she had refused to marry "poisoned or tricked" her, though the overseer attributed her death to consumption. Virginia Hayes Shepherd, a former slave interviewed at age 83 in 1939, described an incident to illustrate how superstitious her stepfather had been: "He believed he had a bunch something like boils. White doctor bathed it. After a few days it burst and live things came out of the boil and crawled on the floor. He thought he was conjured. He said an enemy of his put something on the horses back and he rode it and got it on his buttocks and broke him out." [51]

Black doctors treated many cases of "poisoning" after white doctors had given up. James L. Smith, who grew up in Lancaster County and later escaped to the North, once found his father extremely ill, the poisoning victim of a jealous female slave. His master, William Guttridge, sent for the family physician, who failed to improve the slave's condition. In desperation, Guttridge took another servant's suggestion and hastened ten miles to see an old Negro doctor. This man consulted his cards, correctly explained who had poisoned Smith's father and why—it was a woman whom he had displaced from a position of power within

[50] Bruce, *New Man*, 57, 58.

[51] [A. D. Galt,] *Practical Medicine: Illustrated by Cases of the Most Important Diseases*, ed. John M. Galt (Philadelphia, 1843), 295–96; [William McKean to James Dunlap,] 17 July 1810, Roslin Plantation Records, VSL; interview of Virginia Hayes Shepherd, WPA Folklore File, II, 2, UVA (#1547).

the plantation slave hierarchy—and supplied Guttridge with a bottle of medicine which soon produced a complete recovery. John Walker, who later turned to Thomsonianism, also used a black doctor when all else had failed. His servant Jack had been confined to the house for about two months with severe ocular pains and near-blindness resulting from, they both agreed, poisoning. Doctor Fauntleroy treated Jack for four or five weeks and succeeded only in worsening the condition. As a last resort they decided to send him to an old slave named Lewis, who claimed it was possible to cure Jack. Six weeks later Lewis, who resided across the Mattaponi River in King William County, returned Jack to his master, his sight as good as ever, with instructions to continue taking the herb decoction for several weeks more. Lewis's fee—$10. Incidentally, despite this success with Jack, Walker refused to allow another of his slaves, whom he hired out annually in Richmond, to be treated by black practitioners.[52]

Several of Thomas Jefferson's slaves received medical aid from black doctors, though sometimes with disastrous results. In 1800 Martha Jefferson Randolph reported that Jupiter conceived himself poisoned; the slave consulted one Negro man after his master's drugs had failed to relieve the symptoms. The black physician gave him a dose which he said "would kill or cure." With this suggestion planted firmly in his mind, Jupiter soon fell into a convulsion which lasted for ten or eleven hours. He died after languishing silently for nine days. Within the previous six months two other slaves belonging to Jefferson had perished at this doctor's hand, and a fourth was now showing similar symptoms. "I should think," exclaimed Mrs. Randolph to her father, "his [the black physician's] murders sufficiently manifest to come under the cognizance of the law." Jefferson's Poplar Forest (Bedford County) overseer discovered similar problems among the slaves there in 1819. Joel Yancey learned that Hercules had been obtaining medicines from a local black doctor for the past year, and had, in administering them, caused several deaths and much

[52] Smith, *Autobiography of James L. Smith*, 5–6; John Walker Diary, 25 March, 1, 5 June, 19 July 1833, 30 December 1844, UNC.

illness on the plantation. Slaves had concealed this information from Yancey, no doubt out of fear of the conjurer. When apprised of the situation, however, the local authorities could do nothing under the law; the doctor had not supplied the drugs with any ill intent, nor could anyone prove that those medicines had produced the ill effects reported. Jefferson had to acquiesce in the verdict.[53]

Though most white physicians did not appreciate the competition from root doctors or the abuses which conjurers sometimes perpetrated on slaves, a few were willing to accept their positive contributions. New additions to the white materia medica from slave practitioners were occasionally publicized in professional journals, and lives were saved when white physicians called in black doctors to treat "conjure" cases.[54] Usually, however, black medicine remained discreet and undercover.

Though barred by white law but not by tradition or society from practicing medicine or dispensing drugs, blacks did fulfill certain medical functions legally. Some planters assigned certain "trusted" slaves to the task of rendering medical assistance to all ailing bondsmen on the farm.[55] In most cases, these blacks simply dispensed white remedies and performed venesection and cupping as learned from the master. This was not complete black self-care, but did represent a transitional stage in which Negroes had the opportunity to apply some of their own knowledge of herbs,

[53] Martha Jefferson Randolph to Thomas Jefferson, 30 January 1800, in Edwin M. Betts and James A. Bear, eds., *The Family Letters of Thomas Jefferson* (Columbia, Mo., 1966), 182–83; Joel Yancey to Thomas Jefferson, 1 July 1819, in Betts, ed., *Thomas Jefferson's Farm Book* (Princeton, 1953), 44; Thomas Jefferson to Mr. Clay, 9 August 1819, Edwin L. Stone Manuscripts, UVA (#2117).

[54] Morton, "Causes of Mortality amongst Negroes," 290; Blanton, *18th Century*, 173; Alexander Somervail, "Cases of Negro Poisoning," *AJMS*, 24 (1839), 514–16; interview of Virginia Hayes Shepherd, WPA Folklore File, II, 2, UVA (#1547); Cauthorn, "A New Anti-Periodic," 7–9.

[55] References to plantation nurses may be found in Blanton, *18th Century*, 175; [Harrison,] "Slavery in Virginia," 279; Robert Carter to Dr. Timothy Harrington, 12 January 1787, Carter Letterbooks, Duke; Thomas Jefferson to Joel Yancey, 25 June 1819, in Betts, ed., *Thomas Jefferson's Farm Book*, 44; Andrew Nicol, "Notes on the Sandy Point Estate," *FR*, 9 (1841), 215; Bassett, ed., "Westover Journal," 301 (19 October 1859); "List of Slaves at the Oxford Iron Works," William Bolling Papers, Duke.

etc., gained from elders, in addition to white remedies. These nurses, predominantly women, usually won the respect of both blacks and whites for their curative skills. "Uncle" Bacchus White, eighty-nine-year-old former slave interviewed in Fredericksburg in 1939, attested: "Aunt Judy uster to tend us when we uns were sic' and anything Aunt Judy could'nt do 'hit won't wurth doin." A white lady writing at about the same time provided a similarly romantic view of the black plantation nurse: "One of the house-servants, Amy Green—'Aunt Amy' we children called her—was a skilled nurse. My father [Charles Friend, White Hill Plantation, Prince George County] kept a store of medicines, his scales, etc. so with Aunt Amy's poultices of horse-radish and plattain-leaves and her various cuppings and plasters the ailments of the hundred negroes were well taken in hand." Given such high testimony and devotion from plantation folk, one could hardly dispute the novelist Louise Clarke Pyrnelle's depiction of Aunt Nancy, a fictional antebellum household nurse who claimed, while dosing several young slaves, "Ef'n hit want fur dat furmifuge [vermifuge—worm medicine], den Marster wouldn't hab all dem niggers w'at yer see hyear." [56]

A handful of town-dwelling slaves also acquired and practiced nursing skills both within and without the household. One such woman, Jensey Snow, became a living legend in her home town of Petersburg. On 15 January 1825 Benjamin Harrison manumitted his bondswoman "for . . . several acts of extraordinary merit performed . . . during the last year, in nursing, & at the imminent risk of her own health & safety, exercising the most unexampled patience and attention in watching over the sick beds of several individuals of this town." He further expressed the belief and desire that Jensey "continue, whenever occasion shall require to perform similar acts equally meritorious & praise-worthy." True to her master's prediction, the freedwoman opened a hospital in Petersburg and continued serving the public need.

[56] Interview of Uncle Bacchus White, WPA Folklore File, II, 6, UVA (#1547); White Hill Plantation Books, I, 8, UNC; Louise Clark Pyrnelle, *Diddie, Dumps, and Tot; or Plantation Child-Life* (New York, 1882), quoted in Blanton, *18th Century*, 49.

More than thirty years later the local newspaper printed reports describing operations performed by physicians "at the Hospital of the well known nurse, Jincey Snow." [57]

Some town-dwelling free black barbers and other Negroes who learned the skills became leechers and cuppers or tooth-pullers. These people served all ranks of society from the richest whites to the poorest blacks. One Richmond resident presented an intriguing portrait of a father and son who practiced both professions:

Now-a-days [1856] the profession of dentistry gives lucrative employment in our city to a score of practitioners. In the days of my boyhood, only one Tooth-drawer, who probably never heard the word dentist, did all the work and all the mischief in the dental line.

Peter Hawkins was a tall, raw-boned, very black negro who rode a raw-boned, black horse, for his practice was too extensive to be managed on foot, and he carried all his instruments, consisting of two or three pullikins, in his pocket. His dexterity was such, that he has been known to be stopped in the street by one of his distressed brethren, (for he was of the church), and to relieve him of the offending tooth, gratuitously, without dismounting from his horse. His strength of wrist was such, that he would almost infalliby extract, or break a tooth, whether the right or the wrong one. I speak from sad experience, for he extracted two for me, a sound and an aching one, with one wrench of his instrument.

On Sundays he mounted the pulpit instead of black barebones, and as a preacher he drew the fangs of Satan with his spiritual pullikins, almost as skillfully as he did the teeth of his brother sinners on week days, with his metallic ones.

Peter's surgical, but not his clerical mantle, fell on his son, who depletes the veins and pockets of his patients, and when he has

---

[57] Petersburg Deed Book, 7 (1821–26), 267 (15 January 1825), VSL; Petersburg *Daily Express*, 21 November 1859 (p. 1), 15 December 1857 (p. 1). Luther Porter Jackson, *Free Negro Labor and Property Holding in Virginia, 1830–1860* (New York, 1942), 191, refers to her as Jane Minor. He states that Joseph Jenkins Roberts, future President of Liberia, "married a Petersburg free woman, Ginsey Snow, the daughter of a well-known nurse" (p. 378). Arthur, an Alleghany County slave who had nursed his master faithfully during a long illness, petitioned the state legislature in 1835 for the freedom his master had promised but neglected to include in his will. Legislative Petitions, 28 December 1835, Alleghany County, VSL.

exhausted the latter, the former are respited. The doctor dismisses himself, and as likely as not, carries the malady with him.[58]

To Negro women often fell another legally acceptable task: prenatal and obstetrical care of whites and blacks, especially in rural areas. Midwifery was an art which at least one slave on most large Virginia plantations learned and practiced, not only at home but also throughout the neighborhood. Masters preferred to employ these skilled accouchers in uncomplicated cases rather than pay the relatively high fees of trained physicians.[59] Doctors, remarked one member of the medical profession, attended at less than half of all births in the state. He estimated that nine-tenths of all deliveries among the black population (another physician set it at five-sixths) were conducted by midwives, most of whom were also black. He further asserted that midwives attended half the white women. Physicians often saw obstetrical cases only when problems arose. As a result of this demand for competent non-professional obstetrical services, Negro accouchers flourished in the countryside.[60]

Slave as well as free black midwives delivered both white and black children, and occasionally Caucasian women attended the labors of Negroes. Mildred Graves, living in Fredericksburg in 1939, remembered bringing many youngsters into the world during her years as a slave midwife in Hanover County:

[58] Samuel Mordecai, *Richmond in By-gone Days; Being Reminiscences of an Old Citizen* (Richmond, 1856), 274–75. See also Miller, "Historic Background of the Negro Physician," 102–3; [Galt,] *Practical Medicine*, 206–7; Jackson, *Free Negro Labor and Property Holding*, 142, 165. Jackson (p. 165n) refers to Henry Boyd of Petersburg as a free black physician, though the source he cites for this information (Petersburg Will Book, III, 17) makes no mention of his occupation. The University of Virginia Library owns a manuscript account book (#2120) of Phebe Jackson, a leecher and cupper residing in Petersburg, which runs from 1843 to 1854. Internal evidence suggests that she was a free Negro. Joe McIntosh, a former judge of Liberia's Superior Court, returned to Virginia to become superintendent of the baths at White Sulphur Springs in 1859 (Petersburg *Daily Express*, 30 August 1859, p. 2).

[59] Doctors usually charged $5-20, while midwives charged only $1-3. See, for examples of doctors' bills, Holladay Family Papers, 19 June, 4 December 1843, VHS; and Bohannan Ledgers, p. 58, VSL.

[60] Blanton, *18th Century*, 174–75; Joynes, "Remarks on the Report of the Auditor," 7; C. R. Palmore, "Observations on the Condition of the Obstetric Practice of Virginia," *Steth.*, 1 (1851), 483.

You know in dem days dey didn't have so many doctors. So treatin' de sick was always my job. Whenever any of de white folks 'roun' Hanover was goin' to have babies dey always got word to Mr. Tinsley dat day want to hire me for dat time. Sho' he lef me go . . . 'twas money fo him, you know. He would give me only a few cents, but dat was kinda good of him to do dat. Plenty niggers was hired out an' didn't get nothin'. Sometimes I had three an' four sick at de same time, Marser used to tell me I was a valuable slave. Dey use to come for me both day an' night—you know it's a funny thing how babies has a way of comin' heah when it's dark.[61]

Other masters also secured extra cash or credit by hiring out female servants to local people during their confinements.[62] Some freedwomen earned livings as midwives. Lizzie Purdie, emancipated upon the death of her owner, would have been compelled by law to leave Virginia had not many residents of Isle of Wight County petitioned the state legislature for special consideration. "She is useful," they explained, "in serving sick persons, and especially among ladies."[63]

Deliveries did not always progress smoothly, and it was the midwife's responsibility to recognize her own limitations. When she did not, masters, husbands, and physicians complained, causing the woman to lose her good reputation and (if she was free) perhaps her means of livelihood. Entries in a planter's diary such as "injured by Acoucheur" could be particularly damaging to a lay practitioner of obstetrics. Those like the Halifax County midwife who summoned a physician when her patient's placenta was not expelled after childbirth, thus protecting themselves by

---

[61] Interview of Mildred Graves, WPA Folklore File, I, 2, UVA (#1547).

[62] "Extracts from the Diary of Francis Taylor, of Orange County, Va.," 4 March 1788, 25 July 1786, 2 February 1792, 3 September 1797, 24 January, 20 March 1799, in Blanton, 18th Century, 411, 412, 415, 417; Robert Carter to Presly Self, 22 December 1785, Robert Carter Letterbooks, Duke; E. W. Hubard to Mrs. M. S. Eppes (receipt), 13 October 1859, Hubard Family Papers, box 13, folder 167, UNC; Robert Hubard to Sarah Tulcher (receipt), 1846 (n.d.), Hubard Papers, box 1, UVA (#8708a). This collection contains many more examples of both white and black midwives delivering slave children.

[63] Petition of Lizzie Purdie, 28 January 1839, Legislative Petitions, Isle of Wight County, VSL. Free Negro midwives are also mentioned in Thomas J. Wertenbaker, Norfolk, Historic Southern Port (Durham, N.C., 1962), 93; and Jackson, Free Negro Labor and Property Holding, 82, 99.

taking no unnecessary risks, maintained thriving practices. Some, however, were too timid and lost the respect of their employers anyway. Landon Carter's slave midwife, for instance, took alarm during the labor of a fellow bondswoman; thinking the child dead, she had Carter engage Dr. Mortimer's assistance. The girl, it appeared, was in false labor, and Carter blew up because "Mortimer . . . got a fee of me which he should not have had." [64] Such were the dangers of midwifery.

Blacks did play a significant role in the health care system of the Old Dominion. They legally assisted whites and blacks in delivering children, letting blood, pulling teeth, administering medicines, and nursing the sick. The techniques and drugs they used were overtly derived from white medical practices. But unknown to masters, overseers, health officers, or physicians, blacks frequently resorted to their own treatments derived from their own heritage and experience. Occasionally the white and black medical worlds merged or openly clashed, but usually they remained silently separate.

[64] Account of Joseph Hawkins with Dr. D. Flournoy, 8–14 September 1824, in Blanton, 19th Century, facing p. 99; L. Faulkner, "Cases from My Notebook and Memory," VMJ, 6 (1856), 462–64; Greene, ed., Carter Diary, I, 514 (19 October 1770). Other examples of doctors being called in emergency situations may be found in William H. Ammons to William B. Randolph, 14 September 1833, Randolph Papers, LC; Thomas K. Clarke to Dr. [Charles] Brown, 31 August 1814, Brown Papers, W&M.

CHAPTER 6

Care of Urban and Industrial Slaves, the Aged, and Free Blacks

Medical Care off the Master's Farm

Slaves living in towns or rural industrial sites stood in somewhat different medical positions from their plantation brethren. Unless they somehow learned of and made contact with local black practitioners—an unlikely occurrence for recently hired slaves laboring, for instance, on a public works project, at a mine or at an iron forge in the Blue Ridge—isolated industrial slaves probably had less freedom to treat their own illnesses than did slaves in the cities. Some industrialists and town masters oversaw the health of their charges more closely than others, but those who permitted slaves to live and eat as they wished in Richmond, Petersburg, Norfolk, Alexandria, and the even smaller Piedmont towns had little control over how bondsmen chose to care for their illness.

There is ample evidence in the form of physicians' account books and masters' medical bills to show that, as in the countryside, nineteenth-century urban slaves were often treated by white doctors. Owners undoubtedly employed favorite home remedies in less urgent cases before summoning a professional, thereby subjecting blacks to the drugs and practices of the white medical world. But it must also be supposed that a second, less organized, black medical establishment existed in cities with growing Negro populations like Richmond, Norfolk, and Petersburg, where many blacks had great freedom of movement and little close supervision of their activities. We possess, unfortunately, little proof that such *sub rosa* operations actually functioned in antebellum Virginia towns. One thing we do know is that in addition to the public leechers, cuppers, nurses, and midwives, at least a few black doctors did treat others of their race. John Walker refers to the presence of these practitioners in Richmond in a letter to a free Negro cooper who wished to hire his slave Daniel in 1844: "In case of sickness you must employ Docr Robinson to attend Daniel as I am not disposed to employ a Colored Docr to attend him." [1] The implication is that James Sims, the hirer, would otherwise have called in a black physician to treat Daniel's illnesses. Except for this information, and the knowledge that Negro doctors existed in the countryside, we know little about the urban Virginia black medical world.

Non-agricultural slave-hiring was an important aspect of the peculiar institution. Each January large numbers of bondsmen traveled from their rural homes to cities or industrial sites to begin a year of labor in a new environment. Because this type of hiring often involved the transfer of blacks to distant locations, the problem of supervision in general and health care in particular became a problem. How could a master in Louisa County rest assured that his slaves, hired to work at an iron forge in Rockbridge County or a tobacco factory in Petersburg, were receiving adequate medical attention? Laws, traditions, and written contracts spelled out the rules, but hirers did not always live up to them.

One might first raise the question, how concerned were owners with the health and safety of their hired bondsmen in a distant town or farm? The motives of masters who demanded higher rates and paid-up life insurance policies in return for leasing slaves to dangerous public works projects, rather than insisting on better safety precautions or simply refusing to hire them out, are cer-

---

[1] John Walker to James Sims, 30 December 1844, copy in John Walker Diary, UNC.

tainly suspect.[2] The number of slaves who worked at pursuits generally considered unhealthy or perilous was not small, though hirers did find over the years that they had to pay increasingly higher prices for such workers, or use cheap immigrant labor.

In several instances masters sent sick or injured slaves to their new positions at the first of the year, showing little regard for the bondsmen's health. Joseph Reid Anderson, for example, was mildly angered when Sam, a slave he had hired sight unseen on the owner's recommendation, appeared for work at the Tredegar Iron Works in Richmond with "a very sore leg of long standing." Not only was it "doubtful whether his leg will stand the work he will have to do," Anderson wrote to Sam's master, but he was also "too old to do the work of a hand." He offered to take the man at a reduced price. A Westmoreland County man attempted to rid himself of a chronically ill servant, Edward, by sale or, as a last resort, hire. His agents in Richmond, P. M. Tabb and Son, were unable to find a purchaser because of Edward's condition, but they did locate someone willing to hire him for the year. Though unable to perform farm work, the slave did assist with other labors and partially recovered his health. Tabb returned Edward to Westmoreland County the following year after several further unsuccessful attempts at sale.[3]

While some owners appeared to be indifferent toward their hired servants' condition, many demonstrated concern for both humanitarian and financial reasons. In refusing to return his runaway Negro, Anderson, to a Rockbridge County iron furnace, M. Eskridge of Fauquier County explained to a friend: "It is too far from home to hire servants. I like to hire them where I can see or hear from them if they should be taken sick or any accident happen to them. For the sake of a few dollars more hire a valuable young man may be lost worth a thousand dollars." Another

---

[2] H of D *Jl.*, 1790, p. 131 (11 December 1790); Samuel Drewry to John Buford, 30 December 1854, and agreement between these two parties, n.d. [1854], in Buford Papers, Duke.

[3] J. R. Anderson to C. Hogan, 2, 9 January 1846, Tredegar Papers, Letterbook, VSL; P. M. Tabb and Son to Richard L. T. Beale, 9 June, 21 August, 25 December 1854, 24 February 1855, Beale Letterbook, UVA (#38–105). See also J. R. Anderson to Mrs. E. H. Miller, 30 December 1848, 26 December 1849, Tredegar Papers, Letterbooks, VSL.

owner refused to return his slave to William Weaver's iron forge until the man's leg, which had been injured at work there before Christmas, had healed. John Hartwell Cocke of Bremo took particular pains to insure proper treatment of his hired slaves. In addition to carefully checking their clothing and condition at year's end, Cocke also requested information regarding all sickness so "that the necessary medical aid may be procured." [4]

The basic agreement between lessor and lessee—the hiring bond—stipulated the conditions under which slaves worked and the protection they were to receive from abuse. Surprisingly, not many of these documents made even a fleeting reference to medical care. Most simply stated the amount and length of the hire, and promised to provide adequate food and clothing. [5] Some required the hirer to send for a particular doctor when the slave took sick, or barred the worker from performing certain hazardous tasks, but this was infrequent. There are several reasons for these omissions.

In one sense, there was not much that could be said in the hiring bond regarding sickness, other than that the lessee would attempt to maintain the slave's good health during the year. Even this statement was usually absent from the documents. State laws were strangely silent on the entire matter of hired slaves' maintenance, though the higher courts did hand down several precedent-setting decisions which merely reinforced practices already backed by long tradition. In 1806 the Superior Court of Chancery for the Richmond District ruled that a slave hirer had to pay the full contract price to the owner, even if the slave was sick through no fault of his own. Upon death of a bondsman

---

[4] M. Eskridge to Enos Hord, 16 March 1855, in *Hord* v. *Jordan*, Rockbridge County Courthouse, Lexington, Va. (#74–296); William Staples to William Weaver, 3 January 1830, Weaver Papers, Duke; "Terms of Hiring Genl Cockes Negroes for 1838," 1 January 1838, Cocke Deposit, Cocke Papers, UVA. See also Hez Ford to James E. Cooke, 20 January 1852, Barker-Cooke Papers, W&M; Jno. B. Carrington to Jno. M. Sutherlin, 5 April 1858, Sutherlin Papers, Duke; Bettie West to Mr. Throgmorton, 2 June 1859, Randolph Papers, LC.

[5] See, e.g., hiring bonds between Hugh Hamilton and John Doyle, 29 July 1826; Charles T. Taylor and Edwin Jordan, 1 January 1829, both in Jordan and Irvine Papers, Wisconsin; T. B. Bryant and Leslie & Dunlop, 30 December 1837, Leslie Papers, Duke; Lewelling Jones and William Shepherd, 1 January 1833, Dismal Swamp Papers, Duke.

during the year, however, the lessee was required to pay only for the time during which the slave was alive, whether sick or not.[6] This ruling did little to aid the severely ailing slave who was better off dead than alive to his hirer, despite the fact that owners customarily reimbursed hirers for all medical expenses. It was costly to pay for labor never performed by a slave who remained ill for many months, regardless of who paid the doctor's bills.

The custom of reimbursement for health care costs, though long operative, was not confirmed in the higher state courts until 1847. This practice, observed Thomas Jefferson Randolph, protected slaves from abuse, since "the person not owning the slave [lessee], if he had to pay them [the doctors' bills], might not call in a physician always when needed."[7] Thus, in a contorted, nebulous, and curious way, state law and tradition obviated the need for specific health care stipulations in hiring bonds.

Or did it? Despite this regulation, some hirers did agree to foot the cost of slave health care as part of a hiring contract. For example, the slaves who helped build the University of Virginia at Charlottesville, a slave who worked at Hampden-Sydney College, those who served as attendants at the Eastern Lunatic Asylum in Williamsburg, and laborers hired to the James River and Kanawha Canal Company were all treated at company expense.[8] A historian of Virginia's antebellum iron industry noted that more than half of the hiring bonds he inspected for 1854

[6] *George* v. *Elliott*, 2 Hening and Munford 5. Many people simply ignored the law and entered into agreements which stipulated that sick time must either be made up or deducted from the price of the hire. See, e.g., J. M. Harris to Dr. I. L. Twyman, 18 March 1850, Austin-Twyman Papers (folder 161), W&M; Negro Time Book, 1837–52, entry under "Willis" in 1847, and Account Book, 1828–32 (box 1), 8 April 1829 (re: Noblett's boy), both in Graham Papers, UVA (#38–106); account of John H. Cocke with Buckingham Iron Manufacturing Company, 1835, Cocke Deposit, Cocke Papers, UVA; receipt of D. Watson for labor performed by Maj. Jackson's Negro Jesse, 31 August 1818, Watson Papers, UVA, (#530); Benjamin F. Firebaugh to Maj. A. B. Stuart, 9 February 1844, W. W. Davis Papers, UVA (#378); J. R. Anderson to H. Loving, 24 January 1850, Tredegar Papers, Letterbook, VSL.

[7] *Isbell's Administrator* v. *Norvell's Executor*, 4 Grattan 176; Thomas J. Randolph's Memoirs, Edgehill-Randolph Papers, box 18, UVA.

[8] Annual Reports of the University of Virginia, 1822/23, 1823/24, 1824/25, in H of D Jl., 1823/24, 1824/25, 1825/26; Alfred J. Morrison, ed., *The College of Hampden-Sidney, Calendar of Board Minutes, 1776–1876* (Richmond, 1912),

(seven years after the state courts had ruled otherwise) stipulated that medical bills be borne by the ironmasters.[9]

Some owners, concerned about their hired bondsmen's health far from home, approached the problem somewhat differently. Recognizing that they were ultimately responsible for medical costs, they engaged agents in town to act as surrogate overseers of the slaves' medical affairs. Hiring agents in Richmond were more than willing to perform this task for their country clients in return for a 5 or 7.5 percent fee. Silas Wyatt struck at the heart of the matter in his advertisement of 3 January 1837 in the *Richmond Enquirer*: "It is well known to many who hire their slaves in this place, that they have been much neglected, by not having some one here to attend to them and frequently have sustained heavy losses in consequence—I will therefore hire them out, see that they are properly clad, have strict attention paid them when sick, get the highest prices for their hire, and guarantee all their hires for 5 per cent." For an additional three or four dollars, some of these agents obtained physicians who treated all the slave's illnesses during the entire year.[10]

The system worked well. The same agents' ads appeared in the newspapers year after year, proclaiming gratifying results for previous seasons: "Lewis Hill, Collector and General Agent, Richmond, Va., Again offers his services in Hiring Out Negroes,

---

139 (11–12 June 1851); John M. Galt Medical Diary, 18–19 May 1852, Galt Family Papers (Medical), CW; E. L. [Chirn?], Superintendent, JR&K Canal to Dr. A. Grinnan, 29 March 1855, Grinnan Family Papers, UVA (#49); Elijah Fletcher to Calvin Fletcher, 18 August 1849, in Martha von Briesen, ed., *Letters of Elijah Fletcher* (Charlottesville, Va., 1965), 219. See also agreement between John Buford and Samuel Drewry, n.d. [1854], Buford Papers, Duke; Fletcher M. Green, "Gold Mining in Ante-Bellum Virginia," *VMHB*, 45 (1937), 361–62 (Woodville Gold Mine, Orange County); Richmond and Danville Railroad Company, *Treasurer's Report [for 1853/54]* (Richmond, 1854), 40, 49, 50, 51, 52, 54, 64.

[9] S. Sydney Bradford, "The Negro Ironworker in Ante Bellum Virginia," *JSH*, 25 (1959), 203.

[10] Joseph C. Robert, "The Tobacco Industry in the Virginia-Carolina Area, 1800–1860" (Ph.D. dissertation, Duke University, 1933), 288n; *Richmond Whig*, 24 December 1841, quoted in Frederic Bancroft, *Slave-Trading in the Old South* (Baltimore, 1931), 151. For other advertisements, see newspapers published around the first of each year, e.g., *Richmond Enquirer*, 5 December 1845, p. 3; 2 January 1849, pp. 3, 4; Richmond *Daily Dispatch*, 20 December 1854, p. 1; Editorial, "Practice on Hirelings," *Steth.*, 1 (1851), 677–78.

Collecting Claims. Servants entrusted to his care receive every attention, particularly when sick. And he feels thankful while saying, that during the cholera of 1849, and again this year [1854], he was very successful with those under his charge." Industrialists, many of whom respected the importance of good medical care in obtaining rehires the following year, cooperated with agents whenever possible. For instance, as a regular policy J. R. Anderson, proprietor of the Tredegar Iron Works, informed local hiring agents of sicknesses among his charges: "Tony Wilson," he wrote to P. M. Tabb and Son, "having been taken very sick, I have called in the nearest Physician, Dr. R. Archer, and I write to inform you, so that you may send your own Physician if you desire it." To earn his 7.5 percent commission in 1856, one Richmond agent obtained shoes for Isaac and Tom, a medical recipe for Henry, and sundry medical services for Tom, including a leecher and cupper, a doctor, a room at the Medical College of Virginia Infirmary, and finally, sad to say, a coffin and grave.[11]

Abuses inevitably crept into the system, reducing its efficiency. Doctors objected to being hired as "slaves" for three or four dollars a year. And some agents found less than ideal housing for their charges, further angering physicians who had to treat bondsmen under circumstances unfavorable to their recoveries. Finally, doctors seeing patients in emergency situations frequently experienced difficulty collecting fees because their names did not appear on the hiring bonds as *the* physicians for particular hired bondsmen.[12] Despite these problems, the agents appear to have satisfied most of their customers.

Industrial slave hirers, both urban and rural, also took steps to win the confidence of skeptical masters who viewed certain occupations as particularly dangerous. J. R. Anderson built a hospital at the Tredegar Iron Works to ensure proper medical

[11] Richmond *Daily Dispatch*, 20 December 1854, p. 1; J. R. Anderson to P. M. Tabb and Son, 22 May 1849, Tredegar Papers, Letterbook, VSL; account of John Hackett with George R. Peake, 19 January 1857, Louthan Family Papers, UVA (#38–34). See also P. M. Tabb and Son to R. L. T. Beale, 24 February 1855, Beale Letterbook, UVA (#38–105).

[12] Editorial, "Practice on Hirelings," 677–78.

care of the hundreds of blacks he owned and employed. Proprietors at the Vaucluse Gold Mine in Orange County, and the Midlothian and Clover Hill Coal Mines in Chesterfield County, employed regular physicians to attend the sick at company infirmaries. Like urban hiring agents, the coal-mine owners and some railroad contractors offered to provide medical care for hired slaves throughout the year at a cost of three or four dollars.[13] The physicians of one county even supported the entrepreneurs in their attempts to entice slaveowners to hire out their slaves. In 1853 the Powhatan County Medical Society agreed to permit members the privilege of practicing by the year among operatives in the coal pits and their families, as well as on those laboring at public works projects.[14] Contract medicine of this sort was usually frowned upon.

Slaves residing in some urban areas could, if their masters or hirers chose, take advantage of one source of health care not readily available to their rural counterparts: the hospital. Though several industrial concerns and a few large planters had established what were called hospitals, they were usually small operations tended mainly by nonprofessionals, though physicians did come daily to treat patients when necessary. The city institutions —some public, some private—were run by physicians and were usually open to slaves as well as whites and free blacks. The first of these hospitals, the College Infirmary of the Hampden-Sydney Medical Department in Richmond, began admitting patients in 1838 at the start of medical instruction. It continued in existence, with a name change in 1854 to the Medical College of Virginia Infirmary, throughout the antebellum period, providing educational opportunities for medical students (see chapter 9) and health care for bondsmen, at between four and five dollars per

---

[13] Charles B. Dew, *Ironmaker to the Confederacy: Joseph R. Anderson and the Tredegar Iron Works* (New Haven, 1966), 26; *Plan and Description of the Vaucluse Mine, Orange County, Virginia* (Philadelphia, 1847), 8; Richmond *Daily Dispatch*, 1 January 1855, p. 3; J. Wistar Walke, "Chloroform as an Auxiliary Therapeutic Agent in Cramp and Spasms," *Steth.*, 2 (1852), 59; *Richmond Enquirer*, 25 December 1845, p. 4; 11 January 1859, p. 3; *Harvey v. Epes*, 12 Grattan 153 (p. 156).

[14] "Tariff of Fees, Etc. Adopted by the Physicians of Powhatan County, Virginia," *Steth.*, 4 (1854), 99.

week (private patients higher). In 1854 a competitor, the private Bellevue Hospital, located on Church Hill, opened its doors to slaves for the same rates. Six years later the local papers announced that three physicians were establishing a third medical institution in Richmond, this one devoted entirely to the care of black servants, at the corner of 26th and Main Streets.[15] Little is known regarding this slave hospital, as no further announcements ever appeared and no records of its operation have ever been located. Norfolk also had a hospital which admitted slaves, though this institution was not in existence until the last decade before the Civil War (see illustration).[16]

Other towns probably supported small medical establishments which were not publicized outside the local area or which folded after only a short time. Both Winchester and Worsham had medical school infirmaries, while Thomsonians and botanical physicians operated hospitals at various times in Richmond, Petersburg, and Norfolk during the 1830's and 1840's.[17] Some Petersburgers argued in humanitarian terms for the founding of a public hospital to care for the black and the indigent during the 1850's. Most slaves, they observed, received poor care at their lodgings in the kitchens of private citizens. But their pleas fell on deaf ears.[18] All hospitals and dispensaries treated primarily or exclusively non-epidemic diseases. When smallpox, cholera, or yellow fever struck a town, city hospitals served the community (see chapter 7).

---

[15] S[ocrates] Maupin to Addison Maupin, 2 August 1838, Maupin-Washington Manuscripts, UVA (#2769a); William T. Sanger, *Medical College of Virginia before 1925 and University College of Medicine 1893–1913* (Richmond, 1973), 23; Richmond *Daily Dispatch*, 29 July 1854, p. 1; 26 January 1860, p. 1; *Richmond Enquirer*, 20 March 1860, p. 2. See also Wade, *Slavery in the Cities*, 139–40.

[16] Mariana Bagley, "The History of the Public Health of Norfolk, Virginia, up to 1860" (M.A. thesis, Duke University, 1939), 110–11. Blanton, *19th Century*, 217, hints that another hospital, founded in 1857, treated all classes of patients in Norfolk.

[17] Blanton, *19th Century*, 7-8; *Richmond Enquirer*, 19 June 1838, p. 4; 14 July 1846, p. 2; John Walker Diary, 4 February, 6 March, 18 May, 4 July 1837, UNC; Bennett H. Wall, "Medical Care of Ebenezer Pettigrew's Slaves," *Mississippi Valley Historical Review*, 37 (1950), 463–64.

[18] Petersburg *Daily South Side Democrat*, 12 (p. 2), 17 (p. 2) March 1856, 25 April 1859, p. 1.

INFIRMARY FOR SLAVES.

THE Subscribers beg leave to inform the public that they have rented and fitted up as an INFIRMARY FOR SLAVES, the house in the City of Norfolk, near Calvert's Lane, formerly occupied by Mr. J. Scott.   The location is private and central, and the house airy, well arranged and sufficiently commodious.   Competent Nurses are engaged ; and, in addition to the personal attention of the undersigned, an advanced Medical Student will be constantly in the house to see that the sick are properly ministered to at all times.

The *entire* expense for the treatment of any one case, Medical, Surgical, or Obstetrical, *including* medicines, food and nursing, will be as follows :

Per day.....................................$1 00

"   week.................................. 5 00

"   month..................................18 00

☞ Cases of Small Pox, Measles, and other contagious diseases will not be received.

The advantages of an establishment of this kind, so common in many parts of the South, will he apparent to all who have any experience in hiring out servants. Non-residents, especially, will be saved much trouble and expense by having their servants, when taken sick, sent to the Infirmary, where they will receive the most careful attention and nursing at a comparatively trifling cost.   It also recommends itself to those who have servants in the adjacent counties suffering from chronic diseases, where the remoteness of medical aid renders it more expensive and difficult to be procured as often as needed.

All applications must be in writing, and if from a distance, *post paid.*

WM. J. MOORE, M. D., Office 42 E. Main—residence 15 N. Catharine.

GEO. L. UPSHUR, M. D., Office 57 S. Fenchurch—residence 7 Bermuda.

R. W. SYLVESTER, M. D., Office 20 W. Main—residence 7 S. Granby.

Advertisement for Slave Infirmary in Norfolk, 1851.

SOURCE: William S. Forrest, *Norfolk Directory for 1851–1852* (Norfolk, 1851), 17.

Slaves living or hired out in cities usually had greater medical independence than those residing on plantations or at rural industrial establishments. They lived closer to physicians, had easier access to hospitals, and more readily avoided the watchful eyes of masters when seeking black medical assistance. Whites provided sick slaves living away from home with varying degrees of care, depending upon their conscientiousness and the source of the health care funds.

The Cost of Slave Medical Care

The expense of treating ill bondsmen varied from year to year depending on several factors, including the state of epidemic diseases in the neighborhood, the frequency of accidents on the establishment, the age and sex of slaves, and general working and living conditions.[19] The wide annual variation in medical costs is well illustrated by the experience of Robert Thruston Hubard, a planter with large holdings in Nelson and Buckingham Counties (see Table 11). Hubard retained most of his financial records, including bills and receipts from doctors, dentists, midwives, and suppliers of medicines. Though the information is far from perfect for his Buckingham farms, it is reasonably complete for Tye River Quarter in Nelson County during the 1850's. Physicians' (including dentists' and midwives') bills ranged from a high of $307.85 (1858) to a low of $49.25 (1851), and drugs from $35 (1851) to $1.63 (1856), though the number of slaves remained at 95–100 throughout most of the decade.[20] A look at any doctor's account book or slaveowner's financial journal will demonstrate similar fluctuations.

Because the cost of medical care differed so widely from year to year, it is difficult to determine an average expense per slave. Hubard averaged about $1.45, though some years it was less than $1.00 and others more than $3.00; Hill Carter (Shirley Plantation, Charles City County) paid about $2.00 per slave, excluding drugs, in the 1830's and 1840's; an Essex County man spent about $1.35 per slave (40 slaves) between 1830 and 1834; and George Harrison of Brandon (Prince George County) bragged that during 1836 his doctor bill averaged only 25 cents per slave.[21] In computing the total annual cost of slave maintenance during the mid-1830's, Charles Friend (White Hill Plantation, Prince George County) allowed $3.80 per male and $1.18 per female (this must exclude pregnant women) for doctors and medicine. At the Woodville Gold Mine in Orange County, where the proprietor paid hired slaves' medical expenses, the amount was figured at

[19] For an overview of slave medical costs in the Lower South, see Eugene D. Genovese, "The Medical and Insurance Costs of Slaveholding in the Cotton Belt," *JNH*, 45 (1960), 141–55.

[20] Hubard Papers, UVA (#8708). See also Genovese, "Medical and Insurance Costs," 154.

[21] U. B. Phillips, *Life and Labor in the Old South* (Boston, 1929), 231; Slave Account Book, Mitchell-Garnett Ledgers, UVA (#38–45); [George E. Harrison,] "Slavery in Virginia: Extract from *Slavery in the United States*—by J. K. Paulding, being a letter to the author from a farmer of lower Virginia," *VMHB*, 36 (1928), 281.

Table 11. Medical Care Costs of Robert T. Hubard's Slaves at His Nelson County Farm (Tye River Quarter), 1850–60

	Number of Slaves	M.D. costs	Medicine costs [b]	Total costs [c]	Cost per Slave
1850	53	$ 80.47	$ 7.68	$ 88.15	$1.66
1851	?	49.25	35.00	84.25	—
1852	95	57.38	16.40	73.78	0.78
1853	[97] [d]	133.63	3.46	137.09	1.41
1854	99	90.91	—	90.91	0.92
1855	[100] [d]	92.76	16.59	109.35	1.09
1856	100	62.63	1.63	64.26	0.64
1857	[99] [d]	129.12	2.24	131.36	1.33
1858	98	307.85	33.10	340.95	3.48
1859	[92] [d]	100.37	7.75	108.12	1.18
1860	84	172.36	13.83	186.19	2.22
Total (excluding 1851)	917	$1,227.48	$102.68	$1,330.16	$1.45

[a] Derived from records in the Hubard Papers, UVA (#8708, etc.).
[b] Hubard ordered medicines from a firm in Richmond two to four times a year. Sometimes the orders stated which items went to his Nelson County and which to Buckingham County estates. At other times no distinction was made. The costs in this column are probably low.
[c] Excludes midwives' fees, since these were not regularly recorded.
[d] Estimated number based on known figures for previous and succeeding years.

$6.60 in 1850, though this also included "incidentals," a non-medical category not further defined.[22] The best indicator of health costs was probably the annual rate which Richmond hiring agents were able to obtain from practitioners to care for an individual slave. For the 1830's to 1860 this amounted to three or four dollars per year. Several recent historians of slavery agree with this figure, based on their own estimates for the entire South.[23]

Aside from the cost of having a slave lay by for several days, the most expensive aspect of ill health was the outlay for a physician's care. A visit usually ran between $1.00 and $3.00; medica-

[22] White Hill Plantation Books, vol. III, UNC; Green, "Gold in Virginia," 362.
[23] Robert, "Tobacco Industry," 288n; Editorial, "Practice on Hirelings," 667–78; Starobin, *Industrial Slavery*, 157; Genovese, "Medical and Insurance Costs," 155; Fogel and Engerman, *Time*, II, 117. Alfred H. Conrad and John R. Meyer calculated costs at $1.50 to $2.00, but only for a prime fieldhand. Breeding women, old people, and children usually incurred greater expenses.

tions and special procedures such as bloodletting, bone-setting, surgery, and parturition cost additional sums. Though groups of physicians in towns or counties often jointly established standard rates for services rendered (fee bills), some doctors charged what the traffic would bear. Wrote one man who had hired several slaves to a Danville tobacconist: "If my hands are Sick I wish Dr. Cabell or Dr. Wilbers to attend them, as the acct. you paid is a high one." Another slaveowner, living near Petersburg, discovered that some doctors followed no rules at all in charging fees:

It was not unusual when the doctor called [a Virginia physician remembered many years after the Civil War], after a patient was convalescent and needed no further attention, for the master of the family to bring out a roll of bank notes, or more commonly a bag of specie, Spanish or American silver dollars, and, opening the mouth, dump it down on the table and say, "Doctor, pay yourself," and modestly and trustingly look away for a minute. On the occasion to which I refer, we had been attending a negro slave, very valuable, worth perhaps twelve or fifteen hundred dollars, and as he was sufficiently well to require no further medical service, the Doctor announced the fact to his master, a plain old country farmer, who only owned a few slaves. The old man, as the Doctor anticipated, brought out his bag of specie, and placing it on the table spread the mouth open wide, with the usual remark, "Doctors pay yourselves." The Doctor had a remarkably large hand, and as he went for the "pay," it really looked much larger than usual. The old man noticed it, and his confidence failed him, and just as the Doctor was about to "pay himself," he touched him on the shoulder and said, "Doctor, before you put your hand in that bag, remember there is a God in Heaven looking at you." The arrest was so sudden and unexpected that the Doctor's face was a study, but it did not stop him entirely, and he helped himself. After getting away, however, he asked me if I heard what "that old devil said to him," adding, "he scared me so that I did not get half my pay," and he often recalled the incident afterwards, and enjoyed the recital of it, but he did not enjoy it at the time.[24]

[24] Jno. B. Carrington to Jno. M. Sutherlin, 5 April 1858, Sutherlin Papers, Duke; John Herbert Claiborne, *Seventy-five Years in Old Virginia* (New York, 1904), 123–24.

Fee bills protected the master from overcharges, though even the range of prices for some treatments was as much as $500 (e.g., Caesarean section in an 1850 Richmond fee bill). Nor did all these documents state the price of every procedure, leaving the physician great latitude in the amount he might charge. In most cases the price for treatment of slaves was the same as for whites. Charlottesville physicians (1848), however, exacted only half as much for delivery of a black child as for a white one, and two-thirds as much in the case of slave twins, while Richmond doctors (1850) reduced the cost of vaccinating slaves by one dollar, but maintained equal charges in obstetrical cases.[25]

Some masters looked for ways to cut corners on medical expenses. One man decided to avoid the cost of raising slave children by purchasing only adult males and non-breeding women, while others obtained tax exemptions for all old or infirm slaves.[26] But the best way to fix the doctor's fees was to arrange for an annual health care contract or to sign an agreement defining the cost of potentially expensive slave illnesses as they occurred.[27] Though "deals" of any sort came to be frowned upon by the medical profession in the nineteenth century, some doctors were willing to bargain with patients over the payment of fees.

Slaveowners and doctors usually struck up one of two types of arrangements. Practice-by-the-year was the most important for masters and the most demeaning (claimed practitioners) for physicians. According to the agreement a doctor contracted to attend all slaves owned by the master for a set annual amount, regardless of the number of visits or the amount of medication required. Though complaints from slaveholders were few, the servants' best interests could not have always been well served

[25] Petersburg Fee Bill, 30 April 1800, Hubard Family Papers (box 2, folder 26), UNC; Charlottesville Fee Bill, 9 June 1848, Medical Library, University of Virginia Medical School; Richmond Fee Bill, May 1850, reprinted in George Rosen, "Fees and Fee Bills," *BHM Supplement #6* (1946), 26–29; Powhatan County Fee Bill, 1 August 1853, *Steth.*, 4 (1854), 97–100.

[26] Phillips, *Life and Labor*, 173; Riddick Papers, 31 December 1819 (slave inventory), 14 February 1820 (tax exemption), UVA (#2227).

[27] Wilhelm Moll, "Medical Fee Bills," *Virginia Medical Monthly*, 93 (1966), 657–59; Blanton, *17th Century*, 245–49.

through such a system. Unless physicians were liberally compensated, they probably did not maintain the highest standards in their care of slaves. The only guards against sloppy medical practices were the physician's conscience, the master's watchfulness, the slaves' complaints, and the neighborhood's general opinion of a doctor's level of treatment. Despite its potential drawbacks, contract medicine remained well established in Virginia up through the early nineteenth century.[28]

But as Virginia's physicians developed local medical societies, a statewide organization, and a published organ in Richmond, the system came under sharp attack. The wording of fee bills during this period reflected the new attitude of many doctors. Subscribing physicians had to charge the amounts set forth. The agreements signed by Richmond and Powhatan County practitioners in 1850 and 1853, respectively, contained outright denunciations of contract medicine. A typical statement declared that practice by the year "does not accord with fair competition, nor comport with the dignity of the medical profession." [29]

Dr. John H. Lewis of Jefferson County worked under both systems (contract and fee for each visit) during the first decade of the nineteenth century, and then apparently abandoned the annual fixed arrangement. Others simply modified it by agreeing to charge nominal fees for each visit during the year. But enough contract medicine persisted for angry doctors to continue their campaign against it through the 1850's. George Thrift of Madison County was one of the holdouts. From 1844 to 1858 he treated families for a flat annual rate, exclusive of certain disorders such as female diseases, obstetrical visits, and cases which required more skill, care, or time than most. Entries for families in his account book at the start of each new year read: "Practice by the year with usual Exceptions." Between 1844 and 1848 he received $20 annually from Silas Utz for care of his family, which included a few slaves; in 1850 he received $15 from Joseph Fray, though Fray also paid him $2.50 for a visit to a slave "wounded

---

[28] Blanton, *18th Century*, 167, 298.
[29] Quote is from "Tariff of Fees of Powhatan County," 99. For citations of fee bills, see n. 25, above.

with a pitch fork," and $3 for attending Simon "injured by machine."[30]

Though the editors of the *Stethoscope and Virginia Medical Gazette* reported in March 1851 that "the [contract] practice has long since been scorned down" in Richmond and the rest of Virginia, a doctor in the northwestern part of the state claimed a few months later that the system "prevails to some extent here," although it was, he assured his readers, on the decline. It must have died a long and difficult death, however, for two years later "Celsus" spent a page and a half in the *Stethoscope* describing the difficulties and unprofitability of yearly practice to "younger members" of the profession. Men like Dr. George Thrift, considered "low tradesmen in the profession" and "beyond the pale of respectability" by the editors of the *Stethoscope*, continued to give their clientele what they wanted.[31]

The other type of "deal" which doctors made was the setting of a fee (sometimes dependent on the outcome of the case) for treatment of a slave's particular disorder. Edmund Wilcox of Amherst County, for example, charged Patrick Rose 500 pounds of tobacco in 1780 for curing Cato of "a pox." It took three years. He entered into agreements with Thomas Eads and Philip Bush to treat their slaves, Glasgow and Bob, for yaws, though he was to receive payment for medicines only, unless the Negroes were cured. This sort of bargaining was not only a phenomenon of the eighteenth century. Dr. William B. Price of Brunswick County contracted in 1843 with Mr. A. Kennedy to obtain half ownership of a female servant if he could cure her of epilepsy. He failed. Being a gambling man, however, Price also agreed to attend a Negro woman during her pregnancy for ten dollars, to

[30] Lewis Medical Account Book, p. 1, VSL; R. Powell to John Hartwell Cocke, 1 October 1827, Cocke Deposit, Cocke Papers, UVA; Thrift Ledger, 1844–58, pp. 46, 102, 116 (see also pp. 51, 55, 63, 64, 89, 107, 112). See also Cox Accounts, 1 January 1847, vol. II, front cover, UNC.

[31] Editorial, "Attending Families by the Year," *Steth.*, 1 (1851), 161; North West, "A Voice from the Country on Professional Improprieties," *ibid.*, 495; Celsus, "Year Practice—Hireling Doctors," *ibid.*, 3 (1853), 237–38. Contract practice appears to have remained stronger in the Lower South than in Virginia: see William D. Postell, "A Review of Slave Care on Southern Plantations," *Virginia Medical Monthly*, 79 (1952), 103–4; Martha C. Mitchell, "Health and the Medical Profession in the Lower South, 1845–1860," *JSH*, 10 (1944), 435.

be doubled if she delivered a living child. He also attempted and failed to cure a boy, Richmond, of epilepsy, for one-third of his value.[32]

Neither the annual contract nor the set-fee-for-cure arrangements were adopted by a large portion of Virginia's physicians in the nineteenth century. The pressures applied by the organized profession and the small financial returns realized on an increased patient load worked against continuing those practices. There were, however, a significant number of independent doctors who bargained with their customers for the privilege of treating illnesses on a special basis.

The Old Slave

Acccording to the Virginia mortality census of 1850, and the death registers of four Virginia counties and towns between 1853 and 1860, more slaves than whites died of old age (see Table 9). This same trend is also evident in other portions of the South for that period. Can one conclude from this information that slaves generally lived longer than whites, and that they received better care? In 1956 Kenneth Stampp asserted that the apologists' claim to long and good lives for bondsmen was not borne out by the facts, and that in 1860 a greater proportion of whites, not slaves, were over sixty. Another recent historian reported that some slaveholders did not care for their aged slaves but instead "deposited these unwanted thralls in nearby cities," constantly increasing the number of "retired bondsmen" with whom city officials had to cope.[33] Yet Virginia newspapers frequently reported the deaths of faithful Negroes who had lived to the age of one hundred or more. The editors of a Richmond medical journal bragged that according to the latest census (1850) there were more centenarians among the Negro than the Caucasian race. In all these stories the implication was the same:

---

[32] Edmund Wilcox Ledger, Hubard Family Papers, vol. 13, pp. 40, 63, 23, 65 (also 44, 52), UNC; Price Account Books, I, 1843, accounts with A. Kennedy (April) and Daniel Williams (July and September), Duke.

[33] Stampp, *Peculiar Institution*, 318–19; Ira Berlin, *Slaves without Masters: The Free Negro in the Antebellum South* (New York, 1974), 152–53.

slavery, rather than being a barbarous system which sent people to early graves, was actually quite humane and conducive to long life and good health. Old slaves were not abandoned and left to fend for themselves as were old whites in the North. They were fed, sheltered, clothed, and provided with medical care until their deaths, regardless of the length of their "retirement." [34]

Aging unquestionably posed problems for masters. Not only could those slaves who had become infirm with years contribute little to their owner's operations; they also usually represented a financial drain on resources. Ill health often accompanied old age. The cost of medical care fell to the master, who, unless he had a strong affection for a particular slave, might easily grow to resent frequent outlays of cash on useless chattel. Undoubtedly some white Virginians ignored their responsibilities in the face of financial burdens and provided less than adequate (or less than usual) health care, or perhaps abandoned their bondsmen in a large town. Others simply continued to care for all slaves.[35]

Health maintenance expenses struck particularly hard at the smaller, less wealthy slaveholder for whom a twenty-five or fifty-dollar bill caused a real financial strain. Mrs. Martha Southward of Richmond was probably typical of this group of owners. One of her elderly slaves came down with smallpox in the late 1840's and received treatment at the city hospital. Though thankful that the woman had been cured, Mrs. Southward petitioned the city council for a release from payment of the hospital bill. Her slave could render no useful services due to age and infirmity, she explained, nor could Mrs. Southward herself afford to pay the charges. Council acceded to the request and released her from any financial obligations to the city. As has been mentioned, a few

[34] Editorial, "Mortality Statistics of the United States," *VMJ*, 6 (1856), 95; *Lynchburg Virginian*, 16 September 1839, p. 2; William S. Forrest, *Historical and Descriptive Sketches of Norfolk and Vicinity* (Philadelphia, 1853), 155; Richmond *Daily Dispatch*, 31 July 1854, p. 1; *Richmond Enquirer*, 31 July 1849, p. 4; Petersburg *Daily Express*, 28 June 1858, p. 1; Petersburg *Daily South Side Democrat*, 2 August 1854, p. 2.

[35] For medical expenses, see, e.g., Bohannan Account Book, 43, 176, VSL; account of Mr. McGavock with Dr. Ewing, MS in possession of Jacob McGavock, Max Meadows, Va. (Dr. W. R. Chitwood, Wytheville, Va., supplied me with a copy of this account, for which I express appreciation.) See also Phillips, *Life and Labor*, 175, 240, 246.

owners avoided the humbling circumstance of such an admission by simply releasing aged slaves in cities to tend to their own needs. State law prohibited this practice and it occurred but rarely, claimed one Richmond physician. The press and Richmond City Council, however, indicated otherwise by their several complaints about the matter.[36]

Manumission was an early method of avoiding financial responsibility for superannuated slaves. But a 1782 law forbade emancipation of blacks above age 45 without adequate guarantees that the former owner would provide support in the event they became a burden on the local community; the state legislature reaffirmed this law in 1824 and again in 1848.[37]

Slaveowners handled the problem of the elderly in several ways. Commonly, aging bondsmen were permitted gradually to taper off their duties until infirmity barred them from any further labor. A Fluvanna County man placed an old, disabled servant in charge of his kitchen, to good effect; Charles Friend of Prince George County had Old Jack perform light work around the farm; and Julian Ruffin required that Old Gib only raise chickens, feed pigs, and do other similar tasks for his keep. Many black women cared for young children while parents toiled daily in the fields.[38] The life of Jack Lubbar, a slave of Landon Carter, shows best the gradual transition from full activity to full retirement. Jack served Carter for many years as foreman of a work force at the plantation adjacent to Sabine Hall. In 1734 he suggested that Jack, too old to continue such strenuous work, "by degrees . . . fall astern of the rest"; the man labored at a reduced pace for another twenty years. Carter than moved Jack to Fork Quarter, where he oversaw the work of five hands so well

[36] Richmond Common Council Minutes, XII, 150 (28 March 1849); W. A. Patteson, "Report on Hygiene and Public Health and the Medical Topography and Statistics of Virginia," *Steth.*, 2 (1852), 424–25.

[37] William Waller Hening, comp., *The Statutes at Large; Being a Collection of All the Laws of Virginia from the First Session of the Legislature in the Year 1619*, XI, 39; Virginia, *Supplement to the Revised Code of the Laws of Virginia . . .* (Richmond 1833), 236; Virginia, *Acts of the Assembly, 1847–48* (Richmond, 1848), 118.

[38] T. T. Mayo to John H. Cocke, 8 February 1828, Cocke Deposit, Cocke Papers, UVA; White Hill Plantation Books, 14 June 1845, UNC; Julian Ruffin Diary, 20 January 1843, VHS.

that production of corn, tobacco, and peas doubled, and shoats, hogs, and pigs multiplied more rapidly with fewer losses than ever before. Eight years later the old man and his wife became keepers of the henhouse at Sabine Hall. By 1771 Carter felt Jack deserved complete retirement; he provided him and his wife with a home at Fork Quarter, though, his master reported, "ever active as his life has been, he then became a vast progger in Catching fish, Beavers, otters, Muskrats, and Minxes with his traps." Jack followed this daily routine until his final illness in 1774.[39]

A few masters failed to or refused to recognize the signs of aging in their slaves and expected a level of work far in excess of capabilities. As mentioned above, C. Hogan hired his aging bondsman Sam to the Tredegar Iron Works, only to have his annual rate reduced because the old man could not perform the assigned tasks properly. A similar situation arose at the Bath Iron Works in the Blue Ridge Mountains. Billy, an old Negro hand, proved entirely useless, his hirer complained: "he has not done us more than a weeks work and that of no account, & from present appearances, not likely to render any service. he has a pair of sore Shins which in all probability will never be cured. we have been doctoring & feeding him, and have at length thought best to sent him home. . . ." It was another three months before Old Billy had recovered his health enough to travel.[40]

Some masters solved the problem of aging by transferring the responsibility of daily care to others. The available evidence indicates that most old people remained at home to be assisted by their children and the general slave community. In times of sickness, one slave ministered to all needs, including food, cleanliness, and medication. When Old Rachel developed severe illnesses at White Hill Plantation in 1854 and 1856, Charles Friend had one of the younger women move in with her. Both times the plantation lost use of a valuable hand for several weeks.[41] If

---

[39] Greene, ed., *Carter Diary*, II, 840–41 (27 July 1774).

[40] J. R. Anderson to C. Hogan, 2, 9 January 1846, Tredegar Papers, Letterbook, VSL; Jordan Davis & Co. to William Davis, 17 March, 30 June 1830, Weaver Papers, Duke.

[41] White Hill Plantation Books, 12 December 1854, 28 January–11 February 1856, UNC.

several aged slaves lived together, the more fit undoubtedly assisted the feebler.

A few owners "hired" superannuated slaves to white or black people in return for food, lodging, and maintenance, or paid them a small sum to cover costs. Medical bills were still the owner's headache, but the need to assign a member of the work force to the task of watching over aged Negroes was thereby removed. This approach was rarely taken unless an estate had been broken up and it was otherwise impossible to dispose of old servants. John Walker, for example, took money from his father's estate to pay George Hill for Old Nan's expenses. John Cohoon, administrator of the Nansemond County estate of Jonathan Hargroves, Jr., was able to obtain small sums of money for the hire of Old Dolly and Old Price, though after one year the former could be rented for "victuals and clothing" only. Two old slaves belonging to the estate of Robert M. Riddick, also of Nansemond County, found new homes with black friends and relatives for the remainder of their lives. The executor of the estate provided a small subsistence and medical expenses.[42]

At least a few old people rebelled against the idea of being dependent on others for care. Old Fanny, whose master had moved from Cumberland County to Fauquier County but had permitted several slaves (including Fanny) to remain in the old neighborhood, insisted that she would pay her own hire rather than allow someone to rent her for food and clothing. Hezekiah Ford, her master's agent, reported on Fanny's condition each year. The rate was first set at fifteen dollars, though Fanny, who was now living with her husband, a slave belonging to another estate, found that too steep and "begs that you will not deal so hard with her." Two other younger slaves promised to assist Fanny in paying her hire. She and her husband, Solomon, managed to scrape up most of the required amount the first year by raising corn fodder and a small amount of tobacco, but then began to fall behind in their payments. Hezekiah Ford suggested

<hr />

[42] John Walker Diary, 30 July 1836, 11 April 1837, UNC; Cohoon Ledger, "A List of Jno. Hargroves Jr Negroes as hired out on the 22nd & 27th days of Jany. 1834 till 1st Jany 1835," p. 11, UVA (#8868); entries for Old Mingo, 1820–21 (pp. 36–38), and Jemmy, 1820–27 (pp. 37–44), Riddick Papers, UVA (#2227).

to her master, James E. Cooke, that he reduce the hire as "Fanny is not able to do much," presumably because of her age. She came out two dollars short at the end of the year, but Ford permitted her to add it to the amount due for the following year ($8 for hire plus $2 owed = $10). He also gave her a dollar toward the purchase of a winter coat. Fanny's world caved in the next year, however, when her husband's owner decided suddenly to sell him. In the last available letter of this series, Hezekiah Ford relayed to Cooke Fanny's request that he please purchase Solomon, but as of 6 April 1853 Cooke had still not decided what action to take. The outcome of this incident is not recorded.[43]

Those slaves who were willing to leave matters to their masters often lived relatively pleasant lives in retirement.[44] Having survived the rigors of years at hard labor, some were able to enjoy several years of inactivity in which their lives were their own. Adequate medical care was usually provided, and often supplemented by the slave community, though the master's commitment to cure was perhaps not as great as when the slaves were prime hands. Examples exist of elderly blacks undergoing surgery for cataracts, cancer, and other disorders at their masters' expense, and of owners taking special pains to secure proper treatment for sickly aged servants.[45]

Some, of course, suffered at the hands of their owners in old

[43] Hez Ford to James E. Cooke, 29 November 1849, 23 December 1850, 18 March, 24 December 1851, [—— January 1852?], 20 January 1852, 6 April 1853, Barker-Cooke Papers, W&M.

[44] See e.g., [James K. Paulding,] *Letters from the South, Written during an Excursion in the Summer of 1816* (New York, 1817), I, 24; John Hall, ed., *Forty Years of Familiar Letters of James W. Alexander* (New York, 1860), 1, 352; John Driver to David Jameson, 24 September 1789, Dismal Swamp Papers, Duke; Slave List, 1 January 1826, Wickham Papers (reel 3) UVA (#409); "List of Slaves at the Oxford Iron Works—in Families &c.," 15 January 1811, William Bolling Papers, Duke; Will of Richard Eppes, in White Hill Plantation Books, III, UNC; *Mayo v. Carrington*, 4 Call 472 (old slaves to be provided for after owner's death).

[45] James Bolton, "Bellevue Hospital Reports," *Steth.*, 4 (1854), 459–63, and 5 (1855), 67–69; T. P. Mayo, "Clinical Reports of the Richmond College Infirmary," *VMSJ*, 2 (1854), 274–77; A. E. Peticolas, "Case of Osteo Sarcoma of the Inferior Maxilla," *VMJ*, 13 (1859), 283–84; John A. Cunningham, "Case of an Extra-Uterine Foetus Retained Forty Years," *VMSJ*, 4 (1855), 94–95; John Boswell to Dr. Thomas Walker, 13 July 1787, Rives Papers (box 162), LC; John Watson to Dr. Charles Brown, 11 August 1818, Brown Papers, W&M; John Walker Diary, 15 November 1834, 13 November 1852–19 March 1853, UNC.

age, while others blossomed. The contrast is emphasized by the runaway notice which appeared in a Lynchburg newspaper in 1821, and the letter which an unidentified Williamsburg slave woman, almost blind with age, wrote to her daughter in 1858:

$5 Reward

Runaway from the subscriber living in Amherst County, near Harriss's Creek, on Sunday last, the 6th inst a negro woman named Rose, aged about 60 years. She is somewhat decrepid in her feet. She took them [*sic*] with her two suits of clothing, one of them homespun.

I have every kindness shown me, & have no wish which is not gratified. My fellow servants do all in their power to please me, & even the little children in the yard are glad to lead me about & wait on me. Your old acquaintance Lucy Jones lives with us, & washes; she attends to my room & puts it in order for me every morning. Alex is well & sends love to you. Avena comes to see me once or twice a week; she lives at our old house, & takes care of it; you know there is a beautiful garden there, we are all much attached to the place; having lived ther so many years. Whenever she comes, she brings me a basket of fruit. Oliver's wife & children live with us, & they are very respectful & kind to me, the little children call me Grandmammy, & when I go in the house on Sunday to hear the Bible read, there is strife amongst them, which shall take my hand to lead me in. I have always tried to be kind to all & now all are kind to me.

When I was young, I lived where a large school was kept, & when play time came I always had something nice to give the children: & very often now when I walk in the street, gentlemen & ladies meet me & say they remember with gratitude my kindness to them when they went to school. It is a long time back & those who went to school then have grandchildren now. I am not far from ninety years of age being ten years old at the Seige of York [town].[46]

The Free Black

Free blacks did not really fit into the scheme of antebellum Virginia society. In their anomalous positions as nonslaves

[46] *Lynchburg Press*, 25 May 1821, p. 4; ——— to ——— (My Dear Daughter), 8 October 1858, Galt Family Papers (Personal; reel 9), CW.

in a state where the vast majority of their race was held in servitude, free blacks posed a threat to the stability of the system. But because they played a significant role in the economic life of Virginia, whites could not entirely ignore their presence.[47] As members of the residential community, free blacks were not forgotten for another reason: health. An epidemic among members of this group threatened the well-being of neighboring whites; the illness or death of free blacks, especially those fulfilling important, even if menial, functions, represented an economic loss to the community; and the presence of a poor group of people, such as these Negroes generally were, increased the need for low cost or charitable medical aid sponsored both by the medical profession and by society.

As unsalaried laborers who received the basic necessities of life regardless of the amount of work performed, slaves were usually able to excuse themselves from their daily tasks when sickness struck. Few free blacks enjoyed such luxury. Like whites, freedmen had to pay for medical care and for their food, lodging, clothing, etc. For those with small incomes, sickness meant hardship unless other family members could fill the gap. Black farmers were not in as precarious a position as hired agricultural or urban laborers who received pay only for work performed. Where malnutrition existed among blacks in antebellum Virginia, it was more likely to be found in the free Negro population than among the slaves. Similarly, this group of nonwhites received the worst medical care, though it was not as poor as most recent historians have contended.[48]

As with whites and slaves, free black health care began in the home. Those who could afford them purchased the usual rem-

---

[47] On the position and general importance of free blacks in Virginia, see Luther Porter Jackson, *Free Negro Labor and Property-Holding in Virginia, 1830–1860* (New York, 1942); John H. Russell, *The Free Negro in Virginia, 1619–1865* (Baltimore, 1913); Ira Berlin, "Slaves Who Were Free: The Free Negro in the Upper South, 1776–1861" (Ph.D. dissertation, University of Wisconsin, 1970), and Berlin, *Slaves without Masters.*

[48] For general statements on the poor medical care of free blacks in the South, see Berlin, "Slaves Who Were Free," 304, 391 ("Free Negroes . . . most probably had no access to proper medical care. . . ."); Wade, *Slavery in the Cities,* 141; Alan H. Raphael, "Health and Medical Care of Black People in the United States during Reconstruction" (Ph.D. dissertation, University of Chicago, 1972), 16.

edies of the period—quinine, laudanum, castor oil, vermifuge, paregoric, calomel—at the general store.[49] Others, less well off, obtained what free medicines they could. All probably derived benefits from the bark, roots, and leaves of local vegetation which they used to prepare special medicines.[50] Domestic treatment of sickness was much more important among free blacks than among slaves because, as has been emphasized, many of the former could not afford to pay a physician. A Richmond doctor claimed that practitioners often failed to see the sick of their area because lower-class whites and blacks treated cases of illness, especially among children, from beginning to end with home remedies. Free blacks also had recourse to Negro doctors who abounded in the eastern half of the state, as well as to black bleeders and cuppers.[51] Only a few blacks possessed sufficient time, money, and inclination to take a trip to one of Virginia's medicinal springs or to a prestigious Richmond doctor in search of the proper cure for their ailments.[52]

Physicians' complaints about under-use of professionals notwithstanding, when illnesses became serious or major epidemics struck, free blacks summoned medical assistance in surprising numbers, regardless of their ability to pay. No doubt many blacks, hidden away in shabby rural huts or filthy urban tenement rooms, succumbed to diseases unaided by white doctors. But the medical profession of the Old Dominion was, to its credit, relatively liberal in dispensing aid to those who required it. Free blacks were often the recipients of their largesse.

Among the freedmen who could afford to pay for regular private medical care at home was Alexander Jarratt, a boatman in Petersburg who accumulated bills between 1853 and 1862 totalling at

[49] See, e.g., account of Willis Madden with James R. Brown, 1848–52, Madden Family Papers, UVA (#4120).

[50] See, e.g., Richard S. Cauthorn, "A New Anti-Periodic and a Substitute for Quinia," *Mon. Steth.*, 2 (1857), 8.

[51] L. S. Joynes, "Remarks on the Report of the Auditor . . . ," *VMJ*, 7 (1856), 7; [A. D. Galt,] *Practical Medicine: Illustrated by Cases of the Most Important Diseases,* ed. John M. Galt (Philadelphia, 1843), 206–7; John Walker to James Sims, 30 December 1844, John Walker Diary, UNC; Phebe Jackson Account Book, UVA (#2120).

[52] L. W. Madden to Father & Mother, 5 June 1850, Madden Family Papers, UVA (#4120).

least $80, all of which were paid to Drs. James and B. F. May. Similarly, Lucy Briggs (Madison County) used the services of Dr. George Thrift many times between 1845 and 1850 at a cost of $34.35. In 1851 she even paid him $5 for a practice-by-the-year contract. Shadrack Brander of Petersburg died in 1834 leaving an estate of $583.47, $36.25 of which went to settle his outstanding medical accounts. Henry Boyd, also of Petersburg, specified in his will that his physicians' bills be paid before dividing the proceeds of the estate between two beneficiaries. Though the records are scattered, evidence indicates that free blacks did request and receive medical care from white doctors and did, when possible, pay for it.[53]

But few free Negroes were regular patients of one doctor. Several received medical care as part of arrangements with whites in exchange for labor or goods; [54] the majority saw physicians only in times of extreme need and rarely, if ever, again. Some paid, and some did not, though frequently the financial transactions were not even mentioned in doctors' account books, an omission which causes one to speculate that even those practitioners who listed no freedmen probably treated a few either at no charge or without inscribing the usual "free," "f.p.o.c.," "f.m.o.c.," "f.w.o.c.," "f.n.," or "free negro" beside their names.[55]

There were physicians who went out of their way to serve local poor people, though most probably did not devote as much time and energy to them as to paying patients. One of those sympathetic to the plight of the impoverished sick was Alexander D. Galt of Williamsburg, who, in addition to serving as physician to the

[53] Jarratt Papers, owned by William Jarratt, Petersburg, Va.; Luther Porter Jackson, "The Free Negroes of Petersburg, Virginia," *JNH*, 12 (1927), 369–70; Thrift Ledger, 1844–58, pp. 89, 371, UVA (#9153d); Petersburg Account Book, III (1831–39), 146–47; Petersburg Will Book, III (5 March 1829), 17, both VSL. See also Petersburg Account Book, III, 188 (Sarah Colson); Surry County Will Book, VIII, 19 December 1832 (John Debrix), both VSL; Madden Family Papers, Estate of Hannah Clark, UVA (#4120).

[54] See, e.g., Westmoreland County Deeds and Wills, #35, 28 August 1854, agreement between Philip T. Chandler and Jessee, VSL; Berlin, *Slaves without Masters*, 251; account of John Tucker with Dr. George Thrift, Thrift Ledgers, 1844–58, p. 342, UVA (#9153d); Jean Herron Smith, *Snickersville: The Biography of a Village* (Miamisburg, Ohio, 1970), 48.

[55] f.p.o.c. = free person of color; f.m.o.c. = free man of color; f.w.o.c. = free woman of color; f.n. = free negro.

Eastern Lunatic Asylum, attended to an extensive private practice in the town and neighboring countryside. His biographer, a contemporary acquaintance and relative, described (in exaggerated language) his activities among the less fortunate members of society: "The poor regarded Dr. Galt as their especial friend. . . . Not only was he never known to exact anything from poor patients, but he from his own table furnished them with proper food, that they were unable otherwise to obtain." To substantiate his statement, the writer related a story which, he claimed, circulated among residents of James City and York counties. A rich planter living some distance from Williamsburg took quite ill and sent his servant for Dr. Galt. The doctor was busy with another patient in town and refused to accompany the slave back to his master's bedside. Twice more the slave returned with urgent appeals from the ailing planter for aid and offers of money and land as compensation. Galt, however, became annoyed at these disturbances and repeated his decision not to leave the patient he was attending. The gentleman who had sent for Galt was, according to the doctor's biographer, "the richest planter on James River," while his patient was "an old drunken free negro pauper, who had in a fit of *delirium tremens* broken his thigh bone." Galt fed as well as treated this man for some time, though ultimately he perished of gangrene "in spite of unremitting & anxious care." [56]

Other physicians performed similar services but received less recognition for their trouble. Dr. Stuart Baldwin of Winchester treated, at no charge, several sick adults and many children suffering from whooping cough among a group of 103 prospective emigrants to Liberia who were passing through the Shenandoah Valley on their way to Baltimore. In June 1802 Richmond Common Council noted that two local doctors had, without compensation, inoculated many poor people with the newly discovered cowpox vaccine. And a recently arrived dentist advertised in the

---

[56] William R. Galt, biography of Alexander D. Galt, in Sally M. Galt's handwriting, Galt Family Papers (reel 13, pp. 3–4, 6), CW. Galt's charitable activities may have been overdrawn in this sketch, but the tradition of humanitarianism among physicians like him is accurate.

Williamsburg newspaper during mid-1855 that he would extract teeth for the poor gratis.[57]

As the medical profession within the state became more organized and vocal, discussions revealing the extent of pauper practice, especially among urban dwellers, appeared in newspapers and journals. The increasing population of Virginia's cities in the 1850's, particularly the growing numbers of free blacks in Richmond, Petersburg, Norfolk, and Alexandria, added to the burdens of already busy physicians. What irked them was the frequency with which people teetering on the economic borderline between pauperism and bare subsistence requested medical aid, even though they were unable to afford it. Doctors expected this situation to arise occasionally; as their financial records show, they willingly wrote off these cases to the benefit of humanity. But the volume of charity patients was on the rise in the 1850's, as more common laborers came to towns from rural areas and abroad. People survived well enough until their incomes were suddenly terminated by severe illness. Public almshouses provided for paupers too infirm or old to work, but only doctors, nurses, and apothecaries willing to sacrifice time and money assisted temporarily poor working-class people, among whom were most of the free blacks.

One Richmond doctor reckoned that he had rendered $1,200 in services to the sick poor during one year in the 1850's. Others claimed that the approximately $50,000 in medical labor and time which one hundred or so Richmond physicians devoted to charity patients amounted to an additional "poor tax" of $500 per year per practitioner, which only those in the medical profession were required to "pay." They also calculated that Richmond's twenty apothecaries laid out about $4,000 worth of drugs and medicines for these same indigent sick people, amounting to an extra "poor tax" of $200 per druggist. Similarly, the Petersburg medical faculty (a term used to denote all physicians within the community) estimated that approximately 6,000 of the town's 18,000 residents in 1850 were unable to pay for medical attendance. This,

---

[57] R. W. Baily to Rev. William McLain, 26 November 1851, American Colonization Society Papers (reel 66B), LC; Blanton, *19th Century*, 261; Williamsburg *Virginia Gazette*, 23 August 1855, p. 2.

they figured, resulted in a "tax" on doctors of about $10,000 to $15,000 per year. Again free blacks comprised a large proportion of this indigent group.[58]

Each physician, of course, decided how often he would answer the calls of non-paying patients. Dr. James B. McCaw of Richmond entered information regarding visits to thirteen different free black families between March 1834 and February 1835, only four of whom were charged for the service. Most entries merely stated name, date, nature of visit, and treatment, while excluding any mention of cost. Dr. Thomas H. Dunn of Mathews County collected $16.50 from two free blacks during the years 1852 to 1857, ignoring $52.75 in charges to eleven others. Between 1853 and 1856 a Rappahannock County physician cared for one black paying patient ($9) and for five black families from whom he collected nothing ($22).[59] Undoubtedly most of the thirty-four known free blacks whose cases were described in the Virginia medical press during the 1850's, and of the seven (Virginians only) identified as such in the *American Journal of the Medical Sciences* from 1827 to 1861, received free medical care, though physicians always omitted this information from published articles.[60]

Impoverished and poorly paid free Negroes had several alternatives to this reliance on local physicians' humanitarian instincts. The major source of medical assistance for the totally indigent

[58] Editorial, *Mon. Steth.*, 1 (1856), 498–501; Editorial, "Pauper Practice," *ibid.*, 700–701; Petersburg *Daily Express*, 25 April 1859, p. 1. See also Editorial, "The New Comers," *Mon. Steth.*, 2 (1857), 146; Editorial, *Steth.*, 5 (1855), 742.

[59] McCaw Journal, pp. 33, 44, 50, 54, 56, 74, 76, 77, 94, 97, UVA (#38–54); Dunn Account Books, I, 60, 66–69; II, 14, 15, 18, 60, 78; III, 1, 37, 38, 69, VSL; Holloway Accounts, pp. 49, 77, 82, 95, 98, 104, 106, 116, 117, 123, 189, UVA (#6133b). See also Thrift Ledgers, 1844–58, pp. 2, 89, 162, 229, 279, 371, 412; 1852–58, pp. 33, 127, 129, 290, UVA (#9153d); Ambler Account Book, pp. 4, 5, 8, Hullihen Papers, UVA (#6394); Wilson Ledger, p. 103, W&M; Hubard Family Papers, vol. 13, p. 60, UNC; Day Account Books (Nat Hanby bill, 9 October 1857), VHS.

[60] See, e.g., P. C. Spencer, "The Results of Twenty-eight Operations for Stone in the Bladder," *VMJ*, 11 (1858), 1–7; D. H. Pendleton, "Ergot upon a Blistered Surface," *VMJ*, 9 (1857), 222–24; [Galt,] *Practical Medicine*, 39–41, 206–7, 272; Robert G. Jennings, "Remarks on the Use of the Tampon in Uterine Hemorrhage, with a Report of Two Cases," *Steth.*, 3 (1853), 209; William W. Parker, "Treatment of Erysipelas by a Somewhat New Method, Illustrated by a Few Cases," *VMJ*, 9 (1857), 355–63.

was the poorhouse. County overseers of the poor hired physicians to treat paupers both in the poorhouse and in the community, or reimbursed caretakers for medical expenses incurred. In most cases free blacks received professional attention during times of illness—often better care than their kindred living just above the poverty level.[61] Thus the overseers in York County directed Dr. Alexander D. Galt to visit a "pauper of Colour" who had burned his foot. Galt found the injury so severe as to require amputation, a procedure he was unwilling to undertake but which he believed his friend Dr. Peachy could perform. Dr. J. M. Holloway of Rappahannock County treated five free black pauper families during the mid-1850's for amounts ranging from $2 to $25, and whites for as much (in one case) as $53.75.[62] Doctors hired by county officials attended the poor for all conditions, ranging from childbirth and its complications to the usual common illnesses. Those paupers (black as well as white) residing in areas near medical schools (Richmond, Charlottesville, Winchester, Worsham, and Petersburg) had the dubious additional distinction of receiving treatment before, and sometimes by, interested though inexperienced students (see chapter 9).

Those freedmen neither destitute enough to qualify for almshouse care nor wealthy enough to pay their own medical bills took advantage of the few dispensaries established in some towns prior to the Civil War. One of the earliest opened in Charlottesville in 1826 as part of the University of Virginia Medical School. The professor of medicine treated, in view of students, "all *poor, free, persons, disordered in body, topically or generally . . . gratis.*" Alexandria operated a busy dispensary from the 1830's to at least 1860, issuing drugs or prescriptions for medicines, as well as for leeching and cupping, which the poor carried to local

[61] Auditor's Item #227, Overseers of the Poor Papers, Fredericksburg (box 1), VSL; Richmond Common Council Minutes, II, 73 (16 February 1795), VSL; Editorial, "Professional Remuneration," *Mon. Steth.*, 1 (1856), 633; Bagley, "History of the Public Health of Norfolk," 105–6; Henry Lee Heiskell, "Case of Extra-Uterine Foetation, in Which the Foetus Remained in the Abdomen Forty Years," *AJMS*, NS 2 (1828), 114–16.

[62] Dr. A. D. Galt to Dr. Peachy, 29 November 1821, Galt Family Papers (Personal; reel 2), CW; Holloway Accounts, Index, UVA (#6133b); Staunton City Records, Duke Transfer, in Overseer of the Poor Papers (box 5; reimbursement receipts), VSL.

apothecaries or bleeders. Between March 1857 and March 1858 the city paid $72.75 to a man who leeched and cupped patients sent to him by dispensary physicians. Most other dispensaries were established on an *ad hoc* basis during outbreaks of cholera and yellow fever (see chapter 7).[63]

One final source of medical attention for poor free blacks was the hospital, a place where lower-class members of society could obtain relatively inexpensive but usually good medical care. Most of the medical school infirmaries in Virginia admitted some non-paying patients, as did private hospitals such as Bellevue in Richmond and Montaeri in Petersburg.[64] Black patients usually paid less than whites. Wards were separated by race at the Medical College of Virginia and the Thomsonian Infirmary in Richmond (founded in 1838), and undoubtedly at the other antebellum hospitals.[65] Free blacks not residing in one of Virginia's larger towns had no recourse to hospitals other than those which might have existed in conjunction with county almshouses. For them, a trip to the city was necessary.

It is difficult to assess the quality of medical care that free blacks received. Based on published accounts in medical journals, the treatment was quite good, with some physicians going out of their way to cure patients. But these have to be considered cases in which the doctor put in an extra effort, perhaps just because they seemed worthy of future publication. To second-guess physicians' motives and degrade the humanitarian aspect of all medical care would be unfair. Even today physicians take more pains with some patients than with others for a variety of reasons, ranging from personal involvement and sympathy to prospects of

[63] University of Virginia Minutes of the Rector and Visitors, I, 99 (4 April 1826), I, 168 (12 July 1828), III, 22 (5 July 1838), University of Virginia Manuscripts, UVA; City of Alexandria Papers, UVA (#7146).

[64] "Petition of the Medical Department of Hampden-Sidney College," *Leg. Docs.*, 1848–49, doc. 37, p. 5; Thomas Pollard, "Bellevue Hospital Reports," *VMJ*, 10 (1858), 285–92, 378–82 (not all free blacks mentioned here could have paid for care at the hospital); Blanton, *19th Century*, 221–22.

[65] Hampden-Sidney College, Medical Department, *Catalog* [for 1851–52], 15; *ibid.*, [1844–45], 21; *Richmond Enquirer*, 8 May 1860 (advertisement), p. 3; Blanton, *19th Century*, 222; Bagley, "History of the Public Health of Norfolk," 111; *Richmond Enquirer*, 19 June 1838, p. 4; Petersburg *Daily Express*, 22 May 1860, p. 2.

fame from publication. However, a look at non-publishing physicians' account books for the antebellum period reveals that some doctors did visit their free black patients several times during an illness, despite the fact that the people could not afford to compensate them for their trouble.[66]

Two published papers which appeared in the *Virginia Medical and Surgical Journal* indicate that free blacks, like other patients of the day, did not always receive the best treatment. In 1853 Carter P. Johnson related how a fifty-five-year-old Richmond black man with long-standing "inguinal hernia" died because the doctors who had fitted him for trusses over the years had failed to examine the scrotum closely enough. Autopsy revealed the supposed rupture to be a testicular tumor. The following year a Petersburg physician, R. L. Madison, reported another case of neoplasm, this time in a forty-six-year-old woman who had been seeing doctors for at least fourteen years for uterine symptoms. No practitioner had ever performed a pelvic exam on her before prescribing one or another remedy, until Madison, "being hurried at the time" of his first visit, finally did so some four months later. Her huge uterine polyp was removed and she survived the procedure quite well.[67]

To avoid placing excessive reliance upon the uncertain, inconsistent, and humbling benevolence of the white medical world, some free blacks joined together, both formally and informally, to aid one another in times of need. Isolated rural residents did this in a less organized manner; those in towns such as Petersburg and Richmond founded actual societies. These formal organizations were of two types: benevolent associations and church groups. Private organizations existed for those able to pay the initiation fee and weekly or monthly dues. These benevolent societies, which, according to one man who interviewed former slaves, "existed in every city of any size in Virginia," provided

[66] See, e.g., Bohannan Accounts "C," p. 27, VSL; Ambler Account Book, p. 5, Hullihen Papers, UVA (#6394); Thrift Ledgers, 1852–58, p. 33, UVA (#9153d).

[67] Carter P. Johnson, "A Report of Two Cases Illustrative of the Difficulty Occasionally Met With in the Diagnosis of Scrotal Tumours," *VMSJ*, 1 (1853), 8–10; R. L. Madison, "Case of Fibrous Polypus of the Uterus," *ibid.*, 3 (1854), 185–89.

medical aid in times of sickness, death benefits to members' survivors, and a burial plot in the society's cemetery.[68] Black churches such as the First African Baptist Church of Richmond, one of the largest in the Old Dominion, supported community aid groups from weekly collections and large individual gifts. They provided nursing care and general assistance to diseased and aged blacks.[69]

Benevolent societies and church groups made illness more comfortable to bear for those freedmen with ties to such organizations. Most free blacks, however, simply relied on their own "doctoring" skills. They were usually medically neglected by the white community, except in extreme emergencies, life-threatening sicknesses, or epidemics which might spread through an entire town or rural neighborhood. Though they did receive some medical attention, free blacks were at the bottom of the health care hierarchy.

[68] For fuller descriptions of these societies, see W. P. Burrell, "The Negro in Insurance," *Proceedings of the Hampton Negro Conference*, VIII (1904), 13; James B. Browning, "The Beginnings of Insurance Enterprise among Negroes," *JNH*, 22 (1937), 429–31.

[69] Berlin, "Slaves Who Were Free," 430–31.

CHAPTER 7

Epidemics

Most diseases that struck antebellum Virginians aroused little attention among the general citizenry or local governments. People contracted measles, pneumonia, or dysentery without exciting a public outcry that special health measures should be taken in the community. But the outbreak (or threat of an outbreak) of smallpox, cholera, or yellow fever provoked newspaper editors, city councils, normally dormant boards of health, and individual citizens into almost frantic activity. These three diseases were among the most vicious and fatal of the day, often more virulent than any of the usual childhood maladies or adult disorders. Every possible preventive measure was usually taken. Fortunately for slaves and free blacks, their health counted, too, in terms of maintaining a cheap, menial labor force and restricting contagion from others. Blacks counted heavily in all public health actions of city and county governments during times of threatened or actual epidemics. As a result, under these special conditions, health care was maintained at a higher level for blacks than their circumstances and positions in society would have indicated.

Smallpox (Variola)[1]

Between the Revolution and Civil War sporadic outbreaks

of smallpox occurred throughout the Old Dominion.[2] People generally understood that the disease was a concern of the entire community—that one case might infect a town or farm population, scarring and killing large numbers. Slaveowners wished to protect their investments, and whites feared contagion from the free black and slave sectors. Consequently inoculation and, after 1800, vaccination (see chapter 9) gained popularity and acceptance in Virginia. When a case was reported in the neighborhood, slaveowners called in physicians to vaccinate their Negroes, town councils reestablished boards of health, humanitarian practitioners and public officials offered free vaccinations to the poor (including especially free blacks), and citizens had local governments remove the boards from, or make provisions to rent, a "hospital" in which to isolate victims.

It was well known that isolation of smallpox victims was absolutely necessary to impede contagion. Rural and town folk alike adhered to this practice. Several Buckingham County planters worked together in 1850 during a county-wide epidemic to segregate all those slaves who had contracted or been exposed to smallpox onto one or two designated farms. Residents in a district of Prince Edward County did the same in 1856. Isolation of cases in cities was pursued just as vigorously, perhaps more so, since so many white and black lives depended on it. One of Richmond's first outbreaks after the Revolution occurred in December 1790 and typified the pattern of response. A servant owned by Isaac Lane developed smallpox while working for another man in town. The common council immediately took up the matter in order "to render the Inhabitants secure from the danger" of con-

---

[1] Smallpox at its worst produces confluent or discrete papules (pocks) over the entire body, destroying skin tissue, and causing death from blood poisoning (toxemia). The disease does not always kill patients, especially when it strikes in the milder forms. Infection is most often transmitted through contaminated air droplets from victims' respiratory systems, or through infected clothing, bedding, etc. Blacks are no more or less immune to smallpox than are whites, all other factors (e.g., previous exposure) being equal. For more on smallpox, see C. W. Dixon, *Smallpox* (London, 1962).

[2] John Duffy, *Epidemics in Colonial America* (Baton Rouge, 1953), 16–23, 104–5; Blanton, *17th Century*, 60–61, 126–27; Blanton, *18th Century*, 284–87; Blanton, *19th Century*, 259–64.

tagion. This body procured a house in which to isolate the patient, appointed a guard and attendants, furnished "every thing necessary for his recovery," and paid all expenses out of city funds. Williamsburg town authorities had been following similar procedures for many years.[3]

A second response, in addition to isolation, was inoculation or (after 1801) vaccination of the non-immune population. Again, precedents were set during the eighteenth century for actions which became standard in the nineteenth. Inoculation, a technique imported from African and Asian cultures at the end of the seventeenth century, involved the introduction of live smallpox matter from a patient's scab into susceptible persons to produce, it was hoped, a mild case and subsequent immunity. However, people with light cases still had to be isolated for a period of time, lest they spread the disease to others. Despite the fears of many regarding the possibility of epidemics resulting from inoculated persons being released from isolation too soon, people still requested the procedure when smallpox struck. In 1792, when the disease infected residents of Norfolk and Hampton, the authorities permitted general free inoculation of those indigent residents who desired it. Two Williamsburg physicians even prepared to capitalize on the scare by inoculating, for a fee, all applicants in the countryside between their town and Hampton. The Richmond Common Council dealt with an epidemic in December 1793 both by isolating the original slave and other victims, and by instituting a general inoculation of the populace during the following two months.[4]

After Thomas Jefferson and Benjamin Waterhouse introduced Jennerian vaccination in 1801, this technique became the ac-

[3] Edmund W. Hubard to Sallie E. Hubard, 8, 12, 13 January 1850, Hubard Family Papers, UNC; Captain John Marshall Journal, 24 February 1856, UVA (#2425); Richmond Common Council Minutes, I, 221 (24 December 1790), VSL; *Virginia Gazette* (Purdie and Dixon), 28 January, p. 2; 4 February, p. 3; 11 February, p. 2, 1768.

[4] Mariana Bagley, "The History of the Public Health of Norfolk, Virginia, up to 1860" (M.A. thesis, Duke University, 1939), 31–32; J. Greenhow to ———, 18 July 1792, and Lucretia Craig to Alexander Galt, 20 November 1792, Galt Family Papers (Personal; reel 1), CW; Richmond Common Council Minutes, II, 38 (14 December 1793), VSL; *Calendar of Virginia State Papers and Other Manuscripts, 1652–1781* (Richmond, 1893), VII, 394, 369.

cepted prophylaxis against smallpox. For instance, Martha Jefferson Randolph, the President's daughter, vaccinated her three youngest children and many of the slaves at Edgehill (Albermarle County) when several smallpox cases appeared in 1808 at Staunton, a town on the stage line to Charlottesville (the nearby county seat). The discovery of smallpox on a vessel in Richmond's harbor in 1816 prompted the city fathers "to concert measures for the encouragement of vaccination" at public expense.[5] Slaves and indigent free blacks benefited from the whites' concern for their human property and their own lives.

Isolation and vaccination were the only defenses Virginians had against smallpox. People learned that preparation for an epidemic greatly reduced the chances of its spread, and some, accordingly, took these preventive measures early, even before the disease threatened to strike. Planters vaccinated their slaves and families, and municipal authorities similarly protected the health of town residents, especially the poor, without charge. In rural areas physicians often visited and treated all members of a plantation household at once. Dr. John Spence of Dumphries (Prince William County) was one of the first to obtain vaccine matter after Jefferson's successes in Albermarle in 1801, offering protection to numbers of whites and blacks in his neighborhood. Others vaccinated their large "families" and carefully recorded those which "took" and those which did not, so that revaccination might secure protection. Several planters repeated this procedure periodi-

[5] Martha Jefferson Randolph to Thomas Jefferson, 24 November 1808, in Edwin M. Betts and James A. Bear, Jr., ed., *The Family Letters of Thomas Jefferson* (Columbia, Mo., 1966), 361; Richmond Common Council Minutes, V, 223–24 (19 August 1816), VSL.

[6] John Spence, "Observations on the Inoculation of the Kine-Pock: Communicated by John Spence, M.D. of Dumphries, Virginia, to Dr. Waterhouse," *Medical Repository*, 5 (1802), 381–87; Shirley Farm Journals, 31 March, 1 April 1822 (at end of vol. I), 23 February, 1 March 1825, 26 April 1835, and n.d. [1836] (on 13th page from end of vol. II), LC; Woolfolk Papers, 5 April 1829, [July?] 1837 (folder 29), W&M; Cox Accounts, on page following front cover and on back cover of vol. II, UNC; account of William James with Dr. A. D. Galt, 14 December 1824, Galt Family Papers (Personal), CW; Buffalo Forge Journal, 1859–66, last page, Weaver-Brady Papers, UVA (#38–98); St. George Tucker Coalter to John Coalter, 15 March 1829, Brown-Coalter-Tucker Papers, W&M; John Walker Diary, 29 June 1836, UNC.

cally, as it was known that the preventive effects lasted only for several years.[6]

Richmond, Norfolk, Alexandria, and Petersburg provided free vaccination to the poor at various times prior to 1860, both in the wake of epidemics and when none threatened. Smaller towns followed suit, paying for that procedure and for isolation facilities for smallpox victims.[7] The University of Virginia vaccinated indigent members of the Charlottesville-Albemarle County community gratis during the late 1820's in conjunction with its medical and surgical clinics. And a Richmond physician, responding to a typical panic reaction among the residents of his district, vaccinated 151 people, including 42 blacks, between 3 November 1855 and 7 March 1856, after an epidemic broke out.[8]

Though smallpox was a greatly feared disease, and though outbreaks reported in the public press were constant reminders that it might strike anywhere, anytime, white Virginians were surprisingly lax about vaccinating themselves, their slaves, and their free black neighbors. One physician, whose job as state vaccine agent was to distribute kinepox matter upon request to physicians throughout Virginia, discussed in a long article in the *Virginia Medical and Surgical Journal* how "persons will only consent to be vaccinated under immediate alarm of variola." This situation not only threatened to deplete the available supply of vaccine in the event of a sudden outbreak, but also endangered the public health. There were some who refused to believe that vaccination was an effective preventative against smallpox, but they were in

[7] Bagley, "History of Public Health of Norfolk," 34–37; Richmond Common Council Minutes, XII, 1 (24 January 1848), VSL; Fredericksburg Records, Mayor's Court, 25 May 1834, UVA (#4141); City of Alexandria Papers, 9 October 1845 (receipt of H. P. Howard, M.D.), UVA (#7146); *Lynchburg Virginian*, —— 1847 (in Treasurer's Report); William Browne, "On the Influence of Vaccination in Counteracting the Effects of Smallpox Contagion," *AJMS*, 15 (1834–35), 400–401 (Fredericksburg); James D. Davidson to ——, 25 January 1860, Weaver Papers, Duke (Lexington); Petersburg *Daily South Side Democrat*, 15 December 1855, p. 2 (Lawrenceville); Petersburg *Press*, 13 March 1860, p. 2 (Lawrenceville); *Lynchburg Virginian*, 10 June 1856, p. 3 (Clarksville).

[8] Charlottesville *Virginia Advocate*, 16 February 1828, p. 2; William W. Parker, "Remarkable Consequences of Vaccination during the Recent Smallpox Epidemic," *VMJ*, 6 (1856), 315–16.

the minority. By the 1850's medical authorities and laymen had even recognized the transitory nature of immunity from vaccination and the importance of periodic repetition of the procedure.[9]

But too often people simply waited until the last minute to vaccinate. On the Rappahannock County plantation of Charles Green, thirty of one hundred slaves had been taken with smallpox and one had died by August 1854, with more cases expected among the unprotected bondsmen. A Halifax County man, Jonathan Carrington, who had hired several slaves to Jonathan M. Sutherlin's tobacco factory in Danville, suddenly took alarm when smallpox was reported in that town. Carrington ordered Sutherlin to vaccinate his unprotected slaves immediately. An outbreak in Lexington (Rockbridge County) prompted the overseer of nearby Mulberry Hill plantation hastily to vaccinate all the slaves under his management.[10] Even if they were aware of vaccination and its significance, bondsmen had no access to kinepox matter or to physicians who might have provided them with it. It was the master's responsibility, and all too frequently he hesitated to fulfill it until the last minute. A preventable disease often caused unnecessary deaths among slaves.

Though some whites hesitated to vaccinate because of frugality, distrust of the procedure's efficacy, or an assumption that smallpox would not strike their slaves on isolated plantations, most failed to do so for another reason. Vaccination had lulled Virginians, like other Americans, into a false sense of security about smallpox. After the initial frenzy of vaccinating activity during the first decade or two of the nineteenth century, people began to forget about the disease. It did not strike as frequently anymore, nor did outbreaks spread so widely. Vaccination and isolation effectively controlled cases which did occur. So the prophylactic procedure gradually became less important and less used by the 1840's and 1850's. Public health officials were unable to convince many people to vaccinate themselves or their slaves until epi-

    [9] Arthur E. Peticolas, "The Vaccine Law of the Virginia Code," *VMSJ*, 2 (1854), 450–51; Zachary Lewis, "An Instance in Which Vaccination Protected a Whole Family after One Member of It Had the Disease Fully Developed," *Steth.*, 3 (1853), 144–46. See also "Vaccine Agent," in *Leg. Docs.* 1848/49, doc. 22.

demics startled them back into reality. By then it was too late for some.[11]

Free blacks, especially those in poor financial situations, were in the same dependent position as their enslaved brethren. Those freedmen who knew about vaccination might request it from local physicians or dispensaries, but not all of them understood the need for such protection, or desired it. City governments provided periodic free inoculations to the indigent—a great help to urban free blacks, though even then many were missed. And at least two cities, Richmond and Petersburg, passed ordinances requiring the removal of all free Negroes with contagious diseases to the municipal hospitals for the purposes of separating them from healthy individuals and treating them for the malady.[12] But rural blacks did not have easy access to physicians, or the awareness which some city dwellers had regarding the importance of vaccination and isolation. It is not surprising, then, to find frequent mention of free blacks as victims of smallpox in newspaper accounts, personal letters, and city government reports.[13]

Whites paid for their lax attitude toward vaccinating blacks each time the disease erupted. Town authorities would hastily establish hospitals and provide excellent medical care at great expense. Vaccination programs were not comprehensive enough to reach into all Negro households, leaving a number of residents exposed to contagion. The disease developed in Fredericksburg in 1834, for instance, after a free black steamboat attendant returned from his job in Baltimore for a visit and for recuperation from a bout with smallpox. Some of the scabs were still contagious

[10] Petersburg *Daily South Side Democrat*, 14 August 1854, p. 2; Jno. B. Carrington to Jno. M. Sutherlin, 5 April 1858, Sutherlin Papers, Duke; Ulrich B. Phillips, *Life and Labor in the Old South* (Boston, 1929), 314.

[11] Martin Kaufman, "The American Anti-Vaccinationists and Their Arguments," *BHM*, 41 (1967), 464; John Duffy, ed., *Rudolph Matas History of Medicine in Louisiana* (Baton Rouge, 1958), I, 375.

[12] Petersburg, *The Charter and Laws of the City of Petersburg* (Petersburg, 1852), 68; Richmond Common Council Minutes, XIV, 375 (17 May 1860), VSL. Whites were permitted to provide themselves with suitable accommodations at their own homes.

[13] See, e.g., Socrates Maupin to Addison Maupin, 30 November 1836, Maupin-Washington Manuscripts, UVA (#2769a); Editorial, "The Vaccine Agency," *Mon. Steth.*, 1 (1856), 321; Norfolk *Daily Southern Argus*, 22 March 1849, p. 2.

and none of his family had been vaccinated, with inevitable results. Fortunately none of the family died. When one freedman developed variola in Clarksville in 1856, the village authorities had to quarantine the infected district and remove to an isolated area those who had been exposed. Port Walthall (Chesterfield County) residents paid Dr. Luke White to travel from Petersburg to care for the fifteen blacks and four whites who had contracted smallpox between March and May 1858. Once the disease had erupted in a town, there was no knowing who might develop it. The result was panic with, as one newspaper described it, "people . . . being vaccinated in all directions." [14] Though free and slave blacks ultimately received good care once the disease threatened or struck, many remained unnecessarily exposed and were helpless to change the situation.

Cholera [15]

Thanks to the recurring outbreaks of smallpox, by the time the first cholera epidemic struck Virginia in 1832 residents

[14] Browne, "On the Influence of Vaccination," 401; *Lynchburg Virginian*, 10 June 1856, p. 3; Petersburg *Daily Express*, 29 May 1858, p. 1; Petersburg *Daily South Side Democrat*, 15 November 1855, p. 2. See also George Hairston to Eliza Penn, 5 January 1842, E. S. Hairston Papers, UNC.

[15] The major symptom is diarrhea, caused by a toxin which the *Vibrio cholerae* (a comma-shaped bacteria) releases into the small intestine. In severe cases this may amount to one liter (about one quart) per hour, though it is usually less than half that. As dehydration and chemical imbalance develop, patients become weaker until shock and cardiovascular collapse bring death. The course of cholera is from one to several days, but it may kill within a few hours of onset. Severe illness, however, is not the usual result of infection with *V. cholerae*. Cholera is a disease with many gradations of severity, varying from the extreme form to inapparent infections. These less severe types, not recognized until 1960, help explain the epidemiological pattern seen in the nineteenth-century Virginia outbreaks. Cholera is basically a water-borne disease, contracted through drinking water, foods washed in water, fish or other sea animals and vegetables caught in the water, or fruit, vegetables, and other foods which obtain nourishment from water. There appears to be no racial predisposition toward cholera; however, owing to environmental conditions, members of the lower socioeconomic groups tend to become infected more readily than upper classes. For more on cholera, see Dhiman Barua and William Barrows, eds., *Cholera* (Philadelphia, 1974), esp. 209–19, 359–96; World Health Organization, *Principles and Practice of Cholera Control* (Geneva, 1970); Eugene J. Gangarosa, "The Epidemiology of Cholera: Past and Present," *Bulletin of the New York Academy of Medicine*, 47 (1971), 1140–51.

of the state had already established procedures for handling contagious diseases. Unfortunately, however, isolation of patients, either at home or at hospitals, had little effect on the spread of cholera. Nor were there effective public health measures, such as vaccination, street and house cleaning, or stagnant pond drainage, which could reduce its virulence or invasiveness. Cholera was a new disease of unknown etiology with no known cure. It marched across the eastern and far western portions of the Old Dominion in 1832, by-passing almost everything between, regardless of the steps communities did or did not take to prevent its appearance. Cholera entered the state three more times before the Civil War, and each time it traveled unpredictably, unhampered by human efforts to restrict it. Slaves and free blacks seemed always to suffer the most from its ravages, but whites also felt its effects.

Nineteenth-century white Virginians often related high morals, clean living, and religious orthodoxy to immunity during cholera epidemics. White paupers, free blacks, and slaves, because of their supposed degraded condition, sinful ways, and filthy habits, were regarded as prime targets for cholera—deserving of such a plague. But for an upstanding Caucasian, contraction of the disease threatened not only his life, but also the respected position he had earned in the community. For this reason many white deaths were attributed to diarrhea, dysentery, or bilious fever rather than cholera. For instance, when a prominent attorney and a "wealthy and worthy merchant" of Richmond died during September 1832, the editors of the *Enquirer* disclaimed any connection between their deaths and the prevailing epidemic: "But Mr. French had been previously sick, and much debilitated—and his death did not proceed from the Cholera." "Mr. Archibald Taylor . . . died on Sunday evening, not of the Cholera, but of a bilious Fever." Similarly, the Norfolk Board of Health reported at the start of the 1832 epidemic that three deaths had occurred, all "confined to people of color," classifying the one white death "under the head of 'doubtful.'"[16] Though they did not know that there were gradations in severity of the disease, whites must have suspected that cases of diarrhea during epidemics represented

[16] *Richmond Enquirer,* 25 September 1832, p. 3; Norfolk *American Beacon,* 31 July 1832, p. 2.

at least a mild form of cholera, for they too shuddered at the first symptoms of bowel problems and feared that the plague had descended upon them despite their righteousness. Later, when the diarrhea had passed, they pointed to their illnesses as examples of the kind of disease "proper" people got.

Littleton Waller Tazewell, a respected Virginia statesman, was living in Norfolk when cholera struck in 1832. Both his white and black families escaped illness for about two weeks, and then suffered three cases in four days. His laundress died five hours after the first appearance of symptoms; his gardener took sick while walking in the street and succumbed the following morning; his son developed the premonitory symptoms of the disease but recovered several days later. Tazewell accepted the diagnosis of cholera in his two servants because he expected blacks to contract this malady. "It has been confined," he wrote to a friend in Richmond, "very much to the negroes, altho' a few whites in that class of society next above the slaves in condition have also fallen victims." But when the doctors informed him that his own son also had cholera, he denied it then and later, calling it "a simple attack of bilious fever." Such an illness, in his mind, could afflict only the lower classes of whites. Of the twenty whites who had perished from cholera to that point, Tazewell continued in his letter, "there has not been one known to me either by name or reputation. You may infer from this fact something of the true character of the distemper." Though he recognized that mild cases had occurred in Norfolk, he based his diagnosis of bilious fever rather than cholera on his son's recovery: "The event proved the correctness of my opinion, for his fever left him in three or four days. . . ." Cholera, according to some, was a disease of the poor and the dark skinned.[17]

In truth, cholera was more destructive to the black than the

---

[17] Littleton W. Tazewell to J. Wickham, 17 September 1832, Wickham Papers, UVA (#409). I wish to thank Professor Norma Peterson of Adams State College, Alamosa, Colo., for bringing this letter to my attention. For an excellent discussion of social attitudes toward cholera during this period, see Charles E. Rosenberg, *The Cholera Years: The United States in 1832, 1849, and 1866* (Chicago, 1962). Other examples of Virginians' prejudices against the black and the indigent may be found in *Richmond Enquirer*, 2 November 1832, p. 2; 2 October 1832, p. 3; *Alexandria Phenix Gazette*, 26 September 1832, p. 2.

white population of Virginia. We have no way of ascertaining true morbidity rates because many cases went unreported, even in cities which required daily accountings by each physician. But we can assume that it invaded both races extensively, and we can determine in a rough way the comparative virulence of the disease among white and blacks by looking at the available—admittedly imprecise, but nonetheless useful—mortality reports. It is also possible to explain the probable reasons for the greater malignancy of cholera among Negroes.

Epidemics occurred during at least four different years in the state's major cities and surrounding countryside. The two worst were in 1832 and 1849, with more limited outbreaks in 1834 and 1854.[18] Despite valiant efforts by health officials to maintain accurate statistics, neither patients nor physicians were willing to offer full cooperation, with the result that in most cities figures are incomplete. Because the most visible patients were those treated at city pest houses, and because whites were permitted to remain isolated at home rather than move to one of these hospitals, the records (see Table 12) are weighted toward black cases. Despite Caucasian reluctance to diagnose many instances of diarrhea and cholera-like symptoms as cholera, and to report cases to the authorities, all evidence indicates that blacks still suffered the disease's ravages to a greater extent than whites. Not only did they contract it more often, but they also died more frequently; perhaps even at twice the rate of whites, as contemporary statistics showed.

Free blacks and urban slaves usually lived in the lowest parts of town, near rivers or streams, which served both as sources of potable water and as depositories of excrement. Poverty brought with it filth, poor nutrition, and decreased resistance to disease. Intemperance, where it existed, further reduced the possibilities of good health. Were cholera to strike any group more commonly than another, lower-class blacks (and whites) constituted an exceptionally susceptible population. It is not surprising, then, to read comments in letters such as: "The colored are falling fast

[18] A history of cholera in Virginia has yet to be written. There were even smaller outbreaks in 1833 and perhaps annually between 1850 and 1853.

Table 12. Cholera Morbidity and Mortality in Virginia, 1832–54

	Percent of known cases			Percent of known deaths		
	White	Black	N	White	Black	N
			1832			
Norfolk [a]	20.5	79.5	171[*]	26.0	74.0	453 [b]
Richmond [c]	21.5	78.5	121[*]	27.9	72.1	494 [d]
Alexandria [e]	40.5	59.5	42[*]	—	—	—
Suffolk [f]	14.8	85.2	27[*]	15.4	84.6	13[*]
Fortress Monroe [g]	65.5	34.5	58[*]	64.0	36.0	25[*]
Hampton [h]	—	—	—	20.0	80.0	20[*]
Smithfield [i]	14.3	85.7	28[*]	16.0	84.0	25[*]
			1834			
Petersburg [j]	39.3	60.7	135[*]	34.8	65.2	23[*]
			1849			
Norfolk [k]	53.7	46.3	188[*]	33.7	66.3	101
Richmond [l]	42.8	57.2	348[*]	39.7	60.3	224[*]
			1854			
Richmond [m]	—	—	—	43.1	56.9	260[*]
Total	36.7	63.3	—	31.6	68.4	—
(excluding Fortress Monroe)	(389)	(671)	(1,060)	(509)	(1,104)	(1,613)

[*] These are not the complete figures for the entire epidemic in that locality. Newspapers did not always report all cases *during* an epidemic, but then gave mortality totals *when the disease had disappeared.* For this reason the number of deaths in this list sometimes exceeds the number of known cases. It is not possible to compute a ratio of deaths to cases for the same reason.

[a] [Norfolk] *American Beacon*—cases: 31 July to 14 August 1832; deaths: 18 September 1832.

[b] About 35 of these deaths were attributed to causes other than cholera, though details were not supplied.

[c] *Richmond Enquirer*—cases: 7 September to 19 October 1832; deaths: 23 October 1832, p. 3.

[d] About 45 of these deaths were claimed to be not attributable to cholera, though the racial breakdown and probable causes of death were not supplied.

[e] *Alexandria Phenix Gazette*, 6 October 1832, p. 2.

[f] [Norfolk] *American Beacon*, 9 August 1832, p. 2.

[g] *Ibid.*, 11 September 1832, p. 2. Almost all the white cases and deaths were among soldiers.

[h] *Ibid.*, 18 September 1832, p. 2.

[i] *Ibid.*—cases: 13 September 1832, p. 2; deaths: *Richmond Enquirer*, 14 September 1832, p. 3.

[j] *Richmond Enquirer*, 28 October 1834, p. 2; 31 October 1834, p. 2; 11 November 1834, p. 4; *Lynchburg Virginian*, 10 November 1834.

around us." "A few cases have appeared yesterday & to day in this Borough [Norfolk], confined so far *exclusively* to the Blacks." [19] Or to read in Board of Health reports: ". . . a colored woman, named Jemima, aged 50 years, intemperate in her habits, of feeble health, living in a dirty, damp cellar . . . died about 9 o'clock on Sunday morning." [20]

One Norfolk physican noted that during the 1832 epidemic three-quarters of the victims were black, of whom "the greater lived in *low damp* places, in the basements of houses, in cellars and in kitchens without floors." He also commented on the inordinate occurrence of cholera among cooks, the group most closely allied with food handling and, more often than not, members of the Negro race.[21] A look at the residences of Richmond's known free black cholera victims in 1849 shows that of thirty-one whose homes were mentioned, thirteen lived in neighborhoods directly adjacent to docks on the James River or the James River and Kanawha Canal.[22] The combination of racial stigma and poor living conditions made it a foregone conclusion to Caucasians that the Negro would suffer most from the ravages of cholera.

Whites explained the large number of black cholera cases not only on the basis of inadequate housing, intemperance, and moral corruption, but also on the black's apparently casual attitude toward self-care. Officials, newspaper editors, and charitable groups felt that despite their attempts to teach blacks proper precautions and treatments, these people remained imprudent. They refused to change their habits in the face of impending danger, much to the detriment of themselves, their masters, and the public. One of the major complaints was that blacks all too

---

ᵏ [Norfolk] *Daily Southern Argus*—cases: 30 May to 27 June 1849; deaths: 30 May to 1 August 1849.
ˡ Cases: Richmond Board of Health Minutes, 1849, VHS; deaths: *Richmond Enquirer*, 17 August 1849, p. 1.
ᵐ [Richmond] *Daily Dispatch*, 18 July to 26 September 1854.

[19] William Campbell to Laommi Baldwin, Jr., 5 August 1832, Baldwin Family Papers, Harvard (Baker); William McKenney to Charles Howard, 30 July 1832, Maryland State Colonization Society Papers, Maryland Historical Society.
[20] *Richmond Enquirer*, 14 September 1832, p. 3.
[21] Tebault Papers, Lecture Notebook #3, p. 107, UVA (#9926). See also *Alexandria Phenix Gazette*, 26 September 1832, p. 2 (question 3).
[22] Richmond Board of Health Minutes, 1849, VHS.

often ignored the premonitory symptoms and waited until it was too late (i.e., just at the point of collapse) for physicians to treat them before reporting their illness. This infuriated owners and hirers who lost valuable servants. Nevertheless, it is doubtful that purging, vomiting, and bleeding, the usual physicians' treatments for cholera, could have done more than speed the fulminating and severe cases to the grave, or worsen the condition of those with mild or moderate attacks of the disease.[23]

Another sore spot was the Negro's penchant for eating food forbidden by public health officials because of its assumed connection with cholera. According to city authorities such foods— especially fruits and vegetables—were favorite treats of blacks and difficult to remove from their diets.[24] The owner of the first cholera victim in Richmond (1832) informed health authorities that the man had "eaten imprudently of pears" that morning. Later Board of Health reports included similar statements about other black patients: Dorcas had feasted on "meat, cheese, &c. fried together," Sawny on "shoat, chicken pie, apples, &c.," Milly Green on an "improper vegetable diet," Hannah West on "cabbage, boiled the previous day," and Patsey on a "hearty supper of boiled turnips."[25] Even after cholera had struck Richmond for the fourth time, in 1854, whites found blacks disobeying the law. "If any cause shall operate to prolong the stay of cholera among us," grumbled a newspaper editor, "it will be excessive indulgence in eating watermelons by negroes."[26] It was obviously difficult to alter the blacks' eating habits, even when their lives depended on it.

If blacks could not help themselves, either because of indigence or negligence, and in the process exposed whites to the dangers of cholera, then, the leaders of most communities decided, others would have to manage their affairs for everyone's sake. After re-

[23] See, e.g., Norfolk *American Beacon*, 16 August 1832, p. 2. On cholera treatment, see Norman Howard-Jones, "Cholera Therapy in the Nineteenth Century," *JHM*, 27 (1972), 373–95.

[24] *Alexandria Phenix Gazette*, 26 September 1832, p. 2 (question 3).

[25] *Richmond Enquirer*, 11, 14, 18, 21 September 1832, all p. 3.

[26] Richmond *Daily Dispatch*, 8 August 1854, quoted in Ira Berlin, "Slaves Who Were Free: The Free Negro in the Upper South, 1776–1861" (Ph.D. dissertation, University of Wisconsin, 1970), 393.

viewing the problems arising among the black population during
the 1832 epidemic, including poor living conditions, unwholesome
food, intemperate habits, and belated reporting of symptoms,
the Norfolk Board of Health concluded "that the best means of
preventing the spread and also the fatal termination of the disease,
is, close and strict attention to the condition, habits and health
of the colored population." This was attempted in all the large
towns of Virginia. Ordinances were passed forbidding the sale of
specified foods within city limits, such as melons, green corn, and
pineapples in Norfolk (1832), and spoiled fish, crabs, and stale
vegetables in Richmond (1854).[27] Articles were published sug-
gesting that slave quarters and the houses of rich and poor be
thoroughly cleansed and whitewashed. Some towns provided the
wherewithal for indigent blacks and whites to accomplish this
task. One public notice went so far as to recommend that "no
servants be allowed to sleep in cellars or basements," a piece of
advice which undoubtedly caused some stirrings among those
slaveholders who usually lodged their bondsmen in such places.[28]
A third set of measures aimed at improving blacks' and whites'
living conditions required private and public lots, buildings, or
waterways which threatened the community's health to be improved at owner's expense. To this end, Richmond authorities
undertook in 1849 to clean, among several sections of the city,
South Side Basin, the poor residential area near the James River
where many whites and blacks lived. Numerous cholera cases
had already occurred in that neighborhood, raising great fears
among nearby dwellers.[29]

Richmond had an additional problem which other Virginia
towns encountered on a much smaller scale. Because so many

[27] *Alexandria Phenix Gazette*, 26 September 1832, p. 2 (question 3); Norfolk
American Beacon, 26 July (p. 2), 1 August (p. 2) 1832; Richmond *Daily Dis-
patch*, 14 July 1854, p. 2; Richmond Board of Health Minutes, 9 June 1849,
VHS; Norfolk *Daily Southern Argus*, 16 July 1849, p. 2.

[28] *Richmond Enquirer*, 25 May (p. 2), 8 June (p. 1) 1849; Norfolk *Daily
Southern Argus*, 15 December 1848, p. 2; Petersburg Board of Health Minutes,
21 June 1832, Petersburg Public Library.

[29] Richmond Board of Health Minutes, 2, 4 June 1849, VHS; Richmond *Daily
Dispatch*, 15 July 1854, p. 2; Norfolk *Daily Southern Argus*, 8, 19 December
1848, both p. 2; Norfolk *American Beacon*, 31 July 1832, p. 2; Editorial, "Cholera
in Richmond," *Steth.*, 4 (1854), 477.

industries were located in the capital city, and because they often employed slaves from the country on an annual basis, there were large numbers of bondsmen living on their own. Employers frequently engaged in the practice of distributing "board money" to many of their hirelings, forcing workers to secure their own food and lodging. The system wreaked havoc with slave health, since it often resulted in poor housing, inadequate and injudicious diets, and uncertain access to proper medical aid when needed. It was especially destructive during cholera epidemics. During the 1854 outbreak, for instance, one newspaper editor asserted that four-fifths of all black cholera deaths had occurred among those given board money, while few had occurred among servants who were fed and lodged by their masters. Five years earlier the Board of Health had recommended abolition of this practice as pernicious to slave health.[30]

Prevention was only half the problem. Not only did Virginia's urban citizens attempt to protect themselves, their slaves, and their free black neighbors from cholera; they also provided treatment once the illness struck. The pest houses which had been erected previously for smallpox victims now served as cholera hospitals for the poor and the black. Usually the indigent received free medical care at these ad hoc institutions, while slaveowners paid a fee for their ailing bondsmen varying from a low of $2 per day in Norfolk and $2.50 in Petersburg, to $3 daily, plus $2 more for the first day, in Richmond. These hospitals employed a nursing staff and professional physicians, supposedly guaranteeing that treatment would be competent.[31]

Many blacks were assisted in hospitals, but others found even more personalized medical aid in the form of dispensaries, conscientious doctors, and charitable organizations. Norfolk Common Council, for instance, appropriated $500 for help to the poor during the 1832 epidemic. The Petersburg Board of Health organized its city into neighborhoods through which certain citizens

[30] Richmond *Daily Dispatch*, 18 July 1854, p. 2; Richmond Board of Health Minutes, 9 June 1849, VHS.

[31] Norfolk *American Beacon*, 16 August 1832, p. 3; Petersburg Board of Health Minutes, pp. [22, 24] 27, 28, [31] (June-September 1832), Petersburg Public Library; *Richmond Enquirer*, 18 September 1832, p. 3; *Alexandria Phenix Gazette*, August-October 1832; Bagley, "History of Public Health of Norfolk," 41.

passed each day, educating the indigent about cholera and cleanliness and providing them with needed medical aid. In Richmond (1832), physicians at the hospitals decided to dispense free medicines to all who requested them, while in Norfolk the city reimbursed physicians and apothecaries for goods and services supplied to the poor. A group of women in Alexandria, representatives of various religious denominations, banded together into an association that visited indigent families and distributed food, clothing, and money. And physicians throughout the state frequently provided medical care without charge during these distressing epidemics.[32]

Some employers of slaves took additional actions to insure their workers' continued good health during cholera epidemics, especially when worried owners threatened to remove bondsmen from affected cities. Samuel S. Myer of Richmond, owner of a large tobacco factory in 1832, applied extreme measures to protect his slaves from the disease which had originated in and continued to plague the factory district. In a *Richmond Enquirer* article Myer described how he had confined to his factory about one hundred laborers "who could not be relied on for prudence or temperance, or who were known to lodge in damp or unhealthy places." Here he fed them coffee and boiled rice daily, with herring and bacon, fresh beef or mutton two or three times a week, and cornbread and molasses once or twice a week. All food was well cooked. He prohibited them from drinking excessive amounts of water and enforced strict personal cleanliness. While the workers enjoyed their four hours of daily exercise and play outdoors, Myer aired and disinfected the factory. At night a trusted man watched them and reported any cholera symptoms to the proprietor. The system succeeded in preventing any outbreak of the disease among the hands, a fact of which Myer was proud. He compared this with the six cases and three deaths which had occurred among those sixty blacks whom he had permitted to

[32] Bagley, "History of Public Health of Norfolk," 101–2; Petersburg Board of Health Minutes, 23 August 1832 [p. 30], Petersburg Public Library; *Richmond Enquirer*, 12 October 1832, p. 3; Norfolk *Daily Southern Argus*, 19, 21 December 1848, both p. 2; *Alexandria Phenix Gazette*, 12 September 1832, p. 3; Richmond Board of Health Minutes, 9 July 1849, VHS; Norfolk *American Beacon*, 18 August 1832, p. 2.

live at home during the epidemic. Apparently Myer's factory was blessed with uncontaminated water and a cook who prepared foods thoroughly—otherwise his experiment might have been a disaster.[33]

While some industrialists followed Myer's lead, other employers did exactly the opposite. Captain Talcott, commanding engineer at Fortress Monroe (near Norfolk), simply dismissed all black laborers for the duration of the epidemic in order to reduce mortality. A Norfolk newspaper suggested a less drastic measure —suspension of labor during the hottest part of the afternoon, since, the editor reported, excessive perspiration "renders them [workers] more liable to disease." Most of those in charge of bondsmen probably took what precautions seemed most reasonable and effective, such as cleaning work areas, educating laborers about personal hygiene, proper eating habits, and temperance, exhorting them to report symptoms early, and caring for them when ill.[34]

Concern for the health of slaves during cholera outbreaks extended beyond employers to owners. Country masters who had hired out their bondsmen to urban areas naturally worried about their investments. The first instinct was to have them returned home, where cholera did not threaten. Samuel Myer lost about forty workers in 1832 to frantic owners, though some probably returned in the fall. Explained a Fredericksburg man to Messrs. Leslie and Bryden, Petersburg tobacconists: "I should suppose the risk would be very great to the owners of such property [slaves] by allowing negroes to remain exposed to the consequences [of cholera], as it would be hardly possible for the owners of the Factories to give suitable attention to the sick, and think they would be Safer with their Masters." Petersburg experienced an exodus of slaves similar to that in Richmond during the 1832 epidemic.[35]

[33] *Richmond Enquirer*, 5 October 1832, p. 3. Myer is identified as the author of this article *ibid.*, 27 November 1832, p. 3, when his factory burned down.

[34] Norfolk *American Beacon*, 11 September, 7 August 1832, both p. 2; J. F. Tanner to E. M. Mettauer, 2 August 1849, Tredegar Papers, Letterbook, VSL.

[35] *Richmond Enquirer*, 5 October 1832, p. 3; Alexander Henderson to Robert Leslie, 17 August 1832; Doctor Osborne to Robert Leslie, 17 September 1832; hiring bond of Richard Booth with Leslie and Bryden, 5 January 1833; all in Leslie Papers, Duke; Starobin, *Industrial Slavery*, 67.

There were owners who, for one reason or another, left their bondsmen in cities. J. F. Tanner, superintendent of the Tredegar Iron Works, reassured an inquiring Prince Edward County man in 1849 that "Harry is verry well indeed and I have used every precaution with him . . . to protect . . . against Cholera." Harry remained at work through the epidemic, despite the deaths of two fellow slave workers. John Walker of King and Queen County feared contracting the disease himself and consequently left his man Daniel in Richmond, where he had been hired to a free black cooper. He requested that James Sims, Daniel's employer, send the money for the hire as "I am somewhat affraid of going to Richd at the present." [36] Others apparently simply took the chance that cholera would not strike their bondsmen.

The vast majority of cases occurred in cities, and the most publicity about this disease originated there. But cholera sometimes spread fingers of destruction out into the countryside where, despite all precautions, blacks and whites died. Boatmen were quite liable to contract it and to pass it on because they plied the rivers between cholera cities and rural communities. The James River and Kanawha Canal between Richmond and Lynchburg was a perfect avenue for such spread, raising fears among planters and owners of slave boatmen during every outbreak. When one bondsman died on a James River vessel, masters took careful note and debated what action to take. But their reactions were insignificant compared to the panic which residents of towns and farms along the James experienced when cholera erupted in 1832 among boatmen in Cartersville, New Canton, Ca Ira, and other port villages. Neighboring hamlets refused to permit boats to land or even pass nearby "lest they might spread the plague." [37] In 1854 the epidemic reached Scottsville from Richmond, killing at least twenty-five, and probably touched lightly

[36] J. F. Tanner to E. M. Mettauer, 2 August 1849; [J. R. Anderson] by J. F. Tanner to Judge J. H. Overton, 7 August 1849; J. F. Tanner to "Judge Josh" Baker, 28 July 1849; all in Tredegar Papers, Letterbook, VSL; John Walker to James Sims, 12 July 1849, in John Walker Diary, UNC.

[37] [Francis Austin] to John Austin, 19 June ———, Austin-Twyman Papers (folder 12), W&M; *Richmond Enquirer*, 2, 9, 23 October 1832, all p. 3; Leneaus Bolling Diary, 1, 4, 6 October 1832, Randolph-Hubard Papers (box 7), UVA (#2424c).

at Lynchburg, though health authorities there vigorously denied it.[38] The water route also figured prominently in spreading cholera along Potomac River communities where workers were constructing the Chesapeake and Ohio Canal in 1832.[39]

Apprehensive country slaveowners, spurred on by newspaper articles warning of the danger, often took vigorous steps to prevent cholera from attacking their farms. The *Richmond Enquirer* in 1832 published a rural physician's letter admonishing masters to attend personally to diet, lodging, and clothing, since overseers often were not careful about such matters. He also tried to dispel false hopes that epidemics would not spread through the countryside. The usual preparations for cholera included whitewashing and cleaning the slave quarters, maintaining personal hygiene among the hands, and watching for the first signs of disease.[40] Cholera medicines were concocted, days of prayer and fasting were held, and in a few cases crops were harvested early lest they rot in the field from future neglect.[41] Hill Carter, a model planter, deserted his slaves for the medicinal springs in 1832, but he hired a physician to live at Shirley "for fear we should have the cholera here." With almost human perversity the *Vibrio cholerae* refrained from attacking that year, instead unleashing its violence on the plantation in 1849, when Carter was present to observe the suffering. Thirty-one slaves perished within the course of three terrifying weeks.[42]

[38] Petersburg *Daily South Side Democrat*, 29 July, 1 August 1854, both p. 2.

[39] *Richmond Enquirer*, 11 September (p. 3), 14 September (p. 2), 6 November (p. 3), 1832; *Alexandria Phenix Gazette*, 7, 25 September, 8 October 1832, all p. 2.

[40] *Richmond Enquirer*, 2 October 1832, p. 3; Richard D. Powell to John H. Cocke, 18 September 1832; Drury Stith to John H. Cocke, 29 August 1832, Shields Deposit, Cocke Papers, UVA; Shirley Farm Journals, 10–11 October 1832 (marginal note), LC.

[41] "Mr. Mannell Recipe for Cholera. '32," Cocke Deposit, Cocke Papers, UVA; John Walker Diary, 21 July 1832, UNC; Richard D. Powell to John H. Cocke, 18 September 1832, Shields Deposit, Cocke Papers, UVA.

[42] Shirley Farm Journals, 20 August 1832, 27 June to 18 July 1849, LC; "Minutes of the Annual Meeting of the Medico-Chirurgical Society of Richmond, 7 December 1852," *Steth.*, 3 (1853), 40. For more on rural cholera, see, for the 1832 epidemic: Norfolk *American Beacon*, 11, 13, 18, 20, 25 September 1832, all p. 2; *Alexandria Phenix Gazette*, 15 September 1832, p. 2; *Richmond Enquirer*, 14, 18, 19 September 1832, all p. 3; Tebault Papers, Lecture Notebook #3, UVA

There is some evidence that Virginia's blacks did not merely sit back and wait for cholera to strike. Some believed that the epidemic would bypass them entirely because, as some slaves explained to a white woman near Fredericksburg, "it [cholera] was a judgement from the Almighty for . . . [whites'] sins in holding . . . [blacks] in slavery." [43] But, like whites, a number of blacks did take to praying and holding revivals in hopes of somehow warding off the impending epidemic. Occasionally these prayer meetings disturbed residents living nearby, but for the most part the authorities permitted the Negro religious activities.[44] A few slaves fled the cities in fear of cholera, but records of such occurrences are scarce. Once the epidemics were upon them, servants often nursed one another and, in Richmond (1832) at least, some secretly applied for and received Thomsonian medicines.[45] There existed among the black communities a great fear of the city hospitals which had been established mainly for their treatment. During both the 1832 and 1854 outbreaks (and no doubt during the other two as well), some Richmond blacks deliberately avoided reporting sick for fear they would never return alive from the cholera hospitals. To them home treatment was better than death in a pest house.[46]

Cholera was a threat to public health, but, since its mode of spread was not then understood, little could be done to combat it effectively. It was easy enough to isolate smallpox patients and restrict the disease to those who had had direct contact with it.

(#9926). For the 1849 epidemic; *Richmond Enquirer*, 8 June (p. 2), 3 July (p. 2), 20 July (p. 4), 1849; Norfolk *Daily Southern Argus*, 12, 26 June, 6 July 1849, all p. 2; John Walker Diary, 9 June 1849, UNC; Tebault Papers, Lecture Notebook #1, UVA (#9926); Jno. B. Prentis to Jno. R. Kilby, 23 June, 17 July 1849, Kilby Papers, Duke.

[43] "Notes Illustrative of the Wrongs of Slavery, Commenced in 1832," in Blackford Family Papers (control folder), UVA (#6403).

[44] Norfolk *Daily Southern Argus*, 12, 15, 16 June 1849 (all p. 2); *Alexandria Phenix Gazette*, 26 September (p. 2), 29 September (p. 3), 4 October (p. 1) 1832.

[45] Richard M. Harrison to Robert Leslie, quoted in John M. Webb, "Robert Leslie: Merchant Manufacturer" (Ph.D. dissertation, Duke University, 1954), 174; *Richmond Enquirer*, 15 October 1833, p. 3.

[46] Richmond Enquirer, 15 October 1833, p. 3; Richmond *Daily Dispatch*, 21 July 1854, p. 2.

Cholera was different; many who had had daily contact with its victims never developed the disease themselves. This phenomenon puzzled physicians and laymen alike, and left room for theories blaming miasmata, atmospheric conditions, and the low living and moral standards of most patients. Though blacks were considered prime candidates for the disease, according to this last assumption, whites still feared contagion. For humanitarian and selfish reasons they instituted health measures to prevent its spread to "respectable" persons and valuable servants. As with smallpox, Negroes profited from society's need to protect itself against disease.

Yellow Fever

The plague-fly has received its name from the belief that its appearance marks the crisis in the prevalence of epidemic yellow fever. So uniformly is this true in Southern cities, that I have been told the negroes in those cities believe that this fly consumes—actually eats up—the morbific matter which constitutes the immediate cause of the disease.[47]

If the plague-fly did actually exist, it must have been a familiar sight to Norfolk residents by 1855. As Virginia's major port, this city usually had the distinction of serving as entry point for cholera and yellow fever epidemics. But whereas cholera then spread to other portions of the state, yellow fever remained localized, rarely moving beyond the city limits. Norfolk's sister city, Portsmouth, occasionally shared the "black vomit" with its larger neighbor; until 1821 Alexandria, as a thriving port town,

---

[47] George D. Armstrong, *The Summer of the Pestilence: History of the Ravages of the Yellow Fever in Norfolk, Virginia, A.D. 1855* (Philadelphia, 1856), 160. Yellow fever is caused by a virus which enters the body as an infected *Aedes aegypti* mosquito withdraws a blood meal. Once within the bloodstream, the virus causes vascular congestion with frequent small hemorrhages throughout the body, and severe destruction of the liver. At the outset, fever and headache are the most common signs, but soon backache, joint and abdominal pains, jaundice, multiple hemorrhages, and, in malignant cases, vomiting of blood (black vomit) intervene. For more on yellow fever, see Charles Wilcocks and Philip Manson-Bahr, *Manson's Tropical Diseases* (Baltimore, 1972), 376–78.

also experienced outbreaks of the disease. However, Norfolk probably qualified as the sickliest town in the Old Dominion prior to the Civil War.[48]

As has already been shown, the Negroes of Norfolk, Portsmouth, and Alexandria suffered more than Caucasians during cholera epidemics, and at least as much as whites when smallpox cases suddenly erupted. Yellow fever was a different story. For reasons medical scientists have yet to understand entirely, blacks contracted this malady less frequently than whites and experienced much milder cases with fewer fatalities than their light-skinned neighbors. The explanation for this phenomenon may lie in the antiquity of yellow fever in Africa, where blacks had been exposed to the disease for many hundreds of years, or in its endemnicity there, where some blacks had been exposed to it as children. Caucasians had not previously encountered the disease. The situation is roughly analagous to that of increased white resistance to tuberculosis. Specific genetic factors, such as those linking sickle cell genes to malarial immunity, have not been found in relation to yellow fever. However, recent historical research into demographic patterns during yellow fever epidemics in the United States indicates that blacks of West African descent did possess an innate defense mechanism which allowed them to escape the most virulent form of the disease. Though blacks did contract yellow fever, they rarely died from it.[49]

Whites noticed the difference in susceptibility and often remarked about it, especially during epidemics. When a French steamer burdened with a crew of yellow fever victims entered Portsmouth harbor in the summer of 1854, residents observed that nearly every person aboard except native West Indian blacks

[48] For a fuller account of Norfolk's health problems, see Bagley, "History of Public Health of Norfolk," 14–53.

[49] Richard M. Taylor, "Epidemiology," in George K. Strode, ed., *Yellow Fever* (New York, 1951), 447–48, 529–33; Jo Ann Carrigan, "The Saffron Scourge: A History of Yellow Fever in Louisiana, 1796–1905" (Ph.D. dissertation, Louisiana State University, 1961), 396–97; George W. Hunter, William W. Frye, and J. Clyde Swartzwelder, *A Manual of Tropical Medicine* (Philadelphia, 1966), 31; Kenneth F. Kiple, "Black Yellow Fever Immunities, Innate and Acquired, as Revealed in the American South," *Social Science History* (forthcoming).

had been attacked. The following year malignant yellow fever struck both Norfolk and Portsmouth with devastating virulence, causing many whites to flee to safer inland towns. A contemporary historian of the epidemic explained why blacks did not also pack up and leave: "Of the coloured people but few have gone, partly on account of the difficulty of getting away, but more especially because the yellow fever is a disease from which they have, comparatively, very little to fear." It is questionable whether black residents, even if they had recognized this general medical advantage, would have willingly risked their lives by choosing to remain in town during the epidemic. As another writer at that time reported, blacks were just as liable to yellow fever as whites, but they usually had it in a milder form. No one wants to become ill, regardless of the ultimate outcome. Whites, however, had somehow to rationalize their flight to safety because they had left others behind to suffer the consequences of disease. Many blacks *did* perish during the epidemic of 1855, as well as during earlier outbreaks.[50]

Whites noted racial differences in the malignancy of yellow fever and took advantage of them. Blacks were already the major servant class in Virginia; during yellow fever outbreaks they became the exclusive performers of certain menial tasks deemed dangerous to whites. Suddenly hearse-drivers and grave-diggers were elevated to the status of celebrities because of circumstance. Uncle Bob Butt, in normal times a lowly slave with a thankless job, became, in 1855, "the noted grave-digger" whose appearance in Portsmouth one day was considered a good omen, because it meant the number of bodies awaiting burial had decreased. People now bestowed thanks upon him "for his attention to this important part of the debt due the dead." John Jones, another bondsman, continued his usual work in Norfolk during the 1855 epidemic, in the suddenly "high important capacity of hearse-

[50] Portsmouth Relief Association, *Report of the Portsmouth Relief Association to the Contributors of the Fund for the Relief of Portsmouth, Virginia* . . . (Richmond, 1856), 93; George D. Armstrong, *The Summer of the Pestilence: History of the Ravages of the Yellow Fever in Norfolk, Virginia, A.D. 1855* (Philadelphia, 1856), 54–55; J. N. Schoolfield, "On the Yellow Fever of Portsmouth in 1855," *VMJ,* 8 (1857), 381–82. See also John H. Claiborne, "The Negro. 1. His Environment as a Slave . . . ," *Virginia Medical Semi-Monthly,* 5 (13 April 1900), 5.

driver." Contrary to contemporary theory, he too suffered a severe attack of yellow fever; but fortunately (for his own and Norfolk's sake) he survived.[51]

Other blacks served as nurses alongside volunteer white women and physicians. When forced to do this, some slaves rebelled by performing their duties poorly or not at all. In 1800, for instance, Negroes were almost wholly entrusted with the care of Norfolk yellow fever victims, a task which they generally executed, according to one informant, "in a very negligent manner." Several even deserted their sick charges, leaving them to suffer their fates alone. At other times these nurses did a superb job treating patients. During the 1855 epidemic, nineteen unidentified black nurses from Charleston, South Carolina, traveled to Norfolk to assist at the hospital and in private homes.[52] Whites discovered that racial differences in disease virulence sometimes saved their lives.

Despite the frequency with which epidemics of yellow fever struck the port towns of Virginia and the remainder of the South, their mode of spread was never understood. Residents reacted to yellow fever as they did to cholera, by cleaning streets and homes, restricting sale and consumption of foods considered dangerous, and quarantining any vessels suspected of harboring yellow fever patients.[53] Blacks benefited to a degree from all this public health activity, but probably less so than when cholera or smallpox threatened, simply because of their observed resistance to severe forms of the disease. Where poor whites and indigent

[51] William S. Forrest, *The Great Pestilence in Virginia . . . Yellow Fever in Norfolk and Portsmouth in 1855* (New York, 1856), 163, 273. See also Portsmouth Relief Association, *Report*, 139.

[52] Drs. Selden and Whitehead, "On the Yellow Fever at Norfolk (Virginia), in the Summer and Autumn of 1800," *Medical Repository*, 4 (1801), 33; Howard Association of Norfolk, Virginia, *Report . . . to All Contributors Who Gave Their Valuable Aid . . .* (Philadelphia, 1857), 94. See also Charles W. Janson, *The Stranger in America, 1793–1806*, ed. Carl S. Driver (New York, 1935), 395; Fillmore Norfleet, trans., "Norfolk, Portsmouth and Gosport as Seen by Moreau de Saint-Mery in March, April and May, 1794," *VMHB*, 48 (1940), 253.

[53] See, e.g., *Norfolk and Portsmouth Herald*, 20 August (p. 2), 22 August (p. 3), 1821; *Alexandria Gazette and Daily Advertiser*, 17 October 1821, p. 2; J. D. Bryant, *The Epidemic of Yellow Fever in Norfolk and Portsmouth, Virginia, during the Summer and Fall of 1855* (Philadelphia, 1856), 31–33.

free blacks resided in close proximity to one another, a general clean-up did, however, raise the living standards of all.

Cleanliness, quarantines, and increased natural resistance among Negroes did little to reduce the fury of Tidewater Virginia's several yellow fever epidemics. Several thousand lost their lives. While it was true that blacks often contracted milder cases than whites, many suffered and some died during each outbreak. One of the first victims of the 1821 eruption was, in fact, a black cook; likewise, two early casualties of the 1855 epidemic were blacks who had spent a night on the ship which brought the yellow fever to Portsmouth.[54] Statistics on early epidemics are not available, but information on mortality in 1821 (Norfolk) and 1855 (Norfolk and Portsmouth) indicate that even though many whites deserted the cities, Caucasians died at a much higher rate than Negroes (see Table 13). This is exactly the reverse of the situation during cholera outbreaks, when blacks succumbed in greater proportion. Norfolk's 1855 population of approximately 15,000 was reduced to about 6,000 by flight. Almost 2,000 persons died, according to several contemporary estimates (no accurate count was ever made), including as many as two-thirds of all the whites who remained in town.[55] Portsmouth was similarly depleted. Only about 2,000 whites and 2,000 blacks faced the epidemic out of a population normally amounting to some 6,500 whites and 3,000 blacks. Of these, nearly half of the former and only 5 percent of the latter died. One observer estimated that 42 percent of the Caucasians who contracted the fever died, compared with 5 percent of the Negroes.[56]

Apparently the best public health measure against yellow fever was flight, a course which blacks could not or would not take. One white who remained described the desolate picture presented by the business section of Portsmouth at the height of the 1855 epidemic:

[54] Norfolk Committee of Physicians, "Report on the Origin of the Yellow Fever in Norfolk during the Summer of 1855," *VMJ*, 9 (1857), 96; Selden and Whitehead, "Yellow Fever in Norfolk," 335; Portsmouth Relief Association, *Report*, 90.

[55] Though the figures may have been exaggerated, the ratios are probably not far off. See Forrest, *The Great Pestilence*, 205; Bryant, *The Epidemic of Yellow Fever*, 9.

[56] Portsmouth Relief Association, *Report*, 142.

Table 13. Yellow Fever Mortality in Norfolk (1821) and Portsmouth (1855)

| | Percent of deaths | | |
	White	Black	N
Norfolk (1821) [a]	81.2	18.8	160
Portsmouth (1855) [b]	90.6	9.4	1,050

[a] *Norfolk and Portsmouth Herald,* 1 March 1822. Thomas J. Wertenbaker, in his book *Norfolk, Historic Southern Port* (Durham, N.C., 1962), 190, states that mortality was equally divided between the races. He misread the number of black deaths as 80, when it actually was 30.

[b] Portsmouth Relief Association, *Report of the Portsmouth Relief Association . . .* (Richmond, 1856), 185–92.

In passing from the ferry-wharf to Mr. Handy's house [a Presbyterian minister], I had to go through fully half the length of the main street of Portsmouth; and yet in all that distance I met but one white person, and saw but one store open. As I passed the end of the market-house, looking down toward Gosport, in the part of the market usually crowded by the country people, I saw but two market-carts. The negro drivers of these carts were sitting on the curb-stone beside them, and they, with their horses, looked as if wilted down by the heat; and I saw no one there present to buy their marketing.[57]

Much of the activity which formerly centered around the marketplace had been abandoned in favor of the local hospitals, where nursing had replaced bartering and small talk. The Howard Association, a charitable organization, established an infirmary at the old City Hotel in Norfolk to supplement care provided at the city pest house and the Naval Hospital at Gosport near Portsmouth. All admitted black as well as white patients, though the races were kept separate. As in the general population, Caucasians succumbed to the disease at a distinctly higher rate than Negroes, regardless of the quality of care each received. Black and white nurses ministered to the sick at these institutions (which, incidentally, the poor of both races distrusted as houses of experimentation).[58]

[57] Armstrong, *Summer of the Pestilence,* 34–35.

[58] *Lynchburg Virginian,* 8 October 1855, p. 2; Richard C. Holcomb, *A Century with Norfolk Naval Hospital, 1830–1930* (Portsmouth, Va., 1930), 264; Blanton,

Epidemics menaced and humbled white Virginia society as few others things did. They coerced people to consider the sorry state of most poor people, whether Caucasian or Negro; furthermore, because the health of all depended on the health of one, epidemics forced people to act. Thus blacks derived tangential benefit from the white man's selfish fear of disease. Humanitarianism of course played its part, but not usually until people were intimidated by impending outbreaks of pestilence. Slaves and free blacks (and poor whites) were then recognized as important members of the community.

19th Century, 232; Erasmus D. Fenner, "Dr. Fenner on Yellow Fever in Norfolk," Steth., 5 (1855), 696–97; Howard Association, Report, 50; Williamsburg Virginia Gazette, 9 August 1855, p. 2; Armstrong, Summer of the Pestilence, 54. On a yellow fever epidemic in New Orleans, see John Duffy, Sword of Pestilence: The New Orleans Yellow Fever Epidemic of 1853 (Baton Rouge, 1966).

CHAPTER 8

Insanity

White Virginians believed that, as with major epidemic diseases, cases of insanity required direct regulation by local and state authorities. The disruptive behavior of those with deranged minds posed as much of a threat to the tranquillity of public life as any epidemic. There is little evidence to suggest that whites in Virginia misused the insanity label to control dissident blacks. Though the lack of a legal definition of insanity in the state code left the judgment as to an individual's mental competency solely in the hands of local officials, these authorities appear to have applied similar standards to members of both races. They dealt with the problem of mental illness in the same way regardless of the patient's social, economic, political, or racial status. The result was that, as during times of major epidemics, some blacks (those sent to the state lunatic asylum) received better mental health care than their circumstances and position in society would have otherwise indicated.

By far the greatest number of lunatics—white and black—remained at home, confined and cared for by sympathetic or obligated relatives or owners. In cases when legally responsible people were not available owing to death, poverty, or reluctance, or when the insane individual became uncontrollable, officials in the community took charge. The justice of the peace or mayoral or hustings court declared an individual legally unsound of mind and handed him over to the sheriff for further care. "Care" consisted of living in a cell or basement of the county jail or poor house, often chained to the wall with poor food and little companionship, or (rarely) living with a willing family which was paid for the service. All legally insane free persons in Virginia, whether living at home or as public charges, were eligible for care in a state lunatic asylum when space was available. Slaveowners were also permitted to admit their deranged bondsmen to one of these public institutions between 1846 and 1856, at a cost of $1.50 weekly. Here a trained physician and his staff could regulate the life of each patient, providing generally good care to members of both races, both sexes, and all classes in Virginia society.

Slaves and the Concept of Insanity

The consensus among those who owned and observed slaves was that they were much less susceptible to mental derangement than free blacks or whites, and that those who did suffer from insanity usually labored under it for a relatively short time. No less a national figure than Dorothea Dix observed to the Senate in 1848 that there were "comparatively few examples" of insanity in those portions of America chiefly populated by Negroes and Indians.[1] The reason for this low rate of insanity among slaves, explained Dr. John Minson Galt II, superintendent of the Eastern Lunatic Asylum at Williamsburg (ELA) between 1841 and 1862, was their simple lifestyle. Bondsmen were "removed from much of the mental excitement, to which the free population of the union is necessarily exposed in the daily routine of life." They were, after all, fed, clothed, sheltered, and nursed by others, and provided with the opportunity to perform labor which "strengthen[s] the constitution and enables it to resist physical agents, calculated to produce insanity." When convalescing from an attack of insanity, Galt continued, bondsmen recovered more quickly than whites because they immediately

[1] Dorothea Dix, "Memorial Praying a Grant of Land for the Relief and Support of the Indigent Curable and Incurable Insane in the United States," *Senate Miscellaneous Documents*, 30th Cong. 1st sess., doc. 150, p. 2.

returned to the simple, regular, sheltered daily routine of slave life.[2] Dr. Joseph E. Cox, a Petersburg practitioner, corroborated this view of the slave lunatic: "During 15 years practice in and around the neighborhood of Petersburg I can call to mind no case of a slave that remained as a confirmed lunatic."[3]

The white man's view of the slave as a simple, unthinking, animal-like being who was sheltered from the tensions of life, and therefore relatively immune to insanity, resembled the supposition held for many years that mental illness among children was rare. People assumed that childhood was a comfortable period of life, free from the anxieties which precipitated mental crisis. This premise was as false as the belief that the presumed simplicity of slave life and the child-like nature of slaves removed the circumstances which brought on mental illness. Though slaves escaped the tensions of politics and property or the kind of "excessive mental action" which Galt felt were the major causes of insanity among the free population, other potentially troublesome situations did exist.[4] Among the more obvious stresses, in addition to the usual problems of personal adjustment, were the need to repress anger and aggression toward the master, his family, the overseer, and other whites, despite provocation; the frequent absences and public humiliation of parents during a slave's childhood years; and the accommodation to and acceptance of servitude. Also, slave life was no different from the life of free blacks and whites when it came to interpersonal relations. Just as in white society, there were slaves who simply could not cope with the tensions and strains of family or community life.

Case histories of mentally ill persons in antebellum Virginia are scarce primarily because few physicians or slaveowners kept written records on such patients. Even those which are available provide less information than historians or psychiatrists would

[2] John M. Galt II (hereafter referred to as JMG), "Asylums for Colored Persons," *American Psychological Journal* (Cincinnati), 1 (1853), 82–83.

[3] Joseph E. Cox to JMG, 13 March 1846, Galt Family Papers (Personal), CW. Hereafter these will be referred to as GFP, Pers; the Medical Papers as GFP, Med; and the Manuscript Volumes as GFP, MSS Vols.

[4] JMG, "Asylums for Colored Persons," 82.

like in order to diagnose the illness or determine its cause. The records do indicate, however, that slaves possessed no immunity to insanity, nor any natural ability to recover from bouts of mental illness more rapidly than whites. According to observers during that period, a variety of situations existed which exerted severe mental pressures upon some slaves.[5] For example, Dr. Alexander D. Galt of Williamsburg, called in 1819 to treat the servant Dilsy for "symptoms of mental derangement," listed several contributing factors, including the fact that "her mind is . . . labouring under some uneasiness, from her husband's affections being diminished." [6] A forty-year-old Richmond bondswoman, the mother of several children, first showed signs of insanity after experiencing amenorrhea (abnormal cessation of menstruation). She was treated twice at ELA and once at the Medical College of Virginia Infirmary (in Richmond), a temporary cure being effected only with the return of "dem tings," the menstrual flow, while at the Infirmary.[7] William Hunter of Norfolk reported that at least one of his slaves became "perfectly deranged" in November 1852 over the subject of religion, "a consistent professor of which he has been for many years." [8] In the case of Rose, a forty-three-year-old servant living in Williamsburg, the master and mistress's refusal to allow her to see the man she desired as her husband caused her to run away and then lapse into hysterical convulsions. Her owner felt that a straitjacket was necessary to control Rose during her fits.[9]

Organic diseases also caused insanity. Some slaves (and whites and free blacks) suffered derangement secondary to physical trauma, brain tumors, epilepsy, tertiary syphilis, pellagra, or other dietary deficiency diseases, puerperal fever, tuberculosis,

---

[5] The case histories and general principles discussed here concern slaves only. This does not indicate that whites and free blacks did not also suffer from the same types of problems; in fact, they did. In Virginia there were no mental diseases which physicians or slaveowners specifically labeled as peculiar to bondsmen.

[6] [A. D. Galt,] *Practical Medicine: Illustrated by Cases of the Most Important Diseases*, ed. John M. Galt (Philadelphia, 1843), 318–20.

[7] Charles [Kleullen?] to JMG, 22 February 1848, GFP, Med, CW.

[8] William H. Hunter to JMG, 11 November 1852, GFP, Med, CW.

[9] [Galt,] *Practical Medicine*, 320.

aneurysms, hypertension, and a host of other maladies. Emily, a Shenandoah Valley slave, developed symptoms of derangement soon after her overseer struck her on the head with a board. She "talked incessantly" and "her mind would not dwell long upon any one topic, but wandered off rambling, so as to lose speedily all trace of the starting point." Emily lived in this state of mind for eight years until surgeons at the Winchester Medical School attempted to repair the skull fracture, and her insanity. She died a short time after the operation.[10] Charles Friend's slave Mary, living at White Hill Plantation near Petersburg, developed child-bed fever which soon affected her central nervous system. In September 1857 she reported pains in her head; by early November her master noted that Mary's mind was "so affected I fear she will never be of much service." Two weeks later Friend observed that Mary presented "many signs of Lunacy," and he decided to send her to the asylum in Williamsburg.[11]

The number of slaves in Virginia who suffered from insanity was not very large, if census figures are to be believed. The only antebellum census that recorded insanity among whites, slaves, and free blacks, made in 1850, listed 59 slave lunatics out of a population of 472,528 (12.5/100,000). The 1840 and 1860 censuses did not differentiate among the three groups. This number compares quite favorably with the figures for whites (864 of 940,800 or 91.8/100,000) and for free blacks (47 of 54,333 or 86.5/ 100,000), and appears to confirm the statements of antebellum observers regarding the low incidence of mental derangement among slaves. However, slaveowners were often likely to view non-dangerous personality disorders among their bondsmen as simply behavioral problems which required stricter discipline or sale to the trader. As long as the workers fulfilled their daily obligations to the master, quirks of personality were probably ignored. The problem of definition was also important. A slave-owner might consider a slave partially but not totally insane;

[10] Marshall McDonald, "Surgical Cases Presented to the Class of Winchester Medical College . . . ," *VMJ*, 12 (1859), 104–5.

[11] White Hill Plantation Books, September and November 1857, UNC. For other examples of insanity caused by physical disorders, see James C. Deaton to JMG, 14 January 1845, GFP, Pers, CW; [Galt,] *Practical Medicine*, 318–20.

Robert Watson in April and June 1860 viewed his slave Solomon as "slightly deranged," but since he felt that the affliction was only temporary, he did not report him to the census-taker as insane. Within the context of plantation life, Solomon could continue to perform his proper daily functions as a slave. The lines separating mental soundness from temporary and total insanity were necessarily hazy.[12]

Masters treated those slaves whom they considered definitely insane with varying degrees of sympathy and severity. State law required that "any person entitled to the possession of a slave of unsound mind" must prevent him from wandering through town and country and must "provide him with adequate support," under penality of a fine.[13] There is little evidence that insane slaves who were kept at home were maltreated, though this lack of negative information is misleading, since insane whites often received harsh and minimal home care. Beatings, inadequate food, shelter, and clothing, and solitary confinement were not uncommon.[14] Deranged plantation and urban slaves had one advantage over insane whites: they usually had two (or more) families watching over them. What the master's family could not provide in terms of medical, physical, and psychological comfort, the slave community might. Unsound slaves, when not violent, were permitted freedom of the plantation or household and required to perform simple, menial tasks for the master or other slaves. This practice occasionally resulted in brushes with the law, as in the case of William, "an idiotic Negro," who was picked up in Richmond for "going at large" and returned to his master.[15]

For deranged slaves with sympathetic masters, life could be relatively easy. One Richmond mistress sent her "partially de-

[12] Manuscript Census, Louisa County, 1860, UVA. For a brief discussion of this problem, see Gerald N. Grob, *Mental Institutions in America: Social Policy to 1875* (New York, 1973), 248n.

[13] Virginia, *The Code of Virginia* . . . (Richmond, 1849), ch. 104; Virginia, *Supplement to the Revised Code of the Laws of Virginia* . . . (Richmond, 1833), ch. 178.

[14] See Norman Dain and Eric T. Carlson, "Social Class and Psychological Medicine in the United States, 1789–1824," BHM, 33 (1959), 454–65.

[15] Richmond *Daily Dispatch*, 6 July 1854.

ranged" Negro woman to live in the country under the care of
a paid attendant because she couldn't bring herself to sell the
servant—despite the warnings of friends and physicians that
"Aunty's" problem was "a violent temper more than any thing
else."[16] Another owner, of Powhatan County, emancipated most
of his bondsmen in his will, and provided that they assist in the
future support of Milly, the lunatic slave, and her daughter.[17]

Not a few insane slaves, however, led unhappy lives. A servant
at Frances Scott Miller's boarding house for Hampden-Sydney
College students in Farmville usually reacted violently when
struck for impudence or misbehavior. On one occasion she de-
fended herself with an axe and had to be "tied with ropes and
reins to secure her." She was then locked up outside until her
rage subsided.[18] A slave living in Williamsburg found herself in a
straitjacket (borrowed from ELA) after she had suddenly run
into the house and "embraced her mistress most tenderly, and
talked in a very wild strain."[19]

Throughout the antebellum period the physicians' treatment
of insanity consisted mainly in the use of strong medicines, opium,
blisters, and venesection. Only at the two state lunatic asylums
was moral or supportive therapy regularly practiced. Insane
slaves received the same primitive medical care as whites. James
C. Deaton sent one of his plantation slaves to Dr. M. Clarke of
Richmond for treatment of "fits of insanity." Dr. Clark "applied
a Blister to his scalp & treated him with Cal[o]mel Camp[h]or &
opium" for two or three weeks, which seemed to cure the man.
He relapsed back to his former state of periodic insanity, however, after ten days of regular work.[20] A slave patient who had
been sent to the Medical College of Virginia Infirmary in Richmond for wild delirium accompanied by "a continued howl,"
passed into a restful sleep each day under the combined influence

[16] Catharine C. Hopley, *Life in the South: From the Commencement of the
War* (London, 1863), I, 183–84.

[17] *Redford's Administrator* v. *Peggy and Others*, 6 Randolph 316.

[18] Frances Scott Miller Diary, 26 January 1857, Armistead-Blanton-Wallace
Family Papers, VHS.

[19] [Galt,] *Practical Medicine*, 320.

[20] James C. Deaton to JMG, 14 January 1845, GFP, Pers, CW.

of opium and chloroform. On the seventh day of her admission "her bowels were . . . opened for the first time [with a cathartic]." [21]

As the state hospitals did not admit slaves until 1846 and the local jails did not present an appealing alternative, most insane slaves remained at home to be cared for by the master and the slave community.[22] When circumstances warranted, owners consulted with or sent their slaves to physicians for treatment—usually in acute periods of the disease, such as fits of uncontrollable actions, convulsions, delirium, or bizarre behavior.[23] This type of crisis intervention eased the most severe and visible forms of insanity but often did little to cure the underlying disease, whether mental or physical. In the few recorded cases where insane slaves were jailed, the psychological state of individuals deteriorated even further.[24] Only a small number of slaves received the best psychological care available in the state, i.e., treatment at Eastern Lunatic Asylum in Williamsburg.

Free Blacks and Insanity

The kinds of mental illnesses from which free blacks suffered did not differ in form from those of whites or slaves. For example, according to the hospital physicians, those admitted to ELA suffered from anxiety of mind, intemperance, religious perplexity, hereditary insanity, disappointed affection, and marital strife, problems which whites and slaves also experienced. The unenviable social and economic position of free Negroes in a black slave/white master society possibly added an extra psychological

[21] Charles [Kleullen?] to JMG, 22 February 1848, GFP, Med, CW. See also [Galt,] *Practical Medicine*, 319, 320.

[22] See, e.g., "Inventory of the Lands, Slaves and Other Property of the Different Plantations of Philip St. George Cocke on the 1st Day of January 1835," p. 11, in Cocke Papers, Cocke Deposit, UVA; *Cross' Curatrix* v. *Cross' Legatees*, 4 Grattan 257; "Harrison of James River," *VMHB*, 34 (1926), 84–86.

[23] See, e.g., Robert Carter to Dr. George Steptoe, 28 January 1779, and Robert Carter to Mr. Nathaniel Garner, 4 March 1779, both in Robert Carter Letterbooks, Duke.

[24] "Statement of the Number of Lunatics Confined in the County and Corporation Jails," H of D *Jl.*, 1838/39, doc. 33, p. 2; JMG Medical Diary, November 1860, GFP, Med (folder 27), CW.

burden. A Petersburg physician claimed that he had treated many cases of insanity "among the lowest class of free negroes & mulattoes . . . arising from intemperance and want." [25]

As with many white lunatics, insane free blacks often displayed no abnormal behavior—in fact, they fit quite well into community life—until a sudden mental breakdown occurred. Patsy C. of Nansemond had been "moral, industrious & orderly," according to one reliable observer, until she flew into a "violent passion" and attempted to enter the pulpit at a camp meeting in August 1844. From that day on she remained "totally deranged" with "no rational intervals." She had always manifested a great attachment to children, but now made attempts on the lives of several youngsters, including her own. Though impoverished and dependent upon her own labor for support, Patsy (age twenty-two) had presented no prior indication that she was suffering under any mental stress. The actual cause of her insanity was unknown.[26] Another free black, Joseph G., the thirty-year-old son of a New Kent County free woman of color and her North Carolina slave husband, lived, as had Patsy C., a seemingly normal life for many years. Then during 1844 he began to act strangely, disclaiming any knowledge of his parents, denying that his mother and father were his real parents, refusing to mourn for his recently deceased mother because "she was not related to him," and threatening violence to friends and relatives. He spent the rest of his life in state lunatic asylums.[27]

The majority of insane free blacks were poor, whether they lived in rural or urban areas. Whereas slaveholders could generally absorb the economic loss incurred when a slave became ill or superannuated, poor free black families could not as easily sustain the loss of a working member of the household. When insanity or idiocy struck the impoverished free Negro family, it was essential that public charity intervene. According to the 1840 census, for example, the public purse supported 58 of the 384

[25] Joseph E. Cox to JMG, 13 March 1846, GFP, Pers, CW.

[26] JMG, Case Histories of Aslyum Patients, 1844–45, Patsy C., GFP, MSS Vols., CW. First names and last initials will be used throughout to protect identities of patients.

[27] *Ibid.*, Joseph G.

reported insane and idiotic blacks (predominantly, it is assumed, free blacks) living in Virginia. Most of the remaining 326 privately supported Negroes were probably slaves. More than 300 mentally ill Caucasians also received public support.

Local authorities generally permitted free, harmless, insane persons to live without restriction as long as they could somehow support themselves and remain out of trouble. Most of those who lived alone probably received financial aid and charity from friends and neighbors or from the Overseers of the Poor, or performed odd jobs to earn their keep. The strictness or leniency with which deranged individuals were handled depended upon the attitude of local officials in the town or county. Frederick County magistrates permitted Charles T., a free Negro shoemaker who suffered from periodic bouts of violent insanity, to leave jail and pursue his trade during lucid intervals over a period of eight years before finally sending him to ELA for treatment.[28] Another free black, Fanny W. of Petersburg, went to jail twice for "singing, shouting and . . . hollowing" in her neighborhood. She was a reputed alcoholic who, though married, was "entirely dependent on her own labour for support." [29] Milly L., a free Negro of Fredericksburg who had been judged insane by local magistrates but rejected from ELA as an idiot (the asylum refused to admit idiots), found herself at the mercy of the Mayor's Court in June 1831. Joseph Haywood, a resident of the town, accused her of "using insulting & abusive language towards him." Milly "confessed her fault" but was then only admonished and discharged on payment of court costs.[30]

The most notorious case of insanity involving a Virginia free black was that of Christopher McPherson of Richmond. McPherson was an educated, literate free Negro who counted Thomas Jefferson and James Madison among his friends. When he created problems for the Richmond authorities in the first decade of the nineteenth century, he was already an old man. In addition to opening a school for free blacks in town, McPherson petitioned

[28] *Ibid.*, Charles T.
[29] *Ibid.*, Fanny W.
[30] Fredericksburg Records, Mayor's Court, 15, 24 November 1830, 17 June 1831, UVA.

for a new Negro burial ground, and requested that he and his wife, because of their age, be exempted from the city ordinance barring all blacks but servants from riding in hired wagons. To publicize his cause and explain the injustices he felt were being perpetrated against him, McPherson paraded bareheaded through the streets of Richmond, singing and dancing. He also preached as "Pherson, son of God on earth." Hauled into court and declared insane, McPherson spent three weeks in jail before his hearing at ELA. These weeks in May and June 1811 were not spent idly. He wrote letters to kings, presidents, and other prominent world leaders warning of the millennium. The warrants of insanity from Richmond officials and an interview with McPherson did not impress the directors of ELA, who refused him admission and affirmed his sanity. Free once again, McPherson returned to Richmond to continue preaching and to recover his lost prestige. It was a hopeless cause; he finally gave up and left the state.[31]

County and city jails in Virginia were not equipped, nor were their personnel trained or prepared, to provide adequate care for the insane. Though superintendents of mental institutions and a few enlightened physicians understood the needs of these people, most sheriffs and their assistants held the view that the insane required strict discipline, little food, clothing, or shelter, and even less sympathy.[32] Consequently, many jailors treated the insane like caged animals. Francis Stribling, superintendent of the Western Lunatic Asylum (WLA) at Staunton, visited an unnamed Virginia county prison (probably Frederick County) during the summer of 1841 and found eight lunatics living in neglect and filth in a narrow, unventilated portion of the building. Here whites and blacks were treated alike:

A third apartment which opened into a narrow passage, was if possible still more revolting than either of the former, not because it appeared more uncomfortable or cheerless . . . but because it was the abode of *five* insane females, three of whom were white and

[31] Edmund Berkeley, Jr., "Prophet without Honor: Christopher McPherson, Free Person of Color," *VMHB*, 77 (1969), 180–90.

[32] For the general public's views on insanity prior to 1865, see Norman Dain, *Concepts of Insanity in the United States, 1789–1865* (New Brunswick, N.J., 1964), 20.

two black; one of each color was chained in opposite corners of the room, whilst the remaining three were permitted during the day to exercise or labour in the adjoining passage.[33]

In Petersburg a jailor confined a boisterous and violent free Negro resident of the poor house, Harriet V., in a dark room for almost two months without any kind of medical treatment. Another free black, Charles T. of Frederick County, was chained to the floor and handcuffed for four weeks during an attack of insanity.[34]

Limited evidence indicates that insane free blacks were not detained in county jails any more frequently or for longer periods than whites. Of thirty-five lunatics confined in the county and corporation jails of Virginia during the 1837/38 fiscal year, one was a slave, six were free blacks, and the rest whites. Aside from Julia Ann J. of Shenandoah County, who had been insane since childhood, the other free blacks had been confined for several months at most, and had regained or were recovering their sanity. The same was true of the white cases.[35] Many insane Virginians of both races did ultimately receive treatment at one of the two public lunatic asylums.

Admissions Policies at the State Lunatic Asylums

The Eastern Lunatic Asylum at Williamsburg, opened in 1773, was the first state-supported mental institution in America.[36] From the beginning free blacks were admitted to the hospital at a surprisingly high rate. Between 1773 and 1861 (1801–22 ex-

---

1857–58, Doc. #16, p. 20, that on 29 October 1857 there were twenty black males at ELA. (One was the slave, #466, and the remainder were free Negroes.) These four are not included in the discharge and death columns, as their status could not be determined. None appear to have remained at ELA beyond 1860, as all free blacks named on the Manuscript United States Census for Williamsburg can be accounted for without these four patients.

[33] WLA, *Annual Report*, 1841, p. 25.

[34] JMG, Case Histories of Asylum Patients, 1844–45, Harriet V. and Charles T., GFP, MSS Vols., CW.

[35] "Statement of the Number of Lunatics Confined in County and Corporate Jails," H of D *Jl.*, 1838/39, doc. 33, pp. 2–3.

[36] For a history of this hospital from its founding through the Civil War, see Norman Dain, *Disordered Minds: The First Century of Eastern State Hospital in Williamsburg, Virginia, 1766–1866* (Williamsburg, Va., 1971).

Table 14. Admissions of Patients to Eastern Lunatic Asylum, 1774–1861[a]

Year	Total	White	Free Black	Slave	Year	Total	White	Free Black	Slave
1773	6	6	0		1837	27	25	2	
1774	7	6	1		1838	6	6	0	
1775–98	107 [b]	107	0		1839	3	3	0	
1799	12	10	2		1840	28	27	1	
1800	15	15	0		1841	38	33	5	
1801–21 [c]	—	—	2		1842	27	26	1	
1822	20	19	1		1843	42	37	5	
1823	14	13	1		1844	39	35	4	
1824	6	6	0		1845	25	24	1	
1825	34	32	2		1846	37	31	2	4 [d]
1826	21	21	0		1847 [e]	43	35	6	2
1827	3	3	0		1847/48 [f]	34	26	3	5
1828	10	9	1		1848/49	50	42	5	3
1829	2	1	1		1849/50	53	41	7	5
1830	12	11	1		1850/51	45	36	5	4
1831	7	7	0		1851/52	54	38	11	5
1832	19	19	0		1852/53	67	49	10	8
1833	9	9	0		1853–55	160	133	12	15
1834	15	14	1		1855–57	161	149	9 [g]	3
1835	24	22	2		1857–59	167	162	5	0
1836	25	22	3		1859–61	73	71	1	1

— = information not available.

[a] Compiled from Manuscript United Stated Census Returns, ELA Board of Directors Minutes, CW, and Register of Patients in ELA Annual Reports. The number of free blacks admitted is no doubt understated for the period between 1847 and 1861 because the records do not consistently mention race. There were, for instance, forty blacks at ELA in 1862 (Dain, *Disordered Minds,* p. 111), twenty more than can be accounted for on 1 October 1861. It is doubtful that Galt admitted twenty free blacks in one year, when the most he had previously received annually was ten.

[b] This figure is low, as the records for several Board of Directors' meetings are missing.

[c] Incomplete records for this period.

[d] Between 1846 and 1856 slaves were admitted to ELA but usually not entered into the Board of Directors Minutes. The figures in these charts include as whites only those patients whose names or numbers appeared both in the Minutes and in the Register of Patients appended to the Annual Reports during this period. The remainder, except those not discharged or deceased by October 1856, and all free blacks, were assumed to be slaves. The one exception to this rule was #466, whom Galt listed as a slave in his 1850 *Annual Report* (p. 21), but who remained at ELA until his death in 1859 or 1860.

[e] 1 January through 30 September.

[f] 1 October 1847 through 30 September 1848. Same for each year through 1861.

[g] Includes four unknown free black males. Galt states in his "Communication from the Superintendent of the Eastern Lunatic Asylum, in Reply to several Questions of the Governor's Communication," 29 October 1857, *Leg. Docs.,*

cluded due to missing records) at least 112 (7.2%) of the approximately 1,545 patients at Eastern Lunatic Asylum were free Negroes (see Table 14). In the Tidewater area, where the largest concentrations of both blacks and whites resided, free Negroes were admitted to the conveniently located Williamsburg institution at about six-tenths the rate of Caucasians (see Table 15).[37] The state government paid for those Virginians who were unable to bear the expense of hospitalization, a boon to the free indigent insane of both races who would otherwise have languished in homes, poor houses, or jails. About 55 slaves (3.6 percent of the patients) also received treatment at the hospital between 1846 (the year the state legislature passed a law legalizing their admission as pay patients) and 1860.

Though the records are sketchy and incomplete in some instances, they indicate that the ELA Court of Directors appeared to discount race as a factor in their admissions policy except when the quarters designated for blacks were filled. According to John M. Galt II, the directors "have made no differences in their exertions for them [black insane] & for the white population" with regard to admissions.[38] In fact, "no insane individual of such a class has been rejected for several years past, by reason of the want of room." [39] Those who were rejected were deemed as not fit subjects for the asylum—i.e., they were idiots or not actually insane.

The racial policies of the Williamsburg hospital contrasted sharply with those of the Western Lunatic Asylum, established in 1828 at Staunton. Neither state institution could legally restrict admission of patients on the basis of race, but the directors at

[37] "It has been well known for some time now that the tendency, especially in the past, to hospitalize the mentally ill is inverse to their distance from a mental hospital." Herbert Goldhamer and Andrew W. Marshall, *Psychosis and Civilization: Two Studies in the Frequency of Mental Disease* (Glencoe, Ill., 1949), 26. A complete list of all known free black patients, including residence, admission date, length of stay, outcome of treatment, sex, age, estate, marital status, and cause of illness, appears in Todd L. Savitt, "Sound Minds and Sound Bodies: The Diseases and Health Care of Blacks in Ante-Bellum Virginia" (Ph.D. dissertation, University of Virginia, 1975), 535–42.

[38] JMG, [Draft ?] to [?,] n.d. [probably September or October 1848], in GFP, Med (folder 39), CW.

[39] JMG, "Asylums for Colored Persons," 81.

Table 15. Free Black and White Admission Rates to Eastern Lunatic Asylum for 33 Tidewater Virginia Counties, 1822–59 [a]

Years	White admissions	Approximate white population at mid-decade [b]	White admissions per 100,000	Free Black admissions	Approximate free black population at mid-decade [b]	Free Black admissions per 100,000
1822–29	62	148,444	42	7	25,235	28
1830–39	63	152,442	41	7	28,247	25
1840–49	224	158,900	141	22	29,423	75
1850–59	351	178,455	197	41	31,498	130

[a] These counties immediately surround Williamsburg: Accomac, Caroline, Charles City, Chesterfield, Dinwiddie, Elizabeth City, Essex, Gloucester, Greenville, Henrico, Isle of Wight, James City, King and Queen, King George, King William, Lancaster, Mathews, Middlesex, Nansemond, New Kent, Norfolk, Northampton, Northumberland, Prince George, Princess Anne, Richmond, Southampton, Spotsylvania, Surry, Sussex, Warwick, Westmoreland, York. (The cities of Richmond, Petersburg, Norfolk, and Williamsburg are included with Henrico, Dinwiddie, Norfolk, and James City counties respectively.) Most white lunatics from this area who were committed to an asylum went to ELA, though some (6 in 1820's, 3 in 1830's, 73 in 1840's, and 63 in 1850's) went to WLA. The free black population of the state was most heavily concentrated in Tidewater and could only be admitted to ELA.

[b] Population at both ends of the decade (as determined by the census) totaled, and then divided by two.

Staunton did anyway. Betsy T., a free Negro of Lancaster County, was received into the hospital a month after it opened and died there ten years later. Not one other free black resided at the hospital as a patient before the Civil War.[40]

In part, class considerations led to these WLA-ELA differences. As the older institution, ELA already had a large number of long-term pauper inmates by the time WLA opened in 1828. Though both were public asylums and supposed to admit all insane residents on an equal basis, the directors of the Staunton establishment managed, over the years, to accept many more middle- and upper-class paying patients than its sister establishment in Williamsburg. Once WLA reached its maximum patient capacity, those who were rejected, frequently of the pauper class, went to ELA. That hospital rapidly gained a reputation as the institution for the poor, while the Western Lunatic Asylum assumed a position of superiority based on the better class of its patients.[41] The trustees of WLA, striving to build a strong public and professional image of their institution, had no use for free blacks, most of whom were poor and illiterate. At ELA the directors possessed none of these pretensions and simply took in all who qualified as insane, regardless of race or class.

As an additional factor, eastern and western Virginians held different attitudes toward blacks, and these were reflected in the policies of the two state mental hospitals. Tidewater, Piedmont, and Southside Virginians had grown up with slavery and had lived alongside free blacks since colonial days. An overwhelming majority of the state's slaves and free Negroes populated towns and rural areas in the east. Large landowners there considered all persons on the plantation—white and black, slave and free— as members of "our family." Blacks entered into the white man's everyday life in numerous ways. Not so in trans-montane Virginia, where farms and nonwhite populations were usually smaller. The paternalistic tradition toward free and slave blacks was not nearly as strong west of the Blue Ridge. Antislavery and anti-Negro sentiment ran highest in the western portion of the state, as illustrated by the votes between 1829 and 1832 in the consti-

[40] WLA, *Annual Report*, 1828, p. 6; *ibid.*, 1838, p. 8.
[41] Dain, *Disordered Minds*, 105–6.

tutional conventions and in the House of Delegates. It is not surprising, then, that the directors of ELA dutifully admitted and treated their poor, insane free black neighbors, while their counterparts in Staunton did not.

The superintendents of ELA and WLA during the twenty years just prior to Civil War mirrored these sectional attitudes. John Minson Galt II, a twenty-two-year-old medical school graduate, followed the family tradition by succeeding his father as superintendent of ELA in July 1841. The Galts had served ELA in various capacities since its establishment, so it was almost a matter of course that the son of Dr. Alexander D. Galt, physician to ELA, would fill this position. John Galt had grown up in Williamsburg, attended William and Mary College, and then went on, like so many other young southern gentlemen, to the University of Pennsylvania Medical School in Philadelphia. Though Galt's views toward blacks were typical of his section and period, he also sympathized with the plight of the insane of both races and wanted to treat them.[42] Under Galt the admission of free black patients accelerated rapidly. In the previous sixty-seven years about twenty-three (but no more than thirty) patients from this portion of the population had been admitted; during the next twenty years at least eighty-seven free Negroes entered the hospital (see Table 14).

Francis Stribling, who took the reins as superintendent of WLA in July 1836, had no quarrel with Galt regarding the need to treat insane blacks as well as whites. He insisted, however, that the two races be entirely removed from one another in separate facilities.[43] It was his desire to attract upper-class patients to the institution as a means of enhancing the reputation of both WLA and himself. By offering modern and attractive facilities and the lastest techniques in treatment (all for a price, of course), Stribling succeeded in bringing many paying patients to Staunton. Consistent with these goals, he continued summarily rejecting all Negro applicants, a policy which the directors of WLA had informally instituted back in 1828.[44]

[42] JMG, "Asylums for Colored Persons," 88.
[43] WLA, *Annual Report*, 1845, p. 21.
[44] Dain, *Disordered Minds*, 107.

Indicative of Galt's concern for the care of mentally ill blacks was his successful effort, in 1846, to have the state legislature pass a law admitting slaves to ELA. Prior to this, slaveowners had had to care for their lunatic bondsmen as best they could using home remedies, local doctors, and, when necessary, the town or county jail or poor house. Despite the support which slaveowners gave Galt, he encountered strong opposition to his proposal from Francis Stribling's political allies in the legislature. The admission of slaves would have interfered with Stribling's plans for WLA. Only after the bill had been worded to designate ELA as the sole repository of insane slaves did Galt's plan become law. Galt had wanted slave patients, and Stribling made certain that he alone got them.[45]

Eastern Lunatic Asylum before 1841

Until the 1840's free black patients at ELA lived among the white inmates and followed similar routines. Their small numbers did not warrant separate facilities; nor did the other patients object to their presence, as they constituted no more than 12 percent of the hospital population (see Table 16). The institution's physical plant grew over the years, from one building designed for about thirty patients in 1773, to four main buildings and several outbuildings housing about one hundred patients by 1840.[46] The black patient population grew with the institution, from one in 1774 to twelve in 1841.[47] Though the Board of Directors' minutes for the period 1801 to 1822 are missing, other records indicate that no free black lunatic who resided at ELA between 1801 and 1839 possessed an estate from which the state

[45] H of D *Jl.*, 1837/38, pp. 126, 158; *ibid.*, 1841/42, pp. 36, 176; *ibid.*, 1845/46, p. 16; Dain, *Disordered Minds*, 121–22 (Stribling's political connections are discussed); JMG, "A Communication to the Board of Directors," 1 July 1845, GFP, Med, CW; *Richmond Enquirer*, 5 December 1845 (p. 4), 2 January (p. 2), 16 January (p. 1) 1846; Legislative Petitions, Williamsburg, 2 December 1845, VSL; Virginia, *Acts of Assembly*, 1845/46, p. 18.

[46] Dain, *Disordered Minds*, 26; "Report of the Committee Appointed to Examine the State and Condition of the Lunatic Hospital at Williamsburg," H of D *Jl.*, 1834/35, doc. 36, p. 1; ELA *Annual Report*, 1843, p. 1.

[47] ELA, *Annual Report*, 1841, p. 4.

Table 16. Number and Percentage of Black Patients in Eastern Lunatic Asylum on One Day during Each Year, 1822–61

Day	Total patients	Free Blacks	Slaves	Percent free blacks	Percent slaves
12/31/22	56	3		5.4	
12/31/23	61	4		6.6	
12/31/24	—	3			
12/31/25	70	5		7.1	
12/31/26	76	4		5.3	
12/31/27	62	4		6.5	
12/31/28	60	5		8.3	
12/31/29	57	6		10.5	
12/31/30	58	6		10.3	
12/31/31	48	5		10.4	
12/31/32	56	5		8.9	
12/31/33	55	5		9.1	
12/31/34	59	6		10.2	
12/31/35	77	8		10.4	
12/31/36	74	9		12.2	
12/31/37	84	10		11.9	
12/31/38	82	8		9.8	
12/31/39	78	7		9.0	
12/31/40	99	7		7.1	
12/31/41	94	11		11.7	
12/31/42	93	10		10.8	
12/31/43	109	14		12.8	
12/31/44	132	16		12.1	
12/31/45	128	14		10.9	
12/31/46	145	15	1	10.4	
10/ 1/47	164	21	1	12.9	0.6
10/ 1/48	165	21	3	12.7	1.8
10/ 1/49	181	24	3	13.3	1.7
10/ 1/50	193	27	6	14.0	3.1
10/ 1/51	193	30	8	15.5	4.1
10/ 1/52	211	33	8	15.6	3.8
10/ 1/53	218	38	13	17.4	6.0
10/ 1/55	232	30	9	12.9	3.9
10/ 1/57	257	33 [a]	0	12.8	0.0
10/ 1/59	300	25 [b]	0	8.3 [b]	0.0
10/ 1/61	272	20 [b]	1	7.4 [b]	0.3

[a] Includes four unidentified free black males mentioned by Galt in *Leg. Docs.*, 1857–58, Doc. #16, p. 20.

[b] Does not include four free black males discussed in note a, as their presence at that time cannot be verified.

could collect fees.[48] These paupers, along with whites in similar circumstances, lived free from the burdens of financial worry and discrimination which they would have faced outside the hospital.

Professional treatment of the insane at ELA before John Galt's superintendency consisted mainly of purges, pukes, blisters, sedatives, physical restraints for the violent, and an occasional bath. Sympathy, reassurance, and encouragement did not constitute the principal curative approach. Alexander D. Galt, John's father, practiced this physical type of medicine on insane patients until his death. Though admitting the mania (general derangement) was a "very mysterious" disease which often "comes on without any very apparent exciting cause," the senior Dr. Galt conceptualized the cure in physical rather than psychical terms: "It is only by removing the predisposition that the disease [mania] can be cured. We must find out the condition of the system, on which the exciting causes are likely to produce their effects, and remove or counteract them."[49] With this theory of mental illness as their guide, physicians at ELA prior to 1841 visited and examined patients once a week only, prescribed drugs, baths, restraints, etc., to those who required them, and departed the grounds, leaving patients in the hands of the keeper and attendants.[50]

Physicians neither favored nor discriminated against black patients during this period. For instance, when free Negroes Shadrack G. and Jenny C. were patients at ELA in 1799, both were visited by the physician weekly and purged, bled, puked, and bathed along with the other inmates on a regular basis. Doctors carefully followed all cases of physical as well as mental illness in the hospital.[51]

Since the physician attended patients at ELA for only a small part of the day or week prior to 1841, the task of regulating the general environment was left to the keeper (in charge of males),

[48] Accounts with Committee of Estates of Lunatics for Support at Williamsburg Hospital, 1801–39, Auditor's Item 27, VSL.

[49] [Galt,] *Practical Medicine*, 484–85.

[50] A. D. Galt, Notes on Hospital Patients, 1799–1809, GFP, MSS Vols., CW; Dain, *Disordered Minds*, 46–51.

[51] A. D. Galt, Notes on Hospital Patients, 1799–1809, GFP, MSS Vols., CW; A. D. Galt, Notes on Patients, 28 February 1837, GFP, Med, CW.

matron (for females), and ward attendants, all laymen who had gained their expertise on the job. If inequalities in treatment arose, they would have been from this source, rather than from the hospital physicians. These people cared for patients all day, every day, and their personal prejudices regarding particular people or groups affected the conduct of their duties. The matron, keeper, and assistant keeper were white, as were several of the attendants. Hired slaves, however, constituted a sizable portion of the hospital staff. Their tasks included washing clothes, cleaning the hospital and grounds, serving meals to patients and staff, running errands, and performing other menial duties. In addition, these hired slaves tended to the needs of patients, delivered medicines to them from the pharmacy, and often acted as attendants. By the nature of their duties, servants had more intimate personal contact with patients than did the keeper or the matron. Free black hospital inmates perhaps derived benefits from this situation: their low status as free Negroes in a slave society did not change in the eyes of the white patients, but they probably received kind treatment from the slave attendants.[52]

Accommodations for white and black patients did not differ during this period. Up until the early 1840's each inmate occupied a private room in the main hospital building;[53] only servants and a few convalescent female patients lived in outbuildings.[54] The hospital rooms were not designed for comfort, having no fireplaces or other sources of heat and no bedsteads. Patients slept on straw-filled mattresses placed on the floor and covered themselves with small blankets which were often inadequate for cold weather. At dark the hospital attendants locked all inmates in their own rooms; at daylight the servants washed and dressed patients and led them to warm sitting rooms until mealtime. No one—servants, attendants, matron or keeper—remained on the hospital wards through the night to care for patients in emer-

---

[52] Minutes of the Court of Directors of Eastern State Hospital (hereafter referred to as ESH Mins), 30 December 1794, 13 December 1826, 10 December 1835, 14 January 1836, 15 December 1840, CW; "Report of the Committee Appointed . . ." H of D Jl., 1834/35, doc. 36, pp. 1–9.

[53] "Governor's Communication to the Boards of Directors of the Virginia Lunatic Asylums, and Their Answers Thereto, 1857," Leg. Docs. 1857–58, doc. 16, p. 19.

[54] "Report of the Committee Appointed . . .," H of D Jl., 1834/35, doc. 36, p. 1.

gency situations or to guard against accidental fires or escapes. At mealtimes the lunatics returned to their rooms and ate their usually wholesome meals in solitude. A House of Delegates Committee, visiting the institution in 1835, was "surprised to find that they [the patients] were furnished with no kind of amusement, by which these unfortunate persons might pass off their hours of dreary confinement." There were few books or newspapers (probably useless to the free black inmates anyway), and a dearth of other diversions. In fact, the committee concluded that, though clean and healthful, "the hospital exhibits too much the appearance of a well regulated prison, where the prisoners are well fed and clothed, and excluded from all rational employment or amusement." [55]

For its first seventy years, then, Eastern Lunatic Asylum provided custodial care for all its patients, discriminating but little between white and black, rich and poor. Curative efforts were limited to the administration of a few standard drugs and some personal interaction between patients and professional staff. Attendants, many of them hired slaves untrained for their jobs, served as the patients' primary source of contact. Free blacks benefited from the situation, since most had lived at or near the poverty level prior to admission and had probably received little sympathy from whites. At ELA they were fed, clothed, and cared for at no charge, and perhaps received extra benefits from those slaves who served as their attendants. With the arrival of John Galt in 1841 as superintendent, however, the life of the free black at ELA began to change.

Blacks at Eastern Lunatic Asylum after 1841

Under John Galt's administration ELA expanded its facilities for Virginia's free blacks, and after 1846 it admitted slaves as well (see Tables 14, 16, and 17). However, it also began separating patients by race and altering its treatment of blacks. Whereas Alexander D. Galt and his predecessors had followed no particular theory of psychological treatment of the insane, John

---

[55] *Ibid.*, pp. 1–3; ELA, *Annual Report*, 1842, p. 9.

Table 17. Admissions, Recoveries, and Deaths of Patients by Race at Eastern Lunatic Asylum, 1822–59

ADMISSIONS

Year	Number of whites	Number of free blacks	Number of slaves	Percent free blacks	Percent slaves	Percent of black in total
1822–29	104	6	—	5.5	—	5.5
1830–39	138	9	—	6.1	—	6.1
1840–49	316	34	14	9.3	3.8	13.2
1850–59	612	59	40	8.3	5.7	13.9
Total	1,170	109	54	8.1	4.1	12.2

RECOVERIES [a]

	Number of ELA patients [b]			Number recovered			Percent recovered		
	White	Free Black	Slave	White	Free Black	Slave	White	Free Black	Slave
1822–29	151	8	—	39	2	—	25.8	25.0	—
1830–39	189	15	—	47	1	—	24.9	6.7	—
1840–49	387	41	14	91	8	10	23.5	19.5	71.4
1850–59	776	83	43	163	23	17	21.1	27.7	39.5 [c]

DEATHS

	Number of deaths			Percent of deaths		
	White	Free Black	Slave	White	Free Black	Slave
1822–29	52	0	—	34.4	0	—
1830–39	78	7	—	41.3	46.7	—
1840–49	126	7	0	32.6	17.1	0
1850–59	255	26	14	32.9	31.3	32.6

[a] Prior to 1841 all discharges were counted as recoveries because the Board of Directors Minutes did not mention the state of each patient discharged. After 1841, the Register of Patients in each *Annual Report* stated which discharged patients had been cured and which had not.
[b] The number of patients present on the first day of the decade, plus those admitted during the decade.
[c] All slaves but one were discharged by 1 October 1856.

Galt, young, well read, and innovative, brought with him to ELA the latest European concept in the treatment of insanity, "moral management." Francis Stribling had been employing this mode of therapy for several years at WLA with great success. Galt described the principles of moral management in his annual report for 1843: kindness; sympathy; minimal use of restraints; positive engagement of mind and body in active pursuits such as labor, amusements, reading, writing and religious observance; and proper medical treatment, diet, and living accommodations.[56] The previously custodial, strict, and cheerless hospital now became a more open, industrious, and pleasant "home" for the insane.

Though white inmates at ELA derived substantial benefits from Galt's policies and treatment, free blacks found them to be a mixed blessing, despite the new superintendent's statement that "nearly the identical rules of moral and medical treatment are applicable to the colored insane, which are demanded for white persons similarly affected." [57] Along with a more congenial atmosphere, blacks also found segregated quarters and a lower, servant's status. These changes proceeded from Galt's interpretation of the theory of moral management and from prevailing attitudes toward blacks. One of the cardinal tenets of the new therapy was the placement of patients in familar settings which corresponded to their style of living at home. Galt assumed that free blacks, being mainly indigent laborers, required "comparatively cheap

[56] ELA, *Annual Report*, 1843, pp. 11–19. Several recent historians and physicians have raised questions as to the purpose, usefulness, and success of nineteenth-century asylums and the practice of moral therapy in them. Whether or not these institutions are viewed as having assisted or repressed patients, the fact remains that at ELA blacks received as good care, within the context of the system, as whites. They were admitted at almost the same rate and for similar reasons, and were treated under the same rules. Though moral therapy may have been as coercive, degrading, and brutal as some writers have claimed (it probably wasn't), the insane of both races at ELA had an equal opportunity to experience it. For more on the debate over the asylum movement, see Michel Foucault, *Madness and Civilization: A History of Insanity in the Age of Reason* (New York, 1965); Thomas S. Szasz, ed., *The Age of Madness: The History of Involuntary Mental Hospitalization Presented in Selected Texts* (Garden City, N.Y., 1973); David J. Rothman, *The Discovery of the Asylum: Social Order and Disorder in the New Republic* (Boston, 1971); and Grob, *Mental Institutions in America*.

[57] JMG, "Asylums for Colored Persons," 86.

accommodations," and such menial employment as "assisting the servants of the establishment who had external duties to perform." [58] These chores included, for the women, washing clothes "and other outdoor duties," sewing and binding clothes, housework, and "job work"; for the men, working in the garden, woodyard, and occasionally in the carpenter's and shoemaker's shops. During 1844 and 1845 at least half of the twelve black female patients had as their assigned task washing, while two of the four or five men performed odd jobs around the grounds.[59] The white patients, responding to this situation, viewed the free blacks "pretty much in the same light as they do the servants." [60] Galt did not pursue this policy blindly, however. There were black patients who simply were not suited for physical labor owing to age, disability, or temperament. He allowed these people (three in 1844–45), usually long-term patients, to remain idle.[61]

To illustrate the success of this policy Galt pointed to the extreme case of a black woman who had arrived at ELA in the chains she had worn for eight or ten years. Once the chains had been removed, she became "rather excited, which she would chiefly evince by vehement gesticulation, and pulling up the fragmentary bricks of the court, arranging them in circles; she soon left off the latter habit, after we had given her employment; is now occupied daily, being generally calm and quiet, and has become one of the most useful persons in the asylum." [62]

Though the separation of blacks from whites was not one of Galt's major concerns, it is obvious from his writings and actions that he expended much effort in the task of ordering race relations at the asylum. Not only did outdoor labor serve to cure Galt's black patients; it also "render[ed] their isolation from the white patients a very easy matter . . . [as] they would thus be scarcely

[58] Ibid., 86, 87.
[59] ELA, Annual Report, 1843, p. 14; Lists of Male and Female Patients' Duties, in JMG, Medical Case Histories of Asylum Patients, 1844–45, GFP, MSS Vols., CW.
[60] JMG, "Asylums for Colored Persons," 87.
[61] Lists of Male and Female Patients' Duties, in JMG, Medical Case Histories of Asylum Patients, 1844–45, GFP, MSS Vols., CW.
[62] ELA, Annual Report, 1843, p. 14.

in the wards at all during the day." [63] As the number of free black patients grew, Galt felt compelled to provide entirely separate wards for the two races.[64]

In all regards save housing Galt conscientiously applied the principles of moral management equally to both races. Blacks received kind and sympathetic treatment; adequate food, shelter, clothing, and medical attention; task assignments to occupy their hands and minds; and adequate leisure-time amusements, including participation in religious observances. But because of the policy of racial separation, blacks were not classified as to the character of their illnesses or assigned living quarters with others of similar temperament. Galt considered classification and grouping of patients, especially of violent, mild, and convalescent persons, an important aspect of therapy for whites;[65] however, he placed all black males in one ward and females in another. The superintendent rationalized this policy by falling back upon current attitudes regarding the differences between the races: "Although amongst the colored insane as with others, a just classification is preferable, yet we do not consider the principle to assume here that extreme importance, which it holds as regards insane whites." [66]

Galt buttressed the moral management of blacks and whites with a liberal amount of traditional treatment. Despite attempts to introduce modern therapeutic techniques, he still found it necessary to rely heavily on such standard drugs as opium and its derivatives, on quinine, and on warm or cold baths, to treat patients. He employed morphine to maintain control over difficult patients like William B., who struck one of the slaves at the hospital in January 1855, and Henry T., who eloped from the establishment in August of that same year.[67] He cured Josephine, a young free black from Norfolk, with a combination of showers,

[63] JMG, "Asylums for Colored Persons," 87.

[64] ELA, *Annual Report*, 1844, pp. 3, 10; JMG, Case Histories of Asylum Patients, 1844–45, GFP, MSS Vols., CW; JMG, Medical Diary, 24 September 1854, GFP, Med, CW; ELA, *Annual Report*, 1854–55, p. 47.

[65] ELA, *Annual Report*, 1843, p. 12.

[66] JMG, "Asylums for Colored Persons," 85.

[67] JMG, Medical Diary, 29 January, 7 August 1855, and Treatment List for August 1855, GFP, Med (folder 27), CW.

warm baths, drugs, and special diets, in addition to the usual moral therapy.[68]

Sometimes Galt also prescribed a calming type of treatment known as "riding out" for those requiring it. A month after Margaret F., a nineteen-year-old black woman from Loudoun County, had been treated with medication and baths, Galt ordered that she "ride out in the little carriage regularly" with a servant. This apparently had a soothing effect which Margaret soon came to rely on. She complained to the superintendent several months later that the ward attendants had been neglecting this aspect of her therapy. Though she suffered occasional relapses—at one time she struck an attendant—Margaret F.'s mental condition improved under Galt's treatment.[69]

The superintendent constantly observed or received reports on the behavior of all patients, especially the violent or self-destructive ones. His primary concern was to maintain the patients in a controllable state, with or without drugs, baths, and physical restraints. Control was the key, and it was elusive with some patients; two free blacks who had been at the hospital for fifteen or more years remained as unpredictable and "wild" in 1845 as they had been the day they had entered.[70] Once he felt that a patient had stabilized, Galt attempted to become acquainted with each individual's personal needs and feelings. His own sensitive nature was ideally suited for this. Of one free Negro woman Galt reported:

> April 30. [1844]. She possesses delicacy & other feelings in a degree, & still cannot converse at all. . . . Sept. 30. Perhaps shows feelings rather more evidently.
> March 31. [1845]. I observed her use several words lately that I never noticed in her previously.

And in another black woman he noted these characteristics:

---

[68] JMG, Medical Diary, December 1854-May 1855 (treatment lists), GFP, Med (folder 27), CW.

[69] JMG, Medical Diary, 6 January, 1, 10 February, 4, 5, 28, 30 June, 9 July 1854, GFP, Med (folder 27), CW.

[70] JMG, Case Histories of Asylum Patients, 1844–45, Hannah C. and James C., GFP, MSS Vols., CW.

Aug. 9th [1844]. Answered questions tolerably, but appeared to
have an inward train of thoughts in which she was wrapt. . . .
Sept. 30. [1844]. Still laughs vacantly, hollows & sings.
Nov. 30. [1844]. Has just ceased asking daily for rings.[71]

Regardless of the person and type of derangement, Galt's general
approach remained the same: control behavior, become acquainted with the individual, apply the principles of moral
management, and use any other techniques which suit that particular patient. In this way patients became integrated with the
rest of the hospital community.

Throughout his tenure as superintendent Galt had a strong and
sympathetic interest in the activities of black patients at the
hospital. He noticed, for instance, that one woman who was prone
to diarrhea had been eating green apples and drinking too much
water. Another had suddenly become "melancholy, abstracted &
[was] refusing food." A third was "giving ice to the little coloured
children [of the hired slaves]." He treated their physical as well
as mental ailments,[72] and even hired two former patients to work
at ELA, one, a slave, as a special ward officer.[73] This new slave
attendant was hired to "devote his time to the colored patients of
the male sex in a similar mode as the [white] officers . . . [who]
were attached to the management of white patients in the same
department." He not only provided sympathetic care to the black
male inmates, but also took "those of the colored residents to
walk who were quiet enough to enjoy the liberty." [74] The staff at
ELA provided for free Negro patients even in death. When one
old male inmate passed away in 1858 after thirty-six years at the
hospital, the directors met and "ordered that a head stone be
placed at the grave of James C. . . . to be paid for by private sub-

[71] *Ibid.*, Patsy C. and Fanny W.
[72] See, e.g., JMG, Medical Diary, 22, 28 September 1853, 3 May, 14 June
1854, GFP, Med (folder 27), CW.
[73] ELA, *Annual Report*, 1853–54, pp. 22–23. The former patient was found
"accidently drowned" in College Pond near the College of William and Mary
three years after a change in the state law required the directors to relieve him of
his duties at the hospital. See Williamsburg *Virginia Gazette*, 26 July 1855, p. 2.
His home prior to admission had been Richmond (city).
[74] ELA, *Annual Report*, 1853–54, p. 22; JMG, Medical Diary, 21 October 1854,
GFP, Med (folder 27), CW.

scription from the members of the Board." [75] The black patients at
ELA were not neglected during Galt's administration.

The Results of Galt's Treatment of Insane Blacks

How successful was Galt's approach to the care of mental
derangement among blacks? During his first twenty years of
service (1841–61) to the institution, he treated no fewer than 100
free Negroes [76] (including at least 9 admitted prior to, but remaining there on, 1 July 1841). Of the 94 whose outcome is known,
almost 40 percent (37) were long-term incurables who remained
in the hospital for more than five years (none recovered), and
another 25 percent (23) died within five years of admission (15
within the first two years). Only about 30 percent (29) actually
regained their sanity and left the hospital cured (two later returned for additional treatment). Though these figures appear
gloomy, a closer look at the overall statistics for the hospital
provide a somewhat different perspective (see Table 17). Both
before and during Galt's term free blacks died and recovered at
about the same rate as whites. Free blacks, who constituted 8.5
percent of the total patient population between 1840 and 1859,
contributed 9.3 percent of all recoveries (31 of 312), 7.7 percent
of all deaths (33 of 428), and almost 13 percent (35 of 280) of
all long-term patients from 1841 to 1861.

A larger proportion of the black inmates were, however,
chronic cases; there is no simple explanation for that situation.
Only three of the 37 were over fifty years old at the time of
admission, eliminating age or senility as a cause. Perhaps Galt's
moral treatment was not truly applicable to blacks, who had,
after all, a lifestyle, heritage, and culture different from that of the
physician and the other patients. He placed all blacks in separate
quarters and put them to work at menial labor as part of his
attempt to duplicate their former living conditions. This may
have been a mistake, since, by his own admission, the whites began to treat the free blacks as servants. An additional factor was

[75] ESH Mins, 10 November 1858, CW.
[76] For an explanation of the problems encountered in enumerating free blacks
at ELA, see note "d" accompanying table 14.

the reluctance of indigent free black families to lose a working member of the household as long as that individual was able to earn money. Whereas slaveowners and non-pauper whites more willingly sent patients to the hospital in hopes of a rapid cure, poor free blacks and whites could not afford the luxury of surrendering an income earner, even if the person was partially deranged. They waited until the illness worsened before taking such drastic action, thereby greatly reducing the chance of recovery.

Slaves, on the other hand, presented a brighter picture. About 55 were admitted to ELA as patients between 1846 and 1860. Not only did they usually enter very shortly after displaying symptoms of mental derangement; they also recovered at a greater rate and died less frequently than did the free blacks or whites (see Table 17). Galt recognized this, explaining that the nature of the slave system protected bondsmen from protracted untreated mental illness: "The fact of their [slaves] being property, induces their masters to call in medical aid early in the disease. . . . They are also from the fact of their being property, sure of being attended to." [77] Most slaveowners did obtain medical help from Galt soon after the symptoms of derangement appeared in their bondsmen. One Norfolk master requested his slave's admission to ELA within a week of the man's behavioral changes, explaining, "I am anxious to get him in the Institution, at once, so that the disease may not get too strong from want of taking it in time." [78] Of twelve cases for which records are extant, eight had shown their first symptoms less than three months prior to commitment. Galt's treatment of slaves was similar to that of free blacks. He believed that physical labor, being the slave's "usual avocation," ought to be included in the slave's therapeutic regimen, along with medication and kindness. [79]

Galt considered himself something of an expert in the matter of treating and managing insane blacks, especially after researching and writing the report of the Committee "On Asylums for Colored

[77] JMG to [William M. Awl, superintendent of the Ohio Lunatic Asylum, Columbus], [Draft ?,] n.d. [late January 1846], GFP, Med, CW.
[78] William H. Hunter to JMG, 11 November 1852, GFP, Med (folder 25), CW.
[79] JMG, "Asylums for Colored Persons," 83; JMG to [John Rutherford, Richmond], 12 June 1846, GFP, Med, CW.

Persons" for the Association of Medical Superintendents of American Institutions for the Insane in 1846. He vehemently opposed the establishment of separate institutions for the two races—a suggestion which his fellow committee member and Shenandoah Valley neighbor, Dr. Francis Stribling, favored. Galt felt that black institutions would not attract suitably qualified personnel or generate sufficient public support to function on a level equal to white institutions. By segregating patients of the two races, either in separate buildings or in portions of regular wards, any asylum would be able to function smoothly and efficiently. ELA was one of the few mental institutions in the nation to admit more than a handful of blacks, so Galt undoubtedly felt that it was necessary to provide a model to prove the points expressed in his report.

Though he subscribed to the "peculiar doctrines of Mr. Calhoun" (favoring slavery and states' rights),[80] Galt also had real compassion for the plight of insane blacks. Most superintendents across the country opposed the admission of blacks to white asylums, however, and rejected Galt's ideas and approach. They even refused to consult him for advice on the subject after the 1846 report. In 1852, when the government announced plans to construct a federal hospital for the insane, the superintendent in charge of the project, Dr. C. H. Nichols, bypassed Galt and corresponded instead with Stribling on "the best manner of caring for the colored insane." [81] And Dr. Thomas Kirkbride of Philadelphia, a prominent member of the superintendents' association, publicly dismissed Galt's ideas at the 1855 annual meeting in Boston: "The idea of mixing up all colors and all classes as is seen in one or two institutions of the United States, is not what is wanted in our hospitals for the insane, although it maybe regarded by . . . [Galt] as a desirable kind of liberty." [82]

Another blow to Galt's program of treating black lunatics came

[80] William Galt, biographical sketch of JMG, in Sally M. Galt's hand, GFP, Pers, CW; Dain, *Disordered Minds*, 112.

[81] C. H. Nichols to Francis Stribling, 13 December 1852, WSH Archives (folder IV), WSH.

[82] "Proceedings of the 10th Annual Meeting of the Association of Medical Superintendents of American Institutions for the Insane," *American Journal of Insanity*, 22 (1855), 43.

from within his own institution. A section of the 1846 law permitting ELA to admit slaves as patients stipulated that "no insane slave shall be received or retained in said asylum to the exclusion of any insane white person being a resident of the state."[83] On 16 December 1854 Galt announced to the Board of Directors that he had refused entry to two Richmond female slaves and a white woman from North Carolina because "we are full in the sense of a Hotel being full, and a [white] patient from our State might have to be rejected" were any of them admitted. When the problem had arisen six months earlier, in July 1854, Galt had then reluctantly proposed to send home all slave and out-of-state patients, but the directors had rejected the plan. They again overruled the superintendent in December by deciding to accept the North Carolinian.[84] For another year and a half, despite what Galt called "the plain requirements of [the 1846] law," the board continued to admit slaves and citizens of others states to the hospital.[85]

Their reluctance to bar these patients was probably based more on financial self-interest than on sympathy for the insane. Paying patients brought extra income to the hospital, money which the directors, no longer of the leading Williamsburg families since an 1851 state and local political shake-up, used to run the institution and to fill their own pockets. Galt never worked well with these men—he was in fact frequently at odds with them—in matters concerning the hospital's administration.[86] The slave issue was one manifestation of this discord between superintendent and directors. Finally, however, the latter succumbed, voted to comply with the law, and sent home all slave and non–state resident patients as of 10 October 1856, leaving only in-state whites and free blacks.[87]

No one felt sorrier than John Galt. He watched bitterly as white female patients transferred their belongings to the slaves' former rooms in the building where free Negro women continued to

[83] Virginia, *Acts of Assembly*, 1845–46, p. 18.
[84] JMG, Medical Diary, 16 December, 19 July 1854 (folder 27), GFP, Med, CW.
[85] *Ibid.*, 16 December 1854, 21 June 1855.
[86] Dain, *Disordered Minds*, 142–61, esp. 151–52.
[87] "Governor's Communication to the Board of Directors . . . ," *Leg. Docs.*, 1857–58, doc. 16, p. 19.

reside—a symbol of the state legislature's broken promise to provide for all of Virginia's insane blacks: "The general assembly first passes a resolution, very philanthropic to be sure, as though they would provide for the colored insane, whilst still insisting on sending the slaves home, notwithstanding the slight expense involved in their accommodation; and moreover themselves bring on a measure [the mixing of white and black female patients in one building], for which we are prepared for them to censure us." [88] Though he made a few exceptions after 1856, Galt generally adhered to the law regarding slaves. Insane bondsmen once again lived with their masters or in local jails, untreated by professionals.[89]

Galt continued to treat insane free blacks at ELA until his death in 1862. During his superintendency he had significantly improved the nature of that treatment and increased the number of blacks who received it. Through his efforts Virginia became one of the leaders in the treatment of insane blacks before the Civil War.

[88] *Ibid.,* p. 20.
[89] JMG to [Robert Saunders], 26 November 1860, GFP, Med (folder 33), CW.

CHAPTER 9

Blacks as Medical Specimens

In the modern-day pursuit of medical knowledge, patients serve several necessary and useful functions. Incidental to the recovery of their health, sick people, especially those in hospitals, clinics, and public institutions, become "cases." Upon them medical students, student nurses, interns, and residents learn the basic treatment of disease, medical researchers test new procedures, and attending physicians demonstrate medical and surgical skills. Patients with interesting or unusual diseases, or those chosen as parts of ongoing studies, are "written up" (anonymity retained) in the medical journals, thereby enhancing the reputations of individual doctors, statisticians, and other health professionals. Those who die, either at home or in the hospital, often become pathology specimens from which doctors further observe the disease process, or anatomy-class cadavers upon which students perform dissections as part of their introduction to the workings of the human body.

Patients have served in these various capacities ever since physicians commenced practicing their trade. Today members of all classes of society may be tapped for any of these functions, though the poor predominate. In the late eighteenth and entire nineteenth centuries a similar situation existed, and again the poor were the primary source of medical specimens. In Virginia blacks became subjects more frequently than whites. They served, in times of sickness, not simply as patients, but also as experimental subjects, specimens for clinical instruction, and objects of public display. Slaves and the free poor of both races had little choice in the matter; the former had to abide by the master's decision, and the latter, by the physician's (since treatment was without charge).

There were enough of these sick people in antebellum Virginia to provide physicians with abundant clinical material upon which to observe, experiment, or demonstrate. Only a small number of Virginia doctors took advantage of these opportunities once they had completed their training. The ones who did, however, either for true scientific or for exploitative purposes, wrote and published frequently enough to make their names and achievements familiar to many of the state's practitioners as well as to other interested observers.

The Medical School's Need for Clinical Material

The medical school at Richmond, founded in 1838 as the Medical Department of Hampden-Sydney College, was the largest consumer of clinical material in the Old Dominion. This school, which in 1854 became the Medical College of Virginia (MCV), required living subjects upon which professors could demonstrate operative techniques and the course and treatment of diseases, as well as corpses for anatomy dissections. Blacks comprised a substantial proportion of the former and almost all of the latter. The four other antebellum Virginia medical schools—University of Virginia (1825-present), Prince Edward Medical Institute (which became the Medical Department of Randolph-Macon College in 1847 [1837-61]), Winchester Medical College (1825-29 and 1847-61?), and the Scientific and Eclectic Medical Institute of Petersburg (1846-47?)—had similar but less extensive needs.[1]

Understandably, medical school hospitals did not enjoy a high

---

[1] Walter Fisher, "Physicians and Slavery in the Antebellum Southern Medical Journal," *JHM*, 23 (1968), 36–49, argues that these practices existed throughout the antebellum South. For more information on the medical schools, see Blanton, *19th Century*, 5–68.

reputation among some of the state's residents. "Respectable" citizens viewed them as suitable only for the poor; the impoverished feared them as places for dying or experimentation. Thomas Jefferson's conception of such an institution, typical of that era and no doubt substantially accurate, explains why people were reluctant to utilize hospital facilities:

> And I will ask how many families . . . would send their husbands, wives, or children to a hospital, in sickness? to be attended by nurses hardened by habit against the feelings of pity, to lie in public rooms harassed by the cries and sufferings of disease under every form, alarmed by the groans of the dying, exposed as a corpse, to be lectured over by a clinical professor, to be crowded and handled by his students, to hear their case learnedly explained to them, its threatening symptoms developed, and its probable termination foreboded?

Not many resorted to medical school hospitals willingly, but for some there was no alternative. According to Jefferson, "it is poverty alone which peoples hospitals."[2] He might have added slavery, too, though bondsmen learned early to maintain a high and distant regard for public infirmaries. In 1854 the editor of one Richmond newspaper explained the Negroes' attitude: "Among them there prevails a superstition that when they enter the [medical college] Infirmary they never come out alive; (although servants are no where better treated and taken care of than in that establishment;) therefore they will not complain, but will often conceal their real condition until too late to do good."[3]

Regardless of people's aversion to medical school hospitals and clinics, enough patients did attend them to supply each institution's needs. During its early years the University of Virginia actively solicited impoverished whites and free blacks, as well as slaves, to present themselves as patients at the Rotunda on selected days of the week. Students of the medical school assisted the professor of medicine at these clinics, which were free for the

[2] Thomas Jefferson to James C. Cabell, 16 May 1824, in Nathaniel F. Cabell, ed., *Early History of the University of Virginia as Contained in the Letters of Thomas Jefferson and Joseph C. Cabell* (Richmond, 1856), 310.

[3] Richmond *Daily Dispatch*, 21 July 1854, p. 2.

poor and fifty cents a visit for others (including slaves).[4] Even
after the dispensary had been disbanded, medical students attended many of the surgical cases treated by their professors.
Similar arrangements existed at both Randolph-Macon and
Winchester Medical Colleges; slaves and the poor probably provided the bulk of their cases.[5]

Richmond's Hampden-Sydney Medical Department rarely
lacked living or dead patients for its students. In addition to the
invalids at the infirmary, professors and pupils obtained access,
with the blessings of the city fathers, to the sick at the almshouse,
pest house, and state penitentiary.[6] Physicians at the medical
school recognized from the start that blacks, especially industrial
and urban slaves, would form a convenient and sizable population
from which to draw patients for both the infirmary wards and the
anatomy rooms: "From the peculiarity of our institutions, materials for dissection can be obtained in abundance, and we believe
are not surpassed if equaled by any city in our country. The
number of negroes employed in our factories will furnish materials for the support of an extensive hospital, and afford to the
student that great desideratum—clinical instruction." [7] To attract
patients from outside the city, the faculty placed advertisements
in the country editions of Richmond newspapers informing rural
slaveholders of the hospital's facilities. Slaves were even cared for
at a lower rate than whites.[8]

Always seeking new sources of clinical material, in 1848 members of the faculty contemplated establishing a hospital solely for

[4] Minutes of the Rector and Visitors of the University of Virginia (typescript),
4 April 1826, I, 99, UVA; Charlottesville *Virginia Advocate*, 16 February 1828,
p. 2.

[5] Blanton, *19th Century*, 34; Marshall McDonald, "Surgical Cases Presented to
the Class of Winchester Medical College, Session of 1857–58," *VMJ*, 12 (1859),
96–107; Medical Department of Randolph-Macon College of Virginia, *Catalog,
Session of 1851–52*, p. 7 (in Walter Hines Page Library, Randolph-Macon College Archives, Ashland, Va.); *VMSJ*, 1 (1853), 455–62.

[6] "Petition of the Students of the Medical Department of Hampden-Sydney
College for an Appropriation in Aid of That Institution," H of D *Jl.*, 1841/42,
doc. 24, p. 4.

[7] "An Address to the Public in Regard to the Affairs of the Medical Department
of Hampden-Sydney College, by Several Physicians of the City of Richmond,
1853," appendix I, quoted in Blanton, *19th Century*, 38–39.

[8] See, e.g., *Richmond Enquirer*, 8 May 1860, p. 3.

blacks, "thereby affording valuable means for clinical instruction." [9] Though this proposal was never acted upon, the idea of situating a large teaching hospital in Richmond, one which treated only the poor and slaves, was not abandoned. MCV could not afford to admit many indigent patients, so one Virginia medical journal attempted to stir up legislative and medical society interest in the plan in two editorials during 1853 and 1854. Recognizing that "the rich need no such institution," the editors suggested the founding of "a Virginia *Free* Hospital for the benefit of its *free* poor population"—with, of course, an annex for slaves (whose masters would pay). This would, not merely by coincidence, benefit the Medical College of Virginia as well as the indigent patients, and "present to the Southern medical student . . . an ample field for clinical practice." [10] Again, nothing ever came of the plan. But the faculty seemed determined to increase the supply of patients for the students, especially in the face of new competition from Bellevue, a private hospital which opened its doors in June 1854. Both catered to similar populations and charged modest rates.[11]

The faculty devised one scheme aimed specifically at those unable to pay for medical care. In 1858 the city government considered constructing a work-house to accommodate Richmond's poor. The professors at MCV offered to "take all sick and infirm paupers into the College Infirmary" in exchange for "a sum equal to what would be requisite to build a work-house" (to be used for construction of a new MCV hospital), plus the amount the city annually expended upon medical and surgical care at the present almshouse.[12] Though the plan failed to win approval from the city fathers, the state legislature deemed the college's

[9] "Notes of the Hampden-Sydney Medical Department Minutes," in William T. Sanger, *Medical College of Virginia before 1925 and University College of Medicine 1893–1913* (Richmond, 1973), 8.

[10] Editorial, "A State General Hospital," *VMSJ*, 1 (1853), 173–74; Editorial, "The Virginia Free Hospital," *ibid.*, 3 (1854), 275; "Annual Reports of Sundry Colleges and Academies, 1850," *Leg. Docs.*, 1850–51, doc. 32, p. 11.

[11] Blanton, *19th Century*, 222. Many blacks were treated at Bellevue. For a sampling of cases, see Thomas Pollard, "Bellevue Hospital Reports," *VMJ*, 10 (1858), 285–92, 378–82; 11 (1858), 448–55; 12 (1859), 375–79.

[12] Medical College of Virginia, Faculty Minutes, 1854–74, 4 December 1858, MCV.

need for clinical material sufficiently important to appropriate
$30,000 toward construction of a new hospital in 1860.[13] With the
onset of war in 1861 large numbers of patients entered MCV hospital.

The Medical School's Use of Clinical Material

None of the Virginia medical schools' hospital records
survive today, so it is impossible to discover the exact proportion
of free black, slave, and white patients treated. However, from
1851 to 1860 the medical journals published in Richmond occasionally included descriptions of cases presented at the local
infirmary, and (rarely) at the Winchester and Randolph Macon
Medical Colleges. Of 109 patients mentioned over the ten years,
63.3 percent (69) were blacks (37 slave and 15 free; the status
of 17 could not be determined).[14] This represents only a small
sample of the 150-250 patients who received treatment at MCV
hospital annually, but perhaps indicates a trend in patient utilization of the facility.[15]

Medical students had the opportunity to observe and treat disorders and surgical cases as they appeared in both black and
white Virginians. If, as was claimed, there were medical differences between the races which required special attention from
the physician, then the young physicians attending the state's
medical schools had ample chance to learn about them. Each
MCV medical trainee served as a "resident student" at the infirmary for a specific period of time. Patients assigned to him

[13] Blanton, *19th Century*, 213.
[14] *Steth.*, 1 (1851), 139–42, 144–47, 147–50, 267–71, 656–59; 2 (1852), 64–67,
139–41; 3 (1853), 103–4. *VMJ*, 6 (1856), 108–11, 185–88; 8 (1857), 177–85;
9 (1857), 21–23, 307–9, 365–69; 11 (1858), 188–90, 269–92, 352–54, 466;
12 (1859), 96–107, 112–15, 378–88, 455–57; 13 (1859), 16–19, 109–10, 211–12,
282–84, 370–73. *MVMJ*, 14 (1860), 456–58; 15 (1860), 136–39, 292–99, 360–63.
VMSJ, 1 (1853), 8–12, 29–32, 119–22, 364–65, 386–88, 455–62; 2 (1853–54),
274–77, 380–83; 5 (1855), 20–24, 109–12, 193–95.
[15] L. S. Joynes, "Report of the Dean of the Faculty of the Medical College of
Virginia," *Leg. Docs.*, 1857–58, doc. 23, p. 4; Blanton, *19th Century*, 213. This
might also reveal a tendency on the part of physicians to report cases about the
relatively nonvocal black minority, rather than about "respectable" paying white
patients.

became his responsibility: he kept the records, prepared and dispensed medicines, examined and observed the medical patients, and dressed the surgical patients. Though the professors made daily rounds, the students carried out their directions and worked most intimately with the patients. One resident was required to be in the building at all times. Despite the fact that the hospital admitted slaves, no resident student could "strike or maltreat any patient or servant of the Institution." During their rotation through the infirmary, MCV students cared quite closely for many patients of both races.[16]

It is not surprising that the lower classes and the slaves comprised most of the patient population. Why would a white person who could afford to pay a private physician to come to his home place himself or his white family under the care of a group of inexperienced physicians-in-training? Though people often expressed distaste for medical school hospitals, they still found them useful—even superior to private treatment, in some cases. The schools did employ skilled surgeons and experienced practitioners who could handle cases which others found too challenging. The operating facilities were usually good, and extra ward personnel allowed for post-operative care. At MCV, where medical students assisted surgeons during operative procedures, some middle- and upper-class white patients even came, paying $5–$15 per week. Typical of the "better" class at MCV was a fourteen-year-old white boy sent to the infirmary as a private patient after he had stuck a penknife into his thigh. He entered the hospital in October 1856 and departed four weeks later entirely cured, despite the fact that he was treated in part by medical students.[17]

Though helpful in most cases, hospital staff members occasionally abused their positions and performed excessive or unnecessary demonstrations on patients. The frequency with which this occurred was apparently greater than the public might have suspected; a Richmond physician, editor of the *Virginia Medical Journal*, claimed to have heard "of several surgical operations that had been performed during the past year [1855] most wantonly,

[16] Medical College of Virginia, Faculty Minutes, 17 July 1856, MCV.
[17] Arthur Peticolas, "Surgical Cases Treated at the Infirmary of the Medical College of Virginia," *VMJ*, 11 (1858), 292.

in cases utterly hopeless, as well as in others not requiring but actually forbidding such operations, as being needless." The most blatant known case of mistreatment involved a slave whose master sent him to an unnamed medical school hospital for cure of a tenacious leg ulcer, originally caused by a burn. The wound would not yield to the staff's ministrations, so the surgeon decided to amputate his leg—an extreme remedy in such a case. The servant believed that "his leg was cut off just to let the students see the operation, and to bring the doctor, as well as the medical college . . . into notice." The editor, who met and spoke with the servant, condemned the entire procedure as unnecessary and denounced the surgeon, name not given, as "a heartless monster" who "should be mulcted with heavy damages for malpractice." Nothing more on the matter appeared in print, despite the vehemence of the editor's censure.[18]

The decision to operate or not was usually an obvious one which most physicians and even experienced medical students could make. At MCV, however, the faculty took steps to ensure the elimination of needless surgical procedures by requiring the surgeon to consult with no fewer than two other professors "in every case requiring an operation which may hazard the life of the patient or maim him." [19] This 1854 rule was designed to protect the unsuspecting or unwilling patient from abuse at the hands of medical school staff.

The question of patient consent for surgery did not usually cause difficulties in the treatment of slaves, since relief of pain was the major concern for both master and bondsman. For example, Jordan, a thirty-year-old slave, developed a large, painful tumor of the jawbone which both he and his master wished removed. They granted Dr. Charles Bell Gibson at MCV Infirmary permission to operate in March 1857, and within a month Jordan was back home.[20] Just before Christmas of the following year,

[18] Senex [either James B. McCaw or George A. Otis], "On Surgical Operations," *VMJ*, 6 (1856), 110–11.

[19] MCV, Board of Visitors Minutes, 1854, p. 13, MCV.

[20] Frank Cunningham, "Surgical Cases at the Medical College of Virginia," *VMJ*, 9 (1857), 21–23. See also A. E. Peticolas, "A Case of a Loose Body in the Knee Joint," *VMSJ*, 5 (1855), 20–24; John P. Mettauer, "Surgical Cases Successfully Treated," *ibid.*, 1 (1853), 455–62.

however, this same surgeon encountered a case of consent which posed a moral problem. Phil, a Negro employed in Richmond, suddenly developed a hernia which could not be repaired by the usual means. Dr. Gibson discovered, upon surgically exposing the affected area, that an undescended testis obstructed the replacement of the intestine. He described his dilemma and decision in an article published the following year: "I confess now to some hesitation as to what should be done with the testis, and to a decided inclination to remove it. But an unwillingness to risk complication of the danger of the operation, besides the feeling that *I had no right to castrate a man without his consent, or that of his master,* prevailed against the temptation to lop off this misplaced testis." [21] His predicament well illustrates the ambiguous dual position of the slave in Virginia as both person and property. Six years earlier, Gibson did take advantage of a white patient's helpless situation to perform a castration before students even though he had never attempted it before, in order to utilize a newly developed technique about which he had just recently read.[22] Nothing could prevent instructors from using "captive" patients to demonstrate medical practice or surgical techniques for students; nor was there an effective means of eliminating patient abuse, especially when the recipients were the poor, the lower classes, and slaves.[23]

Colleges did not constitute the sole source of medical education in Virginia. Many doctors taught young apprentices the art and mystery of physic in small town offices and patients' homes, and learned about the approaches and important discoveries of colleagues at state and local medical society meetings. In an area where more than 40 percent of the population was slave or free black, the Negro inevitably weighed heavily in every private physician's caseload. Nevertheless, there is no evidence to indicate that local physicians demonstrated their skills on black patients any more frequently than on whites. Especially in small

[21] Charles Bell Gibson, "Surgical Cases," *VMJ*, 13 (1859), 16–19 (italics added).

[22] *Steth.*, 1 (1851), 144–47.

[23] Poor whites may have suffered more from such abuse than slaves, inasmuch as bondsmen were property and were, when possible, watched closely by their owners. Whites had no such advantage.

towns, when the local doctor was about to perform an unusual or delicate operation the entire population knew of it, and prominent citizens often observed, along with the physician's apprentices. For example, in Fredericksburg in January 1814 Dr. Robert Wellford trepanned (bored a hole to relieve pressure in) an eleven-year-old slave boy's skull one Sunday after church; observers included the owner, the doctor's son and three students, another physician and his pupils, "and many others . . . some [there] from sympathy & many from curiosity." [24]

At regular medical society meetings practitioners exchanged information regarding the management of diseases and occasionally displayed specimens from recent cases for the education of colleagues. Of seventeen cases known to have been discussed at Richmond medical society gatherings between January 1853 and June 1854, ten involved black patients. The only organs displayed during this period had been removed from five Negroes. Though white cases were mentioned, no specimens were produced to illustrate these diseases. [25]

Physicians' apparent reluctance to use clinical material from whites for public display continued even after the patient's death. As a result, blacks served most of the needs of Virginia's medical community for autopsy and dissection cadavers. When a person died, the attending physician, for his own or his students' education, might request permission of the decedent's family for an autopsy. This would confirm or disprove the diagnosis made during life and determine the extent of disease in the body. Whereas free whites and blacks usually had friends or relatives to convey the former patient's wishes regarding autopsy, slaves had recourse only to their owners. Even if the slave's family objected to the procedure, the final decision lay with the master. For example, in the case of a slave woman who died in early 1856 with what was suspected to be puerperal fever and peritonitis, the decedent's husband, also a slave, requested that no post-mortem examination be performed. The physician's desire to discover the actual cause

[24] Robert Wellford Diary, 30 January-6 February 1814, Wellford Papers, UVA. For an example from Alabama, see Fisher, "Physicians and Slavery," 47.

[25] The proceedings of the Medico-Chirurgical Society of Richmond City appeared in the *Stethoscope* during this period.

of death notwithstanding, nothing could alter the decision of the owner, who was, according to the frustrated doctor, "unwilling to do violence to his [slave's] prejudices and feelings." [26] Not all masters were this sympathetic. When death occurred away from home, the owner made a decision without consulting the black family.[27]

Derelicts and free persons with no known relatives were in positions akin to that of the slave. If they died while being treated, they were particularly susceptible to autopsy.[28] At MCV the rules required that "no body must be removed or interred until 24 hours have elapsed after death except at the express request of the friends or by direction of the attending Physician or Surgeon." [29] This regulation provided medical students interested in pathology with the opportunity of examining the organs of the friendless and homeless.

Autopsy was not the only possible fate of a person's body. Anatomical dissection, illegal in Virginia until 1884, was nevertheless pursued quietly and vigorously in the state's medical schools throughout the antebellum period.[30] Most dissections were performed on blacks, though the poor of both races were likely subjects. Medical students, professors, and hired graverobbers disinterred bodies from pauper and Negro cemeteries, mainly in Richmond, Norfolk, Petersburg, Alexandria, Charlottesville, Prince Edward County, and Winchester. Authorities usually ignored these illegal but necessary activities unless an irate citizen filed a complaint.

Cadavers were not always readily procurable in small towns such as Charlottesville, seat of the University of Virginia. As early as 1832 the medical department there was dealing in bodies with

[26] A Young Practitioner, "Report of a Case of Disease Supposed to Be Peritonitis," *Mon. Steth.*, 1 (1856), 364.

[27] George William Semple, "Case of Extra-Uterine Foetation," *MVMJ*, 14 (1860), 7; Thomas Pollard, "Report of Three Cases," *Steth.*, 2 (1852), 185–87; Peter B. Reamey, "Post-Mortem Examination of a Case of Tabes Mesenterica," *ibid.*, 2 (1852), 380–81.

[28] Arthur E. Peticolas, "Surgical Cases Treated at the Infirmary of the Medical College of Virginia," *VMJ*, 11 (1858), 269–92, case 11.

[29] Medical College of Virginia, Board of Visitors Minutes, 1854, p. 16, MCV.

[30] Virginia, *The Code of Virginia* . . . (Richmond, 1849), ch. 196, sec. 13; Blanton, *19th Century*, 69–74.

"certain low and bad men" in Richmond. These grave-robbers exhumed bodies from the poorhouse cemetery (reserved for blacks and indigent whites) and delivered them to the university's Richmond agent, who paid the men and forwarded the corpses to Charlottesville. In one six-month period (September 1831 to February 1832) sixteen graves were relieved of their contents in this manner, outraging the city fathers.[31] The university continued procuring cadavers in Richmond and elsewhere, at least until the Civil War, because of the difficulty in obtaining specimens locally.

A leading figure in this trade during the late 1840's and 1850's was anatomy professor John Staige Davis.[32] Davis used former students and professional acquaintances in at least three eastern Virginia towns (Richmond, Norfolk, and Alexandria) as agents to hire resurrectionists for the university. These men met with varied success in their efforts, for several reasons: grave-robbers were not particularly reliable, the authorities occasionally tightened up security around cemeteries, bodies putrefied rather quickly, and the competition with Hampden-Sydney for bodies in Richmond was fierce.[33] With the signing of an agreement in 1851 between Davis and the anatomist at Hampden-Sydney to share the available supply of bodies in the Richmond-Petersburg area, cadavers (predominantly black) became more plentiful at UVA.[34]

Little is known of cadaver sources for the Randolph-Macon, Winchester, and Petersburg medical schools. According to one Virginia medical historian, Randolph-Macon medical students obtained corpses from a nearby black cemetery: "Anatomical material was not lacking, for hard by was the old colored grave-

[31] Records of the Richmond Common Council, 13 February 1832, p. 334, VSL.

[32] I am indebted to James O. Breeden of Southern Methodist University for calling to my attention the John Staige Davis Papers at UVA, and for providing me with an advance copy of his article, "Body Snatchers and Anatomy Professors: Medical Education in Nineteenth-Century Virginia," VMHB, 83 (1975), 321–45.

[33] See, e.g., H. L. Thomas to John Staige Davis, 3 November 1849; Lewis W. Minor to Davis, 30 November 1850; A. E. Peticolas to Davis, 26 January 1852; T. C. Brown to Davis, 5 March 1857; all in John Staige Davis Papers, UVA. See also Breeden, "Body Snatchers," 326–43.

[34] Breeden, "Body Snatchers," 337–38.

yard at Mercy Seat, and the medical student of that day was resourceful and self-reliant." [35] The editor of the official organ for the Scientific and Eclectic Medical Institute of Virginia in Petersburg boasted that "in relation to clinical practice and material for dissection, we possess superior advantage over any other reformed school in our country." [36] One can reasonably assume that the "advantages" alluded to included Petersburg's sizable black population. There is little doubt that most of Virginia's dissection subjects were procured from midnight graveyard expeditions, and that most of these cadavers were black. Medical schools and students in Virginia thus made great use of black patients, both living and dead.

Experimentation

As a further service to the medical profession and to some scientists, many blacks, as well as some whites, submitted unknowingly to human experimentation, while others permitted themselves to be placed on public display or described in newspapers and medical journals. Usually the end result was notoriety for the physician and anonymity or oblivion for the patient.

Medical experimentation in Virginia was not nearly so blatant or dramatic as J. Marion Sims's use of Alabama slave women to develop an operative technique to cure vesico-vaginal fistula, or so cruel as Dr. Thomas Hamilton's tests conducted upon the slave John Brown in a makeshift open-pit oven in rural Georgia to discover the best remedies for sunstroke.[37] In at least one instance, however, the results were significant for the state and ultimately for the entire nation.

Thomas Jefferson was not a physician, although he took a great

[35] Blanton, *19th Century*, 33–34. He does not document the source of this information.

[36] Editorial, "The College," *Southern Medical Reformer*, 1 (1847–48), 239.

[37] J. Marion Sims, *The Story of My Life* (New York, 1884), 226–46; John Brown, *Slave Life in Georgia: A Narrative of the Life, Sufferings, and Escape of John Brown, a Fugitive Slave, Now in England*, ed. L. A. Chamerovozow (London, 1855), 45–48; F. N. Boney, "Doctor Thomas Hamilton: Two Views of a Gentleman of the Old South," *Phylon*, 28 (1967), 288–92.

interest in medical science and, of course, in the health of his own slaves. In December 1800, upon receipt of a letter from Dr. Benjamin Waterhouse of Boston requesting consideration of his pamphlet on vaccination, the Vice-President replied that he was already familiar with the physician's attempts to introduce Jenner's new technique into New England and was sympathetic to the cause of public health.[38] Jefferson had previously protected his slaves and family against smallpox by inoculation (also called variolation), a dangerous and unreliable technique introduced into this country one hundred years earlier.[39] He now believed, in light of Waterhouse's experiences in New England, that vaccination was superior to variolation and ought to be made available to persons in all parts of the nation.

During the spring of 1801 Waterhouse sent some cowpox vaccine to the President in Washington, who in turn forwarded it to a Georgetown physician, Edward Gantt. Gantt attempted to vaccinate several persons throughout the summer but was unsuccessful; either the matter was inert or his technique was faulty.[40] Jefferson, believing that "it will be a great service indeed rendered to human nature to strike off from the catalogue of its evils so great a one as the small pox," decided to introduce vaccination to central Virginia that summer. (The President was one of many Washington residents who left town during the "sickly season,"

[38] Jenner had discovered that cowpox, a mild eruptive disease of cattle, when transmitted from the cow's teat to human hands, remained localized and benign; however, it somehow also conferred immunity to smallpox upon those infected. The correspondence between Jefferson and Waterhouse and a narrative of their efforts to establish vaccination in this country are contained in Robert H. Halsey, *How the President, Thomas Jefferson, and Doctor Benjamin Waterhouse Established Vaccination as a Public Health Procedure* (New York, 1936). This first exchange of letters, dated 1 December and 25 December 1800, appears on p. 17.

[39] Ola Elizabeth Winslow, *A Destroying Angel: The Conquest of Smallpox in Colonial Boston* (Boston, 1974), 32–37, 44–58, 94–111; Halsey, *How the President and Dr. Waterhouse*, 3; Thomas Jefferson to Martha Jefferson Randolph, 9 April 1797, in Edwin M. Betts and James A. Bear, Jr., eds., *The Family Letters of Thomas Jefferson* (Columbia, Mo., 1965), 143.

[40] Jefferson to Waterhouse, 26 June, 25 July, 14 August, 17 September 1801; Waterhouse to Jefferson, 28 August 1801; all reprinted in Halsey, *How the President and Dr. Waterhouse*, 28, 31, 34–35, 36, 41. See also Edward Gantt to [Jefferson], 17 August 1801, in Thomas Jefferson Papers, LC.

August through October.)[41] He received fresh matter at Monticello on 6 August, a week after his departure from the capital, and "immediately [had it] inserted into six persons of my own family."[42] This was the start of what Jefferson termed "our experiment."[43]

The President devoted much time during the summer of 1801 to this project. His subjects were about two hundred slaves— "seventy or eighty of my own family," the same number owned by his son-in-law, Thomas Mann Randolph and John Wayles Eppes, and some belonging to his neighbors.[44] Of the first six patients (all from Monticello) whom Dr. William Wardlaw, a local physician, vaccinated on 7 August, two developed the pustules indicating a successful take. Jefferson had another slave vaccinated from one of these pustules, and five of the original subjects plus one new slave were injected on 13 August with fresh matter "received from Boston & some from England via Boston."[45]

[41] Jefferson to Waterhouse, 25 July 1801, in Halsey, *How the President and Dr. Waterhouse*, 31; Jefferson to Martha Jefferson Randolph, 16 July 1801, in Betts and Bear, eds., *Family Letters of Jefferson*, 207.

[42] Jefferson to Waterhouse, 8 August 1801, in Halsey, *How the President and Dr. Waterhouse*, 32.

[43] Jefferson to John Vaughan, 5 November 1801, *ibid.*, 44.

[44] *Ibid.*

[45] Jefferson to Waterhouse, 14 August 1801, *ibid.*, 34–35; Jefferson to [James Madison], 14 August 1801, in Thomas Jefferson Papers, LC. Nowhere in his correspondence does Jefferson explicitly state that slaves were used in this "experiment" to the exclusion of his white family. The implication, however, is there. Some ambiguity exists as to whether the first six persons vaccinated included whites as well as blacks. At this time the whites in his family consisted of his two daughters, Mary (Maria) and Martha, and his four grandchildren, Anne, Thomas, Ellen, and Cornelia. Anne and Thomas had been variolated several years earlier in Richmond and had not been vaccinated as late as 19 December 1808 (Anne Randolph Bankhead to Jefferson, 19 December [1808], in Betts and Bear, eds., *Family Letters of Jefferson*, 371), leaving the two younger grandchildren and the two daughters unaccounted for. It is unlikely that Jefferson would have included them in the initial round of vaccinations and then refer to them so coldly in letters as "subjects" (Jefferson to Dr. Edward Gantt, 21 August 1801, in Thomas Jefferson Papers, LC) or "patients" (Jefferson to [James Madison], 14 August 1801, *ibid.*). Although his lack of specific mention of names and his constant use of impersonal terms in correspondence throughout the summer suggest that the President vaccinated his slaves before attempting the procedure on his own white family, no positive proof exists.

Four of the patients vaccinated with 13 August vaccine developed sores on their arms, and fourteen of fifteen who received matter from the first two subjects "very evidently have the infection." Now that the procedure had succeeded on twenty slaves, Jefferson hoped that others in the neighborhood would request Dr. Wardlaw "to introduce it in their families." [46]

The mass summer vaccinations in Albemarle County were not attended with any undue problems, though many of the slaves did lose a day or two of labor. Only one patient developed high fever and delirium; others experienced various combinations of headache, swollen glands, and slight fever. Two or three developed more than one pustule on the vaccinated arm, and only three or four of the two hundred failed to become infected at all. Jefferson kept all subjects at their regular tasks when possible and did not alter their daily routines or diets. He even allowed nursing women to be vaccinated, noting later that "suckling children did not take the disease from the inoculated mother." [47]

Many Virginians still remained unconvinced that injection with cowpox would effectively prevent infection from smallpox. To prove his point Jefferson, when back in Washington (5 November), had the live virus introduced into a vaccinated patient. The man did not develop smallpox. Relieved and elated, Jefferson conveyed the news to his daughter Martha in Albermarle County in order to "place our families & neighbors in perfect security." [48] The experiment had succeeded. To hasten the dissemination of information regarding vaccination, the President not only recommended it to his local acquaintances but also sent live matter to Richmond, Petersburg, and several other parts of the state.[49]

As a result of Jefferson's efforts, vaccination became an established procedure in Virginia. By endorsing Jenner's technique, the President hastened its popular acceptance and thus indirectly helped to reduce the mortality from this dread disease. Few white

[46] Jefferson to Waterhouse, 21 August 1801, in Halsey, *How the President and Dr. Waterhouse*, 35–36.

[47] Jefferson to Mr. John Vaughan, 5 November 1801, *ibid.*, 44–45.

[48] Jefferson to Vaughan, 5 November 1801; Jefferson to Waterhouse, 25 December 1801; Jefferson to Martha Jefferson Randolph, 17 January 1802; all *ibid.*, 45, 47, 52.

[49] Jefferson to Waterhouse, 17 September 1801, *ibid.*, 41.

people then realized that the vaccine matter which entered their bloodstreams and saved their lives often came from the arms of such blacks as Jefferson's slaves. And few people today recognize the significant role that blacks played in the introduction and acceptance of vaccination in America.

Another major medical breakthrough of the nineteenth century involved at least one, and probably more, Virginia Negroes. Dr. J. Marion Sims of Alabama originated the first reliable procedure for the cure of vesico-vaginal fistula, a communication between bladder and vagina which permitted the uncontrollable escape of urine from the former into the latter rather than into the urethra. But John Peter Mettauer, a Prince Edward County physician and surgeon, had actually performed a similar operation fifteen years earlier, using lead rather than silver sutures, though his results were not as consistent as Sims's. Mettauer, like Sims, attempted the operation numerous times on a small number of women, including a twenty-year-old slave, but never received the publicity that Sims later did. After reporting his initial success in 1838 on a local (but unidentified) woman, the doctor presented details on only two other cases, one of which was a failure. Nothing is known of the twenty-five additional women upon whom he operated prior to June 1855, though it is probable that many of them were bondswomen, as Prince Edward County was a large slave-holding area.[50]

The third patient whom Mettauer treated for vesico-vaginal fistula, and his only recorded failure in twenty-eight cases, was a twenty-year-old slave whose condition had resulted from a "tedious and poorly managed labor." This woman suffered through at least ten unsuccessful surgical attempts by Mettauer to correct her condition; his two other detailed cases had been cured with the first procedure. Though the physician admitted that her particular kind of case, "in which extensive sloughing [of the tissue] had taken place," was particularly difficult to cure, he also partially blamed the patient for something no nineteenth-century

[50] John Peter Mettauer, "Vesico-Vaginal Fistula," BMSJ, 22 (1840), 154–55; "On Vesico Vaginal Fistula," AJMS, NS 14 (1847), 117–21; "The Prophylaxis of Traumatic Inflammation," VMSJ, 1 (1853), 8; "Contributions to Practical Surgery," VMSJ, 4 (1855), 454.

white woman would have permitted her physician to print: "I believe this case, nevertheless, could have been cured in process of time, more especially if sexual intercourse could have been prevented, which intercourse, I have no doubt, defeated several of the operations." [51]

Not all those who used blacks for medical experimentation gained fame from their successes. Often what at first appeared to be a positive causal correlation between treatment and cure actually represented a remission of the disease resulting either from natural body processes or from other medications. If a cure reported in one of the medical journals could not be duplicated elsewhere, then it never attained widespread usage despite the number of lives, white or black, that the experimenter claimed it had saved. Two such instances occurred in Virginia during the 1850's.

Epidemic typhoid fever struck many families, especially black households, in one area of Halifax County during the warm months of 1832. The disease was usually the result of filthy living conditions, contaminated water supplies, and infected foods; hence it affected the slaves of large planters, as well as impoverished free blacks. Residents of the area pressured one local physician for immediate action—not only would their laborers lose many days of work, but whites might also develop the disease. Dr. Robert G. Jennings of Church Hill explained to these anxious people that the medical profession "knew of no reliable remedy" for typhoid fever, but that he wished to test a theory for protecting those not already affected. The secret weapon turned out to be smallpox vaccine, its "virtues . . . as a prophylactic [against typhoid infection] having never . . . [been] tried." Much to Jennings's surprise and pleasure, not one of the approximately thirty slaves and free blacks who were successfully vaccinated in three separate infected families developed typhoid. As an added bonus, three or four blacks suffering from the disease recovered shortly after receiving his new treatment; in contrast, those whose vaccinations did not "take" suffered with "a long spell" of typhoid. To further prove his point, Jennings purposely withheld the vac-

[51] Mettauer, "On Vesico-Vaginal Fistula" (*AJMS*), 121.

cine from one person in a twelve-member slave family living in a double house. This individual was the only one in the entire household to actually develop a case of typhoid fever (aside from the original case). No logical explanation can be offered for Jennings's success, though it is unlikely that wholesale smallpox vaccination prevented the spread or eased the course of typhoid fever. His claim generated little excitement in the Virginia medical community; no letters or comments on the subject ever appeared in any state medical journals up to 1861. But he did have the opportunity to test his theories on a captive population, and, as far as he was concerned, the experiment had been successful.[52]

During the winter and spring of 1846–47 another physician, Dr. Walter F. Jones of Petersburg, took advantage of a group of patients from Prince George County to test a remedy for typhoid pneumonia. His report is silent as to the number and make-up of the experimental population, though both patients discussed in detail were blacks. The treatment resembled a form of torture rather than a curative measure, especially in view of the degrading position which the patient was required to assume. Jones described its application upon a very sick and weak twenty-five-year-old male slave, understating its effect almost humorously: "The patient was placed [naked] on the floor on his face, and about five gallons of water at a temperature so near the boiling point as barely to allow the immersion of the hand, was thrown immediately on the spinal column, which seemed to arouse his sensibilities somewhat, as shown by an effort to cry out; he was well rubbed and wrapped in blankets, and removed to bed." If necessary, the treatment was to be repeated in four hours. Somehow (Jones claimed by "re-establishing the capillary circulation"), many of his patients recovered from typhoid pneumonia.[53]

Physicians were not the only whites who tested medical theories on blacks. Slaveowners worried about their slaves' health and

---

[52] Robert G. Jennings, "Remarks on the Use of the Tampon in Uterine Hemorrhage, with a Report of Two Cases," *Steth.*, 3 (1853), 209. The last three paragraphs of this article deal with the typhoid epidemic.

[53] Walter F. Jones, "On the Utility of Applications of Hot Water to the Spine in the Treatment of Typhoid Pneumonia," *VMSJ*, 3 (1854), 108–10.

treated their illnesses with home remedies. In a sense, masters experimented each time they administered personally developed curatives to slaves suffering from unknown or undiagnosed illnesses. Some, of course, dosed blacks with medicines explicitly for the purpose of discovering their effects. For example, John Walker, a small planter of King and Queen County who became an avid Thomsonian in the 1830's, decided to attempt to cure his servant's frequent fits with Thomsonian medicines: "My Servant Anderson has been subject to having fitts all his life—he had one the 13th. I conveyed him through a Thompsonian Course of Medicine the next day. I wish to see what effect it will have & how long before he has another from this time." If the drugs worked, the cure was only temporary, for eight months later Walker recorded in his diary: "Anderson had from Sat. last to Tuesday night fitts almost continually—three men had to stand & hold him down. I think he had at least 100 or more—he has been mending since." [54]

Physicians used this empirical method of treatment quite often in their own practices but never labeled it experimentation. For example, when Dr. Alexander Somervail of Loretto, Essex County, was treating a black woman for fever, he was told that the medication he used had also relieved her of suppression of urine. Spurred by his initial (though accidental) success, Somervail treated at least four other patients (two black and two white) for this problem, with similar results. He then wrote two short articles for the prestigious *American Journal of the Medical Sciences* strongly proclaiming the efficacy of camphor and muriate of ammonia in the treatment of urinary suppression. [55]

The trial-and-error approach was employed not only for developing treatments, but also for evolving new surgical techniques, as has been shown with John P. Mettauer. Another surgeon who gained renown in Virginia by publicizing the results

[54] John Walker Diary, 14 February, 6 October 1855, UNC.

[55] Alexander Somervail, "On the Efficacy of a Mixture of Camphor and Muriate of Ammonia in the Treatment of Suppression of Urine," *AJMS*, 14 (1834), 113–15; "Case of Retention of Urine Cured by a Solution of Muriate of Ammonia," *ibid.*, 16 (1835), 250.

of his operations was P. C. Spencer of Petersburg. His specialty was bladder stones, a painful condition with a painful cure. Stones in the male urinary tract caused unbearable agony and often suppressed the normal passage of urine, a double problem. Spencer adapted and mastered an efficient and relatively safe technique over the course of several years, using twenty-eight patients and a French instrument, the lithotome cache. Three of his first four operations were performed on blacks, one of whom died. To keep the medical profession abreast of his accomplishments, Spencer submitted three interim reports between 1850 and 1858 in Philadelphia and Richmond journals.[56]

In none of the instances of medical experimentation uncovered in Virginia was there any indication of maliciousness or malevolence toward the black subject. Certainly nothing as horrifying and blatantly brutal as Dr. Hamilton's experiments upon John Brown in Georgia appears to have occurred in the Old Dominion. The purpose of these explorations into unknown medical territory was, ostensibly at least, to improve man's knowledge of the treatment of diseases. In some cases, most notably vaccination and vesico-vaginal fistula, experimentation paid off and mankind gained valuable information. Other attempts failed, and people died at the hands of the experimenters. Poor people in general, and slaves in particular, constituted a captive population in Virginia. They had little choice but to submit to the physician's treatment and trust that he would not harm them. Rarely did they realize when an experiment was being conducted upon them.[57]

Public Display

During the 1850's the Virginia medical establishment supported one, and for a short period two, monthly journals devoted

---

[56] *AJMS*, NS (1850), 103–6; *VMSJ*, 4 (1855), 89–93; *VMJ*, 11 (1858), 1–7.

[57] Other examples of subtle experimentation on whites and blacks may be found in H. Dorsey, "Case of Traumatic Tetanus, Successfully Treated," *AJMS*, 18 (1836), 529–31; John Peter Mettauer, "On the Use of the Unripe Fruit of the *Diospyros Virginiana,* as a Therapeutic Agent," *AJMS*, NS 4 (1842), 297–300.

to the improvement and continuing education of the state's practitioners.[58] The Richmond-based editors solicited articles from the general medical community and received manuscripts from a few active physicians living mainly in Tidewater and Southside. Their purpose in taking the time to write varied: some sought to establish fame or reputation by constant re-exposure in print; some wished to describe an interesting or unusual case for the benefit of the profession; some desired to teach or illustrate a principle of treatment; and some simply wrote for the pleasure of it. Blacks played a prominent role in Virginia's medical journals because physicians frequently used their Negro cases to explain or illuminate a point. Of 357 original articles, communications, or reports published during this period (excluding Maryland articles from the *Maryland and Virginia Medical Journal*), 174 (48.7%) mentioned the treatment of black patients. Some Virginia physicians published outside the state. One Philadelphia quarterly, the widely read *American Journal of the Medical Sciences*, carried 66 such articles between 1827 and 1861. Almost 40 percent (26) mentioned blacks in illustrating a disease or treatment.[59] The number of blacks used for this purpose was not out of proportion to their number in Virginia (usually 40-45% of the population.

Some medical writers did, however, take advantage of legally helpless blacks by printing statements about them which a white person would have considered unacceptable. Dr. A. E. Peticolas, a professor at MCV, used these flippant remarks to introduce a discussion of two case histories of jaw tumors in slaves:

> I must confess that I approached Manuel's jaw bone with the greatest reverence. I *read up* with becoming assiduity, and had very serious apprehensions raised by Vidal de Cassis, that if the patient failed to choke himself to death by swallowing his tongue just after the operation, which I took good care to prevent, he would most

---

[58] *The Stethoscope and Virginia Medical Gazette*, 1851–53; *The Stethoscope*, 1854–55; *The Virginia Medical and Surgical Journal*, 1853–55; *The Virginia Medical Journal*, 1856–59; *The Monthly Stethoscope and Medical Reporter*, January 1856-May 1857; *The Maryland and Virginia Medical Journal*, 1860–61. See also Blanton, *19th Century*, 427.

[59] Walter Fisher, "Physicians and Slavery," 43–46, suggests that this use of blacks was more widespread in the Deep South.

assuredly die of a sort of chronic suffocation. I am happy to say, however, that both Manuel and Lucinda have visited me within the past three months, looking sleek, amiable, and grateful.

He would not have written in this manner about a white patient. Nor could Theodore P. Mayo, also of MCV, have suggested in so irreverent a manner that his twenty-four-year-old patient Roy, complaining of testicular atrophy and bladder stones which "were undoubtedly ordinary *leaden shot*," was actually a hysterical male:

> All of us have heard of, and many see, cases where some women with a predisposition to hysteria, insert cinders and other foreign substances into the vagina. . . .
> This boy was a great buck among the dark damsels, and so far as I can learn, had some serious notions of matrimony; and the fact of his testicles "drying up" as he expressed it, might have had such an effect upon his nervous system, as to produce these hysterical symptoms.[60]

This derogatory style resembled that used in the local news sections of some Virginia newspapers.

Medical journals across the country never failed to publish accounts of unusual phenomena, especially those relating to genital organs and gross congenital birth defects. Of eleven such oddities submitted to the Virginia medical press in the 1850's six involved blacks, including five of the six most delicate. There were two cases of hermaphrodism (black), one of precocious puberty (black), two of Siamese twinning (black), one of birth monstrosity (white), one of extra-uterine fetus retained for forty years (black), two of hydrocephalus (white), one of congenital displacement of the heart (white), and one of birth of quadruplets (white).[61] Interestingly, no white cases of hermaphrodism, precocious puberty, Siamese twinning, or other oddities turned up in the state's medical journals. The same was true of the Virginia cases reported in the *American Journal of the Medical*

---

[60] A. E. Peticolas, "College Infirmary Cases," *VMJ*, 12 (1859), 379; Theodore P. Mayo, "Case of Nephritic Colic, with Remarks," *VMSJ*, 5 (1855), 111.

[61] *Steth.*, 1 (1851), 99–101, 263–67, 275–76; 2 (1852), 394–95, 439; 4 (1854), 330–32, 389–91, 573–74; *VMJ*, 9 (1857), 30–32; 10 (1858), 197–99; *VMSJ*, 4 (1855), 94–95.

Sciences: five of nine cases printed here featured blacks, including one hermaphrodite (the same one described in the *Stethoscope*), one woman who could urinate through her umbilicus (navel) owing to a congenital defect, and another forty-year fetus. Among the six remaining cases were three less exotic birth malformations (two white, one black), one simultaneous uterine and extra-uterine pregnancy (black), one birth monstrosity (white), and one penile deformity (white).[62]

Authors felt no compunction about presenting minute descriptions of these freaks of nature, especially those with personal body abnormalities, almost all of whom were black. The supposed hermaphrodite, a Mecklenburg County slave named Ned, reluctantly submitted at least twice in three years to a complete physical examination in order to satisfy the professional curiosity of local physicians. Dr. S. H. Harris of Clarksville wrote, with some levity, of Ned's sexual life (he was eighteen at the time): "Whether his amorous advances to the dusky maidens around him, has ever resulted in any practical display of virility, is unknown. In the absence of all information on the subject, it is fair to conclude, that no seminal discharge has, or ever will take place." Similarly, the personal life of another slave, a young female living in Woodville, Rappahannock County, was exposed in an article relating "precocious development of the female reproductive organs and appearance of the menses" at age four.[63] Of course, every member of the medical profession in the Richmond vicinity conducted his own personal examination of both sets of Siamese twins (one pair alive, the other stillborn) when

[62] *AJMS*, 2 (1828), 114–16; 11 (1832–33), 346–54; 19 (1836–37), 269–70; NS 4 (1842), 43–57; NS 14 (1847), 121–24; NS 15 (1848), 313–14; NS 18 (1849), 407–8; NS 19 (1850), 114–16; NS 20 (1850), 370–74. Another Philadelphia journal, the *Medical Examiner and Record of Medical Science*, published a report on the birth of twins, one mulatto and one black, to a Virginia slave woman under the title, "Case of a Negro woman, who gave birth to twins of different color." She had had sexual relations on successive days with a white man and a black man, and the author speculated that the result was two-color twinning. R. Carter, NS 5 (1849), 523–24.

[63] S. H. Harris, "Case of Doubtful Sex," *AJMS*, NS 14 (1847), 121–23; Charles R. Kemper, "Remarkable Case of Precocity—Menstruation Occurring at Four Years of Age," *Steth.*, 2 (1852), 439.

they were placed on exhibition.[64] The attitude of physicians seems to have been that blacks, being property, or free but inferior, could be used for medical display and publicity, whereas whites with similar anomalies required privacy and anonymity.

Occasionally doctors found a case so unusual that they could not resist the temptation to go beyond mere description and exhibit the subject to the medical and even the lay public. Usually this took the form of specimen preservation in a medical school or hospital, or presentation at medical society meetings. Again, most display objects were obtained from black rather than white patients. When, for example, a thirty-five-year-old Pittsylvania County slave woman carried twins, one in her uterus and the other in one Fallopian tube, her physician packed up the entire specimen after extraction and shipped it off to his colleague, Dr. Hugh L. Hodge at the University of Pennsylvania. Similarly, Dr. Philip Claiborne Gooch of Richmond donated a premature stillborn child, still in its fetal membranes with placenta attached, to the local medical college. Its mother, he reported, was "a most respectable negress." [65] Not one of the five extraordinary white cases published in the antebellum Virginia medical journals was ever placed on display.

In several instances living black patients actually went on tour to exhibit their anomalies. The Siamese twins, born of a North Carolina slave woman but followed closely by the Virginia medical profession, toured portions of the state in 1852. They had been born in July 1851 and were just a year old when placed on exhibition in Richmond. Eight months later, after the excitement had died down and the twins had returned to North Carolina, the editor of the *Stethoscope* complained in his journal that "the greatest physiological phenomenon now in the world, are scarcely known." He recommended that someone "of any spirit or enter-

[64] [P. C. Gooch,] "The Carolina Twins," *Steth.*, 2 (1852), 394–95; William B. Ball, "A New Edition of the Siamese Twins," *VMJ*, 10 (1858), 197–99.

[65] William G. Craghead, "A Remarkable Case of Double Pregnancy—One Ovum Entering the Uterus, the Other Being Arrested in the Tube," *AJMS*, 19 (1850), 114–16; P. Claiborne Gooch, "A Case of Premature Labor—Inertia of the Uterus—Liquor Ergotinae," *Steth.*, 2 (1852), 65–67.

prise" ought to publicize and nationally exhibit these children. Millie-Christine, as the twins were called, did tour the United States and Europe, and gained world renown during their sixty-one years of life.[66]

One of the most striking changes to which blacks were subject was whitening of the skin. Late eighteenth and early nineteenth century observers of this phenomenon could not but wonder at nature's marvelous ways. One of the most inquisitive investigators of "white negroes" was Thomas Jefferson, who, in his Notes on Virginia, raised the subject of black albinism in the state, having pursued it in letters to owners of such persons. He described the seven black albinos of whom he had knowledge, and also one Negro man who had been born black but whose skin gradually turned white over a large portion of his face and neck.[67]

There is no evidence that any of the people Jefferson described were placed on public display, though other Virginians were. Most famous was Henry Moss, a free black who had served in "a corps of pioneers" during the Revolution.[68] At age thirty or forty he began to turn white, so that within a short time most of his body was covered with large areas of white skin and small brown spots. He decided to secure his fortune by displaying his body and so traveled throughout the country for at least several months in the mid-1790's. For a period during the summer of 1795 or 1796 Moss was the rage in Philadelphia, to the extent that Charles Caldwell, a young and later famous physician, took him into his home for a few weeks in order to perform, with Moss's consent, experiments on his skin.[69]

[66] [Philip Claiborne Gooch,] "Editorial," Steth., 3 (1853), 157; African Twins Collection, North Carolina State Archives, Raleigh.

[67] Thomas Jefferson, Notes on the State of Virginia (Richmond, 1853), 78–79. See also Henry Skipwith to Jefferson, 20 January 1784, and Charles Carter to Jefferson, 9 February 1784; both in Julian P. Boyd, ed., The Papers of Thomas Jefferson (Princeton, 1953–), VI, 473–74, 534–35.

[68] Duke de la Rochefoucault Liancourt, Travels through the United States of North America . . . (London, 1799), II, 134.

[69] Charles Caldwell, The Autobiography of Charles Caldwell, M.D., ed. Harriot W. Warner (Philadelphia, 1855; reprinted, New York, 1968), 163–64, 268–69; Rochefoucault, Travels through the United States, II, 133–34; Winthrop Jordan, White over Black: American Attitudes toward the Negro, 1550–1812 (Baltimore, 1968), 521–22.

Less notorious than Henry Moss was the case of a "perfectly black" male servant owned by Major Banks, a Williamsburg lawyer, who began to turn white in 1806. Despite repeated offers, the slave steadfastly refused emancipation until, as an old man in 1821, he agreed to place himself on exhibit in Norfolk, so that the proceeds could be used to manumit his wife and children as well as himself. One Williamsburg physician, anxious to promote the enterprise, assured a Norfolk relative that it "will excite the wonder and curiosity of every one." [70]

Though it cannot be denied that blacks were exploited as medical subjects for medical students, dissection demonstrations, experiments, and exhibitions, the fact remains that poor whites were also used for similar purposes; nevertheless, the frequency with which white specimens appeared at medical society meetings and in medical school classrooms was strikingly lower than that for free blacks and slaves. This situation existed as a result of the degraded condition of blacks, both free and slave, in Virginia. Physicians could jocularly describe the sorry medical plight of a nonwhite with complete impunity, whereas such printed reference to a white person could well have resulted in a court suit. With an abundant supply of black clinical material on hand, the state's medical profession utilized white specimens only with great reluctance; it was as if an unwritten agreement had been consummated between white patients and their doctors, and among practitioners in general. In return, most blacks received free or low-cost medical care. Though the situation may have been (and probably was) worse in the Deep South, it was bad enough in Virginia to conclude that blacks had served the state's medical profession well.

[70] A[lexander] D. Galt to Alexander [Galt], n.d. [1821], Galt Family Papers, Medical, CW.

Afterword: Medicine, Slavery, and the Historian

Despite the fact that historians have written many words on the health care and diseases of antebellum southern blacks, the overall picture has been unclear. Journal articles have been either too broad in scope, with only limited or selective evidence,[1] or too narrow in coverage, focusing only on one plantation, one state, or the medical profession.[2] The writers of state medical histories have included some references to blacks in their works, but even those on Louisiana and Virginia (the only two really adequate state studies) present unclear and incomplete pictures.[3] William Dosite Postell's monograph on slave health is informative but restricted to plantations.[4] In most book-length studies of American slavery the subject of health care and disease has tra-

[1] See, e.g., Victor H. Bassett, "Plantation Medicine," *Journal of the Medical Association of Georgia*, 29 (1940), 112–22; Mary Louise Marshall, "Plantation Medicine," *Bulletin of the Tulane Medical Faculty*, 1 (1942), 45–58.

[2] See, e.g., Bennett H. Wall, "Medical Care of Ebenezer Pettigrew's Slaves," *Mississippi Valley Historical Review*, 37 (1950), 451–70; Weymouth T. Jordan, "Negro Peculiarities," in Jordan, *Ante-Bellum Alabama Town and Country* (Tallahassee, 1957), 84–105; Charles Sydnor, *Slavery in Mississippi* (New York, 1933); Walter Fisher, "Physicians and Slavery in the Antebellum Southern Medical Journal," *JHM*, 23 (1968), 36–49; John Duffy, "A Note on Ante-Bellum Southern Nationalism and Medical Practice," *JSH*, 34 (1968), 266–76.

[3] John Duffy, ed., *The Rudolph Matas History of Medicine in Louisiana* (Baton Rouge, 1958–62); Blanton, *19th Century*.

[4] Postell, *Health of Slaves*.

ditionally been relegated to a separate chapter, where discussions have usually served two purposes: to round out the picture of slave life, and to provide a means for measuring the benignity or harshness of "the peculiar institution." Included are descriptions of basic physical comforts (food, housing, clothing), provisions for health care (hospitals, plantation hygiene, plantation health rules, plantation nurses and midwives, home remedies, and physicians), diseases and epidemics, the cost of medical care, and vital statistics (morbidity and mortality). This material is usually presented in such a way that it supports the writer's general assessment of slavery as practiced in the South.

Though these approaches have been useful, they have failed to make full use of the data available on antebellum black health conditions. Other questions can and must be asked of the materials at hand in order to gain a better insight into the institution of slavery. It is necessary first to understand the nature of disease, the principles of public health, and the state of antebellum medicine before attempting to tie medicine and slavery together. Many historians of slavery have neglected to do this. Descriptive statements of conditions under slavery explain little about their effects on bondsmen. If slaves were provided with hats, what did that mean in terms of health and well being? Did it really matter if a slave wore rags or new clothing? In what way? How important was the slave community as a promoter of disease contagion or of black medicine and self-care? It is necessary to go beyond the simple restatement of slave death rates, cabin counts, disease lists, physicians' accounts, food distribution statements, and letters between slaveowners in order to draw conclusions from medically related sources.

Some of the early writers on the matter of slave health, for instance Ulrich Bonnell Phillips in 1918,[5] discussed plantation medicine from the planter's point of view (i.e., the economics of slave health care) without much comment on the sufferings or needs of the slave. Their major sources were the records kept

[5] Ulrich B. Phillips, *American Negro Slavery* (New York, 1918). See also Bassett, "Plantation Medicine," and Marshall, "Plantation Medicine."

on several large, well-run plantations and included planters' accounts, diaries, instructions to overseers, and agricultural journal articles. Their findings led to the conclusion that slaves were happy, well fed, and adequately cared for. After all, the argument ran, slaves represented a financial investment; how could slave-owners treat them otherwise?

The answer came from Kenneth M. Stampp in his book, *The Peculiar Institution*,[6] in which he devoted twenty-five pages to a description of the deplorable living and health conditions which, he asserted, slaves endured on plantations. Stampp claimed that the incidence of disease and death was much higher among blacks than whites because slaves were poorly fed, clothed, and housed, and that those in charge of the general maintenance of slaves on plantations did a poor job.

A third, intermediate position appeared as early as 1930. Richard Harrison Shryock pointed out that health and health care in the South were less than ideal for whites as well as blacks; he observed that many slaveowners made an honest effort to care for their slaves, but that the "argument for slave health, in terms of property interest, has only partial validity,—men have been known to neglect even their livestock." [7] Of the two most recent general treatments of slavery, one, Eugene Genovese's *Roll, Jordan, Roll*,[8] skirts the issue of health care and hardly evaluates the medical significance of slave living conditions, though emphasizing the role of paternalism in master-slave relationships. The other, Robert Fogel and Stanley Engerman's quantitative study, *Time on the Cross*,[9] relies on previous historians' non-quantitative evidence and evaluations (including Shryock's assessment of slaveowners' good intentions) and on a few standard planters'

[6] Stampp, *Peculiar Institution*, 279–321.

[7] Richard H. Shryock, "Medical Practice in the Old South," *South Atlantic Quarterly*, 29 (1930), 160–78. See also Martha Carolyn Mitchell, "Health and the Medical Profession in the Lower South, 1845–1860," *JSH*, 10 (1944), 424–46; Felice Swados, "Negro Health on the Ante-Bellum Plantations," *BHM*, 10 (1941), 460–72; Wall, "Pettigrew's Slaves," 451–70.

[8] Eugene D. Genovese, *Roll, Jordan, Roll: The World the Slaves Made* (New York, 1972).

[9] Fogel and Engerman, *Time*, 109–26.

and overseers' records. Its section on medicine is the least statistical part of the book, and often simply repeats statements from
traditional historical and literary sources.

What new and useful information can be learned from a study
of health care and diseases in a slave society? Illness has always
been viewed as an enemy of mankind. At the very least it causes
personal discomfort; at worst it results in death. Between these
two extremes are varying stages of disability which affect not
only the patient, but also his family, friends, employer, and (in
the case of epidemic disease) community. Because an individual's
sickness generally impinges on the lives of others, a study of
medical care and illness in the antebellum South can illustrate,
through the reactions of people in that society, the attitudes and
interactions of masters and slaves.

The situation in Virginia typified conditions throughout the
pre–Civil War South. Regardless of the setting (rural, urban,
industrial) few white or black Virginians lived in total isolation
from society. As parts of a community all were occasionally
exposed to communicable diseases. This was no less true of the
slave-quarters community of a large plantation than of residential
areas in Richmond or Norfolk. Masters' and slaves' insistence on
(or laxity regarding) cleanliness had an impact on the health of
others; hence living and working conditions were important determinants of the state of black Virginians' health. In addition to
sanitary arrangements and personal contacts among sick people,
such matters as housing construction, food intake, clothing quality, type of labor, environmental conditions of labor, modes and
severity of physical punishment, and psychological environment
all contributed to a slave's well-being or ill health. These determinants were applicable to all members of society but were
of special significance to blacks because black people often had
little control over them. Each slave encountered a different set
of circumstances and reacted differently. In most cases whites
established the ground rules from which slave living and working conditions evolved.

Bondsmen did have a measure of freedom in the area of disease
treatment. Though masters, mistresses, overseers, and regular
and irregular physicians had primary responsibility for the care

of ailing slaves, blacks engaged, with or without white permission, in a certain amount of self-care. Again, the situation varied with the persons involved and appeared to be looser in the urban than in the farm or plantation setting. Black medical treatments were not uncommon, though they were often hidden from white view. Whites themselves fulfilled their responsibilities toward unwell slaves with varying degrees of conscientiousness. Some waited until all home ministrations had failed before calling for professional assistance; others gave immediately and unstintingly of their time, money, and feelings.

Whites demonstrated their attitudes regarding blacks in several other "medical" ways. While treating sick slaves, for example, some people perceived differences in black susceptibility to certain diseases and conditions, in the severity of black cases, and in black tolerance to various forms of treatment. Whites used these observations to justify Negro slavery and the manner in which slaves were cared for. A number of white Southerners also demonstrated their feelings toward blacks as members of society by using them as medical specimens.

In most cases the responses to the stress of health problems were based on self-interest. Slaves and freedmen were considered the lowest members of society; they were frequently reliant on whites for the necessities of life. Medical independence often had to be expressed out of sight and earshot of physicians, owners, and public officials. Though most masters provided slaves with adequate medical treatment, they often based it on a varying combination of benevolence, duty, and the need to maintain property in good working order. Free blacks also received professional health care, not on a regular basis, but primarily in personal emergencies or when their illnesses threatened the public's health. Slaveowners and health officials generally took pains to clean up black living areas, regulate black food intake, and vaccinate blacks only when disease threatened to cause economic loss or high mortality.

Though paternalism may have been important in some aspects of the master-slave relationship, in the medical sphere individual associations had to be and were submerged by the group needs of a white-oriented slave society. Whites managed the medical establishment. Though blacks often found some slack in the system, the reins could be, and occasionally were, pulled tight. Diseases frequently resulted from conditions arising within the slave community; treatment often depended upon society's or individual slaveholders' needs for financial or medical protection.

Note on Sources

In any historical study of health conditions, adequate primary sources are a necessity. Records for antebellum Virginia fulfill that requirement admirably. Numerous collections of manuscripts are available, in addition to much published primary material. The most valuable of the latter are state papers, medical journals, newspapers, and edited, indexed collections of letters and diaries. State papers include the annual reports of the two lunatic asylums, the state penitentiary in Richmond, the board of public works, and the state auditor, as well as miscellaneous reports from various legislative committees, minor public officials, and governors. It is necessary to page through every volume of legislative papers for the antebellum period to obtain all useful medical information contained in these documents. The same is true of medical journals; any page might mention black health in one context or another. Newspapers provide basic information on epidemics, especially statistics and public health measures. They also reflect the attitudes of whites toward the black man during this period. Human interest stories frequently relate tales of slave or free black accidents, local court actions involving blacks, and recent slave misdeeds. Advertisements—for runaways with deformities, hospitals which treated blacks, urban agents willing to provide for the total care of hired country slaves, and industrial owners looking for Negro workers to enter their "healthy" tobacco factories or coal mines—are also quite useful. Further sources of medical information are the family health guides, many of which were published throughout the South. These are important not so much for their scanty references to black health as for their descriptions of prevalent diseases and their listings of home remedies. Recollections and travel accounts, especially those of former Virginia slaves, also constitute an indispensable body of information on black health and care, as well as on the attitudes of both races toward medical treatment.

It is difficult to write intelligently about diseases without some understanding of the basic processes which determine human health and sickness. One must be conversant not only in the jargon of medicine; one must also know where to find the printed literature on a given medical subject. *Index Medicus* and its predecessor, the *Index Catalogue of the Library of the Surgeon General's Office,* 1st series (Washington, D.C., 1880–95), are indispensable tools for this purpose. A large body of medical literature has been cumulatively indexed by subject and author for many years in these publications, providing easy access to printed materials. Such a system would be a welcome addition to the bibliography of history. Since the early 1960's the scientific community has taken another giant step forward with the publication of *Science Citation Index,* a compilation of all works cited in the footnotes of articles published during a given quarter or year. Historians wishing the latest judgments on, for instance, the susceptibility of blacks to frostbite, need know the title of only one important article on the subject (located through the use of *Index Medicus*) to bring their bibliographies up to date.

For those wishing to know the most useful manuscript sources used in the preparation of this book, a bibliography follows.

Major Manuscript Collections

NORTH CAROLINA

Duke University, Durham
 William C. Adams Diary
 William Bolling Papers
 John Buford Papers
 Robert Carter Letter Books
 Dismal Swamp Land Company Papers
 Robert Leslie Papers
 John L. Mertens Letters
 William B. Price Medical Account Books
 William T. Sutherlin Papers
 William Weaver Papers
University of North Carolina, Chapel Hill (Southern Historical Collection)

Thomas Edward Cox Account Books
Hubard Family Papers (includes Dr. Edmund Wilcox Ledger)
Edmund Ruffin, Jr., Plantation Diary
Francis Taylor Diary (typescript)
John Walker Diaries (part in typescript and part manuscript on microfilm)
White Hill Plantation Books
North Carolina State Archives, Raleigh
African Twins Collection

SOUTH CAROLINA

Medical University of South Carolina Library, Charleston
H. Perry Pope, "A Dissertation on the Professional Management of Negro Slaves," presented to the medical faculty of the Medical College of South Carolina in 1837.

VIRGINIA

Augusta County Courthouse, Staunton
William Weaver v. *Thomas Mayburry*
Colonial Williamsburg, Inc., Research Library, Williamsburg
Eastern State Hospital Court of Directors Minutes, 1770–1801, 1822–66 (photostat)
Galt Family Papers
Medical College of Virginia Library, Richmond
Medical College of Virginia, Board of Visitors Minutes, 1854–1906
Medical College of Virginia, Faculty Minutes, 1854–74
Medical College of Virginia, Miscellaneous Letters, 1859–89
Petersburg Public Library, Petersburg
Petersburg Board of Health Minute Book, 30 June 1821–23 August 1832
Randolph-Macon College Archives, Ashland
Papers Relating to the Randolph-Macon College Medical Department
Rockbridge County Courthouse, Lexington
William Weaver v. *Jordan, Davis & Co.* (file #108)
John Alexander v. *John Irvine's Administrator,* etc. (file #125)
Enos Hord v. *S. F. & W. H. Jordan* (file #74–296)
University of Virginia, Alderman Library, Charlottesville
City of Alexandria Papers (#7146)
Ambler Family Papers (#1140)
Anderson Family Papers (#38–96)
Baylor Family Papers (#6056)

Richard L. T. Beale Letterbook, 1854–56 (#38–105)
Blackford Family Papers (#6403)
Leneaus Bolling Journal, January-March 1814 (film #517)
Carr-Cary Papers
John Hartwell Cocke Papers
John C. Cohoon Account Book (#8868)
John Staige Davis Papers (#1912)
Edgehill-Randolph Papers
Fredericksburg Records, Mayor's Court Proceedings, 1822–37 (#4141)
Gilliam Family Papers (#2608)
Graham Family Papers (#38–106)
Graham-Robinson Ledgers (#38–107)
Grinnan Family Papers (#49)
Jacob Haller Medical Accounts (#981)
Harris-Brady Collection (#38–597)
Heth Papers (#38–114)
J. M. Holloway Accounts (#6133b) (includes account book of Drs. William Amiss and William S. Alsop)
John Hook Collection (#145)
Robert T. Hubard Papers (#8708 and others)
Hullihen-Standard-Kline Family Papers (#6934) (includes account book of Dr. R. C. Ambler)
Fountain Humphrey Farm Notebook, 1819–20, 1828–31 (#1623)
Richard Irby Plantation Diary (#1965)
Irvine-Saunders Papers and Journals (#38–33)
Phebe Jackson Account Book (#2120)
Thomas Jefferson Papers
Louthan Family Papers (#38–34) (includes medical account books of an unidentified physician)
Louthan Family Papers (#1800)
James Brown McCaw Medical Journal (#38–54)
McCue Family Papers (#4406)
Madden Family Papers (#4120 microfilm)
Captain John Marshall Journal (Farm Book) (#2425)
Maupin-Washington Manuscripts (#2769a)
Callohill Mennis Papers (#1993a)
Mitchell-Garnett Ledgers (#38–45)
W. B. Pendleton Medical Account Books (#442)
Perkins Family Papers (#38–53) (includes account book of Dr. Robert Henderson)

Pocket Plantation Papers (#2027) (includes account book of Dr. George W. Clement)

Randolph-Hubard Papers (#4717, etc.)

Robert Riddick Papers (#2227)

Saunders Family Deposit

Edward L. Stone Collection (#2117)

Edward Tayloe Farm Journal, 1850–69 (#38–62)

Tayloe Family Papers (#38–630)

Alfred G. Tebault Papers (#9926)

George N. Thrift Medical Ledgers (#9153d)

University of Virginia, Minutes of the Rector and Visitors; Proctor's Records

Watson Family Papers (#530)

Weaver-Brady Papers (#38–98)

Wellford Family Papers (#3682)

John Wickham Papers (#409)

WPA Folklore File (#1547)

University of Virginia, Medical Library, Charlottesville

Physicians' Fee Bill, Charlottesville, 9 June 1848

Virginia Historical Society, Richmond

William Harrison Armistead Letter

Armistead-Blanton-Wallace Family Papers

Lewis Webb Chamberlayne Medical Account Book, 1835–36

Philip St. George Cocke Plantation Papers, 1854–71

William Benjamin Day Account Books, 1853–89

Eastern State Hospital Account Book, 1841–52

Harrison Family Papers (item #2485a 280–83)

Thomas Eugene Massie Commonplace Book, 1855

Richmond, Virginia Board of Health Minute Book, 1849

David Ross Letterbook

Julian Calx Ruffin Diary, 1843–47

Horace Dade Taliaferro Medical Diary, 1847–60

Virginia State Library, Richmond

Auditor's Item #27—Accounts with Committees of Estates of Lunatics for Support at Williamsburg Hospital, 1801–39

Auditor's Item #152—Papers Relating to the Care of the Insane, 1785–1860

Auditor's Item #227—Overseers of the Poor Papers

Charles J. F. Bohannan Medical Account Book (#25508)

James H. Conway Medical Account Book, 1817–21 (#25114)

Thomas Henry Dunn Medical Account Books, 1852–57 (film on
  reel #59 of Middlesex County records)
Jones Family Business Accounts (#21359)
John H. Lewis Medical Account Book, 1805–12 (#22243)
John K. Martin Papers
Richmond Common Council Minutes, 1782–1862 (film)
Roslin Plantation Records (#23873a)
Staunton City Records
Tredegar Company Papers
Union Burial Ground Society Papers, 1831–51 (#22514)
Virginia County and Corporation Records (includes, on films,
  county registers of births and deaths)
Virginia, Executive Papers
Virginia, Legislative Papers, Petitions
Dr. B. H. Walker Diary (#20800)
Nelson S. Waller Medical Account Book, 1855–65 (#22975)
Washington and Lee University, Lexington
  Reid-White Papers
Western State Hospital, Office of the Medical Director, Staunton
  Western Lunatic Asylum Papers
William and Mary College, Swem Library, Williamsburg
  Austin-Twyman Papers
  Barker and Cooke Papers
  Richard Blow Papers
  Dr. Charles Brown Papers
  Brown-Coalter-Tucker Collection
  Shenandoah Iron Works, Time Book of D. & H. Forrer, 1851–66
  Southall Papers
  Tucker-Coleman Collection
  Joseph Wilson Medical Ledger, 1845–71
  Woolfolk Papers

WASHINGTON, D.C.

Library of Congress
  American Colonization Society Papers
  Robert Carter Papers
  Miscellaneous Manuscripts, Virginia Smallpox
  Physician's Account Book, 1824–39 (#0069)
  William B. Randolph Papers
  William Cabell Rives Papers
  Shirley on the James Farm Journals

WISCONSIN
State Historical Society of Wisconsin, Madison
    James D. Davidson Papers
    McCormick Collection (includes Jordan and Irvine Papers, and
        Jordan and Davis Papers)

PRIVATE COLLECTIONS
T. T. Brady, Richmond, Va.
    "Names, births &c of Negroes [at Buffalo Forge, 1864/65]"
William Jarratt, Petersburg, Va.
    Papers of the Jarratt Family
Jacob McGavock, Max Meadows, Va.
    Medical bill from Dr. H. McGavock Ewing to Joseph McGavock's
        Estate
W. R. Chitwood and Mrs. Mary Kegley, Wytheville, Va.
    Fleming Rich Papers

Index

Abortion, spontaneous, 33, 119
Accidents, 106, 142, 143-45, 164-65, 172-73
Accomack County: case of ascaris (worms) in, 66
Aged blacks, 96, 173, 201-7
Ague and fever. *See* Malaria
Albemarle County: typhoid outbreak, 61; example of poor sanitary conditions, 61; slaveowner's attitude toward sick slave, 151; doctor claims never to have lost a patient, 171. *See also* Brown, Charles; Jefferson, Thomas; Minor, Charles; Randolph, Martha Jefferson; University of Virginia
Albinos, 306
Alexandria: dispensary, 214-15; graverobbing, 291-93; vaccination, 223; yellow fever, 240-41
Alleghany County: misleading mortality statistics collected, 136
Ambler, John: overseer comments on housing and slaves' diseases, 82; describes sick young slave, 129; overseer's medical skills discussed, 158-59
Amelia County: cases of venereal disease, 78
Amherst County: yaws and syphilis, 76; venereal disease, 78, 79; contract practice of physician, 200; aged slave runs away, 207
Animal diseases: communicable to slaves, 104-6
Anthrax, 105

Appomattox County: waste disposal facilities, 59
Arthritis, 135
Ascaris. *See* Worms: ascaris
Asylums. *See* Eastern Lunatic Asylum; Western Lunatic Asylum
Augusta County: tuberculosis, 43; scrofula deaths, 45; mortality statistics, 139-46
Autopsy. *See* Cadavers

Bath County: mortality statistics collected, 136
Baths. *See* Medicinal springs
Bedbugs, 51, 71
Bedford County: typhoid outbreak, 62; black conjurer, 178-79
Beef: as slave food, 93, 101-2
Beriberi, 88
Beverley, Robert: on yaws, 76
Birth statistics, 136
Bites, animal, 135
"Black vomit." *See* Yellow fever
Bladder stone, 135, 301
Blanton, Wyndham B.: on black medical differences, 9; on yaws, 74
Bloodletting, 12-14, 157, 181, 182n
Bones: disorders of, 135
Brain fever: trichinosis mistaken for, 69
Brown, Henry Box, 152
Bruce, Henry Clay: on slave diet, 97; on conjurers, 176-77
Brucellosis, 105
Brunswick County: typhus epidemic, 73; contract practice of physician, 200

323